The Fruits of Their Labor

The Fruits of Their LABOR

Atlantic Coast Farmworkers and the Making of Migrant Poverty, 1870-1945

CINDY HAHAMOVITCH

The University of North Carolina Press

Chapel Hill and London

The paper in this book meets the guidelines for permanence
and durability of the Committee on Production Guidelines
for Book Longevity of the Council on Library Resources.

Library of Congress Cataloging-in-Publication Data

Hahamovitch, Cindy.

The fruits of their labor: Atlantic coast farmworkers and
the making of migrant poverty, 1870–1945 / by
Cindy Hahamovitch.

p.   cm.

Includes bibliographical references and index.

ISBN 0-8078-2330-9 (cloth: alk. paper).

— ISBN 0-8078-4639-2 (pbk.: alk. paper)

1. Migrant agricultural laborers — Atlantic States —
History.   I. Title.   II. Title: Atlantic coast farmworkers
and the making of migrant poverty.

HD1527.A9H34   1997

331.5′44′0975 — dc20

96-41762

CIP

01 00 99 98 97   5 4 3 2 1

Contents

8 sept.

10 sept.

Illustrations and Maps

MAPS

Acknowledgments

In 1988, when I was in graduate school at the University of North Carolina at Chapel Hill and I was supposed to be doing something scholarly like writing a dissertation, I was actually spending a good deal of time agitating for better pay for various folks, including myself. On one particular occasion, while I was going door to door in the history department, pointlessly collecting faculty signatures on a petition calling for raises for graduate students, I happened to meet the southern historian George Tindall for the first time. He asked me what my work was about, and I answered, rather sheepishly, that I was fishing around for a topic and would probably write on nineteenth-century convict labor. He responded not by complimenting me on my choice of subject but by asking, quite out of the blue, if I knew when the farm labor migrant stream had started on the East Coast of the United States. He assumed that it had begun during the Great Depression but had been asking this question of similarly aimless graduate students for fifteen years without getting an answer. I had actually done some research on Florida's citrus industry as an undergraduate at Rollins College, but I did not know the answer to his question either. All the workers I met while in Florida were Mexicans, and I did know that Mexicans had only arrived on the scene a few years earlier.

My adviser, Leon Fink — always willing to brave new waters — approved the subject switch, and five years later I had Tindall's answer, although my response was probably about 500 pages longer than what he had had in mind. When I began looking into the subject, farmworkers had been migrating for over 100 years in the East (although in a number of "streams," not one coherent movement). In the 1880s most of them were African Americans from the South and Italian Americans from Philadelphia, although there were smatterings of other peoples, such as Poles around Baltimore and Bahamians around the edges of South Florida. They were drawn to various points along the coast by the rise of the truck farming industry in the decades following the Civil War. Tindall was right about the importance of the 1930s, however, for the Great Depression greatly increased the numbers of people searching for agricultural work and created what contemporaries called the "permanent transient," the migrant farmworker whose home was a Belle Glade flophouse, a grower's tent, or the back seat of a jalopy. How many migrant farmworkers there were at any particular moment was impossible to ascertain. They presented moving targets to census takers who were rarely known to knock on car doors. Trying to find out how many were women was even more frustrating as various observers would note the presence of women and leave it at that. Migrant labor history and quantitative methods go together like fruit and frost.

There was still a lot I did not know, and what I did learn for certain was not at all what I expected. Knowing that farmworkers had been excluded from New Deal collective bargaining legislation, the Social Security Act, and the Fair Labor Standards Act, I had presumed that twentieth-century farm labor relations would be a sort of throwback to the nineteenth century, when industrial workers were similarly unprotected and usually unorganized, and when employers were less restrained in their use of violence. Studying farmworkers, then, would allow me to see what happened to workers who were completely abandoned by the state.

I was right about some of it. I certainly found evidence of unrestrained violence on the part of growers, and I rarely found agricultural labor unions that lasted more than a few weeks or a few months. But I was dead wrong about the role of the state. What I found to my surprise was that federal officials were very much involved in the affairs of farm labor relations in the twentieth century. Their involvement began in a small way at the end of the previous century and expanded dramatically during the two world wars and the Great Depression. Federal officials created an employment exchange for agriculture, urged southern mayors to threaten black workers with the draft, built labor camps for migrants, froze farmworkers in their home counties, and recruited and transported farmworkers from the United States and abroad. This federal presence was sporadic and often internally contradictory, but it was also far more pervasive than I had imagined. When I finally sat down to write, I realized that my project was not just to describe farmworkers' experiences but to describe the relationship between the state, growers, and farmworkers; explain how it evolved; and show what effect it had on the fortunes of Atlantic Coast farmworkers.

ACKNOWLEDGMENTS

If graduate funding was on my mind at the genesis of this study, it was no less an issue in the following years. I could not have completed this project without the support of several grant-giving organizations. The New Jersey Historical Commission funded my research and writing for a year with a very generous dissertation fellowship. The Kaiser Foundation paid my way to the Walter Reuther Labor Archives, and the history department at the University of North Carolina at Chapel Hill awarded me a George Mowry Graduate Research Grant. Later I received a National Endowment for the Humanities Summer Fellowship, as well as support from the College of William and Mary.

The success of this project also depended on the guidance and support of librarians at many institutions, including Davis Library and the Southern Historical Collection at the University of North Carolina, the Walter Reuther Library at Wayne State University, the Boca Raton Historical Society, Special Collections and Archives at the State University of New Jersey in Rutgers, and the National Archives in Washington, D.C. I am particularly grateful to the interlibrary borrowing departments at UNC and William and Mary, and to the reading room staff of the Suitland Branch of the National Archives.

Many friends suffered through drafts of these pages. My deepest appreciation goes to Katherine McPherson, Doris Bergen, Bryant Simon, Lynn Hudson, and Laura Edwards for invaluable advice, criticism, and moral support. Thanks also to William Barney, Peter Coclanis, Gil Joseph, Jacquelyn Dowd Hall, and Tera Hunter at UNC for their comments and encouragement. My new colleagues at William and Mary— Carol Sheriff, Leisa Meyer, Lu Ann Homza, and Bob Gross—used time they did not have to give me their thoughts and suggestions. I am also indebted to Robert Zieger and Donna Gabaccia, who read the manuscript for UNC Press and helped make this a much better book. Special thanks are also due to Lewis Bateman, for believing that a book on farmworkers was worth publishing; to Ron Maner, for shepherding the manuscript through the various stages of production; and to Stephanie Wenzel, for doing an excellent job of copyediting the book. My adviser Leon Fink has been a great source of inspiration, guidance, and friendship since the day I met him. Although he has always treated me as a colleague, I will remain his student and continue to depend on him for advice, humor, and Labor Day picnics. Thanks also to my parents, Tina and Don, and my sisters, Beth and Jessica, for their high expectations and unending support. My sister Jessy read the very first draft of Chapter 1 when I pounded it out on a manual typewriter over Christmas break almost a decade ago. She was the first nonhistorian to suggest that what

I had to say made some sort of sense. Let's hope she was right. My son, Renny, taught me the true meaning of labor and more than I ever thought I'd learn about love.

My greatest debt, of course, is to Scott Nelson, who probably never wants to read another word about farmworkers. Not only did he read this manuscript in all its mutations, but he suggested many of the ideas around which it is organized and continued to shape the project as I wrote and rewrote. For a great editor, partner, friend, and dad, I save my deepest thanks and love.

Abbreviations and Acronyms

AAA	Agricultural Adjustment Administration
AFL	American Federation of Labor
CIO	Congress of Industrial Organizations
CIR	U.S. Senate, Commission on Industrial Relations
FERA	Federal Emergency Relief Administration
FSA	Farm Security Administration
IWW	Industrial Workers of the World
NAACP	National Association for the Advancement of Colored People
NIRA	National Industrial Recovery Act
NLRB	National Labor Relations Board
NRA	National Recovery Administration
STFU	Southern Tenant Farmers' Union
UCAPAWA	United Cannery, Agricultural, Packing, and Allied Workers of America
USDA	U.S. Department of Agriculture
USES	U.S. Employment Service
USIC	U.S. Industrial Commission
WFA	War Food Administration
WMC	War Manpower Commission
WPA	Works Projects Administration

The Fruits of Their Labor

Yet the migrant cannot be a semi-ward of the state forever. Since political trends frequently reverse government policy, he cannot always be leaning on the crutches of bureaucratic good will and legislative gifts. He must eventually stand on his own feet. But since agriculture is so highly mechanized and requires thousands of workers, he cannot stand alone but must organize with his fellows. . . . Until the rural proletariat is organized, the progressive forces of America will be forever weak and the forces of monopoly will predominate. Yet when that day comes and the migrant and industrial worker see that their destinies are intertwined, they will unite to remove the shadow of monopoly which today lies over the factories and fields of America.

DAVID S. BURGESS, *New Republic*, 1944

Introduction

LONG BEFORE DAWN on a winter morning in Belle Glade, Florida, white farmers drive from their homes or hotel rooms to 5th Street, where rows of flatbed trucks wait idling in the dark. There they are met by the bean pickers, some 2,000 black men and women who emerge out of the crowded, shedlike apartment buildings and ramshackle houses of the "Negro quarter." Murmuring sleepy greetings to one another, men in rubber boots carrying leather knee pads walk alongside women wearing long-sleeve blouses over flowered dresses and pants tied at the ankle to keep out the dry dust of "the muck."[1]

As the pickers converge on the rows of parked trucks, the sound of the crowd grows louder. The rumble of voices stops only when a farmer, standing beside his truck, shouts the first offer of the day: "First picking! Bountifuls! Good stand! Fifty cents!" If this seems an attractive wage for picking a hamper of beans, and if the farmer is known to be honest and his foreman humane, a few men and women will hesitantly board the truck, keeping alert for better offers. Another farmer makes his bid: "Tendergreens, second picking, good yield! Sixty cents!" This is more money per hamper, but any picker knows that filling a hamper takes longer in a field already picked once. Shrugging off this offer, the pickers resume their conversations and wait for a better deal. More growers add to the din as they raise their voices to be heard over the engines of the trucks. As the flatbeds fill with workers, they roar off one by one into the waiting fields.

The crowd seems to hang back from the remaining trucks, so the growers begin to employ one of several schemes to reverse their fortunes. Black men hired for their gift of gab start to trumpet the glories of particular fields, using the truck beds as their stage. A farmer signals a picker in the crowd, paid off earlier, to climb enthusiastically into a particular truck and encourage others to follow. Another gives the go-ahead to a picker paid to malign a competing grower's field or foreman. Eventually, though, the remaining farmers are forced to outbid their colleagues, and they drive off hurriedly once enough pickers have scrambled off other trucks and onto theirs.[2]

So might go a typical day in Belle Glade during the Second World War, when the green beans were plentiful and the pickers scarce. But when the proportions were reversed during the 1930s, the predawn scene in this migrant town looked very different. The growers would save their bribes and cut short their descriptions of their waiting fields. Though they offered only 15 to 25 cents a hamper (down from 40 cents in the 1920s), their trucks were soon crammed with pickers; those not quick enough to get onto the flat beds were reduced to hanging onto the sideboards or lying across the hoods. When the weight of the pickers was so great that a truck could not move from the loading area because the sagging floorboards pressed into the tires, the driver's helper would circle the vehicle, beating the hangers-on with a stout piece of wood until enough pickers loosened their grip so the truck could pull away.[3]

In Belle Glade, Florida, and everywhere migrant farmworkers harvested crops along the Atlantic Coast in the late nineteenth and early twentieth centuries, labor supply meant everything, and everyone knew it. While for other sorts of workers, decent wages, full stomachs, and prospects for the future depended in varying degrees on skill, shop-floor control, ethnic communities, kinship networks, and even the ballot box, migrant farmworkers were rarely skilled, had no shop floors to control, often migrated away from their kin and communities, and could seldom vote in the states through which they passed. Their struggles for power occurred at the moment they sold their labor to a grower for a day, a week, or a season. And their success in those struggles turned on the relationship between the supply of labor and the supply of work.

Labor supply is the crux of farm labor conflict, but it is also an old problem in American history, indeed in human history. The willingness of Europeans to subjugate Africans solved the problem of labor supply in the colonial period and relieved planters of the necessity of having either to repress or to bargain with white laborers. The closing of the slave trade in the early nineteenth century, just as world demand for cotton boomed, created a renewed labor supply problem for southern planters. Later in that century, employers' demand for labor in North and South America brought Europeans and Asians across oceans to lay track and dig mines. The problem of labor supply is very old, and the enslavement of Africans and the beating of African Americans clinging to a grower's truck were simply two sides of the same coin. This book tells the history of struggles over farm labor supply along the Atlantic Coast from New Jersey to Florida from 1870, when changes in agriculture began to create migrant streams, to 1945, when federal officials had finished crafting the labor and immigration policies that would shape farm labor relations for the remainder of the twentieth century.

Labor supply has long been a contentious issue in American history, but in the second half of the nineteenth century, growers' labor demands took a new form as new urban markets and large, heavily capitalized grain farms in the West transformed agriculture in the East. East Coast farmers struggled out from under a deluge of cheap western grain by turning to "truck farming," the growing of vegetables and berries for "truck" — or trade — in urban markets. Truck farmers sold their produce to the denizens of the nation's largest cities. They did not just grow a small patch of vegetables to feed themselves and perhaps sell the remainder; they cultivated the land intensively, making a business of enlivening the diets of urban dwellers.

The nation's first truck farming regions were established in the Northeast after 1870. Southern New Jersey's proximity to three very large cities — New York, Philadelphia, and Newark — permitted the early transformation of small family farms. In the decades that followed, truck farming spread southward down the Atlantic Coast as refrigerated railway cars made it possible for farmers to grow fruits and vegetables at greater distances from urban markets. In the 1920s the draining of Florida's Everglades exposed soil that could bear three vegetable crops in succession while northern farms were under snow.

The rise of these intensively cultivated farms tied to urban markets brought a particularly strained sort of labor relations to United States agriculture. While much of the production process could be mechanized, vegetables, fruits, and berries almost always had to be picked by hand. This meant that truck farmers' labor needs, more than any other farmers', were concentrated around the harvest. They were thus dependent on laborers who arrived just when they were needed and left when they were not. Truck farmers ignored the problem of labor supply at their peril.

Like the expenses of industrial manufacturers, growers' costs were almost all fixed. Only by integrating vertically or forming cooperatives could farmers affect the price of seed, fertilizer, or machinery. But unlike industrial producers, truck farmers could not spread the production process over a year or control when their products hit the market. One cost growers could affect, however, was the wages they paid farmworkers. When a harvest was upon them, truck farmers had every incentive to squeeze down the price of labor.

The problem was the same on the West Coast, but the solution differed. Truck farms in California were large-scale enterprises from the outset and, thus, had much larger labor needs. As a result, California growers imported armies of workers who remained isolated from the rest of the workforce. Mexican Americans, Chinese, Japanese, Filipinos, and Mexicans have all dominated California agriculture at one time or another. Eventually, however, these workers would either organize or abandon agricultural employment to buy land, return home, or seek industrial jobs. Their actions would force growers to seek a new source of cheap and tractable labor.

On the East Coast, in contrast, the smaller scale of the truck farming industry forced growers to tap into functioning labor markets on a seasonal basis. New Jersey berry growers had to hire Italian hatmakers and garment workers during their summer slack seasons. Other New Jersey growers came to depend on African American men from the Upper South, who left their wives and children to tend tobacco and cotton fields while they ventured North to dig up potatoes. Florida growers relied on the sons and daughters of sharecroppers in the Lower South for their harvest labor. Thus the smaller size of the truck farming industry in the East distinguished Atlantic Coast agricultural labor relations in several ways: it blurred the line between agricultural and industrial work; it tended to equalize wages and conditions north and south; and it forced East Coast truck farmers to worry constantly about whether they would have enough labor come harvest.

As a result, East Coast farm employers struggled mightily to increase the number of workers they had at their disposal. Through much of the late nineteenth and twentieth centuries, they employed various strategies, including laws prohibiting the "enticement" of labor, rounding up men and women using loosely defined vagrancy statutes, and threatening farmworkers with the draft. They used prisoners of war and labor importation schemes, all in the name of "stabilizing" farm wages.

Likewise, farmworkers found that their fortunes rested on the supply of labor as well. Because truck crops ripened at different times in different places, and because the timing of harvests was as unpredictable as the weather, farmworkers wandered blindly into regions oversupplied with labor at *their* peril. Still, they had more to gain from labor shortages than other kinds of workers. Unlike iron rails or textiles, truck crops are extremely perishable, and farmers became more open to negotiation as

6

their crops ripened in the fields. Farmworkers have been able to exert considerable pressure on their employers during periods of panic over labor scarcity.

Thus this book aims to bridge the rather disparate fields of labor and agricultural history. Farm labor history has traditionally occupied a blind spot between them. Labor historians are often unfamiliar with even the best studies of West Coast farm labor relations, and agricultural historians tend to ignore farmers in their role as employers. Set apart by labor historians and students of agriculture, the history of migrant farmworkers was left largely to writer-reformers, authors whose aim was to reveal farmworkers' poverty.[4] These reformers' books have helped to bring public attention to migrant farmworkers, but their accounts tend to be more descriptive than analytical. From the muckraking exposés of the Progressive Era to Edward R. Murrow's documentary *Harvest of Shame*, the time line of the twentieth century is dotted with such periodic "discoveries" of poverty.

discover
+
ignore

This study aims to move the history of migrant workers out of the no-man's-land of poverty studies. Although it is hard not to be shocked by the conditions under which farmworkers have lived (and still live), the project here is to tell their history, to explain more and lament less. Rather than seeing farmworkers as a lumpen proletariat, appropriately left to the margins of American history, it attempts to place them at the center of current scholarly debates over the relationship of labor and capital to the state.

As farmworkers and growers struggled to make a living at each other's expense, federal officials in Washington, D.C., increasingly intervened in their affairs. Whose interests the policies they fashioned served and what impact they had at the local level are crucial concerns here. This study necessarily engages questions of state theory, then, but it seeks to do so without privileging national policy makers' actions over the daily lives of local people. Rather, it reveals the ways in which farmworkers triggered decisions made in Washington boardrooms and the ways in which those decisions affected life on the ground.

I hope to join, therefore, the growing number of social historians who are trying to move beyond interpretations of individual social movements toward new syntheses of U.S. history. These newest social historians have begun to "put the state back in" to labor, women's, and African American history as a way to break down the barriers that isolate each field from the others. The result has been new thinking about the very nature of the state, how it came to be, and whom it serves. In the 1960s and early 1970s, New Left scholars and activists tended to define

power structure/ structured social inequality

the state as the political wing of capital.[5] Today few left-leaning scholars (the post–New Left?) accept such instrumentalist notions of state power. But while most would agree that the state is not the board of directors of the bourgeoisie, these scholars disagree on what the state's relationship to capital is. Many now accept the notion of "relative state autonomy" developed by Nicos Poulantzas, Theda Skocpol, and others. In their telling the state is autonomous in the sense that "state-managers" take actions that sometimes defeat the interests of individual capitalists. But this autonomy is relative because, ultimately, the state shares an "essential identity" with capitalism and serves the interests of capitalists "as a class."[6]

Still, there are key differences even among those who accept the idea of relative state autonomy, differences that suggest antithetical courses of action. Christopher Tomlins, for example, argues in *The State and the Unions* that the New Deal left the working class dependent on the state in a three-way bargaining process, in which the federal government forced employers to the table in exchange for workers' docility. Collective bargaining received the state's sanction, not because it was "a desirable end in itself," but as a means to achieve industrial stability and labor peace. The state, as Tomlins envisions it, is a sort of Mafia don, offering protection in exchange for silence and loyalty.[7]

While by implication Tomlins seems to call on American workers to steer clear of men in dark suits offering bargains, Theda Skocpol and her students lean in the opposite direction, emphasizing the power of autonomous state actors to act quite independently of the demands of capital. They point to the good that has been done by autonomous (and often female) state actors. Skocpol's recent book *Protecting Soldiers and Mothers* notes the power women wielded in Washington before they could even vote and their effectiveness in creating what she calls "maternalist" policies: protective legislation, mother's pensions, and maternal health programs. Likewise Kenneth Finegold points to New Deal agricultural policy, stressing the role of disinterested economic experts in the making of New Deal crop reduction programs.[8]

Other scholars, however, have challenged this new emphasis on state autonomy, with considerable success. Linda Gordon, for example, agrees that women created programs for other women, but, she argues, this does not mean these programs were in fact good for women. Likewise, agricultural economists in the Agricultural Adjustment Administration may not have been beholden to growers' lobbies when they devised the New Deal's crop reduction programs, but it is hardly coincidental, as Jess Gilbert and Carolyn Howe point out, that the programs they created benefited large-scale growers at the expense of sharecroppers and black farmworkers.[9]

While Skocpol dismisses such outcomes as "unintended consequences" of well-meant state actions, Gordon, especially, challenges us to look beyond the surface of federal policy, to consider the ways in which state structures were shaped by state managers' unspoken beliefs about women's true natures or their preconceptions about who among the poor deserved aid. State policy has been shaped, she cautions, not just by ideas, political debate, compromises, and corruption, but by the values and prejudices of people in positions of power. Likewise, other scholars have begun questioning the motives and independence of state officials and lawmakers, asking, for example, whether the New Deal was meant to bolster white supremacy or whether the creators of the Social Security Act willfully reinforced patriarchal family relations.[10]

[handwritten margin note: one cause of structured social inequality]

These exciting new areas of inquiry help to throw a little fertilizer on the study of farm labor relations (although hopefully not enough to pollute the narrative stream). While it might be easy, when one is immersed in hundreds of thousands of national archives records, to exaggerate the significance of federal policies to the everyday lives of ordinary people, the actions taken by federal officials have had grave significance for farmworkers' efforts to bargain up their wages. Many farmworkers labored without ever coming into contact with the U.S. Employment Service and without ever taking shelter in a Farm Security Administration (FSA) camp for migrant laborers, but farmworkers nonetheless encountered the workings of Washington when they arrived at a field overcrowded with labor or when they counted the numbers of workers clinging to the side of a grower's truck. Farmworkers have not been able to reap the benefits of their power to strike because, over the course of the twentieth century, the federal government has expanded its role in farm labor relations and ultimately compensated for growers' Achilles' heel.

State action toward agricultural labor has taken two contradictory forms. Since growers first complained of labor shortages in the 1890s, federal officials have attempted to behave as labor suppliers, or padroni, jumping at growers' complaints of labor shortages and leaping into the breach. The Departments of Labor and Agriculture tried to act together as padrone to the nation during the First World War, but lacking an administrative structure to carry out their plans, they failed. Instead of supplying growers with workers, the U.S. Department of Agriculture (USDA) resorted to recommending that local governments use coercive "work-or-fight" campaigns to keep black field workers in the fields. During the late 1930s, however, New Deal liberals began to act on the concerns that self-appointed farm labor advocates had been raising since the Progressive Era. New Dealers responded by making farmworkers wards of the state, settling strikes that turned sour and establishing a migratory labor camp program to uplift and provide shelter for the transient poor.

The paradox is that the liberal reforms of the New Deal era ultimately did farmworkers the most good and the most damage. The state's forays into labor contracting during the First World War were ineffectual, but New Dealers, acting on a policy of welfare reform, built an administrative structure of staff, buildings, operational procedures, and contacts. That apparatus reached directly into the regions where migrant farmworkers labored, providing shelter, food, and safe transportation to the fields. During the Second World War, grower advocates in the USDA commandeered that interventionist welfare apparatus and used it to operate a large and very effective labor supply effort, which replaced militant migrants with farmworkers imported from abroad under no-strike contracts.

[margin note: the Bracero program]

It is quite clear from this story that we cannot talk about the state as either autonomous or not.[11] The federal government was not a monolith. Indeed, the USDA and the FSA often worked at cross purposes, although the FSA began and ended as part of the USDA. The officials of the USDA saw themselves as spokesmen and advocates for growers, not farmworkers. Indeed, the USDA and the growers' organization, the American Farm Bureau Federation, were born of the same womb. The USDA's agents at the county level were funded by both federal and local tax dollars, and growers formed farm bureaus all over the nation to influence the activities of the USDA. Some county agents went so far as to write their correspondence on farm bureau stationery, demonstrating unabashedly the symbiosis between state and landed capital. This relationship could well support the most vulgar instrumentalist theory of the state.[12]

In contrast, the ties that bound liberal reformers in the FSA to the underdogs of agriculture—small farmers, sharecroppers, and migrant farmworkers—were much more tenuous. While there were former growers working in the USDA, the FSA officials who set up labor camps for destitute migrant farmworkers had never been farmworkers and were rarely, if ever, associated with farmworkers. Rather, these advocates for the nation's rural poor were intellectuals whose political commitments led them to apply their legal, managerial, and administrative talents to reform agendas. If USDA officials were "organic intellectuals" in the Gramscian sense—advocates for their own class—the liberal reform-

[margin note: not really listening to farmworkers or knowing their needs]

ers of the FSA were "traditional intellectuals," self-consciously disconnected from any class interests, proponents only, they thought, for the
common good. If any state officials were autonomous, in Theda Skocpol's sense of the word, the FSA's advocates for sharecroppers, migrant
farmworkers, and poor farmers surely were.

This study reveals two weaknesses inherent in liberal reforms not born
of popular movements.[13] First, such autonomous reformers did not necessarily represent the needs and desires of the people they sought to
help. Second, even when they did, their power was not grounded in
organized movements of voting workers, so their presence in federal
agencies was ephemeral. They held their positions by the grace of congressional whim and fleeting public concern. As one historian recently
put it, "While reform intellectuals are important because they can help
to shape an agenda, there are others who wield more power — who control economic resources, or can deliver large voting blocs and can command [the] attention of lawmakers."[14] In this case New Deal liberals
created a welfare apparatus designed to serve migrant farmworkers, but
farmworkers saw that apparatus used to house and transport the foreign
workers who displaced them during the Second World War. Thus New
Deal reformers were dangerous, not despite their autonomy, but because of it.

That the state intervened more and more extensively in farm labor
relations over the course of this century will, I hope, soon be evident.
Why the state took this course is less clear. Part of the reason has already
been mentioned. When growers were confronted by rising labor costs,
they could do a great deal more than curse into their account books.
They had a strong, Cabinet-level agency at their service as well as powerful allies in Congress. Still, this is simply the most obvious explanation for
the willingness of state officials to play padrone to the nation's farmers; it
is not the only explanation.

Just as compelling is the role of race in the political economy of American agriculture and the political culture of the nation. Just as colonial
planters turned to African slaves when English servants proved unruly,
farm employers in the late nineteenth and twentieth centuries have
relied increasingly on people of color to keep their labor costs low and
conditions on their farms out of the public limelight. They have averted
criticism and conflict by importing workers who can be exploited without apology or protest.

Proponents of the notion of a racialist state have suggested that the
New Deal did not just leave Jim Crow untouched but actually exacerbated racial inequality. They have been criticized for mistaking policies

that were discriminatory in outcome for those that were discriminatory in intent.[15] Federal farm labor policies have certainly been discriminatory in outcome, but what is more remarkable about them is the unthinking, reflexive, even automatic nature of the racism that shaped them (which is why the word *racialist* works better than *racist*, although the result may have been the same). When African American workers in the East and Mexican American workers in the West responded to labor shortages by demanding higher wages or better housing, growers called on federal officials to hold down farm wages or find other sources of cheap and uncontroversial labor. Federal officials obliged, excluding farmworkers (and domestics) from New Deal collective bargaining legislation, opening the border to Mexican and Caribbean migrants during the First World War, and actively importing them during the Second. There seems to have been little if any consideration of the fact that the exclusion of farmworkers and domestics from the Wagner Act's collective bargaining provisions would hurt African Americans disproportionately, no debate before the creation of Jim Crow migrant labor camps, and no notice of the fact that only people of color were imported under no-strike contracts by the federal government during the Second World War. Indeed the absence of discussion about race and federal policy speaks volumes about the depth of racist thought in the United States. Racism was not the engine that drove the state; federal officials did not devise migrant policy with the intention of suppressing people of color. But it was the driver's license that permitted that policy to proceed unimpeded and the map that sent policy makers down some roads and not others.

This story suggests the racialist nature of state policy and the dangers of dependence on liberal reforms, but it should not lead us to the conclusion that farmworkers were better off out from under the state's protective wing, as Tomlins's reasoning might suggest. By looking at the vulnerability of those excluded from the three-way bargain between labor, capital, and the welfare state, we can reconsider what the Wagner Act meant to organized labor. Unions may well be in crisis now, but the gains they made after 1935 are all the more striking when compared with those of workers whom New Dealers thought to uplift but not empower. Congress ranted about high labor turnover in industry *and* agriculture during the Second World War, for example, but only farmworkers were frozen in their jobs and ordered not to leave their home counties without the permission of USDA county agents. Industrial employers also complained of labor shortages during the war, but the organized migration of foreign workers into the United States served agricultural, not industrial employers. Unable to organize legally, farmworkers' movements were easily defeated, and without them, farmworkers were unable to oppose an immigration policy tailored to growers' needs. Having the right of collective bargaining may not be a panacea for farmworkers or industrial workers, but it does appear to be a prerequisite for sitting at the nation's table.

Uninvited to that table, farmworkers were unable to make substantive changes in wages and working conditions. This does not mean that they did not make the attempt. There were real battles in the fields of truck farms along the Atlantic Coast, some as momentous and moving as any miners' war or autoworkers' sit-down strike. But these farmworkers struggled without federal sanction, and as a result they were fatally weak. At their moment of greatest power during the Second World War, farmworkers who successfully struck for higher wages found themselves replaced by foreign workers imported on American battleships by the U.S. government.

Even today the annual invasion of poorly paid, unprotected, and often undocumented immigrant farmworkers is often justified by the uncontested assertion that there is simply some work that Americans will not do. This is mystification, of course, for Americans have done this work. It would be more correct to say that Americans will not work under the conditions offered on the nation's farms as long as they have any alternatives. These conditions, which are as desperate as they ever were, are not the inevitable consequences of a seasonal industry or the result of some pathological tendency on the part of farmworkers to migrate, but a product of a specific and alterable relationship between farmworkers, farmers, and the state.

1

A Perfectly Irresistible Change

The Transformation of
East Coast Agriculture

THERE IS NOTHING particularly new about migrant labor in North America. The continent's earliest human inhabitants were nomadic hunters who crossed a land bridge from Siberia as early as 40,000 years ago in search of caribou and woolly mammoths. The first Europeans who came "to Plant an English nation" at Roanoke 500 years ago were followed by thousands of immigrant workers: farmers and artisans, servants and slaves. Indeed, American history is in large part the saga of successive waves of migrant workers and the conflicts and cultures they wrought. What distinguishes labor migrations in the "Age of Capital" from earlier movements of working people is less the total absence of woolly mammoths than the preeminence of wage labor. By the nineteenth century more people than ever were moving great distances to sell their labor power at a price.[1]

What was new also in the late nineteenth century was the growing importance of migrant labor to agriculture in the United States. In the hops fields of California, the beet farms of Michigan, the strawberry fields of Virginia, and the potato farms and cranberry bogs of New Jersey, farm owners relied on men, women, and children who would appear in time for the harvest and disappear thereafter.

Agriculture the world over had always been characterized by short seasons of intensive labor. But in the decades after the Civil War two changes transformed agriculture more dramatically than anything since Jethro Tull invented the plow. The first was the widespread availability of

14

horse-drawn agricultural machinery. The second was the rapid world-wide rise of cities, whose inhabitants had to be fed. These changes led American farmers to plant new crops in new ways and sent them scurrying in search of new sources of labor.

New Jersey farmers were particularly well placed to supply perishable produce to city people as their crops grew in the shadow of New York, Philadelphia, Newark, and a score of smaller industrial cities. Their success made South Jersey the ideological center of "progressive" agriculture and transformed farmers in the Garden State into buyers on the international labor market.

The labor they bought was sold to them by Italian immigrants — mostly women and children who lived in nearby Philadelphia — and African American men from the upper South. Farm labor was unpleasant work, but for those who enjoyed few other opportunities, it was a way to earn quick cash in a world of account books, pawnshops, and eviction notices.

THIS STORY BEGINS, however, not in New Jersey but in the vast, sparsely settled lands of the Dakota Territory's Red River Valley, where mechanized farm production first reached massive proportions. When economic depression struck in 1873, the directors of the Northern Pacific were left with railroad tracks that ended in what seemed to be the middle of nowhere. The Sioux had recently been expelled from the region, but the vast expanse of prairie that the federal government conquered and then gave to the railroad was uncultivated and apparently infertile. Not certain if they were optimists or fools, the railroad's directors and investors gambled that, if they could demonstrate the land's fertility, they could both profit from the sale of wheat and attract settlers to the valley. Once settlers were ready to ship their own grain out of the region, the railroad would be back in business. Together the company's officers traded their nearly worthless bonds for large portions of the railroad's land, hired an experienced wheat grower and ex-lawyer to manage their operation, and ordered him to turn the land almost exclusively to wheat.[2]

Others soon followed their example. The Grandin brothers of Pennsylvania also exchanged their Northern Pacific securities for 100,000 acres of rich, black Red River Valley soil. Seemingly undaunted by the vicissitudes of a crash-and-boom economy, the Grandin brothers made the Dakota Territory their Palestine and reconsecrated their faith in the holy trinity of men, monopoly, and machinery. They hired the same ex-attorney and wheat grower to manage their colony, supplied him with steel plows, cultivators, and harvesters, and ordered the land planted, not with settlers, but with 61,000 acres of wheat. The seeds of hope and profit that had failed with the Northern Pacific were thus replanted on the enormous, highly mechanized estates that soon came to be known across the nation as "bonanza farms."[3]

These massive, mechanized estates of the West were not typical of late nineteenth-century agriculture. In fact, they were not even typical of landholding in the Dakota Territory, which came to be characterized by much smaller, family-owned farms. But it was the bonanza farms, not the family farms of German and Swedish settlers, that captured the imagination of the nation's prophets of progress and symbolized the boom in agricultural production that would flood grain markets the world over. Indeed the bonanza farms monopolized the nation's dailies and magazines, much as they monopolized the best lands of the West. There they were presented to contemporaries as harbingers of a new era of harmony between agriculture and industry and as models of efficiency and productivity.

The Grandin brothers and other absentee bonanza farm owners may have been captains of agricultural industry, but they were less innovators than they were the beneficiaries of fifty years of improvements in farm implements. John T. Alexander's 80,000-acre estate, capitalized at perhaps a half-million dollars, employed 150 steel plows, 75 breaking plows, and 142 cultivators.[4] But what had occurred in the preceding half-century was not so much a revolution in farm technology as it was an application of the intellectual and material products of industry—size, steel, and speed—to agriculture. The horse-powered machines of the Civil War era hardly differed in concept from the scythes, sickles, plows, and flails that had been in use in agriculture for a thousand years, but the strength and durability of steel over wood gave postwar farmers increased power, speed, and proficiency.[5]

Although John Deere's all-steel plow went on the market in 1847, agricultural mechanization remained relatively unimportant until the outbreak of the Civil War. Once the war was under way, however, the dearth of labor and spiraling grain prices catapulted the farmers of the West and Midwest into the machine age. Over 100,000 reapers were used in 1861, and the mechanization of all operations between plowing and harvesting followed with a flurry of new patents and improvements.

The urgency with which improvement followed improvement was assured by the inflexible schedule imposed by nature. The production of a crop involved five tasks: preparing the soil, seeding, cultivating, harvesting, and preparing the harvested crop for market. No matter how great the demand for a particular product, the amount that could be planted was always constrained by the amount of labor needed to cultivate and harvest the crop. Any change in the machinery available for one of the five operations affected the rest. Improved plows made it possible for farmers to plant greater acreage, but growth was still limited to the amount that could be harvested by scythe and cradle. The mechanization of the soil preparation process thus created a bottleneck that could only be solved by the mechanization of the other four operations. The greatest bottleneck was the harvest, which had to be accomplished in the least amount of time and required the greatest amount of labor.[6]

By the end of the Civil War almost every demand of grain production was met by a whirl of horse-drawn steel. Perhaps 250,000 reapers harvested the grain that fed the Union army, and plows, harrows, drills, planters, binders, spreaders, and threshers all assisted in the process.[7] The ability to mechanize every stage of wheat production was thus the bonanza farmers' inheritance. They simply took this bequest and used it to hold down the largest expense of wheat production after land and equipment: labor.

Mechanization dramatically increased the productivity of labor. An early McCormick reaper could cut twelve to fifteen acres of wheat in a ten-hour day, while an individual could cut only one-half to three-quarters of an acre with a sickle. But machines still required operators, and on a farm five times the area of Manhattan, one could hardly call on one's neighbors for assistance.[8] On the Grandin estate the workforce ranged from only 10 men during the five coldest months of the year to 200 to 500 during the harvest in August and September. Harvesting and threshing crews traveled from estate to estate, starting in Kansas and following the ripening wheat northward into Dakota, Minnesota, and sometimes Canada.[9]

Having demonstrated the fertility of the land by producing as many as 5,000 bushels of wheat for every 100 inhabitants of the valley, the Northern Pacific joined with the Milwaukee and North-Western railroads "and with one accord flooded the country with literature," wrote an observer for the *World To-Day*. As if by summons the settlers arrived. When they reported home that opportunities had not been exaggerated, "others came flocking into Dakota and Minnesota by hundreds and by thousands." "Marvellous the change," *Harper's New Monthly Magazine* heralded, "in 1869 a furrowless plain; 1879, a harvest of eight million bushels of grain—ere long to be eighty million." In another five years the region's population had increased 279 percent and wheat production was up 645 percent; every 100 inhabitants now produced 11,500 bushels of wheat.[10]

"How invention has simplified husbandry," the nation's magazines marveled: "The employment of capital has accomplished a beneficent end, by demonstrating that the region, instead of being incapable of settlement, is one of the fairest sections of the continent."[11] The Red River Valley was not alone in its bounty. In the United States as a whole over 21.5 million more acres were devoted to cereals in 1890 than just ten years before. Between 1860 and 1910 the number of farms and the acreage of improved farmland trebled.[12]

Wheat production increased beyond all expectations, but the nation's wheat growers did not get rich. By the turn of the century the nation's farmers were producing six times more wheat than they had harvested a half-century before, but their share of the nation's wealth was less than half of what it had been in 1860. The railroads' reports of opportunities in the West had, in fact, been exaggerated. From 1875 to 1883 "uniformly large yields and high prices prevailed," but this was more a matter of good fortune than the magic of machines. Wheat prices were uncommonly high because Europe's wheat crop had failed several years running, and yields were encouraged by unusually wet weather and a brief lull in the voracious attacks of grasshoppers. By the mid-1880s rising taxes, drought conditions, and falling prices proved to absentee owners that speculation in large-scale farming was at least as risky as speculation in railroads. By the 1890s the bonanza farms were virtually gone, broken up and sold off to German, Swedish, and native-born families brought west by the Northern Pacific on special excursion trains. Only on the Pacific Coast did such massive estates remain.[13]

The settlers who bought pieces of the bonanza farms found that rising interest rates on mortgaged land ate away their savings about as fast as a grasshopper could chew through a stalk of wheat. Without cash the necessity of buying machines and hiring men forced them quickly into debt.[14] With railroad directors out of the wheat-growing business, farmers also found freight rates less favorable and storage prices nearly criminal. As farm sizes shrank and tenancy, indebtedness, and bankruptcy rates expanded, western farmers responded by growing more wheat. Even as they organized farmers' alliances and channeled their frustrations into the populist movement, western farmers flooded world markets, including East Coast markets, with wheat.

The most immediate, obvious, and lamented effect of western wheat production on the East Coast was the abandonment of eastern farms.

"Sacked wheat produced in the West awaiting shipment to world markets"
(*World To-Day* magazine, 1905)

With eroded soil and small farms broken up into plots "hardly larger than a Western corral," eastern growers were unable to compete with the staples produced on the vast, fertile, and less costly lands of the West. Peculiarly unsuited to large-scale mechanization because of their uneven terrain and rocky soil, northeastern farms were transformed by mechanized staple production in the West, not because northeastern growers emulated its example, but because they lost their markets to the volume and cheapness of western grain.[15]

While the number of farms in the nation increased throughout the second half of the nineteenth century, the North Atlantic region alone reported a decline. From 1880 to 1890 twenty-six states increased their acreage in cereals, while northeastern farmers took over 5 million acres out of production and produced over 10 percent less grain. In some northeastern regions the decline was far more dramatic. Between 1860 and 1899 New England's wheat production plummeted from 1 million bushels a year to just 137,000.[16]

To contemporaries the effects of western competition were tragic. As one observer noted in 1890, "The New England farmer has found his products selling at lower prices because of the new, fierce, and rapidly increasing competition. One by one he has had to abandon the growing of this or that crop because the West crowded him beyond the paying point." The *Nation*, after considering "a cumulative mass of evidence that is perfectly irresistible," determined that the state of Massachusetts's agriculture could be summed up in two words: "rapid decay." Among the signs were absentee owners, sagging productivity, lower wages, "a more ignorant population," and increasing numbers of women employed at hard outdoor labor, "the surest sign of a declining civilization." Maine's Board of Labor counted 3,398 abandoned farms in 1890. Massachusetts published *A Descriptive List of Farms . . . Abandoned or Partially Abandoned.* Connecticut released a *Descriptive Catalogue of Farms for Sale,* and Vermont issued a *List of Desirable Farms at Low Prices.* Farther south the warnings were just as dire. In New Jersey, Gloucester County officials reported to the State Board of Agriculture in 1890 that land values had fallen 40 percent in twenty years due to overproduction; the opening of cheap, fertile lands in the West; and increased railroad facilities, "which bring all parts of this country in competition with us." Such were the symptoms of a seemingly incurable affliction. Despite their proximity to urban markets, eastern growers simply could not compete with the volume and prices of western products.[17]

Even the nation's monthly magazines, which usually devoted their space to glowing accounts of resort towns, joined in the lament for East Coast farms. *Century Magazine* blamed the "rich and level Western prairies, with their farm machinery and cheap transportation," for the decay of the stony, hilly farmsteads of the East, which once furnished wheat and corn for an eastern market "and grew their half-scores of sturdy girls and boys." "If possessed of spirit," the boys had long since moved to the wide prairies, the magazine reported, or else they chose other vocations. All this was due not to a love of change or a hatred of hard work but to the hard economic fact that "almost anything pays better than farming." Always determined to find a silver lining under the manure pile, however, the more fashionable magazines, illustrated with charming cottages and snow-covered fields, published lengthy advice columns on hunting abandoned farms for summer homes, faculty retreats, and artists' colonies.[18]

While some abandoned their farms or sold out to city-weary vacationers, however, others managed to stay afloat and even prosper by turning from staple farming to either dairying or truck farming, the intensive production of vegetable and fruit crops for commercial markets. Even *Cosmopolitan Magazine* touted the prospects of abandoning general farming in favor of specialized, commercial agriculture geared to meet the demands of urban markets.[19] *Cosmopolitan* may not have made its name as a farmers' almanac, but in this case its prediction was reliable. New England farmers vastly increased their production of butter and milk, which were too perishable to be supplied by more distant farmers. In New York, Pennsylvania, and New Jersey, growers within a day's journey of the nation's largest cities devoted their efforts to the production of small fruits and vegetables. From 1879 to 1899 Pennsylvania "market gardeners" or "truck farmers," as they were alternately called, increased the value of their state's vegetable and small fruit crop by 275 percent to almost $5.5 million. New York's crop was worth more than twice as much, and New Jersey's followed closely behind.[20]

The turn to dairying and truck farming had the same cause but different effects. Dairy production did not disrupt local labor patterns because dairy farms operated year-round (milk cows do not have a harvest season, after all). In contrast, truck farming had a transformative effect on northeastern agriculture, as the case of New Jersey reveals.

The success of New Jersey farmers in providing perishable produce to nearby cities and the boosterish support of state officials won New Jersey fame as the nation's "garden state," even if New York farmers actually produced slightly more truck crops. In its first annual report in 1874 the New Jersey Board of Agriculture staked out its role as a promoter of intensive farming and declared New Jersey its national leader. "With a great variety of soils and a varied climate, populated with an industrious and energetic people, with great railroad and steamboat facilities, wedged as we are between the two largest fruit and vegetable markets on the globe," the board concluded, New Jersey well deserved the title "banner garden state of the Union." Thirty years later, in 1904, the board's secretary reaffirmed his faith in truck farming as the salvation of northeastern agriculture: "With these millions of people in touch of our farms, people who must be fed three times each day, if farming will not pay in New Jersey, where in the wide world will it pay?"[21]

The crops to which New Jersey growers turned were hardly new to the Northeast. City people had long grown vegetables on tiny garden plots, and farmers grew vegetables and fruits for home consumption. But the growing congestion of urban neighborhoods made city cultivation an impossibility even as hundreds of thousands of new immigrants arrived demanding the foods — such as tomatoes, eggplants, and peppers — to which they were accustomed. When W. T. Woerner's father arrived in Woodridge, New Jersey, in the mid-1820s and began growing vegetables for city markets, his neighbors looked on him as a wizard, but his productive capacity was actually quite limited. He had to grow his own seed because suppliers were few and their products unreliable. Peruvian guano, the only commercial fertilizer available, was too expensive to even consider purchasing, and markets were small and virtually inaccessible. Roads were rarely more than dirt tracks that were impassable in rainy weather, and even when a grower could reach a town or city, the demand

New Jersey and Surrounding Area

for vegetables was slight. "My father set out 400 [tomato] plants in 1836, the younger Woerner wrote, and had enough fruit for all New Brunswick, Perth Amboy and Rahway, and still had enough to feed two hogs."[22]

Fifty years after Woerner Sr. fed his hogs surplus tomatoes, New Jersey truck farming had become big business. While Woerner's father thought it "a big thing" if he could sell one basket of tomatoes on a Saturday in New Brunswick in the 1830s, the same city in the 1870s required 1,000 baskets a day during the two-month harvest season. While in 1834 200 or 300 head of lettuce would have supplied the city for the season, 120,000 were needed to meet the demand a half-century later. The same was true of celery, spinach, and asparagus.[23] Such figures needed no further comment, the secretary of New Jersey's Board of Agriculture remarked to the readers of his annual report in 1882. The key to survival and success was self-evident: with the cities filling up with immigrants who brought new tastes and traditions, farmers had to "be prepared to meet new demands." "Make your own market," he counseled the state's growers. With the expansion of the market for vegetables, the value of land devoted to intensive farming skyrocketed. In 1892 an acre planted in wheat was worth $9.91 and an acre in corn $10.48, but an acre planted in truck crops was valued at an average of $163.00.[24]

What was new about truck farming, however, could not simply be measured in numbers of tomatoes, although truck farmers did vastly increase the productivity of their land. Truck farming involved an intensive use of land whereby crops were planted in succession on the same acres and soil exhaustion was countered by generous applications of recently developed commercial fertilizers. Truck farmers might plant strawberries, tomatoes, and cabbages one after another on the same soil, and sometimes one between the other in alternating rows. Moreover, those who could afford glass and irrigation equipment could continue through the winter, growing high-quality vegetables in heated greenhouses and selling them at fabulous prices to the nation's rich.

Even as New Jersey staked its claim as the Garden State, its leading growers spread the gospel of "progressive farming." By the last decade of the century, truck farming had spread along the entire Atlantic Coast from the eastern shore of Maryland and Virginia to Key West and around the Gulf of Mexico to Mobile and Galveston. The Atlantic Coast Gulf Stream made the air mild and humid, and sudden changes of temperature — the bane of the truck farmer — were relatively rare.[25] With locally produced commercial fertilizers, rapid freight travel, and refrigerated cars, southern truck farmers could put quality produce on the market while northern fields were still covered in snow. Although most of the South suffered the evils of land monopoly, absentee ownership, soil erosion, and the one-crop system, the wealthier farmers of the South's periphery escaped the bounds of cotton, share-tenancy, and crop liens by providing northern markets with a bounty of fruits and vegetables.[26]

In eastern North Carolina, where truck farming followed the path of the Atlantic Coast Line Railroad, the center of vegetable cultivation was New Bern, from where 100,000 barrels of early Irish potatoes were shipped north as early as late May. These were followed by peas, cabbages, snap beans, cucumbers, and melons. Around the town of Mount Olive the dark, moist loam was particularly suited to strawberry cultivation. Farther south in Chadbourn a settlement of Michigan residents devoted their energy to strawberries "with wonderful success." Chadbourn and Mount Olive strawberries were sold at the train stations; no growers ever had to incur the cost of shipping them. The dealers would stand by their refrigerator cars, examine a wagonload of berries, bid for them, put them in the car, and hand the grower a check payable at the nearest bank, a scene that might have brought tears to a sharecropper's eyes.[27]

The mildness of southern winters gave growers along the South Atlantic Coast a jump on northern markets and access to northern cash, that most precious southern commodity. However, few southerners abandoned cotton for truck crops, though they were often accused of stubbornness and stupidity for not doing so.[28] Because truck farming required a substantial capital outlay, the experience of receiving cash from the hand of a northern buyer was simply out of the realm of the possible for most southern farmers. In Raleigh, North Carolina, the owners of the Hackburn and Willett truck farm irrigated sixteen acres by overhead pipes through which they pumped water with steam pressure. In winter they protected six of these acres with wooden frames covered by cotton cloth and planted them with lettuce. They received over $2,000 for the lettuce in December and immediately replaced it with early beets. They followed the beets with melons and then lettuce again. On the other acres they also planted lettuce, manuring heavily and spreading the furrows between the plants with 1,500 pounds per acre of high-grade fertilizer. When the lettuce was cut out in early spring, the land was devoted to cucumbers, then Irish potatoes, and then it was manured again before being returned to lettuce. The Hackburn and Willett farm produced $3,000 worth of produce per acre in a year, but it required an outlay of $1,000 an acre for seed, fertilizer, equipment, and labor.[29]

Describing the Hackburn and Willett operation to New Jersey truck farmers, W. F. Massey, a successful Raleigh grower, reported that "the South has made great advances in market gardening and other lines of horticulture, [but] we are really at the very beginning of a great development in these lines." "We have the soil and the favorable climate," he noted, "land is cheap and in the greatest abundance, and we need only energetic men with capital to carry on the industry to greater and greater dimensions." Men with capital were, unfortunately, the one thing the South surely lacked. Although by 1899 the South's vegetable and small fruit crops were worth $80 million a year, no amount of "energy and intelligence" alone could have made truck farming the salvation of the New South.[30]

Truck farming thus remained a minor part of southern agriculture, but it was the salvation of progressive farmers in the Northeast, particularly in New Jersey. It kept many growers in business and prospering while general farmers went under. Still, it meant more than abandoning old methods and old crops. It meant finding new sources of labor, for truck farmers created their own labor problems even as they raked in record profits.

The principal problem was that truck farms did not offer enough year-round work to keep rural people from leaving for city work and industrial wages. To the readers of *Cosmopolitan* the depopulation of the countryside meant summer homes available on the cheap, but to truck farmers the loss of rural neighbors meant shortages of farm labor for planting, cultivating, and particularly for harvesting.

Occasional farm labor shortages were not new, but the problem was far more intense than it had been in the eighteenth century when northeastern farms were highly diversified. At that time farm families not only produced food but also raw materials for household production, necessitating the labor of family members and year-round hired hands. In the early nineteenth century the rise of manufactories took one industry after another off the farm, reducing to a few months the time during which a hired man or woman could be profitably employed. Yet farmhands could still alternate farmwork and manufacturing because mills required water power and were thus scattered about the countryside. Small industries in country towns offered farm laborers employment in winter when work was scarce on the farm. In the late nineteenth century, however, the advent of steam power and the subsequent concentration of factories in cities deprived rural workers of their winter wages, forcing them to follow the factory to the city.[31]

By switching from diversified farming to the cultivation of fruits and vegetables, late nineteenth-century farmers contributed to this outmigration. Flailing and winnowing grain had been the chief winter occupation of northeastern farm families and hired laborers, and as grain cultivation declined, so did the availability of winter work. Growers saved money by cultivating crops that only required hired hands during brief peak seasons, but as they drove away year-round workers, it became harder and harder for them to find local people available for a few weeks' work in summer or fall.

A large majority of New Jersey's "leading growers" surveyed in 1891 by the State Board of Agriculture said farm laborers were fewer than they had been five years earlier and that the workers they were able to hire were "less efficient and intelligent" than those hired in earlier years. A decade later farmers reported to the U.S. Industrial Commission (USIC) that "the agricultural labor throughout South Jersey is not as good as it was a few years ago." Monmouth County farm leaders concurred, noting that "white, native farm-hands are getting fewer every year. They prefer to work in factories or towns."[32]

Truck farmers were not wrong to indict manufacturers for the loss of their traditional sources of labor. New Jersey's truck farms lay near the periphery of northeastern cities, some within a stone's throw of Philadelphia's suburbs. While the proximity of their farms to the nation's largest cities simplified marketing and insured the freshness of their products when they reached the consumer, it also guaranteed that truck farmers competed for harvest labor with industrial employers of the unskilled.

In their effort to bring in their crops, farmers had a limited number of options. They could raise wages to compete with urban employers, but few were willing or able to make the attempt. Wages did rise during the labor-scarce years of the Civil War, but the increases were wiped away by the depression of the 1870s. Wages recovered somewhat in the 1880s and early 1890s, but they dropped again during the depression that began in 1893. Not until after the turn of the century did farm wages return to their 1866 level, and all the while growers complained that they could not keep their sons, daughters, and landless neighbors from the enticements of city life and city wages.[33]

Many growers reduced their labor needs by mechanizing farm operations, but labor-saving machinery, while markedly reducing the need for workers to plant and cultivate crops, ultimately exacerbated labor problems at harvest. Vegetable and berry producers found, for example, that mechanization shortened farm operations and reduced their need for labor only until the point of harvest. Once their crops were ready to be picked, machines became irrelevant and human hands necessary. The Labor Department's comparison of hand and machine labor makes this point dramatically. In the 1871–72 growing season one acre of strawberries required 50 hours of labor and three separate planting operations. The availability of the "transplanter" in the 1894–95 season reduced the three operations to one and allowed growers to plant one acre of strawberries in only 10 hours. The cultivation of the crop was accomplished by weeders and horse-drawn plows in only 94 hours instead of the 1,080 hours of labor required when farmworkers only used hoes. The delicate operation of picking, however, could not be accomplished by heavy-hoofed work horses and steel machines. Picking, grading, and crating the berries took 556 hours in both periods. Thus, if growers were tempted to plant more acres due to the ease with which tasks could be accomplished by machines, they assumed a greater risk of failure if enough workers could not be found at harvest.[34]

Potato cultivation also saw technological changes in the same period that affected the availability of local laborers. Unlike berries and tomatoes, potatoes are hard and covered by a protective skin and could therefore be harvested by machine. Indeed, the potato digger cut the time needed to harvest an acre from forty-two hours in 1866 to just fifteen hours in 1895. But the digger unearthed new problems that made harvest employment less attractive to workers. The machine worked by reaching under the potatoes and throwing them to the surface, after which they had to be picked up by human hands. Picking up a potato is clearly a far less strenuous task than digging one up with a shovel. But potatoes cannot sit on the ground in the heat of the day without being "scalded" by the sun and thus ruined. So potato growers who had mechanized their operation would pay workers to pick up potatoes in the early morning hours until the sun became too hot at around 10:00 A.M. and then lay them off until they could resume work from about 4:00 P.M. until dusk. Thus the potato digger gave new meaning to temporary employment; workers who were often without work for much of the year were now also expected to accept unemployment for six hours a day at the height of the harvest season.[35]

Thus New Jersey farmers' labor problems were both unavoidable and self-imposed. Growers had little choice but to switch to truck farming if they were to stay in business in an agricultural economy dominated by western grain, but these new crops shrank the work year and reduced the likelihood that local sons and daughters could remain on the land. Local workers may have been further disheartened by low agricultural wages, and residents of potato-producing counties were probably dismayed by the indignities of the digging machine. The efficient and intelligent native-born laborer whose passing was so lamented by New Jersey's growers was given little reason to remain.

While they complained of the inefficiency and scarcity of labor, New Jersey growers continued their transformation of the state's agricultural economy. With demand for truck crops brisk and prices high, entire legions of eastern farmers put their eggs in one basket. Just as in Norfolk farmers cashed in on strawberries and in central Florida growers planted orchard after orchard of orange trees, farmers in central New Jersey increasingly grew nothing but potatoes, and South Jersey growers expanded their cranberry bogs and berry fields. Farmers who grew a variety of crops, such as Hackburn and Willett in North Carolina, could control their need for labor by staggering their harvests. But not all soil could support a variety of crops, and the cost of farm machines designed for particular tasks forced farmers to bank increasingly on their mechanized crop. This left growers extremely vulnerable to sudden, brief harvest seasons and shortages of harvest workers.

Thus when New Jersey growers complained of labor scarcity, they were clearly not calling for year-round workers. What they needed was a ready force of harvest workers who could pick up where machines left off. Franklin Dye, secretary of the New Jersey Board of Agriculture, complained to the USIC in 1898 that farmers had to go "to the cities and towns for extra help in busy seasons" for work that used to be done by "the smaller and poorer farm families."[36] What was lost was a rural population available for temporary employment on New Jersey farms. Growers had to look farther afield for workers who would arrive when they were needed and disappear with the last of the produce. They needed migrant workers.

Unwilling or unable to raise wages high enough to compete with urban employers, growers along the East Coast began recruiting labor farther away. Their efforts encouraged workers to migrate over greater distances, some venturing to one region only, others traveling from harvest to harvest and state to state. In the 1890s the Norfolk, Virginia, harvest drew over 21,000 African Americans from Richmond and neighboring North Carolina. French Canadians came from Quebec to pick fruit and nuts in Maine, Vermont, and northern New York. Growers in the Garden State cultivated two distinct sources of labor. The berry growers of South Jersey hired Italian families from nearby cities, and the potato farmers of central New Jersey imported African Americans from the Upper South.[37]

New Jersey truck farmers and the farmworkers they hired were as much buyers and sellers on the international labor market as mine owners and track layers. However, truck farmers had more difficulty than industrial employers in attracting labor due to the wages and the brevity of the work they offered. Initially northeastern growers were fairly successful at tapping the flow of farm-bound migrants from Europe, and they hardly needed immigrants at all during the 1870s when the depression replenished local sources of labor. However, as the tide of unemployed ebbed in the 1880s, growers' labor problems began in earnest. Emigration resumed in step with economic recovery, but the flow of farm-bound migrants from western and northern Europe slowed to a trickle.[38] Most of the "new immigrants" who began arriving from southern and eastern Europe had worked on the land in their native countries, and many intended to do so again; but they turned a deaf ear to growers' pleas for labor and looked instead for industrial work upon their arrival in the United States.

Fortunately for New Jersey's berry growers the rise of truck farming in the Northeast coincided with the outpouring of migration from southern Italy that began with Italian unification.[39] Instead of pursuing agrarian reform as promised, Italy's new national government exacerbated rural poverty by increasing the tax burden carried by Italy's rural provinces. While protecting industry in the north with import tariffs, the nation's leaders left the rural south exposed to a flood of American and Russian grain (the same flood of grain that forced East Coast farmers in the United States to abandon grain agriculture for truck crops). Further burdened by the rise of citrus industries in Florida and California, which left Italy's citrus producers with a vastly reduced market, Italy's growers fell rapidly down the slippery slope from landownership and tenancy to sharecropping and landlessness. Before they reached the bottom, however, many caught sight of American steamships boarding emigrants in Italian harbors and heeded the advice of the labor brokers, or padroni, who stood ready with fast deals and golden promises.[40]

The Italians the padroni recruited — usually men — came to the United States under contracts that committed them to one or more years of work, after which most returned to Italy. By the turn of the century enough Italians had settled in the United States that kinship networks replaced labor contractors as the primary movers of Italian migration. Still, these labor migrants followed their relatives into urban and industrial employment. Despite New Jersey growers' needs, the torrent of migration out of Italy flowed along a riverbed dug by industrial, not agricultural, employers.[41]

Intent on quick earnings and a speedy return home, few Italians sought agricultural work in the United States, though most had been farm laborers, tenants, or farmers in Italy. Only 5 percent of New Jersey's Italian population worked in agriculture at the turn of the century. "It would seem," wrote New Jersey's Commission of Immigration in 1914, "that from this vast number of immigrants coming annually to our shores and to our State . . . there would be an abundance of farm laborers, but such is not the case." For those who worked furiously toward the goal of landownership in Italy, the disadvantages of farmwork in the United States were obvious. Potato harvesters might waste six hours in the middle of the day when the tubers could not be exposed to the glare of the midday sun. Scooping berries in a cranberry bog might pay well, but the work would end in a few weeks, after which time would be wasted in search of another job. Few immigrants found in industrial work the fulfillment of the golden promises that had been made them. Many were swindled, most were poorly paid, and virtually all were put to work on job sites more dangerous than battlefields. But temporary emigrants were often "self-exploiters," workers who would suffer otherwise intolerable conditions, as one contemporary observer put it, in "hope of returning at some period, after they have amassed a sum sufficient to make the remainder of their lives easier."[42] Dangerous work was still preferable to temporary work.

As millions of Italians journeyed to the United States in hope of buying land in their villages, the remittances they sent home raised land values and thus prolonged the time they had to remain overseas. Over the course of the late nineteenth century, migrants had to stay longer and longer to earn enough to change their condition at home. Ultimately many gave up on the idea of returning to Italy.[43] These settled immigrants provided New Jersey's growers with the labor they required. Married men who decided to remain in the United States sent quickly for their wives and children in Italy. Many of those who were still single sought Italian-born wives in the United States or returned home briefly in search of brides. Instead of saving for land in Italy, these permanent immigrants devoted every cent they earned to the "family economy." Friends and family often provided jobs and housing, but the going wages for unskilled work were rarely enough to support a family.[44]

It was the labor of married women and children that made the difference between subsistence and starvation.[45] Unfortunately for these women, but fortunately for New Jersey's berry growers, garment making and artificial flower making — the industries dominated by Italian women — were characterized by long, seasonal slack periods, and the off-seasons in the garment and hat trades would hit just about when crops were ripening in South Jersey. Of the eighty-four Italian families visited in 1913 by members of the Committee on Women's Work, fifty-seven lost three to six months of work every year due to slack seasons. Moreover, slack seasons affected single women in factories as well as married women who worked in their homes. Of 101 flower-making shops surveyed in 1913, only one-quarter were busy longer than eight months a year. "It's busy, busy, busy, and then the work stops like that," one flower maker said, slapping her hand on the table. In more than half the shops surveyed, workers expected a dull period of three to four months every year.[46]

Thus Italian women in Philadelphia took their children to work on New Jersey's berry farms during the long days of summer.[47] "Italians rank with the most frugal people of the world," declared a charity association worker in 1909, "but even their economy cannot make up for the loss of

Symbiotic industries

four or five month's wages." When slack seasons corresponded to harvest seasons, berry picking provided an opportunity to earn the extra money that might carry a family through winter, the most devastating season of unemployment. In one gang of fifty berry pickers interviewed, all the women took "tailor work . . . sweating work in their homes." "Since children and women can work efficiently" in berry picking and vegetable cultivation, Italians made the family "the working unit," the Dillingham Commission observed in 1911. "There are women and children in swarms[;] old, young and middle-aged are found in every field."[48]

Although the Dillingham Commission (or U.S. Immigration Commission, which met between 1907 and 1911) concluded that "the family" was the "working unit" and referred frequently to male "heads of households," many if not most of the berry-picking families left husbands and eldest sons back in the city. In 1909 Italian immigration authorities estimated that in eight months of construction work an Italian man could save a fifth more than in twelve months of farm labor. Only those family members "who have no other gainful occupation" engaged in agriculture, the commission's report admitted. Husbands and children over sixteen who could secure permanent employment in other industries would be absent "when the count of the berry field [was] made." "Young men can not profitably leave a living wage for berry earnings," the commission observed. "It is the family that makes money."

Thus widows and married women whose husbands had work in Philadelphia were the ones who brought their families to the harvest. These were apparently the women performing "hard outdoor labor" that the *Nation* referred to as the "surest sign of a declining civilization." One widow earned $112 in a season, aided only by one child. A family of three women earned $70 in six weeks picking strawberries. A widow and her small daughter earned $44 in less than four weeks. Though the Dillingham report studiously avoided reexamining its definitions of "family," clearly the working units it describes were usually temporarily or permanently absent a male head of household.[49]

The men who did join their families in the fields were usually casual laborers who had little to lose by abandoning the city for harvest wages for several months of the year. "A host of ragpickers are represented," the Dillingham report observed. There were also "many street sweepers, pick-and-shovel men, . . . concrete mixers, hod carriers, garbage handlers, push-cart men, fruit dealers, . . . shoemakers, liverymen, and a large number who report that they 'do anything we can find to do; some day streets, some day railroad, some day hod.' " For the most part, the report concluded, "they are typical Italian laborers of the pick and shovel variety. When asked 'What Occupation?', many simply replied: 'Rags and railroad.' "[50]

Husbands and adult children who had "permanent" employment sometimes joined their families in the berry fields due to the extreme irregularity of industrial work. Bricklayers, carpenters, cement workers, stevedores, and track repairers all worked intermittently in the late nineteenth and early twentieth centuries. In Philadelphia's poorest neighborhoods, 15 percent of the population was unemployed an average of three months of every year in the 1880s and 1890s.[51] Due to the seasonality of women's work, men's high rates of industrial unemployment, and cultural pressures on Italian women to care personally for their children, the needs of Italian families suited the labor demands of South Jersey's growers.

A few even used wages earned from farmwork to buy land in New Jersey, usually in the Italian communities of Vineland and Hammonton. Dillingham Commission investigators found on interviewing fifty male "representative heads of farm families" in Hammonton that only ten had purchased their land on their arrival in the United States. Of the 72 percent who had worked for wages before buying berry farms, half had worked as farm laborers. After they bought land, most of these men continued to work on neighboring farms for a period of one to ten years.[52] Clearly, for some immigrants harvest work was a means to landownership in the United States, but only 5 percent of New Jersey's Italian population chose agriculture over urban life. For the majority who ventured to the berry fields from cities and returned there after the harvest, farmwork remained a short-term solution to a financial problem.

While the pressures of international trade and increased taxation pushed millions of Italian peasants down the road from landownership to sharecropping to emigration, black southerners walked a narrower path. Few African Americans ever enjoyed the independence of landownership. Pressured into signing labor contracts in the aftermath of the Civil War and, like Italian peasants, quickly disabused of the notion that land reform was forthcoming, millions of freed slaves entered sharecropping arrangements. And like Italians, they did so when staple prices were beginning their rapid and enduring worldwide descent. When Italians fell to the bottom of the agricultural abyss, however, there were steamships waiting to take them to America, Canada, and Argentina. African Americans found few such opportunities, and they faced the even greater threats of the chain gang and the lynch mob.

The best many black southerners could do was to use their newly won freedom to move within the South in search of higher-paying work. Plantation records suggest that tenants often left not when they had cleared their accounts but when they were most heavily in debt. Black migrants moved within counties, from one county to another, and more rarely from the low-wage states of the Southeast to the relatively high-wage states of the Mississippi Delta.[53] "One of the most frequent complaints made against the negro laborer of the South," noted the Industrial Commission on Agriculture and Agricultural Labor in 1901, "is that they go about from plantation to plantation whenever they have an opportunity of bettering their condition."[54]

And this was surprising because ...?

Only a small minority of those seeking to better themselves left the South altogether in the decades between the Civil War and the First World War. Sixty thousand migrated north between 1870 and 1880, 70,000 the following decade, and 168,000 between 1890 and 1900, the ten years that saw cotton prices fall to their nadir and lynchings skyrocket.[55] New Jersey received more of those migrants than any other state.

It is ironic that so many black migrants choose the Garden State as their destination, for New Jersey was also known as the Georgia of the North. South Jersey had been a stopping place on the Underground Railroad and the location of several black towns formed by runaway slaves, but it had also had one of the most severe slave codes of the northern colonies and was the only northern state that sanctioned the Fugitive Slave Act and failed to ratify the Thirteenth, Fourteenth, and Fifteenth Amendments to the Constitution. Indeed, the first black person to vote as a result of the Fifteenth Amendment was a resident of New Jersey, and many turn-of-the-century South Jersey communities segregated schools, restaurants, and public accommodations.[56]

African American migrants may only have ventured into such hostile territory because New Jersey's potato farmers and resort owners were willing to get them there by advancing their fares. While many northern employers refused to hire African Americans for industrial work,[57] New Jersey's booming agricultural economy and seaside resorts offered positions that suited what white northerners believed African Americans could do. Black men may have worked in mills, mines, and brickyards and as skilled railroad workers in the South, but they usually found even the unskilled industrial positions closed to them in the North, except during strikes. Wandering rural Middlesex County in search of work at the turn of the century, a former railroad worker or brick mason from

the impact of racist attitudes

North Carolina might have seen over 200 Hungarians and Italians laying track and 160 Hungarians and Russians working on the county's clay-banks. Chances were, though, that the only work he would find would involve walking behind a digging machine, picking up potatoes.[58]

Growers, reporting to New Jersey's Board of Agriculture and to the USIC, confirmed the presence of black southerners in New Jersey agriculture at least as early as 1889. Salem and Mercer County growers claimed to be dependent "almost wholly on southern labor" by the first years of the twentieth century. The Monmouth County Board of Agriculture reported in 1904 that as "white, native farm-hands are getting fewer every year . . . , a great many farmers have to employ colored help from the South, mostly from Virginia and Carolina."[59]

Black women rarely joined the men in the fields because for them work was plentiful on the Jersey shore. Fully half of the state's black women worked outside their homes, and of those who did, 86 percent made their money as servants, cooks, and housekeepers. By 1912 Atlantic City boasted 100 hotels and boardinghouses and hosted 175 state and national conventions every year, relying on a 95 percent black and largely female labor force. The demand for labor in the resorts swelled the black population of "America's playground" from 184 people in 1850 to over 11,000 by 1915.[60]

Black southerners were brought up only for the season, and after the potato harvest and the tourist season ended, most returned south, cash in hand. But some of the migrants stayed. Between 1870 and 1910, New Jersey's black population tripled due to the influx of migrants from the South's coastal states.[61] Some moved to Lawnside in Camden County, the only incorporated black town in the state, where they farmed or sold wood, and most bought homes.[62] By 1920, 156 black families owned farms in Cumberland County, where social life revolved around the new Elks Lodge. In Gloucester County seventy-eight black families bought farms, where they grew the cantaloupes, peaches, and sweet potatoes they had cultivated in the South. A few found steady work in the potato region. Henry Randolph and his wife moved from Virginia to Middlesex County, where he worked year-round as a farm laborer and she cared for their two children in their rented home. A black migrant from North Carolina worked all but two months of the year on George Mount's farm, where he labored alongside Mount's seventeen-year-old nephew. But most African American migrants headed for cities. By 1910 nearly 75 percent of the state's black population was urban.[63]

These permanent migrants brought with them to their new homes the typical problems of rural poverty: high rates of illiteracy and astronomical death rates from tuberculosis.[64] But their children would learn more and live longer. Even South Jersey's segregated schools stayed open during harvests, when southern schools closed.[65] Black residents were not invulnerable to lynch mobs in the Georgia of the North. In 1910, for example, a black man suspected of murdering a white girl was nearly lynched in Asbury Park. At least in New Jersey, however, the police would step between the mob and its intended victim.[66] The invisible barriers that kept African Americans out of industrial jobs probably account for the fact that a large-scale chain migration did not begin until the First World War cut off European immigration, but for those who did migrate to New Jersey in the years before the Great War, life in the North had its advantages.

Thus for both black men from the South and Italian women from Philadelphia, migrant farmwork in turn-of-the-century New Jersey was a temporary solution, a stopgap measure that could tide an urban family over during the winter or provide a stepping stone from rural to urban life. For New Jersey growers, however, migrant farm labor was a permanent solution to the problems they had created when they converted to truck farming. By the end of the nineteenth century, berry farmers were dependent on padroni to supply them with a harvest labor force composed of women, children, and occasionally an unemployed man. Potato farmers might employ one or two year-round workers, both black and white, but they depended on the arrival of much larger numbers of southern migrants in time for the July harvest. Neither sort of grower could ever be sure that harvest workers would arrive at the right time or in sufficient numbers, or that they would stay long enough to finish the job.

These were just some of the many problems that farmers regularly faced; land values, credit, access to markets, and prices also weighed heavily on them. However, their search for labor was not simply a practical concern like the high price of fertilizer or a rotted bag of seed. The experience of locating, hiring, and supervising large groups of workers — workers who were strangers to local communities and often to the growers themselves — gradually changed the way truck farmers saw themselves in relation to the men, women, and children they employed. Dwindling were the days of the "hired man" who took most of his pay in room and board and shared the table with the family who employed him. Considering migrant workers "too base to be introduced into rural homes," growers housed them in barns and stables, paid them by the day or for every bucket or bushel picked, and sent them on their way at the first opportunity.[67] *change in rural social structure — less stable —*

To meet their labor needs, some growers looked to industry as a model. In 1881 Maine's Board of Agriculture advised its readers to follow industrialists in reaping the profits of products produced by hired hands. "No manufacturer ever built up a fortune on the employment of one laborer, or on the employment of his own hands alone," they counseled. "It is the employment of many laborers and in the accumulated profits of those many laborers that he builds up his income. It is precisely so in farming."[68] In fact, it was more so in truck farming because of the concentration of growers' labor needs around the harvest period and the proximity of the harvest to the moment of marketing. If the harvest approached and market prices were low, the grower's principal interest was in pressing downward on the cost of harvest labor. Even when market prices were favorable, labor was the only expense over which farmers had much control. Some farmers went to great lengths to fashion their farms after industrial conventions. In turn-of-the-century New York, for example, some large farmers instituted a time card system for seasonal and year-round workers.[69] However, few truck farmers hired enough workers, even at harvest, to justify such self-conscious mimicry of industrial labor relations. Most just looked for the cheapest labor they could find, and they found it in the sharecropper shacks of the South and the tenements of nearby cities. By the turn of the century migrant labor had become an integral feature of truck farming along the Atlantic Coast.

The burden of western competition was thus an affliction for some and an opportunity for others. But for those who chose to stay on the land, it was the experience of becoming employers, more than changes in methods, markets, and crops, that made a business of farming. To the question, Where in the wild world will farming pay, if it will not pay in New Jersey?, the Board of Agriculture answered without doubt or pause: "If it does not pay in any case, the fault is not with the business, but with the management."[70]

If the experience of hiring migrant laborers made a business of farming, the experience of working as a migrant laborer at the turn of the century kept many African American and Italian families solvent. Yet, harvesting crops in South Jersey was not a way of life for either group; it was not a resting place on the bottom of the Northeast's labor pool, where only the most degraded and destitute settled. Migrant agricultural workers in turn-of-the-century New Jersey, like those who followed them, were movers, strivers, and self-exploiters, willing to take harvest work as a means to their own ends. For Italian women — confined by their gender to the very irregular garment industry — work in the summer meant the survival of the whole family in winter, when jobs were scarce and pantries often bare. It was temporary work, to be endured for a few summers until one's children were old enough to find factory work. For African American men, excluded from most industrial work by their race, picking potatoes in New Jersey meant cash to bring back to a cash-barren society or, in some cases, a ticket to a new life in the North.

The Sacrifice of Golden Boys and Girls

The Padrone System and
New Jersey Agriculture

ITALIAN FAMILIES disembarking from the trains that transported them to New Jersey's berry region brought feather beds, baby carriages, sausages, loaves of bread, and an entourage of reformers, photographers, state immigration authorities, and federal investigators. Fresh from a victorious fight to restrict child labor in industrial workplaces, the men and women of New York and New Jersey's progressive reform movements were appalled to find immigrant children at work alongside their parents on the large and lucrative cranberry bogs of South Jersey. Convinced of the necessity and efficacy of an activist state, they declared farm labor migration a new and insidious trend in modern agriculture, demanded state action against it, and brought the issue to the public's attention.[1]

Concern for Italian berry pickers in New Jersey was a small part of a much larger and more sweeping "progressive movement." Reformers were concerned about so many social ills that historians have had a hard time identifying a coherent movement. If anything united the myriad causes that animated turn-of-the-century reformers, it was concern for order and stability and a willingness to reconsider the relationship between the state and society. The reformers who took up New Jersey's berry pickers as their cause stood firmly within that camp. However, most of the social workers, philanthropists, and clergy who constituted the foot soldiers of the progressive movement were haunted by urban, not rural, issues. They wrestled with the associated problems of unregulated immigration and industrial unrest, attributable, they believed, to the urban character of the "new immigration." Overcrowded slums bred disease and crime. Immigrants huddling together in alien neighborhoods assimilated slowly, if at all, and the influx of unskilled workers depressed wages and continually refilled the nation's pool of unemployed. So obsessed were progressive reformers with urban ills that they might not have stumbled on the squalid berry pickers' camps had they not followed their charges from the Italian tenements of Philadelphia to the cranberry bogs of South Jersey.

Latecomers to the farms of New Jersey, progressive reformers were also not interested in all agricultural workers. While both African Americans and Italians were at work in New Jersey's fields, only the latter group attracted notice and concern. The southern migrants who worked in the potato fields usually came singly and worked on smaller farms, unlike the Italians, who arrived by the hundreds. The southerners were usually single men or at least men traveling without their children, and it was child welfare that most concerned the particular reformers who made rural New Jersey their cause. Moreover, black men traveling alone across the rural counties of the Georgia of the North were far more likely to encounter hostility and fear than sympathy or concern. All of these factors probably played some part in the reformers' neglect of black migrants. But the result, in any case, was that the leading opponents of migrant farmwork ignored one of the leading groups of migrant farmworkers. As far as Progressive Era reformers were concerned, African American migrants were invisible.

What reformers did see, and what became the focus of their opposition to the berry industry, was child labor, or as they put it, the "Sacrifice of Golden Boys and Girls" to berry growers' profits. The employment of families in New Jersey agriculture not only subjected children to long hours of work and unsanitary conditions, according to its critics; it threatened to produce a generation of unassimilated, uneducated, and uncontrollable immigrant children. Reformers blamed the presence of children among New Jersey's berry fields on the padroni—the labor contractors or "bosses" who recruited, transported, and supervised Italian farmworkers. Moreover, they demanded not just state regulation of child labor but a complete prohibition against the use of children in agriculture.[2]

Had they asked the pickers about their views of the padroni, reformers might have been surprised to find the relationship less exploitive or at least more complex than they had imagined. Indeed, the workings of the turn-of-the-century padrone system reveal a great deal about the dynamics of farm labor supply and the extent to which labor contractors served or defeated the interests of farmworkers.

In any case, reformers' demands forced the berry farmers into a defensive position. When the reformers called on the state to enforce health and housing regulations on berry growers' farms, growers insisted that they could not afford to build special housing for temporary workers. When reformers demanded the abolition of child labor in agriculture, the berry growers insisted that they could not compete with other employers for adult male workers. An edict that kept children from the fields, growers argued, would eliminate their only source of labor because the adult women they hired were almost invariably accompanied by children. However much the berry growers defended their use of Italians as berry pickers, they too were frustrated by their dependence on the padroni, and they too demanded an expanded role for the state. They appealed for a state agency that would direct unattached immigrant and unemployed men to New Jersey's farms. Thus, the furor over Italians in the berry fields resulted in the first debate over the proper relationship between the state, growers, and farm labor.

Still, the conflict between berry growers and reformers can hardly be described as a struggle to wrest control of an existing state bureaucracy, for the state in late nineteenth-century New Jersey was skeletal. New Jersey governors held office for a maximum of three years and had little power or patronage at their disposal. Likewise, the state legislature was a part-time body that met for only one or two days a week from January to April and lacked a support staff. The state assembly was further enfeebled by an annual turnover rate of 60 percent. Reformers and growers were trying not so much to influence state policy as they were to create it in what was essentially a legislative and administrative vacuum.[3]

ONE MIGHT EXPECT growers complaining of annual labor shortages to try to attract workers by improving wages and housing conditions, but although some large farmers built barracklike dwellings, this was rarely the case. New Jersey farmers needed workers every harvest season but only for the harvest season; they had little incentive to devote their profits to migrant housing and toilets in the fields. On the contrary, they had every interest in cutting harvest costs to the bare bone. The padrone system served this need in a number of ways. First, it gave growers access to the cheapest urban workers: married women, widows, children, and more rarely, men who were casual laborers or unemployed. Second, it passed transportation costs on to the workers themselves. Finally, it absolved growers of responsibility for housing conditions on their farms.

By the turn of the century the padrone system was a fixture of New Jersey's berry industry. "Wherever Italian laborers are recruited from cities at some distance from the place of employment," the report of the U.S. Immigration, or Dillingham, Commission noted in 1911, "the *padrone* system is in operation." The National Child Labor Committee announced the same year that the acute demand for temporary labor, which sacrificed "many a cranberry crop" to early frosts "because of a lack of hands to gather the scattered harvest," had "been solved from the standpoint of the growers by recourse to the crowded immigrant colonies in our large cities."[4]

The padrone who stood at the center of South Jersey agriculture differed in significant ways from the padrone who had precipitated the mass migration of Italians overseas. In the 1870s and 1880s, padroni worked principally as agents for American railroad and mining companies, recruiting workers in Italy and supplying them to particular employers for a set term. Following an outcry against "white slavery," as the padrone system came to be known, Congress prohibited immigrant labor contracts in 1885. The padroni then bound workers to themselves informally by advancing their cost of passage and by demanding a *bossatura*, or finder's fee, for securing work with an American employer. When the mass exodus of Italians to the berry fields first began in the 1880s, one man, Louis Volker, controlled the recruitment of all pickers in the city of Philadelphia, according to the Dillingham Commission's sources. Workers could not bargain up their wage rates by threatening to take their labor to another contractor; there was only one source of work on New Jersey's farms. Later two or three other padroni entered the business of farm labor contracting. Given free transportation by the railroads, they traveled from one berry center to another making contracts with growers. The Consumers' League alleged in 1905 that "two of the shrewdest Italians in Philadelphia" operated a transportation racket that controlled all the facilities necessary to distribute thousands of pickers over Delaware and New Jersey. The "transportation bosses" would arrange special excursion trains for which pickers would be charged inflated rates. The amount charged above the actual fare would then be divided between the transportation bosses and the padroni.[5]

By the time the Dillingham Commission made its inquiries in 1909, the cutting off of such railroad perquisites and the prohibition of immigrant labor contracts by the U.S. Congress had impoverished the profits of international and metropolitan labor contractors. With the decline of immigrant labor magnates, "a host of 'little' *padroni*" competed for labor among a more seasoned workforce. "More intelligence on the part of the laborers" and weaker padroni led to pettier if not fewer abuses. The "little" padroni, as they were known, did no more than furnish twenty to forty workers, including their own families; boss them during the season, and make a profit on provisions and housing where they could.[6]

Upon receiving orders from farmers, the padroni would begin canvassing Italian neighborhoods door-to-door until they had sealed bargains with enough workers. Once the season began, they arranged the transportation of their crews, receiving a fee for every worker secured for a grower and the *bossatura* from every worker for whom they located a job. Each time a padrone's crew moved to a new crop, he exacted additional dues. Growers relinquished the problems of supervising, housing, and even paying workers to the padroni and their underlings, who were known as "row-bosses," permitting them to operate commissaries and to charge workers for the use of barns, sheds, and stables as shelters. While in the fields, the padrone acted as "spokesman, general manager, and boss."[7]

The prominence of the padrone system was most apparent in Hammonton Township, at the heart of New Jersey's berry region, where strawberries had once been picked by German immigrants and local folk. By the 1880s, according to the Dillingham Commission, "the Germans were busy cultivating berries themselves," and growers began complaining of acute labor shortages during the harvest season. However, between 1883 and 1895, "the flush times of the Hammonton berry grower," the padroni sent as many as 2,000 Italians on special trains from Philadelphia during the picking season. The numbers of workers fell in the 1890s because of low berry prices, but in 1909 the labor force for the berry-growing district just around Hammonton, Winslow, and Waterford was "not far short of 2100," according to the commission's figures. There are no estimates of the total number of Italian harvest workers in the state, but the Newark Bureau of the Associate Charities reported in 1905 that the "yearly exodus of Italian families from Philadelphia" was so large in certain districts "that the lower grades of the public and parochial schools were almost depopulated during the past season."[8]

For growers the padroni were labor contractors and supervisors. But to the pickers they served as an employment bureau, not only locating work but transporting the workers to it. While black migrants traveling alone might lose days waiting for a crop to ripen or wandering into a county already well supplied with labor, the Italian families relied on the padroni to make all arrangements with employers and to move them efficiently from harvest to harvest. This was the service for which they paid a portion of their earnings each day.

The work itself was as varied as the crops they picked. The harvest season would get off to a back-aching start in May as the pickers stooped to harvest strawberries in Delaware and South Jersey. As the strawberry season petered out, gangs of pickers would straighten their backs and climb aboard the padroni's wagons for the ride to the raspberry and blackberry farms of Atlantic and Gloucester Counties. There they could work in an upright position, but picking the small, soft berries from among the thorny bushes was harder work and paid more poorly. They would thus be happy to move on to more lucrative work on blackberry farms, where the plants were tied with stakes and the fruit was more easily gathered. Blueberries, or "huckleberries" as they were called, would ripen next, but they grew wild, so the padroni had no interest in the crop and would return to Philadelphia, taking most of their wards with them. Without the row bosses to guide them, workers who remained became "veritable gypsies," picking the berries for themselves and selling them directly to freight agents for as much as $3.00 a day. Other pickers found work in tomato, pepper, and cucumber fields, while some went to Cape May County to skin tomatoes and peel sweet potatoes and pumpkins for canning.[9]

Finally, in September, South Jersey's harvest season would reach its peak as cranberries began to ripen. The pickers still scattered throughout the state would converge on the desolate cranberry bogs of South Jersey, where they would be joined by "a great many families" brought directly from Philadelphia by the padroni. For the next three to seven weeks thousands of harvesters would work bent over until their heads reached nearly to their knees as they teased the small berries from the tangled mass of vines. The women and children picked by hand; the better-paid men used scoops. The worst part of the job was not the stooping but the mosquitoes, which would breed when a heavy rain turned the bogs into a "vast sponge."[10]

Children as young as five worked alongside their mothers or ran "back and forth bringing empty boxes to the pickers and carrying the filled trays to the berry shed." Children too young to work were left to themselves or in the care of "little mothers." Infants slept trundled in baby carriages at the end of the berry rows.[11]

It was this use of child labor that most concerned reformers. "Men and women are also caught in the bondage of over-work and over-hours

Children of Italian berry pickers on a South Jersey farm
(*Charities and the Commons*, 1905)

saving perishable food at the expense of their own bodies," the authors
of *Children in Bondage* observed, "but it is only for the children that I
speak on these pages. I plead for tired, bleeding little hands, for bent
and aching backs, for weary dragging feet." Reformers separated the
interests of children and parents, recognizing that adult berry pickers
and the padroni who supervised them demanded the wages that children earned. "From the standpoint of the parents," the Consumers'
League observed, "the more children one has at this time, the greater
the income." "Many foreign parents are merciless in driving their little
ones to this long-extended work," the critics insisted; "American parents
are not so merciless." Canneries escaped the age-limit regulations on
"mercantile establishments" by calling young workers "mothers' help-
ers"; farmers had no such laws to circumvent. As a result, "little backs
begin to bend all day in the sun to pick, pick, pick berries, among thorns,
in the marshes, often tormented by heat and insects, and always driven
and threatened and frequently accelerated by curses and blows." The
labor of children, the authors estimated, brought a quarter of a million
dollars annually to New Jersey's cranberry growers alone.[12]

The reformers' fury at the use of child labor was aggravated by the
housing conditions on the bogs. Although some of the larger cranberry
bogs built barracks, most growers simply cleared out barns and sheds
and furnished them with rows of wooden slabs and straw tick for beds.
These "Fresh Air Homes" may have made "an alluring picture" at first,

One of the barracks built for cranberry pickers on a South Jersey bog. According to the National Child Labor Committee, the building contained 26-by-7½-foot rooms and housed more than sixty people. (*The Survey*, 1911)

with their smells of cheese and bologna, wreathes of bread, and strings of onions suspended from the rafters, but overcrowding made housing conditions on a majority of farms "worse than in the congested city districts from which the people [came]," according to the Consumers' League.[13] Wooden shacks, 40 by 36 feet in length, sheltered 130 people and enough rice, macaroni, sardines, and tomato paste to last the summer. Five years after the Consumers' League first exposed this environment in 1905, conditions remained "unspeakable," according to the National Child Labor Committee: "Families of five, six, and even eight were found living in one room measuring six by eight feet, without any sanitary provisions whatever." Barracks measuring 18 by 30 feet housed 60 to 75 people. "The congestion outslums the city," the investigators concluded. Even the barracks on the large bogs were overcrowded and unsanitary. One such new building, which contained 200 bunks for pickers, had been built around a stable. Some shacks were better than this and some worse, the Consumers' League noted, but "very few were seen in which, or around which, the conditions were anything but filthy and improper."[14]

The interior of a shack that sheltered ten families to a side on a strawberry farm, according to a tuberculosis nurse from the visiting nurse association of Baltimore (*The Survey*, 1909)

before antibiotics → *a communicable disease that flourished in overcrowded housing*

To the reformers, the crowding of both sexes into unpartitioned rooms was worse than the filth, congestion, and lack of sanitation facilities. Most migrant housing invited "disease and immorality," concluded Mina Ginger of the Consumers' League: "A glance inside these sheds on a rainy afternoon reveals a promiscuous horde of men, women and children, unpleasantly suggestive of cattle in a freight car."[15]

Even more significant than the threat of rampant promiscuity in the pickers' camp was the cost of a generation of children left to "grow up as foreign as if they had never passed Ellis Island." Because the padroni recruited workers outside the State of New Jersey, New Jersey's truancy laws were not applied to the berry pickers' children. Mina Ginger was the first to expose the loss of three to four months of school by thousands of Italian children working in New Jersey's fields. "They necessarily fall behind their classes, and there are always some who degenerate into chronic truants," she concluded. Teachers and principals in Philadelphia "say the little berry pickers are generally the most depraved children in the schools," and the loss of so much schooling ruined the chances of their "Americanization along [the] right lines."[16]

affected the quality of education

The reformers blamed these conditions on the growers' use of the padroni as labor contractors. According to reformers the padroni were "brutal," "parasitic," and "un-American" taskmasters, who reveled in their power over defenseless workers, "who seldom know English speech or American customs." By leaving the hiring of workers to the bosses, growers turned a blind eye to the problem of child labor, which produced "depravation of mind and morals" and "the perversion of family life" and promoted conditions that bred disease and promiscuity. "The growers do not actually make these conditions, they merely condone them," the authors of *Children in Bondage* argued in 1914. "They pay the parsimonious *padrone*, and ease their conscience by letting him be responsible for the evil herding and harrying of the pickers."[17]

To reformers, then, the relations between pickers, growers, and padroni were clear cut. The pickers were passive victims, like cattle herded into a stockyard, and though they were not slaughtered on their arrival in the bogs, they were surely damaged morally, physically, and intellectually by the time they left. The growers were in league with the padroni, exploiting children for their own gain while denying responsibility for the treatment of the families who worked on their farms. The padroni were evil taskmasters whose domination over the berry pickers knew no bounds. To reformers, the padrone system was a peculiarity of Italian immigration, and the Italian laborers' submission to their more powerful countrymen a racial weakness.[18]

Yet, such labor contracting systems are an established feature of labor migrations. Whenever poor workers travel over great distances, the person who can advance their fares and secure them work wields considerable power over them. This was true of the indentured servitude system in the seventeenth century and of contract labor systems that brought thousands of Chinese workers to the West Coast in the nineteenth century. What stands out about the padrone system in turn-of-the-century New Jersey agriculture was less the padroni's power over workers than their power over the growers.[19]

Because they could rarely communicate with Italians, New Jersey's American-born growers had to rely on the padroni to supervise as well as supply workers.[20] As the Dillingham investigators observed, few Italian growers employed row bosses. "They can give directions in their own tongue, and, going along from row to row are able to keep in touch with the pickers continually." However, "the American is handicapped in this respect. He does not know the language and frequently can not get gangs unless he agrees to pay a row boss, whose family is among the pickers. No matter how small the gang, one boss is required."[21]

Their dependence on padroni as foremen and recruiters left growers perpetually dissatisfied with labor relations on their farms. "A good many complain of the Italian as a laborer for others," the Dillingham Commission reported. "He is said to be a time server, not indolent, but tricky, needs constant watching, and grumbles a good deal about his work and wages." Children were the source of constant grumbling on the part of employers. Growers complained to the commission that children "break up berry boxes, trample down berry bushes and sweet-potato vines, and overrun the garden and orchard like ordinary healthy, lively boys and girls of that age everywhere. In the cranberry bogs they are especially exasperating, breaking down bushes and trampling over the unpicked berries." One large grower reputedly said that he would be thankful if no child under nine years was permitted on the bogs. The commission also added that young Italian men made very unsatisfactory pickers. Gangs of young men, usually from shops or factories shut down temporarily, sometimes came to the fields for a few weeks. "They do not work steadily or rapidly, and it is very seldom indeed that they remain through the season at one place. Having few belongings, they move easily, and as soon as the berrying begins to fall off they leave for easier work." Farmers, the commission reported, were loath to hire them.[22]

Mr. Rider, a member of the State Board of Agriculture, painted a more flattering portrait of the Italian worker, but here, too, the problem of supervision remained an underlying theme. "An Italian won't do as good work as a native, nor as much," Rider argued, "but most of them are willing workers and they eventually learn to do the work. . . . I have been very much pleased with the class I had tried last season. They have been very willing and worked very hard, especially if someone was watching." The person watching was the padrone, and it was with him that Rider had the most complaints. "We are employing from 100 to 200 people during the harvest season," Rider reported to the State Board of Agriculture in 1904, "and we have always had Italians from the country districts up to last year." That year he changed his padrone, and the new labor contractor insisted on providing people from the city: "He said people from the city and country quarrel, and he didn't want any from the country brought there. He brought down city people, and we had more quarreling than we had in 10 years."[23]

"In a good many instances," the Dillingham investigators noted, "the row boss is a real advantage. . . . He knows the members of the gang, can talk to them in their own tongue, exercises more authority than an American employer can, and becomes a real go-between to protect the interests of his proteges." But in many cases, the report observed, the padrone was "worth nothing" to either the employer or the gang; "his only desire is to earn his $1.50 per diem, and carry a big stick with some dignity."[24]

The growers' problems did not diminish over time. The Italians who worked on New Jersey's farms did not come year after year until they were too old to make the trip, nor were they supplanted by their grown children. Immigrant berry pickers were constantly replenished by new emigrants from Italy.[25] Because Italian berry pickers continually withdrew from agricultural labor as other opportunities became open to them, growers faced a perpetual recruitment and supervision problem. Instead of employing a workforce that returned every year, eventually learned English, and perhaps took on supervisory roles, berry growers had to find and manage raw recruits every season, and the problem got worse instead of better. Though the availability and efficiency of harvest workers was only one of many problems that farmers regularly faced, they were spending two-thirds more on labor by 1910 than they had a decade earlier, though farm sizes had decreased and wages were slow to rise. The difference jingled in the padrone's pocket. By 1914 70 percent of New Jersey's growers hired farmworkers, and they remained dependent on the padroni as long as they used Italian laborers.

That growers used padroni to discipline workers is indisputable. Reformers published photographs of row bosses in suits and bowlers, standing watch with heavy sticks over stooped workers. Not unlike southern textile mill owners who hired foremen from among the families and communities that provided their labor, New Jersey growers used Italian-born bosses to bridge the cultural and language gap between themselves and their workers, with the padrone assuming the authoritarian but familiar role of patriarch in fields filled with women and children. Moreover, by leaving Italian workers to the care of other Italians, growers could more readily absolve themselves of any moral responsibility for conditions on their farms. Italians paid, housed, and disciplined Italians; growers merely provided jobs.[26]

Still, the coercive power of the padroni was not unlimited. Although the bonds between foremen and workers could be exploited by employers to discipline workers from afar, workers could also pull the strings of kith and kin. Just as foremen in southern mills could sometimes be held to the standards of the community from which they came, the padroni were part of the Italian community of Philadelphia; they could not escape its bounds without losing their ability to recruit workers in the future.[27] However, the pickers' power to constrain the padroni went far beyond that of southern mill workers over their foremen. Ultimately,

A padrone with stick and bowler supervising Italian berry pickers at work
(*Charities and the Commons*, 1905)

mill foremen were employees of the mills. They could be influenced by
kin and community, but the mills buttered their bread. Padroni were
paid by both growers and workers. If they expected to compete for labor
among other "little" padroni, they could not risk gaining a reputation as
brutal or exploitive row bosses.

The Italian contract workers who dealt with padroni before the abolition of emigrant labor contracts might well have described their experience as a sort of indentured servitude. Separated by an ocean from their
homes and families and indebted for food and fare, they had little control over their daily lives. But the berry field padroni of the twentieth
century were regulated by unwritten rules, enforced by the gossip of
tenement stoops and sweatshops.

This community regulation of the padroni's excesses may not have
been altogether effective, but by the early twentieth century some padroni were behaving more like shop stewards than row bosses. The Dillingham Commission reported an incident, for example, in which a padrone refused to allow a grower to hire an additional gang, though the
padrone had brought fewer workers than promised. "The first gang re-

fused to go out until late in the day, refusing to pick if the grower persisted in employing a larger force," the investigator reported. Though the commission interpreted this as simple stubbornness on the padrone's part, it is quite possible that this row boss was either conceding to the gang's demand or protecting them from the loss they would incur by picking a field with too many workers. Ultimately the grower gave in to the padrone's demand and dismissed the second gang. According to his testimony, however, the remaining crew was too small to bring in the entire crop, and one-third of it was lost. "Many instances of like sort might be cited," the commission added.[28]

The padrone's role was thus ambiguous and dynamic. A padrone might play the role of taskmaster, shop steward, or indifferent mediator, depending on his interests of the moment. Although the padrone secured and supervised workers and allowed growers to deny responsibility for conditions in and out of the fields, growers paid dearly for their dependence on an uncertain ally.

Opponents of child labor did not perceive this ambiguity and were rarely moved by the growers' recruitment and supervisory problems. In 1905 Mina Ginger recommended that the problem might be solved by recruiting workers in New Jersey cities rather than in Philadelphia, so that New Jersey's school authorities could be held accountable for the education of the pickers' children. In the end, however, she concluded that the solution to the problem of child labor "must rest on the consciences of the farmers, in whose power it lies to prevent and prohibit such labor." She did not consider the question of how women could journey to the fields while their children remained in city schools, though perhaps she intended that rural schools absorb the pickers' children during the harvest season.[29]

Six years later, when the National Child Labor Committee made its recommendations, its members rejected the notion that growers could be shamed or cajoled into improving housing conditions and prohibiting child labor. According to Charles Chute's summary of their report in *The Survey*, South Jersey's system of "sporadic family labor" was "inherently bad" and "intolerable." New Jersey labor law should regulate agricultural employment "as it does other forms of work," the committee insisted, and both parents and growers should be prohibited from keeping children out of school. Neither New Jersey's nor Pennsylvania's compulsory school laws should be set aside, they argued, "for the benefit of cranberry growers whose profits are already large, however willing the parents may be to profit by the labor of the children." "The whole sale removal of these families is not for an outing in the Jersey pines, as one of their employers naively expresses it," Chute argued, "but to labor for the support of the family in a region where there are no restrictions as to age or sex, hours and conditions of labor, nor regulated living conditions." Clearly, by 1911 reformers had abandoned appeals for voluntary cooperation in favor of demands for state regulation of agricultural employment.[30]

Unable to win a ban on child labor in agriculture, reformers did convince state officials to envision an expanded role for themselves in overseeing conditions for workers on New Jersey's farms. Despite their studious effort to mediate between reformers and growers without upsetting the latter, the members of the New Jersey Commission of Immigration joined the Consumers' League and the National Child Labor Committee in calling for a state role in regulating employment conditions in agriculture. The commission recommended, for example, that the State Board of Health enforce minimum standards of sanitation and that the Board of Education consider the practicability of establishing special classes for immigrant children whose schooling was disrupted by "summer work in the small fruit industry." The commission also concluded, after consultation with the state attorney general, that state laws restricting child labor in "mercantile establishments" applied equally to agriculture and should be enforced "upon cranberry bogs" by the New Jersey Department of Labor.[31] The New Jersey legislature simply ignored its own commission's recommendations, but reformers had succeeded in creating a role for themselves as expert witnesses to the problem of migrant labor. In that role they continued to assail conditions on New Jersey's farms.[32]

Growers were no more successful in their efforts to shape state policy. Frustrated by the dubious loyalty of the padroni and the controversy they caused, growers attempted to circumvent the Italian labor bosses and recruit labor with the aid of state officials. In 1904 the president of the State Board of Agriculture traveled to Italy to encourage the emigration of Italians directly to New Jersey farms, hoping to secure workers from among the "intelligent, industrious and peaceful" people he found there. He noted happily that the Italians he met were "not of the passionate and ugly kind that infest our cities." Recognizing that he could not arrange the importation of a specific group of workers due to the prohibition against emigrant labor contracts, he argued that "they are coming anyway. My thought is only that they would be corraled [sic] so that they will come to the farm." A member of the board concurred: "I travel almost every day upon the Central railroad," he observed, "and there is not a day passes when there is not from three to 10 to 15 Italians coming."[33] What these leading growers schemed about was a state or federal agency that would redirect immigrants to their farms.

If state officials could not contract with workers abroad under U.S. immigration law, they could at least recruit from among the immigrants who had already landed on American shores. To prevent newly arrived workers from heading immediately to the immigrant communities in northeastern cities, the board proposed the establishment of a state agency that would direct a "fair proportion of the great stream of immigration to our farms." Such an arrangement would "lead to an increase of permanent farm help throughout the state and relieve the cities of a super-abundant population," satisfying "all concerned."[34]

Two year later, in 1906, no such agency had yet been created, but by then the Consumers' League had made public the results of its investigation of labor conditions on New Jersey's farms. As a result, the State Board of Agriculture adapted its recommendations to an audience hardened to growers' concerns by reformers' charges of cruelty and neglect. The state board again proposed a system for the better distribution of immigrants among "the agricultural communities of the state," but this time it also blamed the padrone system for the conditions suffered by farmworkers. In a gesture of conciliation to reformers, the board members suggested a system of cooperation between farmers and "those interested in the welfare of immigrants" as a means to circumvent and ultimately undermine the Italian bosses. Stressing the need to "employ enough of these men and provide such conditions of living . . . as will make them contented," the board proposed that benevolent organizations send immigrants directly to them. The grip of the padrone system, "which has dumped trainloads of Italian families from Philadelphia into the berry fields at the picking season" and herded them into "temporary shacks" "under conditions which often have been degrading," would thus be broken.[35] New Jersey growers failed to win a labor distribution service in New Jersey, but the federal government created such an agency in 1907, stepping into the padrone's shoes for the first time.[36]

Reformers tried to shape a state that would serve as a guardian to immigrant migrants; growers tried to fashion a state that would supply them with labor. By the end of the first decade of the twentieth century, both groups saw the padrone system as a problem and believed that state intervention was required to resolve it. And both were heard but not exactly heeded. As with other causes dear to reformers in the Progressive Era, the debate over migrant labor in New Jersey led to an expansion of the investigative functions of government—in other words, to a lot of talk and little action. By organizing commissions and publicizing their results, reformers prodded state officials to form their own commissions and to conduct their own investigations, but none of these inquiries led to substantive change in state policy. Growers were no more successful in their efforts to create a state bureau that would supply them with labor, although the federal government would soon get involved in labor distribution in a big way.

The turn-of-the-century conflict between New Jersey growers and reformers is nonetheless significant because it placed the issue of farm labor within the purview of state authority and established the parameters of future debates. Farm labor advocates would continue to call for a benevolent state that would protect farmworkers from victimization. Farm owners would call on the state to act as padrone. Yet in no way did this debate give voice to the berry pickers themselves. Farmworkers would remain not so much stuck in the middle as outside the debate altogether. Investigators questioned field workers on various occasions, but they did so to collect data — wages earned, ages of working children, months of schooling missed — not to solicit workers' opinions or aspirations. Had they asked, they might have found that the berry pickers could choose among padroni, that they negotiated with growers through the padroni, and that they were able to limit to some extent how much authority the labor bosses wielded over them. Organized informally in urban tenements, pews, and sweatshops, the women of the berry fields and bogs were not powerless against the men who carried big sticks with some dignity.

Progressives as Padroni

Labor Distribution and
the Agrarian Ideal

ONCE PROGRESSIVE reformers discovered the problems of farm labor migrancy in the Northeast, they might have been dismayed by a host of agricultural ills. They might have seized, for example, on the myriad problems that farmers faced in an industrial economy—declining prices, land speculation, rising tenancy rates, and extortionist interest rates, to name just a few. Some reformers did take up these causes. Known as "Country-Lifers," they raised public awareness to the needs of rural communities. But even as the Country Life Commission, appointed by Theodore Roosevelt, called for reforms to stop the degeneration of rural conditions, urban reformers elevated the idea of agrarian democracy to new heights.[1] Even after exposing housing and labor conditions on New Jersey's farms in lurid prose, the social work profession's leading magazine continued to celebrate the virtues of rural life. "Upon the character of the rural people," the editors of *The Survey* concluded, "their intelligence, morality, ideals, and material well-being—more than on any other one factor depends the general welfare of the nation as a whole."[2]

Despite what they knew about berry pickers' lives, many urban reformers believed that the solution to urban problems lay on the nation's farms. To bring the urban environment under control, they argued, the nation's population would have to be redistributed from factory to farm, from urban cesspools to the clean air of the countryside, and from radical breeding grounds to the fertile soil of democratic citizenship. The

an idealized
version of rural life

U.S. Census Bureau had announced the closing of the American frontier in 1890, but urban reformers were undaunted. They had heard farmers' complaints of labor scarcity and had themselves publicized the abandonment of eastern farms. They had heard western bonanza farms calling annually for thousands of men to operate the horse- and steam-powered machines of the modern harvest. Frontier or no frontier, the American countryside seemed ripe with opportunities for the urban poor and immigrant masses. Labor had only to be redistributed so that a bargain could be struck between the nation's demand and the world's supply.

The task of redistributing the nation's population, however, proved to be overwhelmingly large and complex, and it was thwarted, ultimately, by the unstoppable growth of farm labor migrancy. Labor distribution was tackled by several reform organizations, both public and philanthropic. The U.S. Industrial Commission (USIC), which met between 1898 and 1902, led the drive to channel immigrants into agriculture. The USIC painted an idyllic portrait of the nation's countryside, one in which rural life was the foundation of good citizenship and farmwork a stepping stone to farm ownership and economic independence. Dismissing the advent of farm labor migrancy as an unfortunate aberration in an otherwise healthy economy, the commissioners concluded that immigrants would do well to gravitate to the nation's farms rather than to its industrial capitals. The progressive rank and file took up their challenge, creating societies, agencies, and bureaus to settle immigrants and the unemployed on homesteads and farm colonies around the nation.

The failure of this effort to ease urban congestion and unemployment led reformers to conclude that the federal government bore the responsibility for the redistribution of the nation's labor supply. In 1907 the Department of Commerce and Labor's Division of Information accepted this responsibility and began a federal labor distribution program. It too failed, but its misadventure reveals much about the problems of federal intervention in labor recruitment and supply. Having set out to promote agricultural settlement and to act as a clearinghouse for the nation's unemployed, the Division of Information ended up as a sort of feeble federal padrone, feeding men and women into the shifting army of migrant farm labor.

Thus the labor distribution movement can be seen as having three stages: the USIC's invitation to action, the efforts of progressive activists, and in the wake of their frustration, the launching of the Division of Information's federal labor distribution program. Despite the inefficacy of these attempts to alleviate urban problems by settling and employing workers in rural communities, progressives kept the agricultural icon untarnished in the first decade of the twentieth century. But the luster would not last long. By the outbreak of the First World War few voices still preached the gospel of the soil. In 1914, seven years after the creation of the Division of Information and more than a decade after the USIC published its findings, the last Progressive Era inquiry into the state of the economy took up the question of agriculture. Unlike their counterparts in the USIC, the members of the Commission on Industrial Relations (CIR) found little to romanticize in the state of agricultural affairs. To them agriculture appeared industrialized and agricultural labor seemed impoverished; rural life was not a solution to the problems of an urban industrial nation but part of the problem. Moreover, the CIR's members did not dismiss migrant workers as an aberration in an otherwise healthy economy. Rather, they saw them as unfortunate human casualties of the modern agricultural order. Ripe with opportunity at the turn of the century, rural life smelled of rot by the First World War. The latter part of this chapter seeks to explain why agriculture fell from grace in the years between the glib optimism of the USIC and the grim vision of the CIR.

To Progressive Era social reformers the nation was awash in a sea of immigrants and unemployed people whose poverty left them open to both exploitation and radical suggestion. Progressives distinguished themselves from the eugenic theorists of the Gilded Age, who had attributed such problems to inherited defects and racial inferiority. Without entirely abandoning eugenic notions, turn-of-the-century reformers tended to find the source of social character or "backwardness" in environmental factors. The social environments that most troubled them were the immigrant slums that appeared to produce the associated problems of poverty, disease, unemployment, and crime. "It can hardly be denied," one social critic wrote in 1905, "that this almost mechanical gravitation of the newcomers of all nationalities toward the cities in general, and New York in particular, constitutes the most serious aspect of the problem of immigration in this country." Its results were "congestion, sweated trades, long hours, low pay, child labor, low standard of living, high mortality, immorality and crime." Because immigrants congregated in "Little Italys" and "China Towns," their assimilation and "advancement" were "retarded." Increasing urbanization meant that immigrants and domestic workers competed for sporadic, underpaid, unskilled work, and by overcrowding into unsanitary tenements, immigrants spread disease among themselves and the native-born. These were the problems that most troubled social reformers in the last years of the nineteenth century and the first decades of the twentieth. Their goal was not simply to treat the symptoms that plagued the nation's cities but to prevent urban ills by gaining control over the social environment. Agriculture was key to that effort.[3]

In 1898 Congress charged the USIC with the responsibility of conducting a comprehensive investigation into the state of the nation's economy. The USIC heard thousands of witnesses and produced a nineteen-volume report. Though they gave their greatest attention to the history, membership, and legal standing of labor organizations, the commissioners also heard considerable testimony on the state of the agricultural economy. After investigating and documenting the deep depression of the 1890s, capital's ongoing attack on industrial unions, and the corporate merger movement, the USIC turned to agriculture and agricultural labor.[4] Its report, completed in 1901, painted a portrait of the agricultural economy in which rural life remained the bedrock of good citizenship and farmwork a step on the "agricultural ladder" to farm ownership. "The evidence is overwhelming and conclusive," the USIC reported, "that the farm laborer's condition, financial and social, is superior to that of the city laborer of the same grade of intelligence and skill." The USIC report went so far as to argue that the general condition of farm laborers had improved during the second half of the nineteenth century. "While farm work was rendered less severe than formerly by the use of improved machinery," the USIC noted, "wages have risen. Farm laborers are declared to be as well off as their employers, or, since the fall in the prices of farm products, *even better off than some of the farmers who employ them*." Farmworkers, the commission concluded, had a greater opportunity than before to rise to the level of independent farm owners.[5]

To come to this conclusion the commissioners had to disregard cataclysmic changes in American agriculture. They had to ignore the problems of overproduction and debt that had triggered the Populist upheaval, the decline in wheat prices that forced the abandonment of eastern farms, the rise of tenancy and corporate farming, and the institutionalization of farm labor migrancy on both coasts. One would expect that, however fanciful, this nostalgic portrait of American agriculture would have at least been based on the testimony that the commission heard during its three year inquiry. However, it was not. The farmers who appeared before the commission testified again and again to the scarcity of "reliable laborers," but they had little to say about opportunities for families seeking year-round farmwork. Rather, they complained about the difficulty of finding workers during "short harvest rushes." Though southern planters and northeastern truck farmers both grumbled that "the migratory character of farm labor decreases its efficiency," migratory labor was exactly what they demanded.[6]

This testimony left the members of the USIC in a quandary. They obviously meant to represent growers' concerns — the USIC invited only farm owners, not farm laborers, to testify — but they were also intent on finding a healthy agricultural economy made up of independent family farmers and sturdy year-round hired hands.[7] In the end the commissioners simply decried the growing seasonality of farmwork and the degeneracy of the migrant poor and ignored growers' demands for federal help in securing temporary labor. They did so without pointing out the disagreement between their conclusions and the testimony on which they reputedly were based.

The commissioners justified their refusal to meet growers' seasonal needs with two contradictory rationales. On one hand, they argued that the increasing seasonality of agriculture caused by specialization and mechanization degraded the quality of farm labor and farm life. The harvests in hops yards and orchards and "similar harvest seasons requiring large numbers of hands for a short time" had "a demoralizing effect on farm labor," according to the commissioners. "Such employment demands little skill; the requirements of each are simple and easily satisfied. They constitute a low order of farm labor, if worthy to be classed with it at all."[8] On the other hand, they argued simultaneously that transient and unintelligent farmworkers had a deleterious effect on agriculture.

This seeming confusion over cause and effect becomes comprehensible when one understands the commissioners' equally contradictory views on race. They faithfully invoked environmental explanations for social problems when considering white workers, whether native or foreign-born, but invoked eugenic explanations when considering black workers. When discussing white workers, as above, the commissioners attributed migrants' degraded condition to the instability imposed on them by seasonal work. They did allow, however, that the failure of "transient and nondescript" white workers to rise above their condition might be attributable to inherent defects: "The common labor of the farms, including the transient service in harvest or other operations and the less intelligent of the foreign element, does not appear to be improving in efficiency," they concluded.[9]

When discussing black workers, however, the commissioners limited their analyses to racialist and racist explanations. Migrancy, they argued, "suits the negro tendency to change" short terms of employment and odd jobs with winter residence in "old haunts in a mild climate." "As a race," the commissioners noted, black workers were "kind and docile and good workers" but "careless in their methods" and "naturally averse to improved implements." "The more you pay a negro," the commissioners insisted, "the less efficient he becomes."[10] Southern planters testified that black workers were becoming more transient, "shifting from one plantation to another." Rather than attributing this to the seasonality of agricultural employment, as they did when discussing white workers, the commissioners fixed responsibility on the "migratory disposition of the negroes." "The difficulty in the South, so far as regularity of employment is concerned," they concluded, "seems to be due to the desire of the laborer for a respite from work rather than from lack of opportunity to work." This shiftlessness and other traits peculiar to "the negro race" accounted for the problems of southern agriculture, according to the commissioners. They were clearly influenced by men such as J. Pope Brown, the president of the Georgia State Agricultural Society, who testified that one of the causes of rural depression in the South was "the presence of the negro," who "does not know how to use improved implements, and does not want to know how, and it is almost impossible to teach him. . . . They are averse to making anything in the world except cotton."[11]

The members of the USIC did not entirely miss the contradictions in their analysis. When compiling the final report of the hearings on agriculture and agricultural labor, the commissioners pointed out the disjuncture between the testimony of northeastern growers who hired black migrants from the South and the testimony of southern planters and academics who attributed migrancy to racial inferiority. "Colored labor is represented as superabundant, crowded, listless, and unambitious, lacking inducement to effort," the report noted. "On the other hand, it is shown that many of these laborers go from Virginia to Rhode Island and Connecticut, get \$18 to \$20 per month and board, giving good satisfaction to employers, and returning for the winter." The commissioners reasoned that those who went north in search of work were "probably of more than average reliability and efficiency" but admitted that "they could not get more than half as much wages at home." This caveat aside, the commissioners nonetheless concluded that "the migratory character of farm labor decreases its efficiency." Migrant workers were "excrescences" — abnormal growths — on the "fair face" of farm labor. Given this disposition, it is not surprising that the USIC firmly opposed a state role in supplying growers with temporary farm help.[12]

Though the commissioners refused to promote the hiring of migrant workers, they could not simply ignore the problem of farm labor scarcity after listening to so many growers complain about it. In response the USIC maintained that the nation's foreign-born population was sufficient to solve growers' labor problems. Although they advocated immigration restriction, they also called for an agency that would make those immigrants who did enter the country aware of the advantages of agricultural employment and channel them permanently into labor-scarce agricultural regions. Given the opportunities that agriculture offered, the USIC argued, immigrants would be better off pursuing agricultural employment than congregating in already overpopulated cities.

However well intended, this recommendation left labor-scarce farmers at a loss. They had testified to their need for labor during "short harvest rushes," not to an absence of year-round workers. They would have had little use for immigrant families delivered from New York or Philadelphia to their doorsteps in the dead of winter. For a month or two in late summer immigrants would be most welcome, but after they picked the last berry or peeled the last potato, they would have to join the stream of migrant workers or the ranks of the unemployed.

The USIC's call for immigration restriction had the backing of the American Federation of Labor (AFL) and a minority of social reformers (including most members of the Dillingham Commission). However, the foot soldiers of the progressive movement were usually antirestrictionists. Activists in the settlement house movement, Americanization campaigns, and public health projects, to name just a few of the many organizations that dealt with immigrants, tended to argue that the nation's problem was not an oversupply of labor but a maldistribution of labor, characterized by excessive concentrations of unskilled workers in the nation's industrial capitals. To Jane Addams, for example, immigration restriction was not a solution to the nation's industrial ills but a panacea, and she leapt at the USIC's call for the redistribution of the nation's immigrant population.[13]

Italy's acting vice-consul in New York, Gustavo Tosti, whose job was to promote the out-migration of Italy's poor, best expressed the antirestrictionist position. He could "easily understand that the evils resulting from the unwholesome promiscuousness of tenement life should lead certain observers to entertain a feeling of diffidence and fear toward the foreign invader." But he did not understand "how the dangers of the concentration of alien colonies in the large cities . . . can be used as an argument for a wholesale condemnation of immigration in general." The answer, he countered, was not immigration restriction but immigration distribution. The United States had more than enough room for a constant influx of "vigorous immigration." While Italy had 111 citizens per square kilometer, Tosti observed, the United States had only 8. Immigrants should simply be distributed to sparsely populated regions, where they could find "needed and useful employment and supply equally useful labor."[14]

Most reformers, though differing on the question of immigration restriction, tended to agree that the existing immigrant population would be well served by a rational policy of labor distribution. And where better to distribute labor than to the countryside. Rural life, reformers reasoned, had been the foundation of democracy, independence, and economic stability in the formative years of the republic. Even in an industrial age and a new century, agriculture seemed to hold out the promise of peace and harmony to an economically unstable and socially explosive nation. Earlier generations of immigrants who had settled on the land had been quickly and quietly absorbed into the nation's productive citizenry, reformers argued. Scandinavians, Germans, and Bohemians, "long settled in rural districts, have become so thoroughly American, have so completely lost themselves in the rural population, that they retain very few of their distinctive race characteristics." Why not, too, the Italians, Russians, Poles, and Hungarians of the "new immigration"?[15]

Thus, the idea of labor distribution complemented progressives' notions about the importance of assimilation and environment. Earlier immigrants had blended so easily into the American populace, they argued, not because they were better prepared or more "socially advanced" than more recent immigrants, but because the agricultural life that greeted them in the United States instilled in them the values of hard work and thrift. Progressives pointed to the Italian agricultural colonies of New York, New Jersey, California, and Louisiana for evidence that the new immigrants from eastern and southern Europe were not inherently backward; in the right environment, they too would thrive.

Christenzo Seragosa seemed a case in point. A native of Sicily, Seragosa arrived in Fredonia, New York, in 1894 and applied for work for himself and a friend at a cannery. They were hired, *The Survey* reported in 1911, but due to the local hostility to Italians, they were unable to find housing in the vicinity of the factory.[16] "Undaunted they moved in and by the end of the year had made themselves so well liked, that the numerous Sicilian families which followed found no difficulty in securing houses." What had really drawn Seragosa to Fredonia, the authors noted, was not the cannery but land suited to grape culture. "All that they could save from their wages was invested in land and planted out to

Vineyards," *The Survey* noted. "Now there are 1,200 Italians in Fredonia, many of them owning large vineyards. . . . Their places are well kept, and they have raised the standard of farming in that vicinity—Americans have to hustle to keep up with them."

The Survey's staff had no doubts about the beneficial effects of agriculture on values, morality, and behavior. The hundreds of little berry farms, vineyards, and sweet potato and pepper fields made these Italian communities "real oases in a waste of sand and lowland" and testified "to the ability of the much-maligned South Italian to create wealth and to make progress materially, morally and politically under rural conditions." Properly organized, another author argued in 1905, agricultural settlements were simply more conducive to social uplift and moral progress than urban slums. In the Italian colony of Hammonton, New Jersey, for example, residents were not crowded into unsanitary tenements but soon built two- to four-room dwellings. The children born in the community were large and strong and were forced to attend school by compulsory education laws. Moreover, the work they were given was "healthful in character, not sweat shop labor." All in all, another author concluded, rural life has had "a salutary effect on the Italians." "It has frequently taken an ignorant, abject, unskilled, dependent, foreign laborer and make of him a shrewd, self-respecting, independent farmer and citizen."[17]

Social reformers were so enamored with the virtues of agricultural life that some were determined to bring the farm to the immigrant, if they could not bring the immigrant to the farm. In New York City in 1905, for example, immigrant children could attend Mrs. Henry Parsons's "Agricultural Kindergarten" and mind their own little plots. There, Parsons assured reporters, they are taught "honesty in their work, neatness and order, justice as well as kindness to their neighbors. . . . All the virtues . . . from a little patch of ground not eight feet square."[18]

The one agricultural occupation that offered no such prospects, according to reformers, was that of the migrant farmworker. A comparison of the Italian settlements at Vineland and Hammonton with the squalor of the region's berry pickers' camps was enough to convince reformers of the evils of migrant life. On this question the views of Alexander Cance, the author of the Dillingham Commission's *Report on Recent Immigrants in Agriculture*, reflected a consensus among proponents of labor distribution: "In standard of living, Americanization, initiative, resourcefulness, progressive spirit, civic and personal respect, and general moral tone, the Italian berry picker is far behind the land owning Sicilian for whom he labors."[19] Vice-Consul Tosti agreed. "The question at issue," he argued, "is not how to transform our immigrants into farm workers, but rather how to transform them into farmers and small land-owners." He refuted the idea, advanced "in certain quarters" (New Jersey's State Board of Agriculture, for example), that agricultural distribution should be accomplished "simply through the employment of a large number of Italians as farm workers and farm hands." Migrant work would provide employment for a few months of the year, but "after a comparatively short period of occupation," the migrants "would lapse into enforced idleness, which would undoubtedly drive them back to the industrial centers." The only way to get at "the root of the question," Tosti concluded, "is to transform a large proportion of our immigrants into *land-owners or farmers*."[20]

It was the experience of landownership itself that best accounted for the social and civic progress made by Italian settlers, according to *The Survey*: "The prestige incidental to landed proprietorship, as well as the financial responsibility of an owner, sets the farmer far above the day laborer."[21] The light of this shining example revealed, according to Alexander Cance, "the deadening effect" of rural isolation on immigrant migrant farmworkers: "When the Italians are intermingled with an equal number of American farmers, they assimilate rather rapidly; where there is rural segregation of large groups Americanization is a slower process than in the city." Ranking social environments in order of their progressive potential, then, agricultural settlements were at the top and migrant life was at the very bottom. Even slum dwellings were less harmful than berry pickers' camps, in Cance's hierarchy.

Only poverty and ignorance of rural opportunities could explain immigrants' failure to avail themselves of the ameliorative effects of agricultural settlement, according to these authors. "The alien is prone to remain in cities," one writer argued, "because of ignorance of opportunities and resources in other parts of the country, lack of incentive or the means to live elsewhere, reluctance to leave the small colony to which he first attaches himself and where he can have associates with his own nationality and race and especially with those of his native province." According to Alice Bennett, "the *contandino* comes to friends in one of the overcrowded cities, and with only five or ten dollars capital, he must take the first job that offers." "Thus the man who would be invaluable as a farmer becomes a parasite and menace to the city," she continued. "As sixty per cent of the Italians who come are *contandini*, some plan should be found to deflect them to the land."[22] What was lacking, Bennett concluded, was information published in Italy pointing explicitly to opportunities awaiting the efficient farmer.

In the decade following the USIC's hearings, reform activists orga-nized three distinct reform ventures, all of which fell under the rubric of labor distribution. The first and most widely supported were the efforts to plant immigrants in agricultural settlements, not as farmworkers but as independent farmers. More controversial were programs that ac-cepted migrant farmwork as a fixture of modern agriculture and tried merely to mitigate its worst effects by supplanting or at least reforming the padrone system of labor recruitment and supply. Finally, reformers who worked mainly among the urban unemployed promoted the idea of public or philanthropic labor exchanges that would bring together "men without jobs and jobs without men," even if those jobs were tempo-rary stints on farms. All three efforts soon ran into problems that led their organizers to renew the USIC's call for a federal role in labor distribution.

The most celebrated effort to redirect immigrants to agricultural set-tlements was undertaken by the Jewish Agricultural and Industrial Aid Society, with funding from the philanthropist Baron de Hirsch. Unlike other settlement efforts that simply channeled immigrants with agricul-tural backgrounds into farm colonies, the Jewish Agricultural Society recruited Jewish immigrants who lacked any farm experience. The so-ciety operated an agricultural training school, advanced credit for land, and maintained a constant presence in Jewish farm colonies, such as Woodbine, New Jersey. Despite such well-organized, -publicized, and -fi-nanced efforts, the agricultural settlement movement as a whole had little impact on the problem of urban crowding. By 1912 only 15,000 Jewish settlers lived in rural communities, and the new immigration remained primarily an urban phenomenon.[23]

On behalf of urban-dwelling immigrants, such as the Italian berry pickers of Philadelphia, who were forced to take temporary agricultural work in order to make a subsistence wage, progressives worked to reform the padrone system. One particularly ambitious example was the Society for the Protection of Italian Immigrants, which tried to raise the stan-dard of living among immigrant farmworkers by operating an employ-ment service in competition with the padroni. To rectify the "neglect and indifference to the laborer's welfare," the society "actively entered into the business of supplying employers with laborers and of conduct-ing labor camps through trustworthy agents of its own." According to Charles B. Phipard's article "The Philanthropist-Padrone," the society's object was not so much to replace the padroni but to reform the system by competition and example. The society soon discovered, however, that it was not so easy to entice workers away from the padroni, or as Phipard put it, to wean "the ignorant laborer" from "his habit of believing that the *padrone* is the only one who can supply his needs." Because it was "extremely difficult to win the confidence of the laborer," it was also hard to convince growers to rely on the society to find workers at short notice. As a result, these philanthropist-padroni, like the reformers who promoted permanent agricultural settlements, had little impact either on immigrants themselves or on those who sought to exploit them.[24]

While the organizers of the Society for the Protection of Italian Immigrants operated a labor bureau in hope of freeing Italians from the clutches of the padroni, other reformers opened similar services to alleviate the suffering of the unemployed, both foreign and native-born. They too found that the irregularity of agricultural employment defied their efforts to bring together jobless men and employers. The New York Association for Improving the Condition of the Poor, New York's Bowery Mission, and other charitable agencies tried to alleviate unemployment by placing men in farm jobs. They found, however, that while serving the needs of growers, their efforts could actually harm the families they sought to help. Robert W. Bruere, general agent of the New York Association for Improving the Condition of the Poor, complained in 1909 that employment offers from farms were usually for periods too brief to be of much use: "The work 'peters out' after a planting or a harvesting, leaving the laborers stranded in the rural districts." Moreover, "many of the unemployed have families in the city whom they cannot leave behind, and cannot afford to take with them." Responding in the *New York Times* to the complaints of a Gladstone, New Jersey, cranberry grower whose offer of a $25 a month job, with room and board, had gone unanswered by the association, Bruere explained defensively, "We are continually attempting to secure work for our 3,600 families either in or out of town, and we make a special effort to place families upon farms. . . . But we find it very difficult to secure accurate information from those who turn to us for workers." He then relayed the story of a recent case in which an employment agency had offered to take some families to the country to do farmwork: "We immediately sent five men, heads of families. One of them was rejected because he had too many children, another was told he was too late; another one was rejected because he was inexperienced in farm work. Reports from the two remaining men have not yet reached us."[25]

Unemployed people were quick to see the disadvantages of accepting harvest work, perhaps more quickly than the philanthropists who sought to place them on farms. In 1911, for example, 3,493 Italians applied for work at the Society for the Protection of Italian Immigrants' labor bureau, and 1,425 employers made requests for laborers; however, only

528 placements were actually made. The small number of placements was the result, according to Kate Claghorn of the New York Tenements Department, of workers' reluctance to accept agricultural employment. The society's 1912 report confirms her analysis. Requests for Italian farmhands were persistently made, the society reported, but "not of the kind any capable or intelligent Italian farm hand would accept." "Wages and conditions offered are, as a rule," the report noted, "below any passable living standard, and the Italian farmer has grown to understand that unless a contract or a clear statement is offered him, he is often deprived of his legitimate earning or taken advantage of in some way."[26]

Reformers frequently expressed considerable frustration over their inability to reduce urban congestion and rationalize the labor market, despite their efforts to promote immigrant agricultural settlement, reform the padrone system, and operate labor exchanges. In 1906 the Inter-Municipal Research Committee, a federation of reform organizations, called for a federal inquiry to determine whether "federal employment centers are needed for the better distribution of laborers, especially immigrants."[27] Its demand reflected a sense of exasperation and a growing consensus that only the federal government had the power to redistribute labor on a nationwide basis. Progressives asked, in effect, for the federal government to take on the role of padrone for the nation, but to do so in such a way that workers' welfare would be protected.[28]

Their demands led, in 1907, to the creation of the first federal agency designed to redistribute labor. Located within the Department of Commerce and Labor's Bureau of Immigration, the new agency, called the Division of Information, was charged by its congressional mandate to promote "a beneficial distribution of aliens admitted to the country" by collecting and disseminating "trustworthy data concerning advantages offered settlers in different parts of the county."[29]

The Division of Information's mission rested on the assumption that immigrants would not choose to huddle among their countrymen in the nation's already overpopulated cities if they were made aware of opportunities in other parts of the country. As its name suggests, the new agency was to provide the information needed to guide immigrants to productive lives in the countryside and other labor-scarce regions. However, the secretary of the Department of Commerce and Labor, Oscar S. Straus, had bigger plans. Straus envisioned a labor exchange for the whole nation, a clearinghouse for labor that would reduce unemployment and all its tragic consequences. This would be a padrone system worth its salt. Within a few years of its creation, however, the division generated controversy that far outweighed any advantages that accrued to the nation by its distribution of immigrant settlers and unemployed men into agriculture. Still, the division's history is worth attention because it reveals the problems inherent in federal intervention into the business of labor supply, problems that would reoccur in later decades.[30]

When Congress created the Division of Information in 1907, Oscar S. Straus had only been secretary of commerce and labor for a year. As early as 1888 there had been an independent Bureau of Labor, but in 1903, three years before Straus took office, it had been combined with the Department of Commerce. Though the subordination of the independent Labor Department to the new Department of Commerce and Labor provoked a hostile response from trade unions, it conformed to Theodore Roosevelt's policy of maintaining a balance between capital and labor.[31] Secretary Straus shared the president's view: "Labor and capital were the two arms of industry," he argued, "the proper functioning of which could best be secured by cooperation, which in turn could best be promoted by administering their interest together." To administer the department's new labor distribution service, Straus appointed Terence V. Powderly, former grand master workman of the Noble and Holy Order of the Knights of Labor. Powderly was an appropriate choice for the post, in part because he had recently been commissioner-general of the Bureau of Immigration, but more importantly because the Knights had also promoted a vision of harmonious cooperation between labor and capital, though one which had called first for the abolition of wage labor. However, this vision of industrial harmony promoted by Roosevelt, Straus, and Powderly rested insecurely and uncomfortably on the presumption of a neutral state.[32]

Within months of the Division of Information's creation, the nation was more desperate than ever for industrial peace. In October 1907 the Knickerbocker Trust and the Westinghouse Electric and Manufacturing Companies failed within days of each other, triggering the collapse of the stock market and what became known as the panic of 1907. Compared with earlier and later depressions, the panic of 1907 seems brief and relatively painless. By the spring of 1908 recovery had begun, and the banks and businesses that had closed all over the nation were reopening. However, perhaps because it occurred only ten years after the devastating and lengthy depression that began in 1893, the panic of 1907 seemed at the time a portent of economic catastrophe. Depression in the 1890s had brought the nation four years of widespread unemployment, strikes, sustained business failure, and deflation. The panic of 1907 seemed to threaten more of the same, if the federal government did not intervene to mitigate its effects.[33]

In his position of peacemaker between capital and labor, Secretary Straus tried to do just that. He announced, by way of the nation's leading newspapers, that the Information Division would not only direct newly arrived immigrants to labor-scarce regions; it would also help secure work for the resident unemployed. He envisioned not simply a bureau that would provide information about employment opportunities, but a "kind of clearing house, so that the wage earner may obtain definite employment before moving from one section of the country to the other."[34] In the midst of financial panic and mass unemployment, the division would bring together employers and the unemployed.

Capturing this spirit of optimism, the *New York Times* trumpeted the division's possibilities. "The bureau would gather facts," the *Times* insisted, "not theories or general information, but definite facts—about labor conditions in every part of the United States, and would be in a position to give valuable help to any section where the problem of the unemployed was especially acute." "Socialists may call it the dawning of a new era and humanitarians of other camps may call it the quickening of the social consciousness," the *Times* extolled, "but certainly nowadays the motto of each for himself and devil take the hindmost has fallen into disrepute." Though the *Times*'s celebration of a federal role in serving the welfare of the hindmost was overstated, it was not entirely undue. Just the attempt to create a government employment bureau "for American workingmen" was a significant shift in the relationship between the state and labor; for the first time federal officials had accepted at least some responsibility for unemployment and its consequences.[35]

Not everyone applauded this new state role. Socialists (as they were imagined by the *New York Times*) may have thought the Division of Information the dawning of a new era, but the AFL was immediately suspicious of the division's professed neutrality. In part the AFL's hostility may have had its roots in internecine rivalry—the AFL had, after all, been the chief beneficiary of the rapid decline of the Knights of Labor after 1886. Still, the AFL's opposition to the Division of Information went beyond petty rivalry. The AFL suspected that the division "was a ruse by anti-restrictionists to distract the country's attention from the evils of immigration by dispersing the immigrants over a wide area, thereby making them less conspicuous." Moreover, its leaders accused Powderly of supplying employers with strikebreakers.[36] At a deeper level Powderly's project conflicted with the AFL's belief in voluntarism, that is, that workers were better served by self-activity than by leaning on the arm of the state. Like its parent agency, the Department of Commerce and Labor, the Division of Information was meant to be a judicious and neutral arbiter between the interests of labor and capital. The leaders of the AFL, however, had every reason to believe in the state's inherent partiality, and their fears were soon borne out.

By promoting opportunities for employment or agricultural settlement in sparsely populated regions, the division unavoidably promoted immigration in general. To AFL and other union leaders, this was unforgivable, depression or no depression. As W. S. Carter, grand master of the Brotherhood of Locomotive Firemen and Engineers, said in a meeting with Powderly and the secretary of commerce and labor, the division's value lay in how well it could "convince people of Europe to stay at home," not in how well it advertised opportunities in the United States abroad. As Carter put it, the Division of Information was like a hen that starts to "cluck and cackle" when she finds something good to eat: "Did you ever see your neighbor's chickens fly over the yard fence at that hen's cluck and eat all the worms that your chickens were supposed to eat?" He continued: "Now, I do not want my friend, Mr. Powderly, when he scratches around and finds a good, plump worm, to go to clucking and having our neighbor's chickens fly over here and eat our worms." The AFL's vice-president had a better idea. Instead of clucking and clacking about opportunities in the United States, the division should distribute American unemployment statistics abroad.[37]

Powderly also had difficulties defending himself against the charge of strikebreaking, except to say that his policy of sending workers to companies where strikes were in progress was no different from that of other public employment agencies in the United States or abroad. The division would send employers seeking workers a questionnaire that requested "the class of labor" required, the wages paid, and the hours and conditions of employment. It would also contain the following question: "Do strikes or other labor difficulties exist in your jurisdiction? If so, kindly state cause of same." Job seekers would then be informed of strikes, so that if they accepted jobs vacated by a strike or lockout, they did so knowingly. If the division refused to send workers into such a situation, Powderly reasoned, it would be acting not as a neutral agent but as an aid to the working class. Employers had to be convinced of the division's strict impartiality if they were going to adopt it as their principal source of labor.[38] This notion of state neutrality assumed, of course, that the two warring parties were equal powers.

When Straus and Powderly began to play the part of padrone, they discovered that they could not simply run a matchmaking service for workers seeking jobs and employers seeking workers. The padrone's role was neither neutral nor abstract. Padroni either served the interests of growers or defended the interests of their crews. Similarly, the officials of the Division of Information found that in the attempt to aid in the distribution of immigrants and serve "as a sort of Government employment bureau for American workingmen," they became embroiled in the most basic conflict between workers and employers: their negotiations at the moment of employment over the terms and conditions of work. By the very act of supplying employers with labor, the division relieved them of the necessity of having to improve wages and conditions in order to attract labor or settle a strike.

the state it wasn't really neutral

Opposed by organized labor for acting as padrone for industry, Powderly found his mission limited to two tasks: promoting agricultural settlement for immigrants and supplying growers with harvest labor.[39] He soon had to admit his inability to accomplish the first task as well. Immigrants arriving at Ellis Island were too excited to pay much attention to the division's brochures and displays, and since many were coming to join relatives, their destination was not up for debate. Once settled in the United States, Powderly complained, immigrants would not return to the division's office at Ellis Island for fear of deportation. The division tried opening a branch office in New York City with little result.[40]

Fearful that his critics would defund the division and ignored for the most part by the immigrants he sought to help, Powderly operated the division so inconspicuously that by 1909 other federal agencies knew nothing of its existence. In July of that year, when the secretary of agriculture received letters from farmers seeking harvest workers in Illinois, Iowa, and Ohio, he replied that he knew of "no organized agency for supplying farmers with help for their farms." "It is understood," he concluded, "that the Department of Commerce and Labor, at one time, gave advice to immigrants arriving at eastern ports as to where there was need for farm help, but I am not informed as to whether the practice is still continued." To unemployed men in northeastern cities who wrote seeking help in securing farmwork, the Agriculture Department officials relayed the same message: "The Department of Agriculture has no money or authority to take up the work of helping men get to the farms where they are needed."[41]

In fact, the Division of Labor *was* helping men get to farms. In 1911 it placed 950 men in temporary jobs on New Jersey farms alone, and it made 23,000 placements all told, according to Powderly. But even these small successes added up to a bitter defeat. Touted in 1907 as a beacon of light for the unemployed and a fulfillment of urban reformers' hopes for the redistribution of the nation's labor supply, the Division of Information ended up doing the one thing that the members of the USIC and other progressives most wanted to avoid: adding immigrants to the ranks of the migrant poor. In 1911 the Dillingham Commission lambasted Powderly for his one success, complaining that the Division of Information had been set up to disseminate information about opportunities for settlement "outside the congested cities," not to act as an employment service for farmers seeking short-term casual labor.[42]

The Division of Information had, indeed, become a padrone in a true sense; it had taken responsibility for supplying growers with temporary harvest help. It made no guarantees that conditions and wages were as promised. It made no provisions for workers' return transportation. By reducing the federal effort to the functions of a padrone, the division scuttled the progressive mission to right the wrongs of the industrial world through the healing power of the agricultural idyll.

In any case, agriculture could not possibly have cured the nation's ills because it had enough problems of its own. The USIC's investigators, tenement reform directors, and Bowery philanthropists did not see agriculture's limitations because they did not want to see them. Their nostalgic vision of American agriculture secured their faith that substantial progress could be made in American society without fundamental change. They were in for a rude awakening.

On August 4, 1913, the *New York Times* included a startling report. The day before, striking hops pickers in Wheatland, California, had killed a district attorney and two deputy sheriffs, and state militia had been ordered into the fields. Over the year that followed, the reports of the investigations into "the Wheatland Riot" turned the prophets of agriculture into agnostics. When investigators reexamined the state of agriculture and agricultural labor in 1914 in light of the Wheatland Riot, they no longer liked what they saw. The urban poor could not be baptized in the holy waters of the countryside because the nation's farms appeared to supply as much fertilizer for discontent and radicalism as any urban factory or slum.[43]

In late July 1913 the Durst hops ranch in Wheatland distributed a call for harvest workers throughout California and in Oregon and Nevada as well. The largest agricultural employer in the state, Durst promised the "going price for clean picking" and a bonus to all pickers who stayed to the end of the three- to four-week season. Workers began to arrive on Tuesday, July 29. By Friday as many as 3,000 men, women, and children huddled under ragged, rented tents, gunny sacks, and camp wagons, trying to find refuge from the hundred-degree heat. The eight small toilets provided by Durst were already filthy, and the garbage generated by 3,000 people littered the camp and had tainted the water.

Though Durst's advertisement had promised work to any white worker who arrived for the harvest, it attracted about a thousand more people than he needed. Instead of sending the extra workers away, he worked the whole group intermittently, so that he could justify paying below the going rate of $1.00 per hundred pounds of hops. Pay was 90 cents, with 10 cents per hundred withheld to ensure that workers stayed the length of the season. Those who left in frustration forfeited their "bonus." Those who stayed paid Durst for their tents, for the stew sold at conces-sion trucks, and for the lemonade sold in the fields by his cousin. Durst had them coming and going. No water was available to the pickers, and the two wells in the camp were soon dry. By Saturday dysentery had reached epidemic proportions. As Carleton Parker, the director of the state's Commission of Immigration and Housing, later reported, workers began coming to Wheatland on Tuesday, and by Sunday "the irritation over the wage scale, the absence of water in the fields, plus the persistent heat and the increasing indignity of the camps, had resulted in mass meetings, violent talk and a general strike."[44]

Actually, by Sunday, August 3, the strike was already in its third day. At 5:00 P.M. about a thousand strikers gathered for a rally at which Wobblies Richard "Blackie" Ford and Herman D. Suhr addressed the crowd. Ford took a sick baby from his mother, held him before the crowd, and cried, "It's for the life of the kids we're doing this." The crowd was singing the Industrial Workers of the World (IWW) standard "Mr. Block" when the Yuba County sheriff, the district attorney, and deputies arrived in two cars, one known to belong to Durst. The posse came bearing revolvers, double-gauged shotguns, and a "John Doe" warrant for the arrest of IWW agitators. The sheriff tried to arrest Blackie Ford but was knocked down and "kicked senseless" by the strikers, according to investigators. One of the deputy sheriffs fired his shotgun over the heads of the crowd "to sober them," he later said. Strikers returned his fire. In the ensuing exchange as many as twenty shots were fired. Four people were killed, and many more were wounded. Among the dead were an English hops picker who had been standing in the crowd and a Puerto Rican worker who had disarmed one of the lawmen and killed the district attorney and the deputy before being killed himself. When the shooting stopped, the remaining lawmen beat a hasty retreat.

The following day the National Guard arrived to occupy the camp, and the Burns Detective Agency began an interstate manhunt for Blackie Ford and Herman Suhr. Eight months later Ford and Suhr were caught, tried, and convicted of the murders of the district attorney and sheriff, although prosecutors presented no evidence at the trial implicating ei-

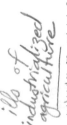

ther man in the shootings and everyone conceded that Ford had not used a gun at all. They were sentenced to life in prison, appealed their convictions twice, and lost both times.[45]

The Ford and Suhr case became a cause célèbre among California progressives and trade unionists, but its impact was felt in much wider circles. *The Survey* published investigator Carleton Parker's report to the governor of California and followed the trial closely. In the spring of 1914 the CIR, which had been meeting since 1912, deputized Parker to investigate the hops field riot for the federal government. The CIR had until that point ignored questions of labor relations in agriculture, but the Wheatland Riot brought the subject to its attention. Parker's findings had two effects: they shaped the CIR's understanding of the state of the agricultural economy and dashed progressives' hopes that rural life would provide a remedy for the ills of an industrial age.

What struck progressives more than the violence of Durst's posse was the incursion of the Wobblies into the countryside. The IWW believed that the working class and the employing class had nothing in common, that there could be no peace so long as hunger and want were found among millions of working people and the few, who made up the employing class, had all the good things of life.[46] The events at Wheatland taught reformers that the irreconcilability of workers' and employers' interests not only applied to agriculture as well as to industry, but *especially* to agriculture.

The CIR met between 1912 and 1915. Its chair was labor attorney Frank Walsh, and it included among its nine members labor economist John R. Commons. While the USIC had glibly reported on growing opportunities for farmworkers to rise to the level of farm owners in the late nineteenth century, the CIR was less inclined to be nostalgic about a bygone era or forgiving of the conditions it found. The CIR reported a growing concentration of landownership, an increase in the ranks of seasonal and casual labor, an "alarming" rise in farm tenancy, and the introduction of industrial methods into agriculture.[47] While the USIC had claimed that farmworkers were more likely than ever to climb the social ladder to farm ownership, the CIR concluded that millions of Americans were falling from the ranks of farmers to those of tenants and landless migrants. Its concern, therefore, was for the growing army of farm labor migrants, who stole train rides, lived in utter destitution, and provided fodder for the class war fomented by the IWW.[48]

The CIR might have concluded that the Wheatland Riot was an isolated incident resulting from the extreme indignities of the Durst ranch. Or it might have concluded, like the USIC before it, that farm labor migrancy was a problem limited to California and parts of New Jersey, a problem that could be ignored, dismissed, or at least reformed. The CIR came to no such conclusion. To its members, farm labor migrancy was a central, not an aberrant, aspect of the agricultural economy. Farmwork was not an outlet for urban congestion and industrial strife but part and parcel of the same problems. "While in some sections agricultural laborers are well paid and fairly treated," the CIR reported, "the condition of the mass is very much like that of the industrial workers." According to the CIR, there were several million migrant workers, including those in agriculture, and their numbers were rising. "A considerable proportion of these migratory workers" were "unquestionably, led to adopt this kind of life by reason of personal characteristics or weaknesses," the commission concluded. "Nevertheless, even if the migratory workers were all men of the highest character and reliability, there would still be a demand from our industries for the movement of the population in almost as great numbers as at present, in order to supply seasonal demands and to take care of the fluctuations of business." Migrant workers, according to this analysis, were a human by-product of industrial instability and seasonal agriculture.[49]

To the CIR, labor migrancy was a national problem that required a national solution. Local efforts to affect the economic, health, and moral problems associated with migrancy had failed, and as a result the movements of migrant workers went "practically unorganized and unregulated." Here, too, the solution called for the state to play the part of the padrone. The CIR advocated a federal labor distribution system extensive enough to coordinate migrant workers' movements nationwide. To eliminate the stealing of rides as well as the unregulated movement of workers, the CIR recommended that the Interstate Commerce Commission provide transportation at the lowest cost to workers who secured employment through public employment agencies. To contend with the problem of those who drifted because of "personal weakness," the report called on states, municipalities, and the Department of Labor to establish sanitary workingmen's nonprofit homes and farms to rehabilitate "down and outs." In response to the long list of abuses to which unscrupulous private employment agencies subjected workers, the report recommended reconstituting the Bureau of Immigration as a Bureau of Immigration and Employment and giving it the funds and authority to license and regulate private employment agencies and to plan for public work projects during seasonal waves of unemployment and depression.[50]

The CIR's plan avoided the problems that Powderly's Division of Infor-

top down organization imposed

a good idea but the devils in the details

racism

mation had encountered because it made no claims to impartiality. The ultimate goal of a federal farm labor distribution system would, according to the CIR, be the organization of migrant workers for their own protection. To the commission, an overabundance of labor was the prerequisite for exploitation. When workers were directed to areas truly in need of labor, they would be able to protect their own interests through self-organization rather than through the efforts of professional reformers and state investigators. Without centralized coordination of the labor market, the best-laid plans of progressive reformers and state regulatory agencies would always come to nought, undermined by workers who migrated blindly into fields and factories already overstocked with labor. Though the commission openly advocated farm labor unionism, its plan would also serve the interests of labor-poor growers because the state would send workers where they were truly needed. Thus the CIR entered the controversy begun in turn-of-the-century New Jersey over whether the state should accede to the demands of growers and take responsibility for maintaining an adequate supply of harvest labor or heed the warnings of progressive reformers and become the watchdog of farmworkers' welfare. The federal role envisioned by the commissioners reconciled these two seemingly irreconcilable positions.[51]

It was not at all clear from the CIR's report exactly how this federal regulation of workers' movements was to work. As we have seen, charitable associations and immigrant protection societies had already tried to place unemployed workers in temporary farm jobs and had found that they could not guard workers' welfare once placements were made. Though the CIR proposed to do on a national scale what had been attempted unsuccessfully in New York City alone, its report offered no insight into the mechanics of operating a labor placement service that would serve the needs of workers.

If the Progressive Era saw the death of the agricultural idyll, it also saw the birth of new notions about race and migrancy. The USIC had distinguished between white and black migrants, presuming that the former were tragic by-products of a new and insidious form of agriculture and that the latter were peculiarly suited to a migratory life. Likewise the many reform agencies that got into the business of labor distribution and attempted to improve the conditions under which farmworkers labored at the turn of the century ignored black workers entirely, although large numbers of African Americans worked on farms in New Jersey as well as New York, Connecticut, Pennsylvania, and Delaware. The CIR, which proposed the most far-reaching reforms of the farm labor supply system, also imagined the nation's labor force as white, perhaps because the Durst ranch, which had caught its notice, had advertised for white workers only. Obsessed as they were with the incursions of the radical IWW, it is not surprising that the members of the CIR reduced all farmworkers to the "bindle-stiffs" of Wobbly legend, the white harvesters who roamed the countryside stealing train rides and living in hobo encampments. The CIR did not exclude people of color from its plans; it simply never mentioned them. Thus the CIR rendered California's primarily Mexican, Filipino, and Japanese migrant population as invisible as New Jersey's African American potato pickers.

So long as farmworkers were imagined as white, reformers expressed concern over their condition and proposed various strategies to alleviate it. But the outbreak of war recolored the nation's landscape. Seemingly overnight the significance of farm labor supply grew exponentially and the geographical center of the debate shifted. Just as President Wilson warned that "the fate of the war" rested "upon the farmers of this country," fears of farm labor scarcity spread like weeds from New Jersey to Texas.[52] While before the war those concerned about the problems and prospects of farmwork focused on immigrant workers in the Northeast and, after 1913, in the West, the outbreak of war drew attention to African American workers in the South. The war pushed federal officials into active involvement in the business of farm labor supply, and the Great Migration moved black farmworkers into the center of farm labor politics. Suddenly quite visible to those who feared farm labor shortages during the war, black Americans had to fight state and federal officials who would have them labor for low wages on southern plantations or face death on some distant battlefield.

The outbreak of war in 1914 cut off the flow of immigration from Europe at the same time that the need for increased agricultural production intensified growers' concerns about labor scarcity and caused them to redouble their demands for state-supplied harvest workers. By the time the CIR published its final report in 1916, the nation was economically embroiled in a war abroad and in meeting employers' labor demands at home. Responding to growers' heightened complaints of farm labor scarcity, the federal government began to act on the CIR's call for federal coordination of the labor supply. The Department of Labor created the U.S. Employment Service to direct the movements of workers from areas of supply to areas of demand. But while the CIR had linked progressives' concerns for workers' welfare with growers' interests in labor supply, these issues did not remain linked in the minds of all those who actually shaped agriculture labor policy during the war. The state threw its energy into mobilizing farm labor for stepped-up war produc-

workers ignored

tion, but those who sought to safeguard workers' welfare were pushed to the side.

The war brought American farmers the greatest prosperity they had ever seen or would see again, but it was not enough to revive the image of the agricultural idyll. The Wheatland Riot had destroyed reformers' hopes for a respite from the turmoil of urban life. Agriculture would be a constant problem, not a pastoral haven from a heartless world.

Work or Fight

The State as Padrone during
the First World War

IN 1918 TAMPA a black woman sitting on her porch found herself in conversation with a white woman who was looking for a domestic. In response to the visitor's queries, the black woman said no, she was not working for anyone, and yes, she could cook. But when the white woman informed her that she wanted to hire her, as she had been unable to find a cook, the black woman wryly replied that she "had experienced the same difficulty" and that she had been about to ask the white woman to cook for her. Not amused, the white woman later returned with the police and had the black woman arrested for refusing work during the war.[1]

This brief exchange, recorded by Walter White of the National Association for the Advancement of Colored People (NAACP), reveals a great deal about the nature of labor relations in the American South during the First World War. In towns and on remote farms, on front porches and street corners, prospective employers found themselves face to face with black men and women who could rebuff their usual offers of a few dollars a week for farmwork and domestic labor. Black laborers were in a position to bargain, and when they did, they sent white employers into fits of frustration. Like the Tampa woman who ran for the sheriff to force a black woman into her kitchen, southern planters found that they required the intervention of local, state, and federal authorities to keep black laborers at work for their accustomed wages.[2]

Although the battlefields of Europe were a long way from the cotton plantations of Georgia, the tobacco fields of North Carolina, and the truck farms of Virginia, the outbreak of the First World War upset the balance of power in the American South as surely as it redrew the borders of Europe. The war cut off European migration, creating hundreds of thousands of new, high-paying jobs in war industries, and triggered a mass migration of black and white southerners to northern cities. The nation's rural population declined by a 1.5 million between 1916 and 1919.[3] In the South, white planters insisted that the African American exodus was draining their farms of labor and that they would not be able to meet the production goals that the federal war machine had placed upon them. Their complaints did not go unheeded. Declarations such as Wilson's left little doubt that the national state would have a role in the affairs of farm labor supply, but what exactly that role would be was still uncertain.

For the first time since Reconstruction the federal government entered the ongoing struggle between white planters and the black farm laborers they employed. During Reconstruction the Bureau of Refugees, Freedmen, and Abandoned Lands had tried to balance the needs of workers and employers by operating a regional labor distribution service to bring labor supply in balance with demand. Agents of the Freedmen's Bureau had moved and monitored black farmworkers until southern whites reasserted their authority over the region and cut off the long arm of Congress.[4] By the First World War southern white planters were less confident of their ability to control black labor. They therefore exploited the sense of national crisis to get the federal government to assist them in their efforts to keep black workers in the South, on the farm, and at work. Yet they remembered the lessons of Reconstruction and applied them to new ends, demanding federal help in the cause of labor supply, but on their own terms.

Two federal agencies took up their complaints. The officials of the Departments of Agriculture and Labor were supposed to act in concert to meet the farm labor emergency created by the war. In fact, they were deeply divided over the question of what constituted appropriate state involvement in the affairs of farm labor relations.

Split from the Department of Commerce in 1913 and directed by Congress to "foster, promote and develop the welfare of the wage earners of the United States," the Department of Labor privileged the question of workers' welfare when considering the problem of farm labor supply. Led by William B. Wilson, a former leader of the United Mine Workers, the department set out to rationalize and stabilize the labor market by expanding the ten-year-old and largely ineffectual Division of Information into a national employment service. However, a federal labor distribution effort would only work, the Labor Department asserted throughout the war, if the nation's farmers made wages and living conditions more attractive to workers. The new U.S. Employment Service (USES) could match unemployed men with farmers seeking employees, but if farm wages and conditions were so poor that workers would choose the relief line over rural life, the employment service would not compel them to do otherwise.[5]

The U.S. Department of Agriculture (USDA), on the other hand, represented the concerns of farmers, not farmworkers, and southern farmers in particular. The USDA's organizational structure grew out of its attempt to combat the boll weevil, which had arrived uninvited in Texas in 1902. The USDA hired local men in communities throughout the South to demonstrate its eradication method to their neighbors, with local governments footing part of the bill. On May 8, 1914, Congress extended the county agent system to every agricultural county in the nation, so long as states matched the federal appropriation. County agents were hired throughout the United States as a result, but the USDA's grassroots organization remained a predominantly southern system. In 1915 more than half of the nation's 1,000 county agents worked in the eleven states of the former Confederacy.[6]

The USDA's decentralized organizational structure made it a very different political animal from the small, Washington-based Department of Labor. Not only were the people at Agriculture often men of southern birth and sensibilities; the whole organization was designed to be responsive to the problems and political predilections of white southern men. Most of the department's officials were appointed and paid in part by the political leaders of the communities that they served. Set up to instruct the nation's farmers in the ways of agricultural progress, the USDA became the mouthpiece of the nation's most reactionary farmers.

Faced with the alternatives of recruiting farm labor by force or by improving conditions and raising wages, Washington chose coercion over conciliation. The role of the USDA in invigorating local forced labor campaigns suggests that the national state does more than create and implement policy; it can also set a moral tone or create a climate of fear, and by doing so it influences the behavior of ordinary people, giving them courage to change or license to hate.

Planters called for help to stem the tide of black migration and to prevent wage increases, and Washington responded. But were there really farm labor shortages in the South during the war? The very notion of a labor market assumes the existence of a point at which supply and demand meet. The only way to measure supply, however, is to calculate how many workers will work given a particular wage. Yet in the South, where growers complained the loudest of labor shortages during the war, farm wages were lower than wages anywhere else in the nation, and they stayed comparatively low throughout the war. This was clearly more, then, than a question of supply and demand.

Indeed, farm experts might calculate the "man-hours" necessary to complete particular tasks, but they could not measure according to some objective standard a person's willingness to work at a certain pay or under particular conditions.[7] The First World War was a time when workers' expectations changed dramatically, but their employers' expectations hardly changed at all. Employers hoped to clear debts and realize greater profits, but they were accustomed to the sight of black workers stooped over in their fields and black women in their kitchens and nurseries. They fully expected to see those sights as long as they lived.

The buying and selling of labor was thus intimately bound up with notions of race. White planters in the South frequently expressed the belief that black people worked less the more they were paid. This "planters' theory of value" was all the more powerful (and long lived) because it combined their belief in the "natural" inferiority of African Americans with "natural" laws of economics. Any increase in wages seemed unnatural — proof of a world turned upside down. What mattered in this climate, then, was not some actual measure of labor supply, but growers' perceptions of labor supply, what might be called the ideology of labor scarcity.[8]

For their part black southerners demonstrated during the war that there was nothing natural about oppression, poverty, and exclusion from industrial jobs. For the minority who left the South, never to return, the war represented a new beginning, an opportunity to strive for equality and a reasonable standard of living in an urban and industrial environment. For the vast majority who stayed behind, among them those who harvested truck crops up and down the Atlantic Coast, the war presented new opportunities to pay off debts and to control how their time and energy would be spent. There was no dearth of labor, as planters claimed, but the war did bring intense conflict over the supply and price of black labor and over the long-held notion that domestic work and field labor were the realm and responsibility of African Americans alone. For black southerners, all the talk of labor scarcity was just that. But it was dangerous talk, for it gave license to white violence and brought federal sanction for forced labor.

EVEN BEFORE THE First World War, southern planters had been complaining of labor shortages (the U.S. Industrial Commission had commented on it in 1901). The deep depression of the 1890s had ended abruptly with the outbreak of the Spanish-American War. Despite the brevity of the conflict, the war triggered a gradual climb in the price of cotton, which by 1900 was bringing growers 25 cents a pound more than they had received throughout the previous decade. By 1904 planters were paying off debts and expanding their acreage, and the good news kept coming. Prices rose gradually but steadily between 1898 and 1914, earning the first decade of the twentieth century distinction as "the golden years of agriculture."

High cotton prices also meant more income for black sharecroppers and farm laborers. However, those who worked the soil and those who owned it responded to high prices in contradictory ways. The boom in cotton prices distracted landowners from diversification efforts they had begun during the depression. In Georgia, for example, planters increased their acreage in cotton by almost 50 percent between 1900 and 1916, while prices rose threefold.[9] Because cotton was more labor intensive than food crops or livestock raising, the expansion of cotton production increased demand for labor.

Had black men and women continued to behave exactly as they had before, white planters might still have complained of labor shortages. But black southerners, too, sought to cash in on agriculture's golden age by using high cotton prices as a stepping stone to better lives.

At the turn of the century "forty acres and a mule" still lay beyond the hopes of most black families. In Georgia, for example, which was home to more African Americans than any other state, 170,000 black men were wage laborers, 70,000 were tenants and sharecroppers, and fewer than 10,000 owned their own farms.[10] Within a few years, however, the cotton boom turned empty dreams into substantial gains. Greater income from cotton shares and wage labor reduced the need for all family members to work for day wages on neighboring plantations during the chopping and picking seasons. Children might thus be kept in school during the harvest (indeed, one study reports that illiteracy among black Georgians decreased from 52.4 percent in 1900 to 36.5 percent in 1910); grandparents might be spared the burden of lifting heavy cotton sacks; and fewer black women would have to work as domestics for white families.[11] But more importantly for the vast majority of black southerners who had always made their living farming other people's land, increased returns made land ownership possible. Between 1900 and 1920 the number of farms owned by African Americans in Georgia increased by 48 percent.[12]

Black southerners who could not buy land responded to the increased demand for their labor as their parents and grandparents had during Reconstruction: they moved about in order to better their condition.[13] Planters complained to the *Southern Cultivator* that their workers had become "boss," leaving or threatening to leave if their needs were not met. One wrote to the *Outlook* in 1903 of his fear that if he dismissed an incompetent laborer, all his kin might leave as well.[14] A Cairo, Georgia, grower suggested that farmers abandon cotton until unemployed black workers were starved into submission. Others schemed of replacing them with machines and immigrants.[15]

Most white planters responded as *their* parents and grandparents had during Reconstruction: they passed and attempted to enforce laws designed to immobilize the black population. In 1903, for example, Georgia's state assembly amended the state's vagrancy law to provide for "a speedier method of pointing out and arresting persons alleged to be vagrants." The new law provided local authorities with a legal rationale for raiding black establishments and sweeping black neighborhoods in search of "idle men." Those found were induced to go to the fields by threat or by force. Between 1903 and 1909 seven other southern states enacted vagrancy laws or revamped their Reconstruction-era statutes.[16]

Southern legislators also set their sights on employers who recruited workers by raising wages (which is, of course, what employers generally do to attract labor). Georgia's new anti-enticement law, also passed in 1903, simply clarified and broadened the language of the 1865 statute that had made it illegal "to disturb in any way" the relation of an employer to his tenant or wage laborer. More significantly, the new law added a "false pretense" clause, which provided that anyone who obtained money or anything of value by contracting for future work and then failed to perform that work would be "deemed a common cheat and a swindler," guilty of fraud. Under this law, tenants who broke their contracts were not just liable for their landlord's expense; they were guilty of a criminal offense for which they could be sentenced to hard labor and forced to serve it back on their landlord's plantation.[17] These laws were meant to make black workers an offer they could not refuse: work for low wages or work for nothing on a chain gang.

THE STATE AS PADRONE

Not every African American suffered at the hands of Jim Crow's justice system, but state legislators' openly partisan role in farm labor relations coupled with the rising tide of lynchings in the same period created an unusually hostile climate for those who struggled for something beyond bare subsistence.[18] Like the post-emancipation statutes that came before them, these laws could not and did not immobilize the South's entire black population. But they did not need to because few black men and women had anywhere else to go. Black migrants who settled in New Jersey were among the relatively small numbers who went north in the prewar period, and their opportunities were also limited.[19] As long as black people had to choose between the troubles they knew at home and unknown troubles elsewhere in the South, black migration remained limited. In this context, draconian labor policies were an effective means of depressing wages.[20]

The outbreak of the First World War altered this delicate balance of power almost immediately. The cessation of the European diaspora forced northern employers to send labor recruiters scrambling to the American South.[21] In this changed context state policies such as Georgia's had unintended results. Instead of proscribing black mobility and depressing wages, draconian laws only spurred migration out of the South. Between 1916 and 1921 probably half a million African Americans left the South for the North and West, more than all the northbound black migrants in the previous forty years.[22] Planters soon complained not just of "unreliable" and "shiftless" black workers but of black workers who left never to return.[23]

Though African American migration from the Southeast was ultimately a movement to the urban North, it began as farm labor migration to the tobacco region around Hartford, Connecticut. In 1915 Connecticut's tobacco planters faced a labor shortage as a result of the absorption of immigrant fieldhands into munitions plants and the return of others to Europe. Their first response was to hire "200 girls" from New York, but according to newspaper accounts the growers and their neighbors found these women lacking in "moral character." The planters then contacted the Urban League to ask for assistance in securing black workers from the South. Established to assist black migrants, the Urban League easily found 1,000 college students with farm experience, happy to work for $1.50 to $3.00 a day for the July-to-September harvest season. The students had to make their own way to Norfolk, but from there the planters paid their fares to Hartford. Glutted with labor due to the boll weevil infestation, the counties of southwestern Georgia sent the first two trainloads of students to Connecticut in May 1916.[24]

The *New York Age*, read widely by black Floridians and Georgians, reported that the students earned $72,000 collectively and that jobs were available year-round in the Connecticut tobacco belt. By midsummer 1917 3,000 African Americans were working in the Hartford tobacco region.[25] Harvest wages in the Hartford area compared so favorably to Black Belt wages that they even attracted men and women not accustomed to field work. When a teacher and a physician from Americus, Georgia, went to see how people from their town were faring in Connecticut, they reportedly found them "well fed, well paid, overcrowded but content." "The only uncomfortable persons they saw," according to the Department of Labor, "were several colored women school-teachers from about Americus who were embarrassed to have their old friends find them at work in the tobacco fields along with their husbands."[26]

The experiment was so lauded by Connecticut tobacco growers and the press that other employers soon followed their example. From the summer of 1916 to that of 1917 the Pennsylvania Railroad imported over 13,000 black southerners, mostly from Florida and Georgia. The supervisor of the Erie Railroad claimed that his line brought 9,000 African Americans from Georgia, Florida, and Kentucky between June and December 1916.[27] From the tobacco fields and railroads the movement became increasingly urban, spreading to steel mills and munitions plants. Newark's black population increased by 100 percent in the first year of the migration. Pittsburgh received over 18,000 black migrants between the fall of 1915 and the spring of 1917.[28]

Though black migrants moved quickly into industrial jobs in northern cities, the migration remained rural at least in part. The Department of Labor reported that over 10 percent of the black farm laborers who went north from Georgia returned every year. Among that 10 percent were the farm labor migrants who followed the truck crop harvests along the East Coast.[29]

The Great Migration coincided with the boom in the South's agricultural economy. Southern farmers harvested record-breaking crops during the war and reaped record-breaking rewards.[30] Prices for cotton, wheat, corn, tobacco, truck crops, and other farm products increased so rapidly that farmers all over the country were able to clear debts and purchase land, tractors, trucks, telephones, and electric lights.[31] In Georgia, boll weevils, bad weather, and growers' restraint kept cotton production down, but prices flew skyward. By the end of 1916, cotton planters had recovered from the bust that followed the news of the war's start in 1914 and were enjoying higher prices for their product than they had ever seen. Still they feared they had everything to lose if they could not control the price and supply of labor.

Farm employers nationwide suffered a reduction in their labor supply, but farmers outside the South were more accustomed to scrambling for labor. Since the 1880s New Jersey growers had been contracting with padroni for Italian harvest workers and advancing the fares of black southerners because they could not find cheap labor any other way. Wheat farmers in the Midwest had long been dependent on a mobile army of harvesters that might or might not arrive on time and in sufficient numbers. California farmers hired Chinese, Japanese, Mexican, and Filipino workers in succession, always in search of the group that would accept the lowest wages. In the states of the former Confederacy, however, planters were long accustomed to a ready supply of cheap labor. In the South the stooped bodies of black cotton pickers were more than an accustomed sight; they seemed a natural part of the landscape.

Thus when war industries, migration, and conscription combined to reduce the nation's pool of farm labor, southern farmers complained the loudest. Eighty-seven of 100 North Carolina counties reported labor shortages before the United States even entered the war. In the summer of 1917 the *World's Work* reported that "the whole South now fears a shortage of farm labor at the precise time when it is most sorely needed."[32] Growers on the Eastern Shore of Virginia warned that the 1917 potato crop would rot in the ground because of labor scarcity. In southwest Georgia black migration "made the change from a surplus of labor to a scarcity," according to the president of the chamber of commerce in Valdosta. "Every man that goes," he claimed, "now creates a vacancy and is missed."[33] Planters elsewhere in Georgia's Black Belt feared that the exodus might spread from the boll weevil infested counties to their plantations, where labor demand was already high.[34]

Suppliers of farm machinery fanned the flames of panic throughout the South. "Has your help left?" asked an advertiser in Atlanta's *Southern Cultivator.* "Wild stories of high wages in the North and about army camps have lured help from the South by tens of thousands." "If the men *you* were depending upon have joined this rush to the North, let us help you." "Munitions plants and factories have steadily drained labor from the fields," warned the Cleveland Tractor Company. "The new regulations place unskilled farm hands in the first draft class." "*You must replace muscle with machine.*" Du Pont Industries even advertised explosive "farm powder" with the slogan "Every idle acre helps the enemy" under a drawing of an army of pitchfork-bearing farmers. Du Pont's Red Cross Farm Powder, the ad declared, "would do more real work . . . in a few hours than ten men could do in a week." International Harvester added that its corn binders and pickers beat hiring men, "even if plenty of men were to be had."[35]

The Labor Department (separated again from the Commerce Department) dismissed as exaggerated such claims of labor scarcity. Federal representatives of the Labor Department's Bureau of Negro Economics, who traveled to southwest Georgia to investigate the causes of black migration from the region, concluded that in those weevil infested counties at least, migrants were being forced to leave by lack of work. According to investigator T. J. Woofter Jr. the transition to food crops enabled planters "to cultivate more land to the plow, and at the same time, do away with much of the family labor which was needed for hoeing and picking cotton." Investigator W. T. B. Williams reported that planters were putting more and more land "under wire for cattle raising." State officials corroborated their reports. Georgia's crop estimator's 1916 report noted that "the Negro exodus has been greatest in the territory that has been infested [with the weevil] long enough to make it difficult to grow a paying crop of cotton."[36]

To planters in the South, however, any reduction in the pool of poor people reduced their leverage in holding down farm wages. And low wages were particularly important since they offset losses caused by the boll weevil. The best evidence against growers' claims of labor scarcity in southwest Georgia is that farm wages remained depressed despite war inflation and the Great Migration. In 1916 farm wages in Georgia ranged from 50 to 80 cents a day, and in 1917 they were little higher. This range was less than half of what the Department of Labor estimated minimum wages had to be to attract labor during the war.[37]

Though claims of labor scarcity in southwest Georgia might be discounted, not all southern planters were crying wolf; there were pockets of severe labor scarcity in the South. In the Norfolk area and on the nearby Eastern Shore in particular, truck farmers competed with port authorities and military construction sites for both labor and rail facilities. Before the war, Norfolk was a vast truck farming region, with 45,000 acres in peanuts and potatoes and over 20,000 farm laborers employed in peak seasons.[38] The war transformed it from a modest port and thriving truck farming region into the military capital of the United States. The new navy base alone was large enough to house over 7,000 men.[39] According to the *Manufacturers Record*, "the truckers had been paying about $1.25 per day" for farm labor before the United States entered the war, and they "suddenly found themselves confronted with the Government as a strong competitor, paying in excess of $2 a day, and a shorter

THE STATE AS PADRONE

day at that." "It may be safely stated," the paper concluded, "that if a potato rots in the ground in Virginia it is because of lack of labor or lack of transportation."[40] "How can we hold our laborers," one grower asked, "when the government contractors offer them $3.50 for an eight-hour day, with 66 cents an hour for overtime? While the Food Administration is urging production, we have hundreds of acres of wheat uncut, whole farms of potatoes undug."[41]

When Norfolk farmers complained of labor shortages, no one doubted them, but southern newspapers tended to assume or at least assert that farmers were suffering similar labor shortages throughout the South.[42] Few planters in Georgia and other southern states suffered such distress. Georgia lost perhaps 5 percent of its 850,000 black citizens to northern cities, but the bulk of the state's black population stayed in the state.[43]

African Americans who stayed in the South enjoyed unprecedented opportunities. Farm laborers could earn cash wages on truck farms up and down the coast as farmers expanded their acreage and clamored for labor. While vegetables grown for fresh produce markets had to be sold within days of the harvest, vegetables preserved in cans could be marketed over a much longer period and shipped over great distances, even to the battlefields of Europe. As a result canneries that had solved the problems of food spoilage and mastered mass production soon dotted the Atlantic Coast, providing new jobs for unskilled labor. Heightened demand for canned products raised truck crop prices and led growers to bring more acres under cultivation. At the same time booming industrial war production escalated railroad shipping rates, making the cost of transporting truck crops across the country from California prohibitive. East Coast truck farmers were thus left with a virtual monopoly on both eastern markets and overseas trade.

With more acreage in truck crops than ever before, farm laborers could harvest their way along the East Coast, with little time lost between jobs and cash wages awaiting them at the end of every day. Traveling south by car or rail, laborers could find work on Florida's bountiful vegetable farms. Others would venture northward to the coastal Carolinas and to the labor-starved farms around Norfolk. From there the truck regions of Maryland and Delaware were in easy reach across the Chesapeake Bay by steamer or sailboat. By late summer, sharecroppers from southwest Georgia would be working on truck farms in South Jersey and Long Island. At that point the stream of workers would divide, one part following the Connecticut River to the tobacco and truck fields of Connecticut and Massachusetts, the other following the Hudson and then veering off to the fruit belt of western New York. Wages earned harvesting crops provided cash to families that had known nothing but debt — cash that might buy a ticket north or a better life in the South.[44]

Workers who looked for opportunities within the South also had much to gain. In Georgia's central and eastern Black Belt counties, for example, cotton production was hardly touched by the boll weevil. With cotton prices nearly four times their prewar level by 1918, sharecroppers quadrupled their income, while their landlords incurred the inflated prices of farm supplies and implements. Improved share settlements meant black families could clear debts that tied them to particular landlords. They could buy supplies and provisions without paying usurious interest rates to furnishing merchants.

Thus the relative scarcity of labor meant far more than a few acres of cotton left ungathered or a few potatoes left to rot in the fields. A decreased supply of labor and the higher wages it wrought threatened the very underpinnings of white supremacy: the economic dependence of black workers. During Reconstruction, planters doubted their ability to control black laborers without the compulsions of slavery. During the First World War they dreaded the prospect of having to control them without the compulsions of debt.

White planters complained so frequently about the difficulties of controlling black people that they belied their own claims that black workers had deserted them. Farmworkers were still present, but they were better able to set the terms of their employment. "The colored people are squeezing the goose which has always laid the 'golden egg' for them, and the limit is reached," complained the editors of the *Manufacturers Record.* "Many a farmer has made a 'declaration of independence' in regard to the labor question" by resorting to farm machinery and family labor.[45] Another observer reported that in Georgia "the Negro tenants are rolling in wealth." They would come into town to "pay their bills and buy more goods with money peeled from great rolls of green and yellow backs. Theirs, indeed, is almost an embarrassment of riches. They seem hardly to know how to handle such masses of currency."[46]

White editorialists frequently invoked the Reconstruction-era edict that black people worked less the more they were paid. "The colored workers in the South have too often demanded increased pay with decreased hours of labor and decreased efficiency and decreased dependability," one writer submitted to the *Manufacturers Record.* Charles Whittle of Atlanta justified raising cotton prices on the basis of the same logic. "Cotton is confronted with labor difficulties that are peculiar to the negro race," he argued, "that is the better wages paid for negro labor the less number of days the negro will work. His wants become satisfied before he has supplied the demand for his labor."[47]

White planters resorted to cherished myths to explain their predicament and to time-tested labor practices to solve it. Unable to prevent African Americans from leaving Georgia using the 1903 vagrancy law, state officials looked for more effective ways to obstruct black migration. Determining that the state had lost 50,000 black residents in just ten months, Georgia's commissioner of commerce and labor resolved to ask the next session of the legislature for further controls over emigrant agencies.[48]

The South's leading newspapermen cautioned the legislature against the use of force to stop the migration. G. F. Hunnicutt, the editor of Atlanta's *Southern Cultivator*, warned against the use of "unjust means to prevent the negroes from leaving," arguing that "it is no more right to force them to stay than it was to make slaves of them in the first place." Both Hunnicutt and the editor of *World's Work* suggested that the migration might "have a good effect on the South." Georgia ought not "reject a blessing which God is trying to send us," opined the *Southern Cultivator*. The *World's Work* reasoned that the labor shortage would compel southern farmers to abandon cotton monoculture in favor of diversified crops, adopt more scientific methods of cultivation, and replace "the negroes" with "men of more progressive races."[49] The *Manufacturers Record* even went so far as to advocate improving conditions as a way to slow migration. "We recognize all of the shortcomings of the negro race," wrote the editors. "We know fully the difficulties in the way of handling them. But we know also that the whites have to a considerable extent fallen short of their true responsibility to the negroes, and in doing this they have injured the South and given an excuse for hundreds of thousands of negroes to leave this section, hoping for better conditions elsewhere."[50] In May 1917 the *Savannah Morning News* came around to the position that white southerners were compelled "to think seriously and calmly about the Negro" by "economic conditions forced upon them by the greatest war the world every saw." Its editors concluded, moreover, that it was "necessary to pay the Negro enough for his labor and to do far more than has been done to make living conditions in his home more attractive and healthful."[51]

African American editors also warned that draconian attempts to immobilize workers would only spur out-migration. The *Savannah Tribune* kept up a bombardment of weekly discussions of these issues from the time the migration began. Without expressing approval or disapproval, the editors continued to insist the solution to the problem lay "always with the white man of the South." "If he will acknowledge his error," they concluded, "and take, frankly and fully — in good faith, the necessary steps to correct the trouble, he can succeed."[52]

Southern politicians ignored all such warnings and listened instead to those who insisted on harsher laws and their more stringent enforcement. Legislators passed laws prohibiting labor agents from removing labor from their states.[53] Southern railroad companies cooperated by refusing to allow northern employment agents to prepay migrants' rail fares, a strategy, according to the *Manufacturers Record*, that effectively eliminated "the labor employment shark of the North."[54]

When these measures proved to be counterproductive and African Americans continued to migrate out of the South, planters had two options. They could follow the advice of those who counseled conciliation — raise wages, improve conditions, discourage lynching — or look for a gun bigger than that wielded by their state legislators and county sheriffs. Most planters reluctantly chose the second option. They insisted that the federal government stop the migration and supply labor to them on favorable terms. This was a difficult road to travel for the high priests of state sovereignty. The federal government might have the power to provide relief, but planters were loath to open their homes to the kind of federal guests their fathers had banished from the state almost fifty years before. They hated the idea of federal intervention, but they feared even more an exodus of the black workers on whom their livelihood depended. Thus they called in Lucifer to drive out Beelzebub or, in this case, to keep him under control at home.

With the entry of the United States into the European war in April 1917, southern planters took their search for a hired gun to Washington. They visited their congressmen, marched into the office of the Department of Labor, even wrote the president. Certain that they could not meet federal demands for increased food production unless they were provided with labor, they insisted that the black migration be stopped.

Three days after the United States declared war on Germany, officials of the Departments of Labor and Agriculture met in St. Louis to draw up a farm labor supply plan. They were well aware of the effects the European war was having on the nation's labor supply, and they feared that American military involvement would contract the labor market even further. Ordered by Herbert Hoover's new War Food Administration to increase food production with less labor, the two departments settled on a plan. The USDA would use its already considerable network of county agents to determine farmers' precise labor needs. The Labor Department would "use its best endeavors to supply such numbers of farm laborers."[55]

The plan was modeled on the USDA's bottom-up organizational structure. In every agricultural community, committees would poll farmers as to their immediate labor needs and report their findings to county-level committees, listing both the number of workers each farmer needed and the names of available farmworkers. The county committees would then assign workers to labor-poor farmers. If everyone's needs were thus met, the system would go no further. But if a county ended up with a surplus or deficiency of farm labor, the committee would report it to a state-level body, which would direct exchanges of workers among counties. State-wide shortages or surpluses would be reported to federal officials. In this way each community, county, and state would function as a clearing-house for farm labor. When interstate transportation of farm labor was necessary, the Labor Department and the USDA would cooperate in moving the necessary "men" (in the minds of federal officials, farm-workers were always men).[56]

The national farm labor exchange plan looked quite workable on paper, but it ran aground on a number of practical and political problems. The most immediate difficulty was that the St. Louis meeting took place just three days after the United States declared war on April 6, and the first major harvest was to begin in Texas in June. Thus the Departments of Labor and Agriculture had two months to accomplish what Terence Powderly's Division of Information had not been able to do in the previous ten years: rationalize the distribution of the nation's farm labor supply.

Another problem was the imbalance between the number of workers who applied for farmwork and the number who either had any experience at it or would accept it once they heard the terms being offered. This was not a new concern. The Division of Information had complained of it earlier, as did the Society for the Protection of Italian Immigrants, both of which tried to place unemployed men on farms. In the spring of 1917 the USES attracted thousands of applicants with appeals to patriotism, but love of country was not always enough to compel city people to board a truck for a brief stint digging potatoes. The Newark, New Jersey, office brought in 250 to 400 applicants a day with posters that read "Enlist in New Jersey's Agricultural Army. Serve your Country, and Reduce the Cost of Living. President Wilson says: 'The Farmer is our First Line of Defense' and 'We need Plows as well as Guns.'" Many of the men who crowded into the office backed right out the door when informed that the jobs advertised were temporary positions that paid $24 to $40 a month with board (wages in the South were half as much). Others had no farm experience and were unacceptable to farm employers. As a result the Newark staff considered themselves successful if they placed forty-five men a day on New Jersey's farms.[57]

A related problem was the lack of a federal apparatus for matching the farmers and farmworkers. At the outbreak of the war there were thousands of fee-charging employment agencies but few public employment services. The only federal bureaus that dealt with farm labor in particular were the Division of Information offices in New York and Houston. To recruit farmworkers in cities across the country, the Department of Labor had to convert the bureaus it had set up to enforce safety legislation in industry into farm labor placement services. Within a month the small staffs of these new USES offices were overwhelmed with work. On May 1 the office in Baltimore reported that "since the middle of last month" its work had increased tremendously, "and anything approaching regular office hours has become a memory." The publicity given to the need for increased food production and the resulting need for farm labor had focused "the eyes of the entire community" on the office, according to its director, "as it logically looks to the Government to offer a solution for the acute situation." He added that he was working "night and day" with a committee appointed by the governor to determine farmers' exact needs and discuss ways to meet them.[58] In New Jersey the Employment Service reported that farm labor recruitment activities were "swamping the present administrative forces." A few days before he made his report, the director wrote, "it was necessary for us to lock the doors as it was impossible to have any additional applicants within its quarters."[59] The Pittsburgh bureau tried unsuccessfully to meet all of Pennsylvania's farm labor needs with its original staff: two inspectors, one director, a stenographer, and a Chinese interpreter.[60]

By June the farm labor program was suffering from the opposite problem as overlapping farm labor supply efforts proliferated. The USES had eighty-eight offices in twenty-eight states. The USDA had county agents and farm demonstration workers employed as "farm help specialists" in 1,350 of 2,800 agricultural counties. There were state labor exchanges in twenty-two states, not to mention forty-five newly organized state councils of defense and hundreds of municipal and philanthropic employment services. For-profit employment agencies also added to the muddle. New York City alone had 1,000 unconnected employment agencies, most operating for profit. To complicate matters even further, county and community committees were beginning their efforts, and the Department of Labor was dividing the country into twenty employment service zones. The Department of Labor warned that it could not meet the demand for workers unless all these efforts were coordinated. One agency might have a farmer in the office demanding twenty farmworkers, and another across town might have twenty former farmhands in the waiting room, but neither had any way to match the workers to the farmer.[61]

Although the lack of a preexisting apparatus was a serious impediment to the federal effort, the biggest obstacle to the Department of Labor's distribution plan was the opposition of white southerners. Southern farmers wanted workers supplied, not removed to parts unknown. Since the USES worked to recruit labor for industry *and* agriculture, and advertisements for industrial employment were drawing farmworkers from the fields, southern planters alleged that they were at the losing end of the labor redistribution effort. As one Virginia farmer put it, "The reason we cannot secure labor on the farms is because better wages are paid men to work for the Government, railroads and every kind of work than can be paid on the farm." All rural workers were tempted by industrial opportunities, planters argued, but black workers, they believed, were particularly susceptible to recruitment campaigns. "Glowing stories that Northern employers stand ready to pay them thirty or forty cents, a sum that represents affluence in their eyes, is enticing them North in droves," one reporter noted.[62]

The Department of Labor tried to assure southern planters that "all real labor needs will be met by the U.S. Employment Service," but they were not placated. Planters had been running labor recruiters out of their communities since the turn of the century; the last thing they wanted was to have private recruiters replaced by employees of the Department of Labor. As a result they refused to cooperate with the Labor Department's efforts. According to Assistant Secretary of Labor Louis Post, growers who required workers exaggerated their needs; those who did not, refused to report "excess workers" available for use elsewhere.[63]

This sort of obstruction left the Department of Labor in a quandary. Its officials could distinguish real labor needs from exaggerated claims of labor scarcity only by taking control of the myriad and disconnected labor agencies and determining for themselves exactly who was needed where and when. In June, two months after the St. Louis meeting, the Department of Labor proposed a reorganization plan that would make all exchanges part of one centralized clearinghouse system. At the top of the heap would sit the Department of Labor in Washington, from where it could "take charge of great movements of wage workers across the country whenever that is necessary."[64]

For southern planters federal intervention into the affairs of farm labor supply was a necessary evil to be tolerated for the duration of the war. However, federal intervention under the guidance of men such as William Wilson, miner and trade unionist, and Louis Post, progressive and follower of Henry George, smacked of carpetbaggery. Planters' opposition was given voice by the USDA. Assistant Secretary of Agriculture R. A. Pearson rejected the Labor Department's centralization plan, arguing "that people throughout the country feel that they are being organized and reorganized too much."[65] G. I. Christie, the director of the USDA's farm labor department, publicly scoffed at the idea that the government could and would " 'furnish' sufficient labor or 'find' sufficient labor for all the farmers at all times." "Just how this was to be done no one was kind enough to state," he quipped, "and the Department was unable to find any magicians in its employ! As a result of persistent presentations of the plain facts the Department [of Agriculture] finally succeeded in dissipating this strange notion."[66]

Without the cooperation of the USDA and southern employers themselves, the Labor Department could not move farmworkers from areas of surplus to areas of demand as it had planned, and as the Freedmen's Bureau had done before it. Instead it had to meet the farm labor emergency by finding farmworkers outside the existing farm labor force.

The first place the Labor Department looked was beyond the borders of the United States. The Immigration Service, which was subordinate to the Department of Labor, simply opened the borders to agricultural workers from Mexico, Canada, Puerto Rico, and the West Indies. Ten thousand men entered Texas from Mexico during July 1918 alone. New regulations waived restrictions prohibiting the admission of illiterate aliens, so long as new entrants worked only in agriculture. American employers had to meet immigrant farmworkers at their port of entry and give written promise that they would abide by housing and sanitation rules and pay the prevailing wage in their community. But as there were no federal employees to inspect housing and sanitation conditions on farms or to determine what "prevailing wages" were in agricultural communities, these restrictions were little more than idle warnings.[67]

Although 72,000 Mexican workers entered the United States between 1917 and 1921 to work on farms, World War I immigration policy relieved labor needs only in limited areas.[68] Mexican immigrants worked in the Southwest; West Indians took farmwork on the east coast of Florida; Canadians helped bring in the harvest in Maine; but the rest of the nation's farm employers had to rely on domestic sources of labor. To assist growers who could not get foreign migrants, the Department of

Labor tried, as promised, to enlist an army of farm volunteers. The department first undertook to organize 1 million boys ages sixteen to nineteen into a United States Boys' Working Reserve, under the direction of William Edwin Hall, president of the Boys' Club Federation. Farm training camps appeared in various parts of the country soon after the United States entered the war, but they were most numerous in the Northeast.[69]

The only organized use of "boy power" in the South, however, occurred on the Eastern Shore of Virginia, where farmers used 800 Boy Scouts to dig potatoes. The experiment was less than a rousing success. According to the *Manufacturers' Record*, "The lack of labor on the part of the farmers prompted them to grasp at a straw, and the love of a 'lark' on the part of youngsters just out of school prompted them to jump in at the prospect of a picnic." Most of the boys were "totally unfitted for any work on the farm," and "the novelty wore off before noon the first day."[70]

Despite the Department of Labor's reluctance to recruit them, women were also involved in the volunteer effort, perhaps more enthusiastically than the boys' troops of the Working Reserve. Women themselves initiated their effort and called it the Women's Land Army.[71] The "farmerettes" did their own recruiting and self-promotion, confident that farmwork "Furnished a Healthful Vacation, a Little Fun Now and Then, Much Valuable Experience, and Cash Wages." As Helen K. Stevens reported to the *New York Times* of her own experience, the farmers of Westchester County, New York, "did not hurt themselves in a mad rush to secure our services that first week." Undaunted, Stevens and the "thirty girls" in the camp planted their own garden and "learned how to use hoe and rake." They were hardening to their eight-hour day by the time the farmers' orders began to come in. "Once they found out what we could do," Stevens reported, "the orders came in so fast that the camp grew like a mushroom. . . . By the middle of March there were over seventy, quartered everywhere . . . and all working out every day."[72]

Despite promoters' efforts to disassociate the Women's Land Army from images of backbreaking toil done by immigrant and African American women, federal officials balked at the idea of advocating the use of women to meet farm labor shortages. A New York "farmerette" wrote to the *New York Times* to dispel the notion that city women would be degraded by participating in the effort. "Why shouldn't they do it?" she asked. "I do not know of a single girl in this camp who is at all likely to develop into a peasant type of woman. . . . Women of intelligence will not degenerate mentally or physically through being farm laborers. Rather they will raise labor to *their* own level, will give it greater dignity."[73] In

preconceptions +
racist/classist
notions

"The College Girl with the Hoe," the president of Mount Holyoke College insisted that "all through the caloric intensities of July and the wilting dog days of August" the fifty-four Holyoke students who did farmwork never forgot their complexions. When summer arrived and outdoor cultivation began, he assured his readers, "hired men with calloused hands will do the plowing."[74]

Despite such testimony, the Department of Labor waited until late in the war to begin its own effort to recruit "college girls and the women of the leisure classes" for farmwork, and even then it only registered women for use in the event that their participation became necessary.[75] The "consensus of opinion," according to the USES, was that it was "unwise to stimulate general interest in the question of placing women on farms" until there was definitely a farm labor shortage.[76] The Women's Land Army continued to operate, but without official backing.

While other campaigns to recruit farm labor volunteers simply fizzled in the South, the idea of encouraging middle-class white women to work on farms provoked a particularly virulent response. In April 1918 the USDA tested public opinion by circulating a picture showing three French women hitched side by side to a plow, in place of horses or oxen. The photograph bore the caption, "In any section of France you can see women of magnificent, noble womanhood hitched to the plow and cultivating the soil. All of agriculture rests upon their shoulders. Uncomplaining, with high devotion, in an attitude which amounts almost to religious exaltation, the woman of France bears the burden."[77] The *Southern Cultivator* responded by hurling back at the USDA the words of its own assistant secretary of agriculture, Clarence Ousley, on the question of mobilizing women for farmwork. "It would be extremely unfortunate," Ousley was quoted as saying, "if we should get the notion or herald the idea that we have come to such a pass in the United States that we must drive our women to farm work." G. F. Hunnicutt of the *Southern Cultivator* agreed. He argued that drafting women for farmwork while men went to war would mean a return to "heathen methods." The *Manufacturers Record* recommended the use of "some of the millions and millions of Chinese farmers and laborers" on American farms rather than letting the burden of increasing foodstuffs fall "upon the women of the land."[78]

The southern response to volunteer recruitment efforts is particularly striking because the Labor Department did not have difficulties recruiting farm labor volunteers elsewhere in the nation.[79] But in the South, whites who were not already accustomed to working in the fields attached to manual labor the stigma of slavery. They continued to assume that if there was work to be done, black people should naturally be called upon to do it, and if not black people, then some other people of color. In an editorial titled "Let Us All Work," the *Memphis Commercial Appeal* noted that "physical labor was regarded in the days of slavery as the special task of slaves." "As a result of this erroneous conception," the editorial concluded, "a stigma was put upon physical labor and ladies and gentlemen were supposed to avoid it." Following this logic and the title of the editorial, one might expect the author to have indicted white people for failing to do their part for the war effort. Instead he indicted "the negro race" for borrowing a distaste for manual labor from southern whites. Physical labor disgraces no one, he argued, "A laboring negro is to that extent an honorable negro."[80] The Department of Labor thus had no success in getting white southerners whose fingernails were clean to dirty their hands for the war effort.

While the Labor Department tried to convince white southerners to assign greater value to farmwork—so that they would either do it themselves or reward others sufficiently for doing it for them—the USDA determined that the solution to the problem was to have black southerners work harder and for less money. Ignoring the Department of Labor's assurances that farmers' claims of labor scarcity were exaggerated and that all vacancies could be filled by the USES, the USDA launched its own mobilization effort beginning in February 1918. Rather than relying on the public's patriotism to bring in "the crops needed to win the war," the USDA accused anyone who failed to find "essential" war work of being a traitor and singled out black southerners as "slackers."

W. J. Spillman, chief of the USDA's Office of Farm Management, insisted that the farm labor situation demanded "immediate consideration." "In some parts of the country," he reported, "information that is coming in indicates a serious labor situation." He cited "one large farm in Virginia which ordinarily employs a hundred laborers at an average wage of about $17 a month and their keep" but now employed only five men and an eleven-year-old boy. The boy was paid $1.50 a day and the men earned $2.00 a day and their keep, he noted, while "at the same time, there is in the community a considerable number of idle men who during the past winter earned enough in two months work on a Government contract to keep them in comfort for a year, and who refuse now to work." Though Spillman drew his evidence from the part of the country where farm labor scarcity was extraordinarily severe, he concluded with the ominous prediction that "unless farmers can be given immediate assurance that the Government will do everything in its power to supply them with labor, the planting program for the coming year will be seriously interfered with."[81]

Assistant Secretary of Agriculture Clarence Ousley also visited the Norfolk area and applied his findings there to the rest of the South. He reported that in a five-county area surrounding Norfolk, truck farmers had lost approximately two-thirds of their labor to army and navy construction sites. "Friday morning we were driven out to the army and navy construction works," he reported. "I sat in an automobile on the roadside and for twenty minutes watched some fifty or more common laborers clearing a piece of ground twenty yards away and on the opposite side of the road about the same distance some twenty carpenters building shacks. . . . I think I never saw such loafing," he told Spillman. The Norfolk farmers "say that they are willing to suffer inconveniences and loss of income by having their laborers taken away for necessary Government work," Ousley noted, "but you can understand their state of mind when they see these laborers receiving $3.00 and more a day for 8 hours work and not rendering a fair service."[82]

Because Spillman, Ousley, and other USDA officials spoke on behalf of growers and based their conclusions on their impressions of the situation in Norfolk, their effort to mobilize volunteers invoked a desperate and even menacing tone. The publicity campaign they generated played first on the guilt of those who remained at home while sons and friends fought abroad. Secretary David F. Houston set the tone: "If soldiers are willing to serve in the trenches, to dig ditches, build railroads, and risk their lives, many civilians can well afford to spare a part of their time to serve in the furrows and in the harvest fields."[83]

In February 1918 Houston delegated responsibility for the USDA's publications and information activities to Assistant Secretary Ousley, who was even more zealous about the campaign to generate farm labor. According to Ousley, "A man who worked less than 20 days a month, regardless of wealth, should be considered a vagrant in time of war."[84] It was Ousley who generated press releases such as the one titled "TOWN DUDES — OR PRUSSIAN CUTTHROATS!": "Failing to increase food production may mean losing the war," Ousley warned, and losing the war "will mean attempted and perhaps actual Prussian occupation of the U.S." "So, which will be worse," he asked, "to have some of the town people working of the farm this summer, or to have the Kaiser's savages there a few summers hence — commandeering its products — bayoneting you should you object to their peculiar sort of 'skylarking' — the kultural kind — the kind poor Belgium knew, and now knows?" In case the threat of invasion failed to move his audience, Ousley also pummelled the public with fictional death lists:

> (Item — Private John Smith killed in action on the field of honor. . . . A husky man, who would make a good hay pitcher, washing dishes. . . . Three miles away a farmer crying for labor — without which he cannot produce food, and without which food we cannot win the war.)

> (Item — Private Bill Jones, dead in the front line trenches; dead — but his squad repelled the Hun's attack. . . . A double-fisted athlete serving cafe breakfasters with soft-boiled eggs and buttered toast. . . . Plenty of women who can do that work. . . . A farmer, within an hour's ride, saying that unless he gets labor he will fail to produce food.)[85]

Despite this propaganda campaign, the USDA's effort to mobilize farm labor volunteers in the South was no more successful than that of the Department of Labor. Farm labor "enlistments" were particularly slow in Georgia, Alabama, Florida, and Virginia, and the USDA concluded that 25 percent more "hands" would be needed for the 1918 harvest in those states.[86]

It took only a sleight of hand to shift the focus of the department's publicity from urging readers to blame themselves for the threat to the nation to urging them to blame someone else. W. J. Spillman introduced the USDA's new direction in "The Farmer's Part in Securing Labor." "In some parts of the country," Spillman argued, "there are gangs of idlers who will not [sic] work as long as they have a little money." He questioned the patriotism of these idlers and called on state and county officials to enforce laws that made idleness a crime.[87] Ousley followed up with a press release that demanded the utmost use of all possible manpower, "coming right down to a 'go to work or go to jail basis,' if that is necessary."[88]

Over the next few months the department's policy took shape in pronouncements and correspondence. At first the USDA simply encouraged state officials to resolve their labor problems by enforcing vagrancy statutes. In late February, for example, Clarence Ousley received a letter from Mandel Sener, the director of the chamber of commerce in New Bern, North Carolina, complaining of labor shortages due to African American migration. "Right now there is greater labor shortage among the farmers, lumber mills, fertilizer plants and other large industries than ever before existed in Eastern North Carolina," Sener wrote. Blaming labor agents for luring away black workers, he asked Ousley for his "views as to the best way to remedy this situation." "As you know," he noted, "the logical home for the negro is in the South, where he was born, receives best treatment and where he has always found his best friends."[89] Ousley's reply to Sener's letter simply advised North Carolina's officials to do what they were already doing. The government could not conscript labor or discourage men from laboring in necessary war industries, he wrote. "The government, through the Department of Agriculture and the Department of Labor, can give information as to labor that may be available here or there, and that will be the work of the farm help specialists," he pointed out, "but when those resources are exhausted then it is up to the communities themselves to make some vigorous sacrifice of convenience, to dismiss their yardmen and cooks, to enforce vagrancy laws, etc."[90]

Southern officials kept up their chorus of complaints, however, because they had been enforcing vagrancy laws, and yardmen and cooks were already scarce luxuries. Moreover, vagrancy laws allowed public officials to arrest individuals who had no jobs and no alternative means of support; they did not permit the arrest of men with money in their pockets. In April the mayor of Charlotte, North Carolina, and the chairman of the surrounding county's board of commissioners made "an urgent call" on Congress "for some legislation which will compel regular work by people who now loaf a large part of their time because they can make enough to live on during a few days of every week." They insisted that "the need of labor on our farms is even greater than in our industries, and the biggest, the most vital, the most urgent task ahead of the American people is digging out of the ground THIS YEAR the largest crop of foodstuffs in all of our history." "The South alone," they continued, "has millions of acres of uncultivated yet fertile land that our patriotic farmers are anxious to bring under cultivation, but they are like soldiers with guns but no ammunitions, for they are unable to command anything like the normal supply of labor." Wages were so high, they complained, that laborers were able to earn a livelihood by working two or three days each week. "We have tried to cope with this condition by wholesale arrests for vagrancy," they insisted, "but because they are earning a bare living we are unable to get convictions. This is particularly true of a part of our negro population, the shiftless, idling class, who merely work enough to supply their own meager needs and contribute nothing in taxes, labor or products toward the support of the Government in this crisis, or of the soldiers who are fighting *seven days a week* for our freedom." They demanded that all men between the ages of thirty-one and fifty and all within the draft age not in military service be required to keep continuous employment.[91]

The mayor of Savannah, Georgia, lodged the same complaint. As a result of high wages, he argued, "the laborers find they can support themselves without working full time and a large number are always absent from work." "We have tried in every way to enforce the loitering law," he reported, "but the problem of getting the men to work a full week seems to be beyond the city's powers to remedy." "We need a thorough arousing of public opinion as the result of an intensive campaign," the mayor concluded, "or we need uniform State and local laws, or we need a national law."[92]

The only law that would address these "needs" would be an extraordinary measure that would require men to work whether or not they had enough money to support themselves and their families. The State of Maryland already had such a law — passed in August 1917 — and it was thus to Maryland that the USDA looked for a model response to farm labor scarcity. By January 1918 Maryland men were "being fined or jailed for failing to work — and being punished regardless of whether they have the means to support themselves or are being supported by others." Maryland's assistant attorney general reported to the *New York Times* that "in past years farmers have had a great deal of trouble with colored laborers, most of whom seem to have acquired the habit of working for a day or two and then taking a vacation until the money earned is exhausted." "This situation," he argued, "greatly hampered the farmers and interfered with the proper care and harvesting of crops. Those in charge of the enforcement of the [work-or-fight] law paid special attention to the needs of the farmers."[93] Maryland also adopted a civil conscription policy by which those determined to be underemployed were registered and assigned to work, either for the state or for private employers "under State supervision." According to the assistant attorney general, while the number of people actually assigned work was nominal, the number driven into jobs "by fear of the penalties provided" was "large enough to justify the statement that the measure is a success and is fully worth the time, labor, and expense which the State has given in enacting it into law and enforcing its provisions." A sweep of Baltimore by the police department, he noted, "resulted in the voluntary and involuntary registration of hundreds of idlers, and there was a scramble for available jobs by the leisurely inclined."[94]

Work-or-fight laws were not unique to the states of the former Confederacy. South Dakota passed a bill in March 1918 authorizing county councils of defense to register and conscript men for labor on farms, imposing a penalty of three months' imprisonment and $1,000 on those who failed to comply. New Jersey's law required that all able-bodied men between the ages of eighteen and fifty hold "some lawful, useful and recognized profession or job until the end of the war." The city of Bayonne led the campaign with the arrest in March 1918 of ten men found in saloons.[95]

The USDA encouraged all states to pass such measures, but its mass mailings to southern mayors and responses to planters' complaints about black migration leave no doubt that the department's chief concern was black labor in the South. Even the USDA's most conciliatory gestures toward black southerners were based on the assumption that they were shiftless and improvident and needed to be inspired to work. In March 1918 Clarence Ousley sent a letter to the directors of the agricultural extension services in the cotton states about "the custom among the negroes of the South to work only five days in the week and to spend Saturday and Sunday in recreation." "On account of the great need for farm labor this year," he wrote, "earnest effort should be made to induce negroes and other farm laborers to work full six days." "It is not possible to effect compulsion," Ousley explained, but much could be done "by local persuasion." "If the negroes are impressed with the importance of working full time," he reasoned, "large numbers of them will respond."[96]

Taking up Ousley's challenge, Alabama's extension service director took the idea of a "Saturday Service Army" to the annual meeting of the USDA's Negro Farm and Home Demonstration agents at Tuskegee College. "[We] hope to stimulate pledges and definite enrollment . . . by the use of appropriate buttons, reward certificates, etc," he reported to Ousley. The "negro agents" responded "heartily," as did the State Council of Defense.[97] Leslie Gilbert, Alabama's farm help specialist, followed up by meeting with African American preachers in May. Together Gilbert and Ralph D. Quisenberry, the country food administrator, performed a "good cop, bad cop" routine. Speaking to the group of over thirty black preachers and pastors, Quisenberry emphasized patriotism and participation, telling "of the need for a maximum amount of food stuff if we would do our duty by the boys in France and our allies with them." He used a soft touch, complimenting his audience for their Red Cross and Liberty Loan work and concluding by expressing his confidence that they could be counted on to maximize the production of their crops. Gilbert's speech took a different tone, suggesting what lay in store for those who could not be counted on for "regular and continuous labor":

"Today over Alabama an immense army of farm hands are spending the day in town, taking twelve valuable hours to do twenty minutes trading, talking, joking, idling or quarreling—while every ounce of man and mule power is needed back on the farm." "The Saturday holiday is a slacker," he concluded, "an economic traitor,—a friend of the Kaiser,— at peace with Von Hindenburg,—and should be outlawed on every farm in the Southland."[98]

By the spring of 1918 the USDA had succeeded in turning the tide of public opinion in favor of force as a solution to farm labor scarcity. White southern editors who a year earlier had cautioned readers "to think seriously and calmly about the Negro" and to avoid "unjust means" to prevent them from leaving the South now led the verbal war on "idleness." "The slacker," declared the *Manufacturers Record*, "is worse than a pro-German; worse than a lustful beast of a German brute. . . . Every man is a slacker, it matters not what he professes, who is not doing his utmost to fight Germany, and who is not as ready to sacrifice his time, his strength, his money, his life itself, as is the soldier who may have to die to save the slacker or the slacker's wife and daughters from the hell of Germany's domination." "Reader," the editors queried, "where do you stand in this hour which tests the genuineness of all claims to manhood and womanhood?"[99]

Moreover, those in Congress who advocated "conscripting labor" were also holding sway.[100] Representative Louis T. McFadden of Pennsylvania, for example, called for men to be drafted and then "paroled" back to the farms. One thing was sure, he warned: the nation's farmers were "not going to plant on promises" during the coming season. Representative Thomas L. Rubey of Missouri won applause from the House by calling for a bill to provide that every able-bodied man in the country between the ages of thirty-one and forty-five who was without an occupation, be "mustered into the United States Army." "Pass a bill of that kind and the pool rooms and the bowling alleys will close their doors because of lack of patronage," he insisted. "Pass such a bill and there will be a dearth of loafers around the saloons and in the gambling dens." William Ramseyer of Iowa introduced a bill that would apply the principle of compulsory military service to industrial service for the duration of the war. "It is high time," he concluded, "that the weary loafers and the well-to-do idlers go to work."[101] On March 16 Congress made its first move to alleviate alleged farm labor shortages by passing a law providing furloughs without pay to enlisted men in the army to enable them to work on farms.[102]

Continued calls for a farm labor draft soon led the executive branch to act as well. In May 1918 Selective Service director General Enoch Crowder issued a national work-or-fight order based on Maryland's law. According to Crowder, "One of the unanswerable criticisms of the draft has been that it takes men from the farms and from all useful employments and marches them past crowds of idlers and loafers away to the army." The remedy was simple, Crowder concluded. Any man pleading exemption from the draft would have to show that he was contributing effectively to the industrial welfare of the nation. Crowder ordered all men who were unemployed or working in "nonessential" industries either to find productive work on farms or in factories or to find their names at the top of the draft lists.[103]

His order did not constitute a labor draft, Crowder argued, because it applied only to men who had already been drafted and deferred, and because it left men free to chose among jobs in essential industries instead of assigning them to particular employers. Among the kinds of workers who would be considered "noneffective" were waiters, elevator operators, doormen, sales clerks, servants, and athletes. Men of draft age holding noneffective jobs had to find essential work immediately or become soldiers after July 1, 1918. "This," said Crowder, "is not alone a war of military manoeuvre, it is a deadly contest of industry and mechanics." He called on "all citizens to report names of idle and nonproductively employed men to the nearest draft board."[104]

In the weeks following the edict, Crowder reported that registrants were complying with the order. He cited a "material increase in the available supply of labor for essential industries" and expected an even greater increase when the regulation deadline passed in July, estimating that 800,000 to 1 million men would be affected by the measure. On the day the federal order went into effect, 10,000 men applied for essential work in New York State alone. The *New York Times* reported that in many clubs, restaurants, elevators, and other workplaces with jobs classed as nonessential, "women were substituted for men." On the same day, law enforcement officials began a sweep of the city, "a shot across the bow for the loafers, to warn them to engage at once in beneficient pursuits." Yet of the seventy-five men subpoenaed to answer the charge of idling, all but three succeeded in clearing themselves the next day.[105]

Press coverage of the work-or-fight campaign in the Northeast makes the whole affair seem more like a vaudeville skit than a compulsory labor campaign. A man who lived off his wife's wealth defended himself from prosecution by arguing that he was employed in tending his wife's property. "Not all men have wives, alas!" the *New York Times* lampooned, "and not all who have them were forethoughtful enough to select wives with estates that required managing."[106] Two young men in the Bronx were turned in by their mother, who found them still in bed late in the afternoon. A man arrested while sitting on a park bench in Brooklyn turned out to be Theodore Roosevelt's second cousin on his way back from taking his mother to visit Colonel Roosevelt.[107]

Despite the jollity of the *New York Times*, Crowder's order led to the proliferation of state work-or-fight orders, and not all state officials interpreted them in the same way. Before the federal initiative, Maryland, New Jersey, South Dakota, and West Virginia had passed compulsory work laws. Afterward they were joined by Georgia, Delaware, Kentucky, Louisiana, Massachusetts, Montana, New York, and Rhode Island.[108] More ominously, the federal order emboldened southern whites who sought to use force against black southerners. Federal sanction for compulsory work measures freed southerners with racist and violent predilections from whatever sense of propriety or legality had been restraining them.

In cities and towns throughout the South, white supremacists revived the mysterious order of the Ku Klux Klan in the name of the war against slackers. The Montgomery, Alabama, Klan announced in October that it was "Back To Life and Very Active After 40 Years" and promised in a morbid poem to "lap the blood of a 'Slacker' out of a spoon." In its first appearance in forty-two years, the Montgomery Klan, 100 members strong, rode through the city in a caravan of cars bearing signs that said, "Work, fight, or go. No slackers allowed in Montgomery. We protect good women — bad ones must go. . . . This is a warning and final notice. Do your duty." The next day city officials followed up with a dragnet operation to round up slackers.[109] On October 18, 1918, the *Montgomery Journal* covered another Klan demonstration in which "white ghost-like figures" appeared in Court Square silently "as fall the shades of night." Each wore a crimson cross on his breast, one carried a revolver, and four held an effigy of a slacker between them. The klansmen ended the demonstration by tying the body to a tree, saturating it with kerosene, and setting it afire. "Admonishing the public to take warning, the figures marched away, followed by none, and soon mysteriously disappeared."[110]

In cities and towns throughout the South, work-or-fight ordinances were applied to black women as well as black men. Police arrested seventy-five women in New Orleans and eight in Tampa, Florida. In Vicksburg, Mississippi, the wives of two black servicemen accused of refusing to work were tarred and feathered by a mob that used the slogan "Make Vicksburg and Warren County 100% American." Likewise, when the mayor's cook quit in Wetumpka, Alabama, one Saturday, the mayor had her arrested the next morning and tried in his court on Monday (he was also the town judge). He fined her $14.00, paid the fine himself, and told her to "go on out to the house" and "quit her foolishness." In Pine Bluff, Arkansas, the chamber of commerce adopted a resolution calling on the secretary of war to extend the work-or-fight order to women. The planters who attended the meeting blamed shortages of domestics and plantation laborers on government allotments to dependents or "supposed dependents" of black soldiers that allowed hundreds of black women to refuse work.

It was "simply the old story of white people not being able to adjust themselves to the new order of things," concluded J. H. McConico, the president of the Mosaic Templars of America, in his report to the NAACP. Black women had not refused to work, he argued, where adequate remuneration was offered. However, they refused to pick cotton for 75 cents to $1.00 per hundred pounds, because they had received that price when cotton sold for 10 cents a pound, and it was now selling for three times as much. "Instead of dodging work," women were working in railroad shops, sawmills, and other establishments, making $2.00 to $3.00 a day. In view of the wages they were making in industry, he concluded, it stood to reason that they would reject work as domestics for $2.50 to $3.00 a week.[111]

The Department of Labor agreed. Adequate numbers of workers were available for all essential tasks, and higher wages would have to be paid by anyone short labor, Assistant Secretary of Labor Louis Post insisted. In April 1918 he released a public statement that asserted, unequivocally, that the American farmer was a "victim of publicity." "So many people have been crying that there is a great shortage of labor that the farmer is beginning to believe it himself," Post noted. "Two-thirds of the farm-labor shortage is imaginary and the other third can be remedied." It was true, Post continued, that farm labor was scarce in many sections. But there were enough idle men in the cities to fill the gaps. "Why, then," he asked, "do they not go to the farms?" The answer, he asserted, was low farm wages and poor working conditions: "We are suffering to-day for the sins of the past. There is hardly a sweated industry in the country which offers so poor a future as farming." Finding a solution, Post concluded, meant making fundamental changes. As a war measure, he advised, the farm had to be made a more attractive place to work. Where there were labor problems, he urged an immediate betterment of wages and working conditions for farmworkers, including minimum wages of $45 per month with board and lodging, better housing, and better food. The Labor Department had solved the labor shortage problem for shipyards, Post argued, and would do the same for farmers, if the farmer would "do his part." "There are plenty of able-bodied men in America to farm American farms," Post concluded, "and the Department of Labor will see that the farms get them."[112]

The USES backed up Post with statistics. Even in Virginia, its investigators reported, there was "an ample supply of labor for all purposes." However, "diligent inquiry" failed to disclose "a single case where the wages offered for such labor was in excess of $30 per month, board and house." "It is absolutely certain," the USES officials concluded, that labor could not be "secured for farm purposes unless the farmers agree to pay more liberal wages than they are now offering." Indeed, the success of the Employment Service's Farm Labor Division in placing workers depended heavily on the wages paid in any particular region. Where wages ranged from $30 to $90 a month, as in Iowa, Wisconsin, the Dakotas, Nebraska, Illinois, Kansas, and Missouri, 70 percent of farmers' calls for help were filled. However, where wages ranged from $15 to $50, as in Texas, Florida, Georgia, Alabama, Mississippi, Louisiana, Delaware, and Tennessee, fewer than 1 percent of the calls were filled. During the week ending April 16, 1918, Alabama farmers applied for 196 laborers, but the Farm Service found only 4 workers willing to take the jobs. Georgia growers asked for 140 workers and received 2.[113]

Labor Department officials asserted, moreover, that southern planters could pay better wages if they chose to do so. Between 1914 and 1918 farmers' incomes increased an average of 120 percent as a result of higher prices for wheat, corn, oats, cotton, and potatoes, and income from truck crops increased 99 percent. Farmers' expenses increased 64 percent due to higher prices for feed and farm implements, but farm wages rose only 35 percent.[114]

To the Department of Labor, then, the southern farm labor shortage was a class struggle exacerbated by racial antagonism. White planters refused to pay competitive wages because they expected black laborers to be pliable and available. Black workers, for their part, were using their improved bargaining position to gain some measure of independence from white employers.[115]

Concerned that the USDA's encouragement of work-or-fight laws would worsen the farm labor problem instead of solving it, the Department of Labor sent Dr. George Haynes, the director of the recently created Bureau of Negro Economics, on a trip through the South in 1918 to "promote closer cooperation between the races and to stimulate among the negroes in particular a spirit of cooperation that will show the value of their daily work to the nation." Haynes's mission was to organize committees of black and white citizens, to be known as "negro workers' advisory committees," which would discuss the role of black workers in the war effort.[116]

Former field worker for the YMCA, creator of a sociology department and training center for black social workers at Fisk University, and founder of the National Urban League, Haynes was eminently qualified for the job. He was, however, African American. His presence and the presence of his staff so infuriated white southerners that they lobbied for the abolition of both the Bureau of Negro Economics and the USES. "Irritation over Negro conciliators" ran high "from the Atlantic coast to Texas," according to the *New York Tribune*. Southern senators called the Labor Department's policy "carpet-bag government" and threatened (ironically) to vote Republican. At a meeting of the National Lumber Manufacturers' Association, the organization's president, John H. Kirby of Houston, Texas, received enthusiastic applause when he reported that he refused to sit with Haynes at a Department of Labor conference. "I shall be glad to confer with Mr. Post, if he wishes to see me," Kirby said, "but I shall not call upon him, and when it comes to sitting in council with Dr. Haynes, a negro, you will have to excuse me: In the South, we do not sit in conference with them and accept their suggestions to us." Congressman Thomas Linsay Blanton of Texas, an "ardent segregationist and relentless critic of the Labor Department," accused the Bureau of Negro Economics of sending black organizers into Georgia, Alabama, Mississippi, and the Carolinas to unionize domestics and farmhands and to encourage them to demand wages of $75 to $100 a month for only seven to eight hours of work a day. "This," he said, "is what is known as Negro Economics." He also accused the bureau's employees of stirring up animosity against whites in the South, whom he said were the "best friends the Negroes ever had on God's green earth."[117]

With Haynes rebuffed and the Labor Department as a whole stymied, black southerners had to combat the work-or-fight campaign on their own. In urban centers and small cities where black residents were organized, their resistance was fairly successful. Two days after the *Pine Bluff Commercial* reported on the campaign by the local chamber of commerce to extend the work-or-fight ordinance to black women, the African American ministers of Pine Bluff, Arkansas (Haynes's hometown), drafted and published a resolution of protest. According to their missive, they protested on behalf "of the twelve million Negroes of the United States and especially those of this section of our country, to which the article mentioned has special reference." "The loyalty of the Negro woman" could not be questioned, they argued, and "the women of the race" protested being "classed parasites, or placed in the class of idlers or slackers." The African American community of Pine Bluff backed the ministers by holding a public forum at the local Normal College, where they were addressed by the mayor, Simon Bloom. The substance of Bloom's remarks, McConico later noted, was that the work-or-fight order applied to all women without specifying any particular race or class. "He soon saw that the audience knew that this was pure buncombe and, in the midst of much embarrassment, closed his address."[118]

The black community's protest took a different form in Montgomery, Alabama. On October 20 a broadside appeared in the city that mimicked the Klan's threatening rhetoric. Addressed to "Slackers and Traitors, Spreaders of German Propaganda" and "Fighters Against World-Wide Democracy," the "Mysterious Order of Dragons" announced that it had organized "to create a love for Country, Race and Fair Play."

> We Have Never Blown UP a Munition Plant; Never Produced a Benedict Arnold, and Never Assassinated a President, but on the other hand, Have Proved Ourselves Loyal to Our Country, We have nursed the Southern White Man from the days of Slavery; We Stayed at Home during the Civil War and Protected his Family; We have Clothed the World from his Cottonfields. And Now, NOW is our time to Tell him our wants and DEMAND PAY—not for Doing Our Duty, but it is time he DID HIS DUTY?

The broadside went on to demand fair play, justice in the courts and "A MAN'S PLACE AMONG MEN!"[119]

When the police sought and arrested a number of married black women in Bainbridge, Georgia, who were not employed outside their homes, the African American community immediately organized a meeting at the courthouse. G. R. Hutto, grand chancellor of the Knights of Pythias and chair of the meeting, demanded that the city attorney say whether the "work or fight bill applied to Colored women alone, or to white women as well." The organizers made clear that the black community of Bainbridge "would not submit to such a law" and that any attempt upon the part of the City officers to force their wives to work against their will "would bring about a race riot, and that we as Colored men would fight them as long as we could get hold of a piece of them." The following day the mayor remitted the women's fines, and the work-or-fight ordinance went unenforced thereafter.[120]

Though work-or-fight measures were defeated in cities and towns where the African American communities were well organized, the measures were used extensively in rural areas, where employers conscripted

collective action (handwritten annotation in margin)

labor for private use rather than for service in the war.[121] Georgia required black men to have employment cards punched by their employers every day, an obvious attempt to revive the old plantation pass system. In Waynesboro a deputy sheriff stopped a black farmer who had come to town in his car on business and demanded his work card. Since he worked for himself, the farmer replied that he did not have to carry a card, whereupon an argument ensued, and the sheriff shot and killed him as he tried to get back into his car.[122]

Though Crowder's order specified that it was not meant to be used to settle work disputes, southern employers made no attempt to hide the fact that they used the measure to intimidate working people. In Lake County, Florida, for example, an orange grove owner sent the sheriff after eight African American orange pickers who left his employ for another grove that was paying a better rate. The sheriff ordered the men "to go back to work at the former place, to war, or to jail," interspersing his remarks with a good deal of profanity, according to Walter White, "that being the recognized manner of white men talking to Negroes in that part of the country."[123]

Although the work-or-fight campaign helped some growers to intimidate labor, African Americans continued to leave the South in increasing numbers. Thus, if the discriminatory and often violent enforcement of compulsory work laws did anything, it appears to have driven black workers away. By insisting on federal support for their own draconian methods and by resisting the state management that the Department of Labor offered, southern planters took their big gun and shot themselves in the foot.

Unwilling to abandon subsistence wages and their accustomed forms of labor relations, southern employers scuttled the farm labor supply effort during the First World War, but their allies in the Department of Agriculture succeeded in promoting a particularly southern solution to a national problem. Instead of advising growers to entice black workers back into the fields by improving wages and conditions, the southern men at the USDA counseled coercion and intimidation. Ironically, then, World War I farm labor policy unified the nation in a way that Reconstruction never did. Instead of remaking the South in the North's image, the First World War did the reverse.

5

The Sunshine State Meets the Garden State

Farm Labor during the
Long Depression

WITH AGRICULTURAL PRICES higher during the First World War than they had ever been before, farmers had hastened to cash in on a flush economy. They had planted every acre that they owned or rented and borrowed to buy more land to put into production. The war boom also encouraged farmers to invest in machinery, motor vehicles, and fertilizers—anything that would make their farms more productive and get their produce to market more quickly. All this cost money, of course, but as long as farm prices held at three and four times their prewar level, credit ran like water from a new irrigation system.[1]

But farm prices were bound to come down, and the fall began in late 1918. The federal government staved off an immediate price collapse after the armistice by buying farm surplus and sending it to Europe to feed war refugees, but the relief effort wound down quickly as European farmers traded their rifles for plows. American agricultural exports fell from a high of $4.1 billion in 1919 to just $1.8 billion in 1922.[2] Prices fell by almost 50 percent in one year. Nonfarm prices also fell, but less drastically, for the terms of trade were once again against farmers. For rural Americans the Great Depression had begun. Thousands of farmers had to pay for land, supplies, and vehicles bought at inflated war prices with half their war income. Those who had nothing saved went bankrupt.[3]

In postwar Georgia and elsewhere in the cotton belt of the Southeast the blow was doubly hard. Cotton prices dropped from 35 cents a pound in 1919 to 17 cents in 1920. Only the boll weevils were undaunted. While the weevils gradually succumbed to eradication efforts in the Southwest, in Georgia the infestation was just getting under way. Crop yields dropped from 1.75 million bales in 1921 to just 588,000 bales in 1923. Between 1920 and 1925 Georgia planters took nearly 3.5 million acres out of production. When the stock market crashed in 1929, it hit Georgia like the inevitable knockout blow at the end of a long, lopsided fight. Farm prices stumbled 60 percent in the following three years, and cotton fell prostrate at 5 cents a pound.[4]

This rapid contraction in farm prices built the modern farm labor migrant stream on the East Coast as thousands upon thousands of Georgians hit the road. The luckiest made the last trains north to industrial and service jobs before the northern market was saturated with workers. African American migration to the urban North peaked in the early 1920s and then tapered off to a trickle as factory gates closed to job seekers in places like Newark, Chicago, and Detroit. Those who managed to make a crop looked for other work at the end of the season. Tens of thousands of other sharecroppers and farm laborers who had worked the 3.5 million acres now idle in Georgia kept moving. They packed their belongings into trucks and cars bought from failing farmers and joined the ranks of the East Coast farmworker migrant stream.

The long agricultural depression that began after the First World War changed the nature of farm labor migrancy on the East Coast in three ways. First, it forced more black southerners, particularly Georgians, to join the ranks of mobile harvest workers. By the 1920s African Americans outnumbered all other ethnic groups in the East's migrant population, and they retained their majority for the following fifty years.

The second change was the rise of commercial agriculture on a grand scale in South Florida. The draining of the Everglades in the 1920s exposed hundreds of thousands of acres of land that could be planted in a wide range of crops—beans, tomatoes, potatoes, and sugarcane, to name just a few—while northern fields were still under snow. By the early 1930s, South Florida agriculture was big business, and the winter harvest in the Sunshine State drew even greater numbers of migrant farmworkers southward. As a result the migrant stream stretched the length of the coast. While draining the Everglades made the success of commercial agriculture possible, it was the flood of poor migrants from Georgia that made agriculture in South Florida profitable at the height of the Great Depression.

The third change was the unhappy consequence of the first two. The farm depression, coupled with the rise of large agricultural enterprises in the Everglades, made it both possible and necessary for thousands of

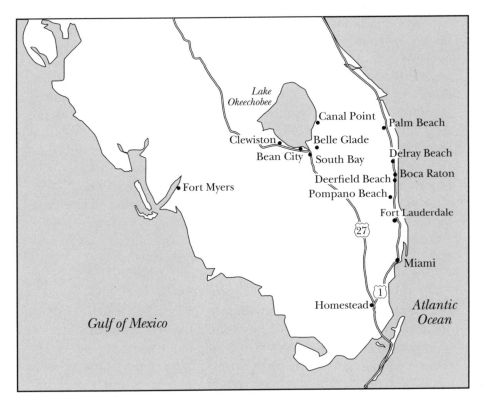

South Florida

black southerners to migrate year-round in search of harvest work. The ③
third change, then, was the rise of the "permanent transient," the migrant farmworker who had no sharecrop arrangement to return to, no
state of residence, and no home to speak of. Most alternated winter work
in Florida with summer work in New Jersey. The considerable distance
involved in this circuit led to increased dependence on crew leaders,
who became more exploitive as they became more necessary. It was
during this long depression between the First and Second World Wars,
then, that the East Coast migrant stream took on its present form and
character.

The expansion of the migrant stream down the length of the coast and
the rising number of African American migrants who made the journey
up and back had an additional consequence. We might call it the southernization of New Jersey or the nationalization of the farm labor market.
Black men had traveled to New Jersey to harvest potatoes in the late
nineteenth and early twentieth centuries because farm wages in New
Jersey compared favorably to anything they could earn in the South and

because Jersey growers often advanced their rail fare to get them there. By the 1930s, however, most black migrants made the journey packed into the back of labor contractors' trucks, and they found, when they arrived, that it had become increasingly difficult to distinguish the Garden State from the Sunshine State. Truck farms in both states were growing in size. In both regions spending one's days in the fields meant spending one's nights in a barn, a flophouse, a chicken coop, or under a rented tent in a grower's field. North and South, state and county officials were at best obviously indifferent and at times openly hostile to the concerns of seasonal harvest workers. Most importantly, perhaps, as increasing numbers of southerners sought harvest work up and down the coast, harvest wages tended to equalize. By the end of the 1930s the only advantage to seeking harvest work in New Jersey was that one might find enough days of work in a year to carry on to the next one.

For African American sharecroppers and tenant farmers forced to find additional work after the meager cotton harvest or forced off farms altogether by the boll weevil, there was no point in searching for temporary work in Georgia. There might be work grading peaches and harvesting tobacco for a few hundred workers, but there were simply too many people competing for too few jobs. After the last peanuts were picked and the pathetic cotton harvest was completed, Georgia's tenants and sharecroppers turned their sights southward to the one southern state that was not in despair: Florida.[5] Their hopes lay not in the turpentine camps and cotton plantations of that part of Florida that is indistinguishable from southern Georgia and Alabama. They had few prospects in the orange groves of central Florida, where jobs were jealously guarded by white pickers and packers.[6] Rather, they looked to the Everglades, Florida's river of grass, which spans the southern half of the peninsula from Lake Okeechobee to the state's southern tip. Here the 1920s brought a new city in pastel colors for the enjoyment of the nation's rich, and massive, new farms on rich black soil for the sustenance of Georgia's poor.

Bounded on the east by a line of coastal sand dunes and on the west by the Ocaloacoochee Slough and the Big Cypress Swamp, the Everglades disappear to the south into mangroves, whose twisted roots hold back the salt water of two oceans. The Everglades are essentially a shallow bowl of limestone, filled with layers of sand, alluvial deposits, decaying vegetation, and sawgrass. Lake Okeechobee, at the top of the Glades, keeps the area's 2.5 million acres of sawgrass wet. Under water for half the year, the rotting vegetation forms a rich black muck.[7]

The Everglades have only two seasons: one wet and one dry. The rains begin in April or late May, reach their peak in August or September, and often end with the bluster of a full-fledged hurricane. What passes for winter in Florida brings on the dry season. The water level falls beneath the roots of the grass, and the Glades dry so thoroughly that a spark can cause wildfires that last until the rainy season begins again.

In the nineteenth century, North Florida farmers dreamed of clearing the grass, draining the water, and planting the muck, but they lacked the means to do it. They planted the sandy soil along both coasts, but only the Seminoles lived in the sawgrass itself. Between 1888 and 1905 the trustees of the state's Internal Improvement Fund received proposals to drain the Everglades, but private capital proved insufficient. Only when the State of Florida took up the project in 1903 did the reclamation begin in earnest. By 1909 two dredges had cut a path fourteen miles into the Everglades from Fort Lauderdale, and by 1911 142 miles of canals crisscrossed the southern part of the state.[8]

Once drainage was under way, speculation in mucklands began with a fury. The state began selling land it had drained at a cost of $1.50 an acre for just $2.00 an acre. R. P. Davie bought 25,000 acres at the edge of the Glades north of Miami and resold them for $30.00 each. Dicky Bolles bought 500,000 acres, reselling them in ten-acre plots at $240 a contract. That meant a profit of 1,100 percent per acre. Using the slogan "ten acres and independence," land agents roamed the country, telling anyone who would listen that they could make a fortune in Florida with a tent, a hoe, and a handful of beans.[9]

Farmers who came to try their luck at mining the muck battled mosquitoes, snakes, and alligators and spent months clearing sawgrass off an acre of land, only to discover that their beautiful crops wilted and died from a strange "reclaiming disease."[10] After the Agricultural Experiment Station discovered that adding copper sulfate to the soil solved that problem, truck farms began to flourish. Truck farmers were soon joined by a few self-proclaimed pioneers who experimented with sugarcane on the shore of the lake. The cane grew so well that by 1921 2,000 growers—cane planters and truck farmers—lived in sixteen settlements around Lake Okeechobee. In winter they were joined by suitcase farmers who came south to plant when the northern season was over.[11]

But there were surprises in store for the pioneers of South Florida. While the bonanza farms of the Dakota Territory had been unusually wet when settlers arrived a few decades earlier, the first flurry of settling, draining, and planting in South Florida happened to coincide happily with several years of unusually dry weather. When the rains returned in

1922, however, the lake rose, filling the new canals and flooding the surrounding fields and towns. Bare Beach, Clewiston, Moore Haven, and Okeelanta lay under water for weeks. The only way sugar growers could see their tall, beautiful cane plants was to row out over them and peer down through the water. Fifteen thousand acres of cane were reduced to 1,000 overnight.[12]

The experience was enough to send the least hardy souls packing, but those who believed that there was gold in the muck remained. While the nation's wealthy spent their millions sailing the intracoastal waterways, playing blackjack in Miami's casinos, lazing on South Florida beaches, and drinking bootleg rum, truck farmers grew $4 million worth of beans, tomatoes, peas, and cabbage on the south shore of Lake Okeechobee. B. G. Dalberg bought out the soggy remains of Glades sugar growers and formed the Southern Sugar Company. Elsewhere in Florida land sold, resold, and sold again. The value of Miami real estate ran ahead even of Wall Street stock. Fort Lauderdale boomed. Fort Myers boomed. Delray, Deerfield, and Palm Beach boomed. Around them tenant farmers grew truck crops, loading onto the Seaboard Railway what they could not sell in local markets. Property values in Miami increased 560 percent between 1921 and 1926, and the streets were crowded with "binder boys," speculators who bought land on the margin, betting on ever-increasing real estate values. The real estate market stood on a flimsy credit structure that could be knocked down by a gust of wind. The 1926 and 1928 hurricane seasons brought winds of biblical proportions.[13]

Unusually dry weather kept the muck on fire during the winter of 1926. Spring brought heavy rainfall that put out the fires and refilled the lake. But in September a hurricane picked up all this water and threw it at the town of Moore Haven. Three hundred people died, and with them went the real estate market. Forty banks closed, and the assessed value of Florida real estate fell by a third. Truck farmers conscripted black workers at gunpoint to clean up the mess and plant new crops. The recovery was short lived. Two years later a nighttime hurricane pounded the southern end of the state. The following day found much of Miami flattened and more than 1,800 people dead in the mucklands south of Lake Okeechobee, most of whom were African American and Bahamian farmworkers who had come for their share of Glades gold.[14]

From then on the Army Corp of Engineers took responsibility for regulating the level of the lake by building a levee around it and locks to control the water level. The new dike worked too well; the muck dried to a powder. The engineers responded by periodically releasing water to irrigate the muck, but this tampering with the Glades ecosystem caused persistent problems. Drained of water, the soil shrank like a dry sponge. The dryness of the soil also brought insects, robbed the land of nutrients, and increased the severity of freezes and the frequency of droughts and muckland fires. Worse, as the fresh water disappeared, salt water began invading the coast at the rate of a foot a year.[15]

The resulting need for drainage and irrigation systems and fertilizers and insecticides, as well as the cost of devastating droughts and freezes, made farming in the Glades an expensive and complex enterprise. Even after the construction of dikes and drainage systems by the Army Corp of Engineers, individual farmers still had to dig ditches on their own property that linked up to the larger drainage system. They also had to run pumps to regulate the water level and run "mole drains" three feet under their fields to carry the water into the ditches.[16]

There were other expenses once their crops were ready for market. The advantage of truck farms in Florida was that vegetables could be grown in winter when northern markets were starved for fresh vegetables. Northern markets were, however, a long way away, and vegetables had to be presentable upon arrival if they were to fetch good prices. In the early years of Glades truck farming, all produce bound for the Northeast had to be sent down canals to one Fort Lauderdale broker. Growers had to pay him a brokerage fee plus money for crates, packing, and shipping. Even then, produce would arrive in New York loosely packed and encrusted with muck. To escape their dependence on this broker and to produce a more marketable product, growers began building their own packinghouses around 1926, and by the early 1930s they were buying expensive grading, washing, and precooling equipment (potatoes and leafy vegetables had to be iced before they could be shipped).[17]

Over the course of the 1930s, then, Glades farmers divided into two groups: those who could afford to pack and ship their own crops and those who could not. As one successful grower, Howard Haney, put it, "The law of economics more or less eliminates those farmers that do nothing but . . . furnish the raw material for the packing house." If a grower was not large enough to do his own packing, shipping, and precooling, Haney concluded, "he doesn't stay in business very long." Farmers who did nothing but produce crops lost perhaps 50 percent of their possible profit, according to Haney, while growers large enough to process their own crops made money even if they took a loss on their harvest operation in a particular year.[18]

Small farmers had to pay others for processing and marketing, but their position was precarious for other reasons as well. Few small farmers actually had title to the land they farmed.[19] Most of them rented land from packinghouse operators, who did not own it either but leased it from absentee landowners. In order to get a piece of land to plant for any one season, tenants would have to agree to buy their fertilizer, crates, and hampers from a particular packinghouse and have their crops graded and packed there. They could not shop around for the best produce prices and the smallest fees. Moreover, the packers preferred to deal in large quantities, so they would insist that the tenants they staked put all their acreage in one crop. The crop the packers preferred was green beans because it made the greatest return for the least investment. However, beans were also the quickest to freeze during a cold snap, so a bean farmer could be wiped out overnight. This was not the packers' concern. Indeed, by intentionally financing too many farmers, the packers encouraged overproduction and depressed the prices they paid farmers for produce. As one "big shipper" commented to federal investigators, "If I loan a man money to grow celery — I ship that celery, and I make 15 cents/crate for handling it — what the hell do I care what *his* net profit is. . . . I get *mine* first. . . . If he goes broke this year, I will finance some other grower next year on the same land. What I want is tonnage, and I don't care what the grower's name is."[20]

Lucky growers made money fast, but a poor market at harvest, a freeze, or a heavy rain followed by a hot sun could mean ruin. In 1936 Joseph Cassellius planted nine acres of beans with seed and fertilizer advanced by a packer/shipper. After two freezes and a flood, he had little left to sell when it came time to settle his account. After the packer took his fifth, plus the money he lent for supplies as well as the cost of the shipping packages and grading, Cassellius ended up owing $80. M. M. Carter moved his family from Arkansas to Belle Glade in 1935 and planted twenty acres of beans. He was "frosted out" the first year and "drowned out" the second. After that he "figured that was enough."[21]

Vegetable farming was such a gamble that growers referred to it as though they were betting at Pompano racetracks or Havana blackjack tables. "Beans is a big crop," Joseph Cassellius explained, "because beans is a quick crop and if you hit it, it is quick money and you can plant right back to something else."[22] Luther Jones, who had considerably more success at the crap shoot than poor Joseph Cassellius, said essentially the same thing: "Vegetables are a gambling game, purely a gamble. . . . In vegetable farming you may be a pauper today and worth $100,000 tomorrow." "A man might lose one year, break even a second year, make a little money the third, and what's known as a 'killing' the fourth," Jones continued, but success involved crop rotation, staggered pickings, and other protective measures that were "not possible to the little fellow."[23]

By the mid-1930s most of the big fellows were improving their odds by diversifying their farms. By doing so, they protected themselves from freezes, staggered their labor demand, and covered their bets in case the market price of a particular crop plummeted. They not only rode out the depression but prospered, making truck farming the state's leading agricultural industry. Acreage in green beans increased more than sevenfold in twenty years, and during the depths of the greatest depression in American history, the value of Florida beans increased from $59 to $86 an acre.[24]

As the truck farming industry grew, however, the gap between small farmers and large operators became even wider.[25] As a federal investigator testified before a congressional committee, by the end of the decade there seemed "to be general agreement in the Lake Okeechobee area that the small farmers are being pushed entirely out of the picture, that the whole set-up is against them, that the very land won't let itself be farmed in small pieces, but responds best when handled in great 640-acre sections, with unified water control and crops breaking just right so you've got stuff hitting the market all along."[26] South Florida's pioneers became increasingly bitter; many of them had "staked their claims to a piece of muck when the only way in or out was by canal and the mail boat brought the wife's letters once a month." They had "toughed it out through hurricanes and flood when Lake Okeechobee stood ten feet deep all over Belle Glade. They have the idea that they built the country up and ought to have some title to it."[27]

Legally, in fact, small farmers rarely had title to it, and as the 1930s wore on, they were less and less likely to have any attachment to a particular piece of land. While in 1929 in Palm Beach County 42 percent of the harvests took place on farms of fewer than 50 acres, ten years later only 8 percent of the harvests took place on farms that small. Small farm owners were simply disappearing. On the other hand, harvests on farms of over 500 acres increased sharply from under 14 percent to 53 percent.[28]

The collapse of the land boom, the hurricane of 1928, bank failures, and falling crop prices in the early 1930s merely facilitated the transition from small-scale enterprises to large-scale "factory farms." Between 1920 and 1940 the number of Florida farms over 1,000 acres almost doubled. By 1940 there were 101 farms with more than 10,000 acres.[29] The most notable of these was the U.S. Sugar Corporation, which bought the failed Southern Sugar Company in 1931 as well as 100,000 acres of muckland. By 1940 U.S. Sugar had 25,000 to 30,000 acres in sugarcane as well as extensive fields in truck crops. It also owned large undeveloped tracts, "nobody seems to know how great an acreage."[30] By the end of the Great Depression, these large farms produced a majority of South Florida's truck crops. In 1939 47 farms in Broward County (6 percent of the total) accounted for 62 percent of the total value of vegetables produced in the county. In Dade County just 40 farms (or 10 percent) accounted for over 70 percent of the crop value. In Palm Beach County, where U.S. Sugar had built a fiefdom, 97 of the East Coast's largest farms (17 percent of the county total) accounted for a whopping 86 percent of the value of the county's total vegetable production.[31]

The consolidation of Florida agriculture into large estates meant that the vast majority of migrant farmworkers worked for a tiny minority of growers. Having conquered the problems of processing and shipping, having pushed back an inland sea, and with chemical and mechanical artillery, having subdued the wildness of the Glades, large growers were free to put their energies into restraining the cost of labor. This proved to be a much simpler task.

The price of labor was important to large and small farmers in different ways. For small farmers, who had to pay a third party to grade, clean, cool, pack, ship, and market their crops, these costs far outweighed the expense of hired labor. In the potato harvests of 1934–35, for example, harvest labor cost growers $4.39 an acre, while the expense of paying third parties to process the potatoes for sale added up to almost $50 an acre.[32] Still, these farmers could not control what they paid for processing; they could influence what they paid for labor, and given their other expenses, they had to.

In contrast, by the 1930s large growers had drastically reduced their processing expenses by doing the work themselves, and they were hiring much greater numbers of farmworkers. Therefore, for them, farm labor represented a much larger proportion of their costs. In the state of Florida as a whole, wages paid to hired farm laborers represented the largest single drain on farm income.[33] Clearly growers, both large and small, had good reason to want to hold down the price of labor.

This was not a particularly difficult task in the 1930s; the fields were flooded with workers. As a federal investigator reported in 1939, if a tenant farmer had a thousand hampers of beans to pick, "he'd as soon that they be picked by two hundred workers as a hundred. The pickers are paid by the hamper, so the important thing is to get the matured beans picked as quickly as possible and without regard for a full day's work for a specific number of laborers."[34] The same was true of large

Migrant farmworkers waiting to be paid for harvesting vegetables near
Homestead, Florida, in 1939 (Marion Post Wolcott, Library of Congress)

growers. Flooding the labor market took no genius or effort. As displaced sharecroppers and tenants poured into the state, growers simply did nothing to dissuade them.

As a result, while the rest of growers' expenses rose over the course of the decade — the cost of seed, fertilizer, and equipment all went up — farm wages remained stagnant or fell, depending on the crop. Growers paid less than $5.00 to harvest an acre of potatoes throughout the 1930s, and by all accounts bean pickers' wages fell dramatically over the decade.[35] As a veteran of harvests in thirty-three states put it, "Florida is the sorriest wages in the United States."[36]

The first paid farmworkers in South Florida were the Native Americans whose ancestors had lived in the Everglades since they fled there to escape removal to the West after 1832. However, they were few in number and susceptible to malaria, brought to the region by settlers from northern Florida and Georgia. They were outnumbered by Bahamians, who had been fishing, sponging, and turtling in the Florida Keys since the 1830s, and who had begun working seasonally as farmworkers on Florida's lower east coast by the late nineteenth century. During the First World War the relaxation of immigration restrictions allowed Bahamians to move back and forth even more easily between the islands and South Florida. Between 1900 and 1920 about one-fifth of the entire population of the Bahamas worked in Florida. In 1920 the commissioner of Watling Island reported to the Bahamian legislative council that seasonal migration to Florida left the island "almost denuded of young men." During the 1920s Bahamians migrated to Florida at the rate of about 6,000 per year; the depression of the 1930s merely intensified this seasonal flow.[37]

Despite the proportions of the Bahamian migration, islanders were soon outnumbered by the Black Belt refugees who poured into the state after the postwar bust. Black and white migrants came for a share of boom wages, driven from cotton-producing regions by the boll weevil and drawn to Florida by the hope of preserving the gains they had made during the war. Jacob McMillan left Georgia "like a lot of them. I went broke, everything went to the bottom and I had to get away."[38] White migrants, like McMillan, found work in the packinghouses or not at all because most growers thought it inappropriate to have white and black people working alongside each other in the fields.[39] Still, South Florida growers rarely faced the prospect of turning away white migrants in need of work, for the vast majority (perhaps 80 to 90 percent) of the poor people who entered the state were African Americans.[40]

The 1920s saw the founding of all-black communities, such as Pearl City (since enveloped by Boca Raton).[41] Pearl City resident George Spain's mother arrived in South Florida from Georgia in 1920. Every winter she picked beans, carrying George with her to the fields until he was old enough to walk by himself. Bud Jackson's father left northern Florida for Miami during the construction boom but found it "too large a city for him." In search of a place to bring his family, he "drifted" up the coast until he found work plowing bean fields on a truck farm in Boca Raton and a place to live in Pearl City.[42]

Black men and women migrated to Florida from all over the cotton South, but most simply crossed the border from Georgia.[43] Some were tenant farmers and sharecroppers who came to Florida during the winter when there was no work at home and returned when Florida's "bean deal" was over. Some, like Pearl City's Ulyssess Brown, came originally as seasonal migrants but eventually stayed. Brown left Georgia in 1935 as a young man of nineteen because he "was tired of plowing a mule all day for thirty cents a day." He headed to Butts Farm in Broward County, Florida, with a couple of friends who had been there before. They worked steadily alongside thousands of other Georgians until there was nothing to do but dig ditches and clear land for $1 a day and his friends wanted to return home: "They kept on cussing at me til they got me to decide to come with them." The next year Brown returned to Butts Farm for good.[44]

The worse the depression in the cotton belt, the more farm laborers crowded into South Florida. Mary Jenkins and her brother, Freddy

Migrant vegetable pickers and their rented shack in South Florida
(Marion Post Wolcott, Library of Congress)

Young, sought an escape from life on a cotton farm in Dublin, Georgia. Growing up, they swore to each other that when they were ready to marry, they would never "talk to a girl or boy that wanted to farm," but in 1935 Freddy returned from Butts Farm with cash in his pocket and his own car. "We all got excited and when they come back we come back with him," Mary Jenkins recalls. However, Butts Farm turned out to be nothing but an ocean of beans, a thousand stooped laborers, and a long row of pickers' shacks. Standing by Freddy's car in the dawn light as the farm's residents readied themselves for work, Mary Jenkins thought that Butts Farm was the worst place she "had ever seen." But with only 50 cents in her pocket, there was no going back until the end of the season.[45]

By 1940 40,000 to 60,000 farm labor migrants came to Florida annually, according to the estimates of the Florida Industrial Commission. Half fanned out along the lower edge of the state in towns like Pearl City, Pompano, and Homestead. The other half flocked to the string of towns that hugged the southern shore of Lake Okeechobee in the heart of the state's vegetable and cane region. They headed, in particular, for the town in Palm Beach County that pulsated with life for half a year and slowed to a crawl the other half.[46]

Belle Glade was by the 1920s, and still is today, the center of activity in

The "Pahokee hotel," housing for black vegetable pickers in Florida during the Second World War (Marion Post Wolcott, Library of Congress)

the mucklands. At the height of the depression in the mid-1930s, migrants paid $4 to $6 a month for the right to camp on a grower's land, or $3 to $4 a week for the privilege of sleeping in a shack without a sink or toilet. They slept, according to one observer, "packed together in sordid rooms, hallways, tar-paper shacks, filthy barracks with one central faucet and toilet, sheds, lean-tos, old garages, condemned and shaky buildings."[47] But from all accounts few people who came to Belle Glade expected to get much sleep.

In season, the "negro quarter" would expand to nine-tenths of the town, stretching its whole length and into neighboring communities. "Drive out in the cane fields," recalled a truck driver, "and you will see them, thick, the families living around in old packing sheds, in all kinds of little shacks, and big boarding houses and barracks. That's the way it is all around the Lake—just one little town right after another, and all settled in between like that."[48] "There are no regular streets," federal investigators Aubrey Clyde Robinson and Glenore Fisk Horne noted in a confidential report to the head of the Resettlement Administration, "just a jumble of houses with alleyways, hodge-podge streets and footpaths, two and three-story buildings most of which are shed-like, barn-like, ramshackle."[49]

After work and on days off, the streets would be filled with people "at the windows, on the porches, in the back yards, standing in the streets until a car can hardly drive through," Robinson and Horne noted. The oil stoves and open fires of outdoor fish fry stands and barbecues added to the congestion and filled the air with hot smoke.[50] As Zora Neale Hurston's characters tell it, "Folks don't do nothin' down dere but make money and fun and foolishness." To the "strange eyes" of a newcomer to Belle Glade, Hurston wrote in 1937, "everything in the Everglades was big and new."[51]

Belle Glade was like a mining town sitting on a mother lode. It was a jook joint on a Saturday night in a decade of Sundays. Wages may have been falling throughout the 1930s, but around Belle Glade at least there *were* wages, cash wages, paid at the end of every day. For people deep in debt to landlords and merchants back in Georgia, North Florida, or South Carolina, a dollar saved and brought back home was simply a dollar in a creditor's pocket. "They made good money," Hurston wrote, "even to the children." "So they spent good money. Next month and next year were other times. No need to mix them up with the present."[52]

Since the price of labor rarely changed, the best a picker could do was try to get work on a field with good pickings, or "first picking," as the workers called a field that had not yet been picked. As John Beecher of the Farm Security Administration explained to a congressional committee in 1940, every morning during the picking and planting season the pickers would gather at dawn in Belle Glade's hiring yard, "a couple of thousand of them crowded into two blocks." The growers would park their trucks along one side of the street. Black men hired as "barkers" or "broadcasters" would use the truck beds as platforms, from which they would harangue the crowd of pickers on the merits of the particular field to which each truck was destined. Beecher recalled one particularly adept broadcaster called "Two Dice." When there were perhaps sixty aboard and it would seem impossible to pack on another person, Two Dice bellowed, "Room fo' fifteen mo'. Bes' fiel' in all de Glades. Beans hangin' thick on de vines. First pickin'. Payin' twenty cents a hamper. Come on folks, ride de prosperity truck. Room fo' fifteen mo'." And fifteen more workers would somehow crowd on, the chain would be fastened across the end of the truck, and it would pull out for the fields. As it moved away, several men would jump onto the outside of the truck and hang on. Two Dice would then get up on the platform of an empty truck and bellow forth "the glories of another field."[53]

As long as there were more workers than were needed, hiring pickers by the day tended to suppress the price of labor. After all, if pickers were hired by the season, those who did not get a position would be forced to leave the area, thus reducing the pool of available workers. Because harvest workers were hired in daily "shape-ups," a great number of workers hung about Belle Glade, picking up a few days' work here and there and keeping wages universally low.

Growers in the mucklands also controlled labor costs by pitting African Americans against West Indians and by controlling the operation of state relief efforts. An "influential Negro leader" in Jacksonville explained to federal investigators that African Americans in his city traveled all the way to South Florida in search of work when they heard "that the Nassauians were getting 25 cents a hamper for picking beans." As soon as the Jacksonville residents got down to the fields, however, growers told the "Nassauians that these Jacksonville folks were willing to work at 15 cents a hamper, thereby bringing the price down in direct proportion to labor surplus. If the Negro after he gets broke doesn't want to work, he has to walk back home."[54]

Relief agencies also helped to control the price of labor, but this was more complicated because farmworkers were rarely eligible for relief. Migrant workers were excluded from the relief rolls by rules that required relief recipients to reside at least one year in Florida and six months in a single county.[55] "These people have learned not to ask us for anything," one county employee noted. Late in the decade, however, state officials began distributing surplus commodities provided by the federal government, but they did it in such a way that the program acted as a subsidy for growers. When growers did not have enough work to hold workers in an area because of a freeze or a flood, and they feared they would lose workers to growers along the coast or farther north, they would take a truckload of pickers to the Palm Beach County welfare office and "certify" that they were in need of surplus commodities. Without such a certification, welfare offices would not distribute commodities to black farmworkers. Once the growers were ready to begin hiring again, they would have the pickers cut off relief, so that they would not be in a position to support themselves while holding out for higher wages. As soon as they received word from growers that the harvest was upon them, Palm Beach welfare officials would begin to reduce their relief rolls. Like growers, they believed that "the Negro will work a few days and get a few dollars and, of course, if he has the commodities . . . he will lay off for a while."[56] "All the way down the East coast," the Jacksonville observer reported, "the relief cut off the Negroes during bean picking and tomato gathering time, because the Negroes, said Relief people, wouldn't work as long as they could get relief."[57]

State and county officials showed their support for Glades growers in even more open and obvious ways. The Belle Glade police regularly kept order during the morning hiring roundup, and they would occasionally be called on to force workers onto the growers' trucks when the pickers collectively refused to accept the prevailing picking rates, even though harvesters recruited in this manner were not apt to be enthusiastic workers. One grower told a federal investigator that "he had quit getting the police to help load his trucks" because it was "always necessary after arrival at the field to beat up two or three before the group would go to work, and then they didn't really work but just made like it."[58]

When growers no longer needed to keep people at work, migrants had little choice but to leave the state, not because the police forced them to go, but because they would starve if they stayed. Residents of coastal towns near tourist resorts like Pearl City were able to remain in Florida year-round by stringing together seasonal jobs and by combining the incomes of all family members. Bud Jackson's father worked year-round as a gardener on some of the wealthy estates, while his mother picked beans on Butts Farm in season. Irene Carswell's mother alternated work as a vegetable packer with domestic service in white people's homes, while her father sharecropped on a truck farm before also becoming a gardener. Louise Williams's father worked as a carpenter for whites in Boca Raton, while her mother worked at home "except in the winter when the bean season was on." Pearl City residents survived the long hot summer by fishing, hunting, turtling, and living off earnings carefully saved the rest of the year.[59]

Pearl City could sustain a small year-round population only because its residents were able to combine farmwork with service work in neighboring Boca Raton. Still, there was only so much need in summertime for gardeners and domestics even in tourist communities, and tourists rarely ventured into the mucklands. In the interior of the peninsula, in the Glades communities on the shore of Okeechobee, there were no golf courses to maintain or resort hotels to paint and clean. There was little to do in the summer but suffer from the heat.[60] As Emma Riggins explains, in the winter when there was a lot of work, people poured in from up north, but in April and May they would go back because the sun was too hot to farm. "By May and June there ain't nothing to do there."[61] Belle Glade could support only a few hundred people in the summer.

As summer approached, most of Florida's migrants returned to their home states for the cotton planting and chopping seasons. A minority joined the East Coast's mobile army of harvest workers or went "up the state," as the pickers called migrating up the coast for other harvest work. Because Florida's growing season took place in winter and early spring, farmworkers could alternate picking and cane cutting in Florida with harvest work in more northerly states. Thus the rise of South Florida's truck farming industry made it possible to work almost year-round as a migrant farm laborer.

For migrants who had homes to return to in Georgia or elsewhere, the wages they earned in Belle Glade were clearly a boon. Compared with what sharecroppers and tenant farmers earned (or owed) in Georgia, they made good money on the muck, as Zora Neale Hurston put it, even if Florida's wages got "sorrier" over the course of the depression. But for those who had to go north in search of other work or go "up the state," as farmworkers called it, the expense of the trip was enough to eat up savings earned in the Everglades. At the end of a year of work and travel, many if not most migrants ended up with nothing to show for their labor. How well they fared usually depended on how they made their way to northern harvests.

Only migrants who had their own cars could literally work their way up the seaboard.[62] Four, five, or even six "free-lancers," as these independent harvesters were called, might travel in a car, pooling expenses. With a car the group could move quickly from job to job in case of crop failures, uncompetitive wages, or the arrival of competing workers. There was a few weeks' work to be found here and there, perhaps digging potatoes in Morehead City, North Carolina, harvesting a variety of vegetables in Pocomoke City, Maryland, or working in a cannery in Berlin, Virginia.[63]

However, free-lancing was not without its drawbacks. Migrants going up the state might spend more days searching for work than actually working. Charting their course on the basis of rumors of ripe crops and high wages, they often found themselves in regions overpopulated with farmworkers or already picked out. Free-lancers were also the bane of growers because they would leave a harvest before it was over and drive off in search of first pickings somewhere else.[64]

Workers who had no vehicle or money to pay for food and gas along the route had to find a grower or crew leader to advance the cost of the trip. Growers would send trucks the length of the coast when they needed workers at the start of the season. Many workers arrived in Florida standing upright in the back of a truck and left the same way. Besides the obvious discomfort and dangers of the ride itself, accepting an offer of transportation from a grower involved other risks. Getting into the back of a grower's truck meant giving up one's freedom to move if conditions proved to be unsatisfactory. Pickers transported by a grower might end up wasting time waiting for a crop to ripen, picking a crop for less than the promised wage, or stuck on an isolated farm and paying the grower's prices for food and shelter.

John Heard left Georgia at the bidding of a Freehold, New Jersey, grower. After graduating from junior high in 1933, Heard had received $12 a week on work relief doing drainage work. He spent one winter in Florida digging potatoes and then worked two years in Georgia as a porter in a drugstore for $6 a week. In 1940 he received a letter from an apple grower in Freehold who promised steady employment for twenty men at $15 a week. So in July Heard left his wife and child in Georgia and made his first trip north. When he and the other men arrived, however, they found that the apples were not ready to be picked and they would have to wait without pay for two weeks. Asked how he liked New Jersey, Heard replied, "I like it all right, when I have something to do."[65]

The crew leader system offered a middle ground between the anarchic wanderings of the free-lancers and the tyranny of the grower's truck. A padrone system by another name, the crew leader system was by the 1930s the farm laborer's principal means of finding work.[66] Crew leaders contracted with growers before the season, so crew members were assured of a job after the long and uncomfortable journey. Crew leader Norman Hall reported to a federal committee that he would pack thirty-three people into the back of his truck and drive all day and all night, stopping only to eat.[67]

The crew leader system was not necessarily exploitive, but it became increasingly so over the course of the depression. Since the 1880s, when black southerners began making arrangements with northern growers to harvest crops in the summer, certain pickers had been acting as crew leaders. The crew leader was merely the person who corresponded with the grower and made the arrangements, gathering as many friends or family members as the grower said he needed. Before the advent of cars, the growers would advance the cost of rail fare and take the money out of the pickers' pay during the harvest. In the 1920s and 1930s, however, the availability of cars and trucks offered pickers who had a vehicle the opportunity to make money by transporting other workers. The more migrants there were who were desperate to go up the state, the more crew leaders could charge them.

Because crew leaders could always find work for their gangs in New Jersey's potato region, working in a crew usually meant a trip to the Garden State. Once in New Jersey, crew leaders assumed all the historic functions of padroni, only in this case the pickers harvested potatoes, not berries. The growers would contract all harvest work to the crew leader and absolve themselves of the responsibilities of housing, feeding, supervising, and even directly paying their workers. The grower would simply contract the entire harvest to the crew leader.

Despite the continuity between the padrone system and the crew leader system, New Jersey agriculture had not gone unchanged since the Progressive Era. In Burlington, Camden, Gloucester, Salem, and Cumberland Counties fruit and vegetable growers continued to hire Italian families from Philadelphia as they had since the 1880s.[68] But by the 1930s the unassuming spud had outpaced berries as New Jersey's principal crop. In 1910 the central New Jersey counties of Middlesex, Mercer, and Monmouth were already the state's leading potato producers, but together they accounted for only 36 percent of the state's annual potato crop. Over the next thirty years, however, potato production in the "three M" region more than doubled. By 1940 central Jersey farmers were producing three-quarters of the state's potato crop, and potatoes made up 71 percent of all the crops produced in the state.[69]

On the rise, moreover, were farmers who grew nothing but potatoes. These were the growers who had invested in the two-row mechanical potato digger. Farmers who grew potatoes along with other crops could stagger their labor needs and do without migrant farmworkers from out of state. Those who mechanized potato production justified the expense of the machine by expanding their acreage in that one crop. The more acres they had in potatoes, however, the more dependent they were on temporary workers, because even mechanically dug potatoes still had to be bagged, cleaned, and sorted by hand. According to a New Jersey Employment Service survey, the commercial potato growers who grew nothing but potatoes hired all of the 4,000 to 5,000 black migrants who entered the state in 1939.[70]

So long as migrants were readily available, New Jersey's potato growers did not have to spread out their labor needs to attract local workers. Indeed, by the 1930s black southerners were said to have outnumbered local farmworkers three to one during the harvest season.[71] This estimate may be inflated, but it is probably not far off. Of the 320 growers surveyed by the New Jersey Employment Service, half said they hired their harvest workers simply by answering a knock at their doors; black southerners were wandering the state asking for work. Asked why they resorted to labor from out of the state, some growers complained that "local help was not available"; others claimed that the federal Works Project Administration had "spoiled" local people. But most insisted that black southerners were the "most satisfactory labor for potato digging" and were "good workers, willing to work at all hours."[72]

In filling out the employment service survey forms, these growers failed to mention that the availability of thousands of southern migrants allowed them to depress the price of labor. As a black school principal noted in a letter to the U.S. Department of Labor, men were "coming in from the South in truck loads to pick potatoes at a very much lower rate of wage than the people in the neighborhood receive." This, he argued, was "bringing about resentment on the part of laborers in the neighborhood, both white and colored, because these laborers from the South work cheaper and lower the standard of living. They live under very bad conditions — some of them out in the open."[73]

There was, in fact, considerable debate over what farm wages were in the potato region during the depression era, but there is little doubt that they were very low, even by southern standards. In 1934 the secretary of New Jersey's Farm Bureau flatly denied that central Jersey potato growers were "employing southern colored laborers at ridiculously low rates." Insisting that he had made a "personal investigation of the labor importations into the state," he emphatically denied that the wages paid to migrants undercut local men. He was "personally acquainted with hundreds of growers in Middlesex, Mercer and Monmouth counties," he said, and knew of none who refused local help "when it is available and willing to work." As for wages, he continued, they were not 3 to 5 cents per 150 pounds as alleged, but 5 cents for a sack of 100 pounds. In July 1940 James C. Ewart, chairman of the New Jersey State Potato Growers Association, suggested that growers would pay at most 7 to 8 cents a bag. Three to 8 cents a sack was about what potato pickers earned in Florida.[74]

Congress entered the debate in 1940 while investigating "the interstate migration of destitute citizens." Testifying before a House of Representatives select committee, New Jersey Deputy Commissioner of Labor George Krueger argued that the potato growers' use of migrant labor reduced employment opportunities for local citizens "to an alarming degree." "During harvest seasons a huge influx of out-of-State labor comes in, willing to work for substandard wages, and when the season is over, numbers of these persons remain, often succeeding, eventually, in getting on relief rolls," he added. He reported that wages in the potato region ranged from 20 to 35 cents an hour in 1939. One of the congressmen pointed out that potato pickers were paid by the bag, not the hour, and that they sat idle for much of the day because potatoes could not be exposed to hot sun. This alone made any calculation of hourly wages irrelevant. The congressman added that when he went into the fields in the course of the investigation, one potato farmer claimed to be paying

25 to 40 cents an hour, but one of his migrant workers said that pickers were paid 3 cents per field bag. A "No. 1 hand" might be able to pick 100 field bags a day, he noted, but few could pick that much. Flustered, Deputy Krueger deferred to the officials of the State Employment Service, who were forced to admit that they did not know what potato harvesters actually received for their work because farmers were often unwilling to report the wages that they paid. Even if they were willing to report the amount they paid to labor contractors, they would not necessarily know how much of this total the workers actually received.[75]

According to Edith Lowry of the Home Missions Council, they received very little. The council, a charitable organization funded by Protestant churches, ran schools and clinics in two New Jersey migrant labor camps as well as in thirteen other states. Lowry also did what the State Employment Service survey takers had not done: she asked the pickers themselves what they received for their work.

Her findings make clear what the crew leader system had become by the end of the 1930s. A contractor would make an agreement with a farmer to dig, grade, and sack his potatoes for so much a 100-bag (usually 8 cents, Lowry said). Of this, the pickers would receive 3 cents a picking sack, which actually held 125–145 pounds of potatoes. The workers who ran the grader would get 25 cents an hour (250 sacks of potatoes per hour and a quarter, or about $1.55 for the five men who worked the grader). This meant that for 250 bags of potatoes, the contractor would get 8 cents a sack from the grower, or $20, out of which he would pay $6.50 for field labor and $1.75 for grading, leaving a profit of $11.25 for himself. This was not all, Lowry added. The contractor also usually got $2.00 from the grower for every worker transported and about $7.00 from each worker for the round-trip passage from Florida. The contractor would also charge for food and shelter, such as it was.[76]

Asked when housing conditions might be brought up to "what might be called standard condition," the chairman of the Potato Growers Association said, "That would depend on how you defined 'standard condition.'" From Lowry's account it would appear that farm labor housing had not improved since reform organizations made their first investigations into New Jersey agriculture in 1905. Most shelters were barns, shacks, or chicken coops. Few had screens or even windows. Flies and mosquitoes were "almost unbearable," and ventilation was poor. No beds or bedding were provided; there were no bathing facilities or toilet paper, and few toilets.[77]

Many New Jerseyians blamed these conditions and the paucity of farm wages in the potato region not on growers but on the migrants themselves. It is hardly surprising that 4,000 penniless "transients" would not be welcome by anyone other than the farmers who employed them in a region already suffering under the weight of the depression. Still, for many New Jerseyians, the fact that the potato migrants were African Americans accounted for their "willingness" to accept such degraded conditions and "ruinous" wages.

State officials echoed these complaints. Testifying before the Tolan Hearings in 1940, H. L. Lepper of the State Employment Service explained that the problem was particularly pressing because, of the approximately 4,000 African Americans who entered the state in 1939, 19 percent failed to leave at the end of the potato season. This figure did not count all those who entered the state in search of work and never found it, he added. "The fact is," Lepper concluded, "that they are here in New Jersey with the idea that they might get work, and in many cases they are persuaded to make the trip into the State by people who charge them $4 and $5 to make the trip from Virginia, and never get a job after they get there. They are our biggest problem."[78]

Even Edith Lowry of the Home Missions Council blamed black migrants from the South for working "too cheaply — killing the potato labor price ruinously." The council's staff found them "crude, and altogether physically distasteful." "The growers who hired through contractors," the council concluded in its report to Congress, "were helpless to control the migrants." "Both white and colored citizens of Cranbury are anxious for the same after effect," the council reported, "that the migrants won't return next year. Everyone heartily dislikes the migrant Negro from Florida."[79]

In blaming black farmworkers for the state's agricultural economy, New Jerseyians unwittingly adopted peculiarly southern explanations for their economic problems. Farm wages were disastrously low because black workers were willing to work for a pittance. Housing conditions were poor because black people did not appreciate modern conveniences. This was the argument made so effectively by the southern planters who testified before the U.S. Industrial Commission in 1898; black people were responsible for the degraded state of agriculture. In 1898 New Jersey growers had dismissed that argument, citing their profitable dealings with black migrants from the South. By the mid-1930s New Jerseyians of all kinds had taken up the litany of the New South as their own.

Still, the southernization of New Jersey was not yet complete. In August 1939 a group of white men crossed the line from litany to liturgy when they expressed their anger and frustration by acting out the ritual of the southern lynch mob in what came to be known as the Cranbury Painting Affair. Late on August 11, 1939, seven black migrant workers were asleep in an isolated one-room shack on a farm near Cranbury, New Jersey, at the center of the potato region. Five men slept on bunks made of old boards padded with picking sacks, and a married couple slept together on the other side of a makeshift partition. They were awakened by the sound of breaking glass and by voices that demanded that they get up and come outside.

Stepping into the light of flashlights, they found themselves facing a mob of white men armed with guns and wearing handkerchiefs over their faces. Stripped naked and with their hands tied behind their backs, the seven were ordered to walk out into the potato field. Jake Preston demanded that his wife be freed, and as a result, he was beaten until she begged him to be quiet.

While their assailants busied themselves with the Prestons, the five single men, their hands still tied, made their break into the bushes. Shots flew over their heads, but they were not pursued. The Prestons were forced into one of four cars and driven several miles to a deserted field. There they were threatened with mutilation and rape and ordered to lie down on the ground, after which their attackers poured white paint on them and beat them with a rubber hose. Screaming at their victims to go back to the South, the mob finally drove away in their cars, leaving the Prestons to make their way back to the farm in the dark, naked and stinging from the paint. They managed to get to a hospital, dressed in potato sacks they had taken from a field. They were refused treatment.

The next day word of the attack spread, and southern migrants across the potato region talked of leaving the state. Frances Preston too wanted to go back south, "where I never had anything like this happen to me." However, Jake Preston and the other men wanted to stay and press charges, and with the help of the National Association for the Advancement of Colored People and the radical lawyers of the Workers Defense League, they did. By pressing charges the Prestons assailed the notion that they were responsible for the sorry state of New Jersey agriculture; they were victims of growers' miserliness, not its cause.

Two weeks later the state police announced that they had arrested nine adult men and one minor. All of the nine were in their late teens and twenties. Five were employed as farmhands; one was unemployed. They were never made to account for their actions; no one seemed to think that what they did required any explanation. The minor was deemed too young to stand criminal prosecution, but the nine men pleaded guilty to charges of assault on Frances and Jake Preston. All nine received suspended sentences.[80] The message was clear: black migrants like the Prestons were the cause of depression wages, and no one could be blamed for trying to send them back from where they had come.

If its lynch mobs were less deadly, New Jersey still seemed to aspire to becoming an honorary member of the New South. While both New Jersey and Florida offered relatively high agricultural wages in the early years of truck farming, by the 1930s growers at both ends of the "stream" were taking advantage of the swelling numbers of migrant workers and offering wages that were roughly equal, and equally low. Farmworkers had to keep moving to keep eating, which meant they spent what little they saved getting to the next harvest. Truck farming, then, had transcended the invisible line that had long divided the nation's labor market along sectional lines. National unity, the Prestons and other black farmworkers discovered, was nothing to write home about.

Black migrants faced more than just violent opposition to their presence in the North. The collapse of cotton prices combined with federal crop reduction programs forced displaced sharecroppers into the migrant stream on a year-round basis. Thousands could alternate summer work in New Jersey, New York, and Connecticut with winter work on Florida's truck farms, but the availability of jobs in Florida proved to be a mixed blessing. The farther farmworkers had to travel to find work, the more they had to depend on crew leaders to get to where they were going. While parasitic in function, crew leaders or padroni were not necessarily dangerous in a tight labor market and when workers could return home easily if they found conditions intolerable. With crew leaders empowered by the depression, however, farmworkers became poorer and more dependent with every mile they traveled. Distance from their families may have made their hearts grow fonder, but it also made labor contractors richer.

While Florida's packer/growers grew wealthier as farm wages fell, and ever more powerful crew leaders cut further into workers' earnings, critics blamed black southerners like the Prestons for the degradation of farm wages. But the Prestons were not the only farmworkers on the East Coast to challenge the notion that black migrants were to blame for the paucity of farm wages in the 1930s. Other farmworkers—black and white, Italian and native-born—joined to protest their treatment and the cheapness of their labor. They found, however, that they would have to fight not just for wage hikes and improved conditions, but for recognition as workers. They would have a hard row to hoe.

6

Wards of the State

Farmworker Unionism
and the New Deal

THOUGH MIGRANT FARMWORKERS were essential to the agricultural economies of New Jersey and Florida, they were "stateless"; they paid no taxes and did not vote. If they did not leave promptly when they were no longer needed, they became more a hindrance than a help. Thus state and local authorities kept migrant workers moving, and as long as they kept moving, no state or municipality could be made to accept responsibility for them. Farmworkers were, however, still citizens of the nation. If any government had an interest in their health, housing, and working conditions, it was the federal government, or so state officials argued on a fairly regular basis. Still, Franklin Delano Roosevelt's administration was uncharacteristically slow to form a policy toward migrant farmworkers. Indeed, farmworkers were excluded from all labor and relief measures passed during the legislative whirlwind of the New Deal's first hundred days. In 1933 when Section 7(a) of the National Industrial Recovery Act (NIRA) gave workers the right of collective bargaining, farmworkers were not specifically excluded by the language of the statute, but field workers were excluded by the president's administrative decree three weeks later (the position of cannery and packinghouse workers was less certain). Congress established a Federal Transient Program within the Federal Emergency Relief Administration (FERA), which made available millions of dollars for the relief of "transients" (defined as "needy persons" who had no legal settlements in any one state or community). However, the FERA specifically excluded migrant farmworkers from its provisions, arguing that federal aid to working migrants would simply subsidize those industries "that existed and benefited in some degree because of the cheap labor supply furnished by migratory-casual workers." FERA funding to state relief organizations required that the states employ the "utmost vigilance" in assuring that the funds went to "bona fide transients," not to migrant farmworkers. When it came to federal relief efforts and labor legislation, migrant farmworkers were defined neither as workers nor as migrants, which left them with no identity to speak of.[1]

Perhaps more confident of their own authenticity, migrant farmworkers refused to behave as nonpersons. If they knew they had been excluded from New Deal legislation, they were clearly undaunted; the passage of the NIRA brought a flurry of strike activity on farms across the nation. There were only ten strikes involving fewer than 3,200 farmworkers in 1932. But as the National Recovery Administration (NRA) announced its goal of a $16-a-week minimum wage just as farm wages reached their lowest point in forty years, farmworkers were moved to action.[2] In 1933 there were sixty-one strikes involving 56,800 workers in seventeen different states. More than 47,000 farmworkers abandoned harvests in California alone. Virtually all of these strikes occurred in the nation's truck farming regions where migrant labor predominated. By 1935 there were ninety-eight agricultural unions, fifty-four affiliated with the American Federation of Labor (AFL).[3]

On the East Coast farmworkers also took inspiration from the NIRA. In Morrisville, Pennsylvania, 1,000 farmworkers on two of Bucks County's largest farms quit their jobs in September 1933 and marched on the office of Starkey Farms, demanding a "New Deal."[4] Similarly spontaneous strikes occurred in the tobacco fields of Connecticut and Massachusetts. In Cape Cod cranberry pickers affiliated with the AFL, and in Florida the membership of the United Citrus Workers reached 30,000 by the end of the year.[5]

In striking, farmworkers exercised a power that they shared with few other workers: the power to devastate their employers' operation in a matter of days. Truck farmers' inability to mechanize harvest processes left them extremely vulnerable to labor shortages. While manufacturers of industrial products might try to wait out a strike, growers of perishable crops could not slow the ripening of their tomatoes or prevent their beans from drying on the vine while workers picketed their fields.

Faced with the loss of their crops and caught by surprise in the first flush of the 1933 strike wave, some growers simply capitulated to their workers' demands. On Starkey Farms workers won a 33 percent pay raise within a few hours. However, few victories came so easily. Once growers made certain that their field workers did not enjoy the right of collective bargaining under the new labor legislation, they felt free to use whatever force they deemed necessary to meet the threat to their harvests.

As a result, farm labor strikes in the New Deal era faced the organized violence of employers.[6] In 1934 farm and cannery workers twice struck Seabrook Farms, New Jersey's largest truck farm. In doing so they brought down the wrath of their employer, armed vigilantes, and the county police. Like the massive cotton pickers' strike the previous year in California, the Seabrook strike quickly came to a violent stalemate.[7]

Though federal law did not protect workers' right to strike at Seabrook Farms, federal officials did intervene. The U.S. Conciliation Service mediated the Seabrook strike as well as thirty-one other strikes in the 1930s.[8] However, in each case its conciliators refused to recognize the legitimacy of farmworkers' unions. Farmworkers had demanded that they be treated as workers. Under federal policy they would be wards of the state.

SEABROOK FARMS, six miles outside Bridgeton, New Jersey, was owned and managed by Charles F. Seabrook.[9] It was, as a reporter for the *New York Sun* noted, "the last word in modernity." C. F., as Charles Seabrook was known, was a native of the Bridgeton area and the son of a Cumberland County farmer. He hated farming. As a youth he showed a flare for scientific farming and experimented with overhead irrigation piping. His venture was successful. On an outlay of $3,500 he realized a profit of $10,000, according to the *Sun*. That was the beginning. In the years that followed, he gradually took over the management of his father's properties, eventually swindling his father out of the business by selling his father's share of the farm to a New York banking family at a price well below the appraised value of the farm.[10] He too was squeezed out of the company in 1919, which was renamed Del Bay Farms, though C. F. retained some land of his own nearby. Instead of farming, however, he returned to what he truly enjoyed, traveling the world as an engineer, even spending several years in the Soviet Union after he was invited to apply his knowledge toward the advancement of the workers' state. He should perhaps have thought more about the state of the workers' finances, for he agreed to work on credit, and when the world economy collapsed in 1929, the Soviet Union stiffed him to the tune of $800,000.[11] C. F. returned to the United States with no choice, as his son Jack remarked, but to "figure out how he was going to make a living from the only assets he had to work with, farmland."

He did more than just make a living. He prospered, buying back the Del Bay farm with the help of a group of Massachusetts investors, receiving a Reconstruction Finance Corporation loan in the amount of $250,000, and buying a cannery from a bankrupt company. By 1934 Seabrook managed Del Bay's 3,400 acres plus 1,000 of his own, five square miles on either side of the highway that ran from Bridgeton to Camden. He also teamed up with General Foods, which had purchased the patented Birdseye process for quick-freezing packaged vegetables in 1930. The Seabrook name became synonymous with large-scale, scientific farming in South Jersey.[12] "Where else," the *Sun* queried, "does one find on a farm a press room for the convenience of visiting reporters and two press agents prepared to serve up facts and statistics?"[13]

With canneries and his own marketing organization, Seabrook could diversify his holdings and undersell his remaining neighbors.[14] By diversifying his crops, he made himself invulnerable to the natural disasters that devastated single-crop operations. By canning, freezing, and marketing his own produce, he not only cut out payments to packers and shippers, but he could wait out poor markets while other truck farmers had to sell the moment they harvested. By 1934 Seabrook had conquered two of the three problems that afflicted the nation's truck farmers. Having done that, he set out to deal with the third: the price of labor.

Seabrook employed about 150 men year-round and as many as 300 additional women and men during peak seasons. According to the *New York Sun*, the laborers in past years had "come, done their work, received their pay and departed." These were not, however, ordinary years.[15]

In the spring of 1934 South Jersey was in a state of turmoil. By the first of April, 6,000 workers were on strike in Camden's soup, ship, and radio plants. Among them were 2,000 cannery workers at Campbell Soup, who were striking for union recognition and a restoration of 1929 wage rates.[16] While black and white cannery workers faced off with police in the streets of Camden, and Campbell Soup prepared to arm its strikebreakers, five farmworkers at Seabrook Farms began meeting and talking union in their barracks just a few miles away. Led by a black farmhand named Jerry Brown, they wasted no time deciding on their grievances. Male farmworkers at Seabrook earned at most $1.75 for a ten-hour day. Women earned even less. They wanted a return to subsistence wages. In the first week of April, Seabrook's workers declared themselves a union and elected Brown president. On April 10 the company fired him for his organizing activities. Three hundred African American and Italian American workers walked out in a body.[17] As striker Primo Busnardo explained, "Hunger pulls people together — prosperity separates." Mack Broadwell, a black striker, noted years later, "We wanted more money — there was no Communism or nothing, we just wanted more wages to live on." "Migrants, and everybody got into the strike," he added, "those that didn't want to, we asked to stay home, and they did."[18]

the power of communist organizing

The strike caught Seabrook by surprise. Unprepared to replace the strikers and faced with the loss of his cabbage crop, he settled and even allowed picketers to warm up in a boiler room. In just four days the fledgling union won a doubling of wages and a written promise that Seabrook would not discriminate against union members. He also pledged in the one-year agreement not to fire black workers first as was the company's custom in slack seasons.[19]

Despite the success of the strike, the union's leadership changed. Jerry Brown was voted out, and two new leaders — one white and one black — were voted in. Why this change occurred is uncertain. Brown may have been intimidated by crosses burned on his lawn and threats made on this life. His supporters attributed his defeat to the intervention of two new organizers: Eleanor Henderson and Professor Donald Henderson, both members of the Communist Party and founders of the Agricultural and Cannery Workers' Industrial Union. Brought into the party by his wife, Professor Henderson had recently been fired from the economics department of Columbia University for his political activities. Brown went out and the Hendersons came in, in the words of one reporter, just as "Seabrook tossed the match into the powder barrel."[20]

Seabrook waited until his summer slack season arrived in mid-June to announce that as of June 25, wages would be lowered to just 18 cents an hour from the agreed-upon 30 cents an hour for men and 25 cents for women. Arguing that the earlier contract had been made "under duress," Seabrook claimed that he had to lower wages to meet the budget imposed by the administrators of his federal farm loan. He also announced the names of the 125 people who would be laid off until the harvest rush; almost all of them were African Americans.

Seabrook must have known that his actions would set off another strike, but this time he was ready.[21] He had assembled a force of vigilantes, who called themselves "A Committee to Combat Communism."[22] He had rallied local law enforcement authorities to his cause and hired an unemployed bootlegger, Jack Saunders, to coordinate the more unsavory aspects of the antiunion campaign. Saunders's job was, in his words, to "create problems" and "crack heads." Moreover, with three

unions = communism

workers for every two farm jobs in 1934, Seabrook had reason to feel confident that he could find replacement workers. It did not hurt that C. F.'s sister was married to Douglas Aitken, Seabrook's lawyer and the county's representative in the state assembly.[23]

The violence began when the strike committee entered Seabrook's office to present their demands and were blackjacked by Seabrook's vigilantes. Reinforced by Seabrook's extralegal agents, Sheriff William L. Brown began wholesale arrests as soon as picketing started on Monday, June 25. Over the next two days picketers were arrested; a group of men tried (unsuccessfully) to break into the Hendersons' house at 1:00 A.M.; and the sheriff accused Eleanor Henderson and a Vineland labor organizer, Vivian Dahl, of possessing dynamite. The charges were later dropped. Though these attempts at intimidating the strike's leaders suggested active opposition on Seabrook's part, his main strategy was to wait the strikers out.[24]

In ten days, however, there was no sign that the strikers would relent, and Seabrook's beet harvest was upon him. On Thursday morning, July 5, an armed and deputized "Constable" Saunders tried to get a tractor though the pickets with the help of the anticommunist committee. Met by a hail of stones, he withdrew, but not before four strikers were injured and deputies arrested Donald Henderson and Vivian Dahl. A local magistrate who was standing by held an impromptu trial in the farm's office, where he arraigned Henderson and Dahl on charges of conspiracy and disorderly conduct and fixed bail at $3,500.[25]

On Saturday morning Saunders again tried to get a tractor through the crowd, this time with official backing. For half an hour women clad in overalls, singing union songs, fought "a pitched battle" with fifty policemen. The police lost ground steadily until reinforcements arrived with tear gas bombs and began hurling them directly at the strikers. The sheriff deputized twenty-seven members of the vigilantes' committee so that they could use their weapons legally and make arrests. He also enlisted the county's firefighters, who turned their hoses on the pickets. "There was no chance of clubbing the wrong person," noted "The Scribbler" in the *Bridgeton Evening News*. "The policemen carried pistols and clubs. . . . The firemen had their hoses. . . . The strikers had stones. . . . The scribes had pencils. . . . The photographers had cameras. . . . Everybody was armed with something."[26] In the ensuing battle Saunders shot one striker in the leg and ended up with a stab wound himself. Police and deputized strikebreakers chased workers through the woods and sealed off all roads leading from the farm. Fifteen-year-old Primo Busnardo was just stepping out of his company house when a tear gas canister was thrown into his neighbor's home. Hearing shouts that a baby was inside, Busnardo ran in and grabbed the baby before he was overcome by gas and had to be dragged to safety by a large woman. By the end of the day, thirty tractors were at work in the fields and thirty men and women had been arrested.[27] Among them were Eleanor Henderson and William O'Donnell, a former member of the state police. Sheriff Brown declared that he believed he had "all the pickets' ringleaders in custody."[28]

After the day's battle, Seabrook tried to add the long arm of the state to the less effective limbs of the local police. Sheriff Brown called on Governor Harry Moore to declare martial law and send in state troopers. Seabrook sent Moore a telegram insisting that he had never reduced wages, that no reduction was contemplated, and that the strike was called "by Communist labor agitators" because he had laid off temporary laborers he had brought in to do seasonal work. He claimed that the farm's regular employees wanted to work but had been "intimated [sic]," and that he was willing to confer with representatives of the "regular employees" to reach a settlement. The governor declined to intervene, saying he would not send state troops to do battle with workers who were earning only 18 cents an hour. The governor did ask Colonel H. Norman Schwarzkopf of the state police to send an observer. In the face of the governor's refusal to declare martial law, David Jaggers, a Bridgeton garage mechanic and head of the vigilantes, informed the sheriff that he would have "500 deputies armed and ready for emergency service at any time their services were desired." That night crosses burned in front of the homes black workers rented from Seabrook.[29]

While Seabrook and the sheriff solicited supporters with varying success, the strikers also appealed for government assistance. They went right to the top, dispatching a delegation of twelve workers to Washington, D.C., to plead for the secretary of labor's intercession.

While the delegation traveled to Washington, the strikers regrouped, beginning the third week of the strike with a Sunday night meeting in the "Negro Elks Lodge" in Bridgeton. There they were joined by members of the United Farmers' League — small farmers organized by local communist Leif Dahl. In a fiery speech, a Salem County farmer denied that any farmers in his county had been deputized the previous day. J. A. Ingalls, a black striker, urged his comrades to forget race prejudice and work in harmony for the success of the strike. "In the eyes of Seabrook officials," he said, "we are either yellow or red. I would far rather be classified as the latter, fighting for my rights, than to be suppressed and live at starvation wages." When the cheering died down, the 400 people packed into the meeting hall signed a petition addressed to the governor and to county prosecutor Thomas G. Tuso. In it they protested "the illegal arrest and imprisonment of the striking workers and organizers of the Seabrook Farms, the deputization of outside thugs, and the spending of thousands of dollars of county funds to aid Seabrook in smashing a peaceable and legal attempt to raise their wages and organize their union." Lower taxes and more adequate relief for the unemployed were in order, they argued, not county funds for strikebreakers. When all 400 names were affixed to the petition, the strikers promised to return to the picket line in full force, despite the arrest of union leaders.[30]

On Monday morning Seabrook tried once again to get tractors into his fields. Three tractors were taken out of their garages and up the highway, but when they returned from the beet fields, they found their way blocked by a crowd of perhaps 250 strikers. This time Seabrook's deputies were out in force. Among them were a state assemblyman, a former state senator, a justice of the peace, and Seabrook's son Courtney.[31] And each tractor bore three men armed with long clubs.

As strikers attempted to rush the tractors, the riders swung their clubs and the drivers steered the machines into the throng. The strikers ran from the path of the enormous wheels but then returned to lob a volley of bricks and stones at the tractors. Sheriff Brown and the vigilantes immediately counterattacked with tear gas, temporarily incapacitating the pickets. As many as a dozen strikers were arrested, and the rest were driven back. The tractors passed through the gates.[32]

The strikers could do little more until about noon, when three more trucks arrived, loaded with Seabrook Farms beets. A group of women jumped aboard and began pitching bushels of beets onto the highway. The "special police" attacked the women with blackjacks, revolvers, and clubs. Male strikers rallied to their defense, tearing down fences for clubs and swinging back at the attackers. According to reporters, "a giant colored man" tried to disarm a Bridgeton policeman but was felled by a club. Unable to scatter the pickets and desperate to increase his forces, Sheriff Brown tried to swear in newspapermen as deputies.[33]

Unable to recruit reporters as a fighting force, the sheriff added nauseating gas to his arsenal as the fighting continued into the afternoon. The strikers retreated to their barracks, but the sheriff's men pursued them, firing tear gas into the buildings and setting one on fire. Firemen from Upper Deerfield doused the embers, then turned their hoses on the pickets. Clubs, rocks, and axe handles took to the air, but the strikers were driven back. The workers then stormed a fire engine, tearing away its hose and flipping the truck onto its side.

The only truce in the day's battle came when a group of the strikers' children were caught in a gas-filled building. The screams of their mothers halted the fighting "as if by magic." "Both police and strikers dropped their weapons and rushed through the frame structures and carried the children to safety." Sheriff Brown disclaimed responsibility for the gassing of the children. "It was just an unfortunate circumstance," he commented to reporters, "It couldn't be helped." As soon as the children were taken to safety, the fighting resumed. By the end of the day nineteen men and seven women had been arrested, none of whom could afford the $1,000 bail set by Bridgeton's justice of the peace.[34]

While Seabrook declared victory, the workers' delegation to Washington bore fruit. About midnight a representative of the United States Department of Labor's Conciliation Service arrived in Bridgeton at the behest of the secretary of labor.[35] As the official representative of Frances Perkins, John A. Moffett had good credentials but little authority. Federal labor law was in a state of chaos in the summer of 1934. No workers could be sure of their rights under the law, but farmworkers had more reason than most to feel uncertain of their status. Congress had passed the NIRA in 1933, which, among other things, conferred on all workers the right of collective bargaining.[36] However, once the act went into effect, it was immediately apparent that the officials of the NRA, which had been created to implement the act, were uncertain as to whether farmworkers were included.[37] Growers' organizations asserted that they were not, and the officials of the Agricultural Adjustment Administration (AAA) backed them up, arguing that the AAA, not the NRA, was responsible for all issues pertaining to agricultural production. A few weeks after the passage of the bill, President Roosevelt tried to settle the dispute by excluding agricultural labor by executive order. This, however, only led to a protracted and unfortunate debate over the precise meaning of "agricultural labor."[38]

In August 1933 the NRA and the AAA agreed on a characteristically lengthy and obscure definition. Henceforth, "agricultural labor" would include "all those employed by farmers on the farm when they are engaged in growing and preparing for sale the products of the soil and/or livestock; also, all labor used in growing and preparing perishable agricultural commodities for market in original perishable form. When workers are employed in processing farm products or preparing them for market, beyond the stage customarily performed within the area of production, such workers [are] not to be deemed agricultural workers."[39] The key to this definition is in the last sentence. Those who processed farm products outside or beyond the area of production were not agricultural workers and were therefore covered by the collective bargaining provisions of the NIRA. Conversely, those who worked within the area of production were excluded from its provisions.

This pithy definition led, of course, to the unavoidable question: What precisely was an area of production? No one was quite sure, but if any laborers worked in the area of production, field workers surely did. So those who plowed, planted, cultivated, and harvested were definitely among those excluded from the NIRA. Seabrook's harvest laborers would not enjoy the right of collective bargaining. That, at least, was certain.

The position of cannery and packinghouse workers was less clear (especially at a place like Seabrook's, where the field labor and processing labor forces often overlapped). In agreeing to the "area of production" wording, the NRA thought it was drawing a line between workers who processed farm products and workers who picked them, a line that would protect existing unions in packinghouses and canneries (unions whose members, perhaps not incidentally, were mostly white). But on a farm such as Seabrook's, where canning and packing were done on farm property, was any work performed beyond the area of production? Florida citrus growers expanded on this very point, arguing that the entire citrus belt was within their area of production and that all citrus workers were therefore excluded from the NIRA.

The AAA and the NRA argued over the definition of farm labor, replaying the First World War conflict between the U.S. Department of Agriculture and the Department of Labor. The AAA supported citrus growers in their effort to limit the number and kind of workers who would enjoy the right of collective bargaining. The NRA tried to revise the wording of the definition to suit the demands of cannery and packinghouse unions. It lost. The question of which workers fell under the NIRA would be determined not by the nature of the work or by the number of workers at a site, but by the location of the site itself.[40]

By the time the first strike began at Seabrook Farms in April 1934, this working definition was in force. When the strikers at Seabrook petitioned Frances Perkins for help, they received a letter informing them that the provisions of the NRA did not apply to agricultural laborers. Consequently, none of the Seabrook workers was in a position to demand that C. F. Seabrook sign a legally binding contract, nor could they appeal to the NRA for support. Seabrook signed a contract to save his cabbage crop, but there was nothing to prevent him from throwing it by the wayside, or into an irrigation ditch as it were, the moment the crop was brought in. By the time the second strike began in July, however, there was no working definition in force at all, the NIRA having been struck dead by the Supreme Court in May. Senator Robert Wagner had drafted what would become the National Labor Relations Act, but it had been tabled, lacking administrative backing, and would not be revived until 1935. This meant that throughout the second strike, there was no federal labor law in force.[41]

So John Moffett's lack of authority. Moffett did settle the strike, but it is evident from the terms of the signed contract that he approached Seabrook more as a supplicant than as a mediator. He did not step between two countervailing, if unequal, powers. He took it upon himself to speak for the workers as someone who had their best interest at heart and could best represent them to their employer. He assumed, in essence, the role of a mother mediating between her rebellious children and a stern and uncompromising father.[42]

Even before he left for the farm, Moffett reported to his boss that he had spoken on the phone with C. F. Seabrook, who "suggested a few proposals be made to the strikers which he desired treated with confidence." When he arrived, Moffett went immediately into a four-hour conference with Charles Seabrook, his lawyer, state assemblyman Douglas V. Aitken, and International Labor Defense lawyer David Horuwitz, there to represent the strikers. The following morning Moffett explained the agreement to union representatives and asked them to urge the strikers to ratify it.[43]

By the afternoon of the same day, they had complied. The ratified agreement provided that Seabrook would reemploy as many of the strikers, without discrimination, as he had work for; that a roster would be made for those for whom he had no immediate work; and that those whose names appeared on the roster would have preference over any others in getting employment on the farm. Most importantly, the agreement stipulated that the strikers would return to work for the wages that they had won in April. The agreement also provided for the establishment of an impartial board of adjustment to settle remaining differences. Both sides agreed that the decisions of this board would be final and binding and that it would consist of two farmers selected by the master of the Pomona Grange of Cumberland County; two "public-spirited" citizens, one to be the county farm agent and the other to be designated by the Cumberland County common pleas judge; and Moffett, the labor conciliator. The Hendersons urged the workers to hold out for equal representation on the adjustment board, but the workers decided to settle.[44]

That afternoon Seabrook announced to the press that he thought the settlement "quite satisfactory." Since the strikers had just won all of their original demands, they must have been surprised by this statement. However, by the next morning it was clear that theirs was a paper victory. Approximately 300 men and women returned to work as agreed, only to find that Seabrook needed only half their number and would not hire back the black workers. Colonel Schwarzkopf of the state police warned all "agitators" to leave Bridgeton within twenty-four hours or face forcible removal, and he left five troopers to patrol the farm on motorcycles. State assemblyman Aitken had already obtained the passage of two laws by the state legislature, one calling on the governor to send state police to the farm to keep order, the other authorizing the appointment of a legislative committee to investigate communist activities among the strike organizers.[45]

That was not all. William O'Donnell, a strike leader who had not heeded Schwarzkopf's warning, was arrested for having uttered "loud and profane imprecations" against county authorities—he had called county prosecutor Tuso "a damned rat" and "scum of the earth" during a speech on the final day of the strike. O'Donnell was convicted and sentenced to six months in prison. Eleanor and Donald Henderson were released from jail but escorted out of town by local police.[46] A group of self-proclaimed minute men, headed by former state senator Albert McAllister, devised a general defense plan "for the quick organization of the farmers in the event of a strike," and police in four South Jersey towns received instruction on the use of tear gas and machine guns.[47]

Given the fact that farmworkers' collective bargaining status was so uncertain in the summer of 1934, the Conciliation Service's part seems more philanthropy than policy. Nothing required Secretary Perkins to send Moffett to Bridgeton. She may have been moved by embarrassment over the news of open class warfare just outside Philadelphia or by sympathy for the strikers, but there was nothing to compel her to take action. Moffett came at the workers' invitation, and in doing so he required that they put themselves in his hands. His "contract" made significant gains for them, providing that they forfeit their union. Without it, however, they were in a poor position to defend those gains. Once their leaders were banished, the workers would not speak for themselves; their speaking would be done for them by "public-spirited citizens," including the U.S. conciliator himself. They were therefore dependent on his vigilance and continued support. The moment they ratified this agreement, the strikers ceased being workers and became wards of the Conciliation Service.

The agreement performed the remarkable feat of recognizing the workers' grievances without recognizing the workers. It addressed their demands and was signed by their representatives without suggesting any role for their union in future negotiations. Looking back on the experience a month later, black workers who continued to meet at the Elks Lodge wondered at their paper success but savored the spirit of resistance. Asked if they claimed victory, Jim Mills responded, "Did we win the strike? Brother, I don't know, and that's a fact. I know we didn't lose it. We ain't got nothin' now, maybe, but we didn't have nothin' befo' — so how could we lose?" A "towering truck driver" found more to celebrate: "The way I look at it is like this," he said, "I've been hanging around this town a good while — too damned long." "I've never seen a colored man get anything for his work but a beating," he continued. "He works his head off all day long, and all he's got is enough to eat on. If he don't work, he's no worse off, because the relief won't let him starve anyhow. I say, if we can't get anything for working, let's see what we can get for fighting."[48]

Although it is not clear what the strikers got for fighting, C. F. Seabrook made concrete gains. The Birdseye Company was willing to pay a high price for the quality frozen vegetables that Seabrook Farms could produce given the climate of labor peace that the U.S. conciliator helped produce. As C. F.'s son Jack later noted, "Once freezing commenced, Seabrook was the brightest spot in the economy of southern New Jersey." Demand was so great that Seabrook Farms hired hundreds of construction workers year-round to add freeze-drying facilities. The building began in 1934 and went on for twenty years.[49]

Farmworkers won what seemed to be a significant victory by striking and by cultivating the concerns of liberal reformers in Washington. The Seabrook strikers got their raises and a promise that the company would not discriminate against black workers. They won an arbitration board designed to avert future conflagrations. But they did not win power for themselves. When the tear gas had cleared and their wounds had been cleaned and work resumed on the farm, the strikers saw their concrete gains disappear before their eyes. Yet despite the ephemeral nature of their victory, the strike was still important, for the U.S. Conciliation Service's role at Seabrook and in other farm labor conflicts in 1933 and 1934 created a model for the federal migrant labor policies that would take shape over the next few years. The federal government would assume the role of guardian, benefactor, protector, even mother to migrant farmworkers, but it would not legally empower farmworkers to protect themselves through collective bargaining.

7

Uncle Sam as Padrone

The Politics of Labor Supply
in Depression and War

THE WAGNER ACT, which was signed into law in July 1935, excluded
field workers and domestics—some 65 percent of African American
workers—from its provisions.[1] Still, field workers were not abandoned by
the state. If New Dealers were unwilling to redress farmworkers' power-
lessness, they were gearing up to do something about their poverty. The
agency that would take up their cause was the Resettlement Administration and its successor, the Farm Security Administration (FSA). The
FSA's mission was to serve the nation's poorest rural people, including
those excluded from or further impoverished by the administration's
recovery measures. The FSA took 10 million acres of marginal land out
of production and resettled the families that had worked them. It created suburban "greenbelt" developments that were designed to increase
rural income by combining cooperative farming and small industry. In
one year alone it lent tenant farmers $260 million in low-interest loans to
enable them to buy farms and gave out over $800 million in rehabilita-
tion loans to prevent failing farmers from joining the ranks of the migrant poor. For those who had already gone bust and hit the road, the
FSA began in 1935 to build migratory camps that would house and feed
farmworkers in truck farming regions on both coasts.

Yet farmworkers enjoyed the guardianship of the FSA only temporarily. It was not long before the agency succumbed to the attacks of its
congressional enemies. It was, in fact, the first casualty of the growing
tide of anti–New Deal conservatism unleashed by the Second World War.

151

As the "economy bloc" in Congress hammered on the need for cutbacks in nondefense spending and demanded the elimination of New Deal "experimentation," FSA advocates argued for the agency's preservation on the grounds of the Migratory Camp Program's contribution to the war effort. In a sense this argument worked too well. By the spring of 1942 the FSA's resettlement projects, cooperatives, land purchase, and small loan programs had all succumbed to the budgetary axe; the migrant camp program was the only FSA project left intact.[2]

With the nemesis agency out of the way, the U.S. Department of Agriculture (USDA) might simply have disbanded the Migratory Camp Program, but it did not. The camp program survived not only intact but vastly expanded. New camps drew migrants to areas where farmers would not or could not house them, and a transportation program helped move migrants immobilized by gas and tire shortages. Instead of serving the needs of America's migrant poor, the camp program retooled to serve the needs of the nation's labor poor.

Yet even though growers benefited from the services of the FSA's labor supply program, they complained of labor shortages. Farmworkers had not vanished; they were using the security afforded by the federal migrant camps to wage informal but effective strikes. Though they proclaimed neutrality, FSA officials found themselves in the middle of a bitter struggle between farmworkers and truck farmers, and in the end they would be caught in the cross fire.

In the spring of 1943 the nation's largest growers responded to farmworkers' militancy by wresting control of federal farm labor policy. Bowing to their demands, Congress did two remarkable things: it took the Migratory Camp Program away from the FSA and denied farmworkers the right to migrate without the consent of county authorities. While American farmworkers were "frozen" in place, the new Emergency Farm Labor Supply Program filled FSA migrant camps with farmworkers transported by the FSA from Mexico, the West Indies, and Puerto Rico, as well as with 120,000 prisoners of war.

While during the First World War the agencies charged with rationalizing and mobilizing the nation's farm labor supply had attempted, unsuccessfully, to build an administrative apparatus from the ground up, the agencies of the Second World War had in the FSA's Migratory Camp Program an administrative structure that could be easily converted to their use. Thus, instead of stemming migrancy as it had planned, the FSA spent its last years in existence facilitating migration, literally shuttling farmworkers from harvest to harvest. Created to protect and defend the nation's poorest rural people, the FSA ended up playing a large part in opening the nation's borders to the poor of other countries.

THAT THE WAGNER ACT would exclude agricultural workers from its provisions was not immediately clear. Indeed, the original draft of the Wagner bill had gone into committee in March 1934, just prior to the first strike at Seabrook Farms, with farmworkers clearly included in its provisions. When it came out of committee two months later, the term "employee" had been redefined to exclude "any individual employed as an agricultural laborer." What happened during those two months is uncertain.[3] What is certain is that the authors of the Wagner Act forced history to repeat itself by failing once again to define what they meant by "agricultural labor." Once the bill came to be law in 1935, the National Labor Relations Board (NLRB), which the act had created, decided not to abide by the definition of agricultural labor that had proved so unwieldy in 1933. Instead of distinguishing between work done within and without an area of production, the NLRB drew a distinction between field laborers and processing laborers. The former group was excluded from the act; the latter, included.[4] So after 1935 the cannery and packinghouse workers at Seabrook Farms, for example, could demand an NLRB supervised election and force C. F. Seabrook to sign a legally binding contract. Seabrook's field workers, who included most of the migrant workers, fell outside the NLRB's jurisdiction. They could vote with their feet by moving on, but they had no collective voice that any court of law would hear.

The NLRB's definition was certainly more easily implemented than its predecessor, but it was just as arbitrary. It seems to have been based on the presumption that the relationship between field workers and their employers was fundamentally different from that between packinghouse workers and their employers. Perhaps reviving the romantic notion that field workers had a personal, even intimate relationship with the "farmers" who hired them, it assumed that they had no need for collective bargaining. Farmworkers and farmers, according to this vision, sealed their bargains with a nod and a handshake. It was precisely on this basis that the Ninth Circuit Court upheld the NLRB's definition in 1940.[5]

The definition made some sense if "agricultural labor" only referred to the declining number of year-round employees on small farms. However, applied to the several hundred harvest workers at Seabrook Farms, the thousand at U.S. Sugar, or the hundreds of thousands of migrant farmworkers who traveled with crew leaders, working a week here and a month there without ever negotiating their wages directly with a farmer, the NLRB's definition was patently absurd. Still, it held. Processing workers would enjoy the right of collective bargaining; field workers would not.

A strike of South Florida bean pickers soon revealed the risks of an unsanctioned strike in a glutted labor market. In the winter of 1936–37, when growers slashed the piece rate for beans from 25 to 15 cents a hamper, thousands of bean pickers refused to board the trucks at Belle Glade's loading area. "We been living up and down the East coast for years," one worker explained, and this "is the first time we have ever seen beans down to 15 cents. We go out and make maybe 30–40 cents a day, and again we might make $1.50 if we had real good picking. . . . We wouldn't go to the fields at the low prices." Although the fact that thousands of desperately poor workers refrained from boarding growers' trucks suggests a high level of organization, growers—with the help of Florida's border patrol—easily defeated the strike. So many people were migrating to Florida seeking work and warmth that the state police had established a border patrol along the main highways, turning back "undesirables" who might flood relief rolls, while taking care not to offend tourists "in better automobiles."[6] After four days without labor, the growers got the bean pickers to return to the fields by promising to raise the hamper rate to 20 cents, but at the same time they alerted the state's border patrol to their "labor shortage" problem. The border patrol settled the issue by flooding the area with labor by simply "letting Negro hitch hikers through." Once there were enough destitute workers in the area to replace the strikers, the growers reneged on their promise. With no strike fund, exorbitant rents to pay, and no other means to survive in a region miles from urban soup kitchens and hundreds of miles from family members who might lend support, South Florida's bean pickers went back to work.[7]

Excluded from the Wagner Act, the bean pickers could not have appealed to the NLRB for a state-supervised union election, had they seen fit to do so. They had, however, been made wards of the newly created Resettlement Administration, although they would see no sign of the administration's migrant labor camp program for four more years. Even then, as wards of the state, they would be housed, fed, transported, and even educated but never organized, politicized, or legally empowered.

The Resettlement Administration was the outcome of a civil war within the USDA. President Roosevelt had populated the USDA with a strange assortment of zealous reformers and arch-conservatives. At the head of the agency he placed the liberal Henry A. Wallace, but the bulk of the top positions in the USDA's newly created subagency, the Agricultural Adjustment Administration (AAA), went to what Sidney Baldwin has called "conservatives and 'sound men,'" including the "energetic businessman" George N. Peek in the head spot. USDA traditionalists got most of the positions, but they were forced to work with the likes of Abe Fortas, Alger Hiss, Adlai Stevenson, and Rexford Tugwell.[8] Tugwell had once cowritten an economics textbook with none other than Seabrook strike leader Donald Henderson. It was not an agency made in heaven.[9]

The AAA itself was the source of most of the conflict. The main thrust of agricultural policy under the New Deal, the AAA sought to achieve "parity prices" by paying farmers who cut back their production.[10] There were a number of issues that split the agency's already divided staff, but perhaps the most divisive was the question of how AAA benefits would be divided among landlords and tenants. To the dismay of the liberal faction, it immediately became evident that landlords were not sharing the rewards of the program with their tenants. When the rules were changed so that landlords were required to share the AAA payments, landlords often evicted tenants and sharecroppers and hired labor by the day. As Mary Hines, a schoolteacher and strawberry picker in Alabama put it, "I don't believe there's going to be any tenant farmers any more, since the government has fixed it so the tenant farmer can get half the subsidy. The landlords will just hire help and you can work it or let it alone which means that most of them will work at any price to keep from starving."[11] The AAA succeeded in raising farm prices and improving the lot of farm owners, but it added to the number of tenants and sharecroppers already displaced by the depression, droughts, and boll weevils. Organized by the Southern Tenant Farmers' Union (STFU), some camped along the roadsides to protest their displacement; others packed up their belongings and headed west to California; and a significant number headed for South Florida for work as packers or pickers, depending on their skin color.[12]

In Washington the AAA's liberal faction conspired to change the agency's policy without the approval of its director. For their efforts they were fired in what became known as the "purge of 1935." The purge made it clear that any attempt to address the issue of rural poverty would need to be done outside the walls of the USDA. So in April 1935 the president, by executive order, created a separate agency called the Resettlement Administration.

Migrant poverty was just one of the many problems that the Resettlement Administration inherited. It was just getting around to implementing its migrant policy when it was reconstituted as the FSA and moved back into the USDA. Thus the Resettlement Administration began and the FSA carried out the first federal effort to meet the concerns of the "350,000 American families" who "were wandering from state to state in a desperate effort to earn a living as migrant farm laborers."[13]

The Migratory Camp Program involved two plans: the construction of permanent camps in areas of concentrated commercial farming and the creation of temporary mobile camps that would literally follow the migrant streams and provide shelter in the form of tents and trailers along the route. By 1936 there were twenty-six permanent camps in operation or under construction that could shelter 7,000 families. By 1942 there were ninety-five labor camps that could accommodate 19,464 families, or about 75,000 individuals, at any one time.[14]

FSA officials did not pretend to be providing good housing or a permanent solution to the migrant problem. Rather, they defended the labor camp program as an emergency, stopgap strategy, merely a small part of a larger effort. "The main effort of the FSA," according to its proponents, was "devoted to stopping unnecessary migration at its source . . . and to help[ing] needy farm families to get a new start in their own communities."[15] This the FSA attempted by providing loans to small farmers who would otherwise face foreclosure and by resettling tenants and sharecroppers on productive land.

Still, despite FSA officials' insistence that the migrant camp program was simply a temporary stopgap measure, there was an optimism behind it, a certainty in the efficacy of reform. If the migrant camp program had simply been about meeting the immediate needs of migrant farmworkers and their children, it would have done no more than build shelters over their heads, put food in their mouths, and treat their many ailments. But the migrant camp program did far more than that. It sought to free farmworkers from poverty by changing their behavior. To this end the camp managers taught lessons in personal hygiene, self-government, thrift, and parenting.

The first FSA camps built on the East Coast were the Jim Crow camps in Belle Glade, Florida, in the heart of green bean country. Eleanor Roosevelt came for their opening in the spring of 1940. The Osceola Camp for white migrants had 176 units, metal frame huts designed to shelter a family. With 356 units, the Okeechobee Camp for black migrants was basically identical in construction, but bigger. By summer three more camps were under construction: two in Pahokee near Belle Glade, one each for white and black migrants, and a camp for black workers in Pompano, farther down the coast. In 1941 the FSA built

Corrine Williams, FSA home management supervisor, helping camp residents
can tomatoes in the utility building of the Okeechobee migratory labor camp
in Belle Glade, Florida (Marion Post Wolcott, Library of Congress)

two more camps in Florida—one in Homestead and another in Canal
Point—and a hospital in Belle Glade. The next camp to open in the East
was in Bridgeton, New Jersey.[16]

Each permanent camp was meant to be a self-contained village. In addition to housing, each site had an assembly building, a clinic, a school, a
nursery, a canning kitchen, and a utility building with laundry facilities.
The schools were staffed with certified teachers supervised by the Home
Missions Council. They offered lessons covering six grades in all the
camps, and at the Okeechobee camp there was a high school as well.[17]
The camp residents themselves opened cooperative stores, and by 1942,
profits from the Okeechobee camp's store paid for both the nursery
school and the school lunch program.[18] Utility buildings provided laun-
dries and sewing machines, where women could make clothes for their
families. Many became so proficient that they made articles for the Red
Cross once the war started, as well as almost 1,500 mattresses and 400
comforters for their own use.

The camps also contained medical clinics that served both the resident population and anyone else who came for treatment. Residents
were required to be tested for venereal disease and to receive treatment
if they were carriers. They were also immunized against typhoid fever,

A women's club group meeting in the assembly building of the Okeechobee migratory labor camp, 1940 (Marion Post Wolcott, Library of Congress)

smallpox, and diphtheria. From 1936 to 1942 camp residents made use of the clinics over 28,000 times.[19]

The camps were, however, more than just a collection of shelters, services, and facilities; they were communities whose populations were constantly changing. Each camp was governed by a council, which was elected by the camp residents and which met in the assembly building, the "seat of democracy in the camp." The community councils were meant to be lessons in self-government and uplift. They met regularly to draw up and enforce rules for the camp population. Hearings might be held when families failed either to pay their rent of $1.00 a week or work the alternative two-hour period maintaining the grounds of the camp. Those who had no reasonable explanation for their delinquency would be evicted by the council. Still the councils also had a more positive role. In the Okeechobee camp for black workers, for example, the council voted to use money contributed weekly by the camp residents to send one boy and one girl to Florida A&M College. To the FSA the councils were an experiment in self-discipline for a people who were often a "real test," in the words of one New York camp manager.[20]

The minutes of one such council meeting, reprinted in the newsletter of the Bridgeton, New Jersey, camp, reveal the extent to which the councils intervened in the daily lives of camp residents. The meeting began with a prayer by the chairman. A council member then read a note from Councilman Rufus Jerido, who wrote to say he had enjoyed his stay in the camp and regretted leaving but that his job in Florida awaited him. The chairman then asked for discussion of the condition of the privies. Carl White said that it looked to him as though someone had deliberately dirtied the privy on his side of the camp. "David Reese thought that we ought to have a watchman to try to catch the people who were messing up as we have a rule to handle those people with." It was decided that each councilman would talk to each household on his street and ask their cooperation in keeping the privies clean, as "we had a lot of new people who didn't know how to act right." The case of "Dr." Black came up next. Having finally caught him, after considerable effort, selling liquor, the council agreed to evict him immediately. John Wilcox reported that there were two houses on his street that would "bear watching," as they were noisy late at night and "quite a lot of people went in and out all the time." To this, Councilwoman Eldor Henderson responded that "a man who drinks with a bunch certainly can't 'turn up the bunch.'" She advised Wilcox to control his own drinking or find himself kicked off the council. Last, the council decided that, although they "didn't feel that they should meddle in family affairs," they would warn "Fats" that he and his wife would have to leave the camp if he fought with her in public or "alarmed" the street again.[21]

When the camp council was not deciding the fate of their fellow residents, assembly buildings would be used for church services, entertainment, movies, and "many wholesome recreational activities" meant to "supplant the native 'jook' joint." Paul Vander Schouw, the supervisor of the Florida camp program, announced happily that the assembly hall activities were so successful that jook operators from Clewiston to Canal Point were bitterly protesting their loss of revenue. By the second year of the Florida programs the various camps were offering Easter egg hunts at the nursery schools; cards; checkers; table tennis; boxing; dances at Camp Osceola; baseball at Okeechobee, Pompano, and the Everglades camp; and camp anniversary celebrations with dances, orchestras, and parades. According to Vander Schouw, the "Everglades Camp has at least a 100 and usually more at the rec. hall every night of the week."[22]

Such wholesome activities and Christian living were not for everyone. Vander Schouw reluctantly reported that black migrants continued to live in slum housing in Belle Glade despite the availability of units in the camps. William Yearby's wife was one who insisted on renting a room in Belle Glade instead of living in the FSA camp; they did not have a car so "she couldn't get back and forth to town."[23] For all the FSA's moral indignation at unwholesome activities, Belle Glade was still a cultural mecca, despite its squalor. Who would travel several hundred miles in the back of a truck for church services and an Easter egg hunt?

Still, sympathetic growers and the camp managers suggested deeper reasons for some black workers' reluctance to try the camps. Howard L. Haney, a substantial Belle Glade truck farmer, noted that "certain unscrupulous white property owners in the colored section of Belle Glade have circulated stories . . . pointing out the restrictions that they would be subjected to in the camp, even going so far as to sell them on the idea that, upon entering the camp, they would undoubtedly immediately be transferred to the Army."[24] Vander Schouw confirmed that some growers discouraged their workers from living in the camps because they feared they would lose contact with and control over their labor. If the workers they recruited settled in the camps, someone else might hire them just as easily.[25]

Some migrants remained suspicious of the camps, but for many others, particularly parents with children, they came as an extremely pleasant surprise. Frank Collins, who had been migrating to Florida, Kentucky, Michigan, and Indiana for three years when the first camps opened, noted that "we have lights and water and showers and everything is fixed very nice."[26] Timothy Farmer came to Belle Glade after working on and off in cottonseed oil and textile mills in Augusta, Georgia, between 1925 and 1937. The son of a renting Georgia farmer, he had also tried sharecropping for three years and had traveled the Atlantic Coast as a potato harvester. In 1937 his brother, who had been "roaming around . . . trying to find something better," urged Farmer to join him in Belle Glade. Asked at the Tolan Hearings what he thought of the FSA camp, Farmer answered that he liked it "fine, fine." He earned $30 a month as the elected chairman of the camp council and also preached to the camp congregation. "I think it is just grand for the colored folkses."[27]

White camp residents echoed this praise. Robert Patton testified that the FSA's Osceola camp was the only good thing about Florida. "It was really pitiful the way the people had to live [prior to the camp]. You take up north, there are no migratory camps at all."[28] Also a veteran migrant, Annie Tompkins had been traveling with her husband and five children between Florida and Michigan for seven years before getting a house at the Osceola migrant camp near Belle Glade. One year they had flipped a coin to choose between Florida and California. The coin sent them to the Imperial Valley. They had heard California was so mild that you could sleep outside every night, but they found it cold and the work hard. They found space in an FSA camp in Brawley, and they met a floating camp on their way to Idaho; but in Salinas the camp was full, and they could not get in.

Back in Florida, the Tompkinses discovered that the camps' greatest advantage was their permanence and low rent. For people who had been shunted from place to place season after season, the camps offered a settled existence and the possibility of saving a bit of money. In the winter of 1940 the Tompkinses found space in the Osceola camp for white migrants, and there they stayed. Annie Tompkins worked in the lunchroom; the rest of the family, in the Belle Glade packinghouses. They had their own garden spot in the camp and could can their produce at the camp cannery. Asked what she thought of these government camps, Tompkins's praise was effusive: "I think they are a splendid thing for the poor people," she replied, listing as advantages everything from canning facilities to bathtubs to school lunches for the residents' children.[29] Mrs. Johnnie Belle Taylor from Talbot County, Georgia, also enjoyed the security that the camps offered. She paid rent on her unit in the Okeechobee camp year-round so that she would always be guaranteed a space, though she continued to pick truck crops in Georgia in the summer. There were no FSA camps in Georgia, she noted. "We just got to live in the house where the people let you stay. Some have to sleep in cars and some few of them have a little tent along with them. . . . We just have to take it as we find it. . . . We just put up with most anyway, just to working, trying to live."[30]

The camps won their converts more slowly than the FSA had hoped, but eventually many migrants were convinced that the disadvantages of life outside the camps outweighed the restrictions within them. For example, James Solomon, originally of Dawson, Georgia, had worked at U.S. Sugar as a cane cutter and lived at the corporation's Clewiston camp. However, after three months of steady work, he was sick for a day, and the foreman insisted that he go to work. His choice was to work or move, so he moved. He spent the next three months in a Belle Glade boardinghouse, but the following season he moved into the FSA camp for black migrants. He went back to work for U.S. Sugar. But when he injured his back and could not carry the cane, he did not have to move again. He simply switched employers and went to work cutting cabbage. Asked if he planned to return to Georgia in the summer, he said, no, he was going to stay in the FSA camp.[31]

Even the migrants who declined to live in the camps benefited indirectly from the camp program. Howard Haney thought that the FSA camps had forced growers who housed their farm laborers "to make definite improvements in their housing facilities in order to keep their

The interior of one of the "permanent" homes for migrant workers at the Okeechobee camp. The photo was clearly staged to demonstrate the uplifting effects of the migratory labor camp program. (Marion Post Wolcott, Library of Congress)

laborers satisfied." "The Farm Security Administration," he continued, "and I believe that most any farmer in the section would substantiate this, is doing wonderful work in improving the health of both white and colored laborers, particularly that of the children, as each camp has a clinic, and a school, and nursery operating 24 hours a day."[32]

Clearly, the FSA offered a real service to the minority of the migrant population that found shelter in its camps. The invasiveness of the camp councils may have been oppressive to some, but the program was an honest effort to empower migrants to improve their lives and the lives of their children. On the other hand, empowering individuals to improve themselves and empowering individuals to act collectively are two different things. However much FSA officials might have been personally committed to the idea of collective bargaining in agriculture (and many clearly were), they were not permitted to advocate or encourage unionization in the camps. Their mission was to guard the welfare of the migrant population. In doing so, they might indirectly affect relations between growers and farmworkers, but this was not their legally defined task.

The fate of the Migratory Camp Program during the Second World War reveals the dangers inherent in a policy of individual, without collec-

UNCLE SAM AS PADRONE

tive, empowerment. FSA officials responded to the exigencies of the depression with proscriptions for devoting the power of the state to the solutions of the nation's ills. What they failed to realize perhaps is how easily the apparatus of aid and reform could be turned to other ends. As a program created solely from above, it could be changed solely from above with ease.[33]

For two years after the outbreak of war in Europe, the conflict had little effect on what the USDA called the "superabundance of labor power on American farms." Indeed, daily farm wages actually fell from October 1939 to January 1940. In early 1941 the Bureau of Agricultural Economics estimated that if the United States entered the war, more than 1.5 million farmworkers could leave agriculture without impairing the nation's agriculture production.[34] As long as depression conditions persisted, the camps presented little threat to growers' position. To a small portion of the migrant population, the camps offered a dry place to sleep, medical care, and regular meals. Even the camp managers' efforts at behavioral modification seemed to benefit growers. As Glades truck farmer Howard Haney pointed out, "You will get a much more reliable type of laborer out of the camps" because of the restrictions the camps imposed on the conduct of residents.[35]

Still, by the winter of 1942 truck farmers were less complacent about the supply of labor. Triggered perhaps by federal demands for increased agricultural production or by news that the Migratory Camp Program might be defunded, rumors of farm labor shortages spread like kudzu. Growers began bombarding Washington with threats that they would cut back production if they were not guaranteed a harvest labor supply.[36] Maine prepared to import French Canadian laborers for the potato harvest in Aroostook County. Vermont recruited high school and college students for a Volunteer Land Corps. Massachusetts officials discussed the use of conscientious objectors as seasonal laborers, and South Jersey growers reported acute shortages and "considerable" loss of asparagus. Maryland and Alabama had already reenacted their World War I work-or-fight laws, and Delaware reported that just the threat of the draft was "used in some instances to scare indifferent labor to accept jobs."[37] Growers wrote to Washington from all over the country complaining of labor shortages and suggesting solutions: close the schools during harvests, recruit businessmen, redraft all men classified 4H for farmwork, revive convict lease systems.[38]

While growers declared that a farm labor emergency had begun, federal officials continued to report that the nation's supply of labor was adequate to meet the needs of increased farm production. Farmers had only to pay attractive wages to assure themselves an adequate labor supply. One farmer made it clear that he intended to do just that. In Oceana, Virginia, Frank P. Whitehurst noted to a reporter from the *Norfolk Virginia-Pilot* that he intended "to pay labor on a competitive basis." "Farming not only is a business," he stated, "but it is the most vital of businesses, and it is a mystery to me why so many people think agricultural labor should be the lowest paid of all." To illustrate, Whitehurst explained that just a few weeks earlier he had been paying his spinach cutters 5 cents a basket. "Somebody else hiked the price of labor to six cents, and Mr. Whitehurst kicked the ante to ten without hesitation. He finished his cutting, and his labor made high pay. One Negro woman was paid as much as $9.56 for one day's work," the *Pilot* reported. He called cheap labor the "greatest curse to agriculture in the United States." "The farmers use cheap labor to grow surplus crops, which glut the markets and knock prices down."[39]

Whitehurst may well have been the only truck farmer to advocate openly paying higher wages for farmwork. Still, to make him out to be the only reasonable farmer along the East Coast is unfair. Truck farmers were honestly fearful of labor shortages due, in part, to the nature of farm labor employment in their industry. Except for the farmers who hired the same people year after year, few growers had any contact with their workers before their harvest rush began. Some made advance arrangements with crew leaders, others sent out a truck a few days before they expected their harvest to begin, and some just counted on migrants to appear when they were needed. For the preceding twenty years truck farmers had had little reason to doubt that they would have adequate numbers of workers when they needed them. However, with a war on, with rumors of labor shortages in circulation, and with federal officials counting anything that moved, farmers were understandably fearful that workers would not appear on schedule as they had in the past.

They often cited rising wages as an indication that the labor supply was dwindling rapidly. Wages did rise slightly after Pearl Harbor, but as in the First World War, they were lowest where growers complained the loudest. In 1941 average hourly wages were 31 cents along the coast from New Jersey to Maine. But along the southern coast from North Carolina to Florida, wages were among the lowest in the nation at 12 cents an hour. In Delaware, Maryland, and Virginia average hourly wages were just 22 cents in 1941, yet farmers there were threatening to plow over crops for lack of labor. Virginia's war board reported a "real shortage of labor," and Maryland authorities felt compelled to drag "several hundred colored people" before county magistrates "to explain why they would not accept farm work."[40]

If labor prices are taken as a measure of farm labor supply, then it is difficult to explain why truck farmers complained of labor shortages when they were apparently well supplied with labor. However, the notion of a "labor market" that operates according to the law of supply and demand ignores the impact of custom and culture, of deeply held assumptions about what labor is "worth." Farmers, as the Interbureau Coordinating Committee pointed out, were accustomed to "a great oversupply of workers." Some had "come to consider this over-supply as the normal supply, and to consider any reduction in the surplus supply as a shortage." Over the past year, the committee found, "there was some confusion in the use of the term 'shortage,'" and a tendency in some cases "to identify increases in wages, irrespective of the number of workers available, as a shortage."[41]

From the perspective of federal officials, an anticipated labor scarcity was just as important as an actual dearth of labor, for growers who expected harvest labor shortages would plant fewer crops when more were needed. If this occurred on a wide scale, as USDA officials feared in the winter of 1942, the nation would fall short of its war production goals. Thus federal officials not only had to figure out where there might be "real labor shortages" and be prepared to meet the demand; they also had to assure all farmers that the federal government was prepared to deal with a nationwide labor shortage of immense proportions. They had to create a labor supply program adequate to meet the real and *imagined* labor needs of the nation's farmers.

As a result, federal farm agencies began to mutate in the name of war mobilization, as they had during the First World War. Administrations, divisions, committees, and subcommittees reconvened, expanded, combined, and were renamed at an alarming rate. Seemingly every official who had ever set eyes on a farm laborer or at least on a farm labor statistic got into the act of directing and redirecting the nation's migrant population. All in all, World War II bureaucrats went a long way toward recreating the administrative muddle that had proved so daunting during the First World War.

For the officials of the FSA the growing hysteria over labor shortages represented both danger and opportunity. As the "war emergency" deepened, the FSA, like other welfare agencies, faced the loss of its funding. Congress, the public, and the president were concerned about labor shortages, not labor surpluses, wage spirals, not starvation wages.

However, growers' fears of farm labor scarcity presented the FSA with an opportunity to save itself while other New Deal agencies waited in line for the axe. If a case could be made for the FSA's potential role in maximizing agricultural production, the agency might lift its head off the budgetary chopping block.[42] Four months after Pearl Harbor the FSA began to use the problem of labor shortages as a justification for the Migratory Camp Program, "incorporating that slant" into its official pronouncements, as one staff member put it.[43]

FSA officials adopted the argument that the Department of Labor had used to so little advantage during the First World War. The root of the farm labor emergency, they insisted, was not a shortage but a maldistribution of farm labor. The solution was to expand the Migratory Camp Program and use it to draw farmworkers to areas where they would not otherwise go for lack of housing. The director of the FSA's labor division warned that "such a program presupposes an organization of the farm labor market that has heretofore never been accomplished." Still, FSA officials believed they were up to the task. The result was a shift in the agency's emphasis from improving farmworkers' lives to maximizing farm production.[44]

the interest of the growers

FSA officials drew up a laundry list of justifications for the program's preservation and expansion. "Under a system of area to area transportation," a memo to the war manpower commissioner stated, FSA camps would serve as "important links in the movement of agricultural workers." Sanitary facilities would increase morale and thus productivity. Nurseries would free adults for work. Many farmworkers had been immobilized by gas and tire rationing and required transportation if they were to follow their usual migratory patterns.[45] On these grounds the FSA was able to hold on for one more year.

On January 23, 1942, the FSA and the U.S. Employment Service (USES) signed a joint statement of policy to coordinate their farm labor activities. The role of the USES would be to identify areas of labor surplus and demand and to recruit farmworkers willing to be relocated from the former to the latter. The FSA would launch a transportation program to move the workers to wherever the USES directed them and provide them with food and shelter along the way. All this was announced publicly to assure farmers that they could expand their spring planting without fear of labor shortages come summer.[46]

The FSA quickly expanded the Migratory Camp Program in order to demonstrate to farmers and to its congressional adversaries that it could meet the labor needs of truck farmers on both coasts. By July 1942 it was operating 89 camps, 43 of which were mobile. Six additional mobile units were already under construction, and 140 additional sites had been proposed to be served by 90 camp units, almost entirely mobile.

The sheer magnitude of the labor supply effort was remarkable. In 1942, for instance, the USES reported that the Eastern Shore area of Virginia needed 900 workers for its fruit, vegetable, and berry harvests. The FSA quickly readied mobile camps in preparation for what it called "Migrant Soldiers on the Food Production Front." The USES then located workers in Florida who had been rendered superfluous by a flood in the Lake Okeechobee area.[47] For every county and every crop, the USES had to know when labor needs would peak and when they would wane, how many workers would be required, and how many could be spared. Once workers were readied for relocation, the FSA had to move them, house them, feed them, babysit their children, and tend to their illnesses while it continued to move other workers to other locations. It was an operation that rivaled troop movements and battle maneuvers in scale and complexity.

Even though the FSA demonstrated that it was willing and able to reconstitute itself as a federal padrone, the agency faced fiscal dismemberment on the floor of Congress. FSA opponents, led by the American Farm Bureau Federation, argued that, with the exception of the Migratory Camp Program, the return of prosperity made FSA programs unnecessary. According to the Farm Bureau, FSA efforts to bolster small farmers merely forestalled the inevitable; large-scale commercial farms were "the wave of the future." As for the migrant camp program, the Farm Bureau argued that it should be turned over to the locally administered Agricultural Extension Service.[48] This position was reiterated in Congress by the aptly named Joint Committee on Reduction of Nonessential Federal Expenditures[49] and by the House Appropriations Committee, which joined the attack on the FSA in January 1942. FSA advocates were fighting for the very life of the agency.

Secretary of Agriculture Claude Wickard came to the rescue, arguing that it "not only was a poor time to decrease the activities of the [FSA]" but that Congress should be expanding its activities, "not only for the family-sized farm of the small farmer but the migratory labor camp, so that we can more fully utilize the agricultural labor we have." Despite his plea, the final debate devolved into a floor fight on the subject of whether FSA director C. B. Baldwin was a communist.[50]

The FSA had all but abandoned its social welfare mission and converted itself to a war footing, but its congressional enemies would not forgive. Its only hope for survival was to do what no other agency had yet done: find growers a new source of labor. With this in mind Secretary

Wickard quietly left the country for Mexico City, "ostensibly," according to one account, "to address an inter-American conference on agriculture but actually to initiate negotiations with the Mexican government on importation of Mexican farm workers."[51] His mission was a success. The Mexican government agreed to let the U.S. government transport Mexican citizens to the United States for work on American farms. Wickard gave full responsibility for the program to the FSA. Tempted by the prospect of foreign workers and unwilling to alienate the secretary of agriculture by demanding that another agency control the program, the Appropriations Committee gave the FSA another six months to live.

To the chagrin of growers, however, the agreement between the FSA and the Mexican government came with strings attached. Growers would have to make individual contracts with workers under the supervision of the FSA, and they had to sign "performance bonds" to guarantee that they would fulfill their end of the bargain. Workers not housed in FSA camps would have to be provided minimum standards of housing. No more than three single workers or four family members could be housed per 12-by-14-foot floor space, and facilities for cooking, sleeping, laundry, bathing, toilets, and waste disposal were to be provided. Growers could charge rent, but at a rate agreed upon before recruitment and included in the contract of employment. They would also have to pay a minimum wage of 30 cents an hour or the prevailing wage, whichever was higher. If the grower failed to pay workers' wages, the FSA would be required to support them. Moreover, to induce workers to accept employment and to justify the high transportation costs (to be shared by the workers, the growers, and the U.S. government), the agreement required that employers offer at least thirty days of work. If weather or other factors cut short their need for labor, growers would still have to pay the transported workers for 75 percent of the period covered by the contract. If the FSA had taken on the role of federal padrone, the Mexican government had acted as a shrewd union representative, negotiating the most comprehensive farm labor contract in the history of American agriculture.[52]

Oddly enough, this Labor Importation Program, which became known on the West Coast as the Bracero program, helped the FSA to reclaim its sense of mission, for the agency seized the opportunity to win these gains for American workers as well. Arguing that they could not transport foreign workers under conditions superior to those extended to domestic workers, the FSA immediately announced that the terms of the Mexican agreement would also be applied to its domestic labor transportation program. FSA critics in Congress could hardly argue that

American workers should be transported under terms inferior to those enjoyed by foreign workers imported at federal expense.

Transportation of domestic and foreign farmworkers began in the fall of 1942. By February 1943 4,000 Mexicans had been transported to harvests in California and Arizona, and 6,808 American workers had been moved to various points around the country. The FSA dove into the importation project with the same spirit of reform it had brought to the camp program. Mexican importees enjoyed educational and recreational facilities, even fiestas organized to make the work season less tedious.[53]

Along the East Coast many small truck farmers felt relief, particularly those who depended on the labor of migrants who passed their farms on their voyage between northern and southern commercial farming centers. These were the growers most at risk if domestic farmworkers were immobilized by gas or tire rationing. When the FSA asked for "good testimonial stories which show the need of our migrant camps," many growers were only too happy to oblige. The farmers of South Erie County and Chautauqua County, New York, wrote that they were "extremely interested in one phase of the FSA Program and that is the Migrant Farm Labor Camp." Letters requesting that the program be extended came from Bellcross, Hendersonville, and Elizabeth City, North Carolina. T. B. Griggs, from Currituck County, North Carolina, wrote that "the camps were very satisfactory," adding that he "don't hardly know what we would have done . . . without them." During the potato digging season the "U.S. Employment man" came by almost daily "to see if we had the labor we needed." Griggs added that he hardly saw the use of planting a new crop if the program was not going to be renewed. At a meeting in Hendersonville in the summer of 1942, tobacco farmers passed a resolution asking for the capacity of the local FSA camp to be doubled. When the regional camp manager reported that the FSA lacked the $1,200 needed to do this, two of the largest growers in the region "immediately placed that amount of money in the hands of the County Agent." The mayor of Wallace, North Carolina, the "World's Largest Auction Strawberry Market," wrote to urge the FSA director to do his "dead level best to have the camp kept intact and ready to start the . . . program next season." "Please tell every one," he closed, "by Damn it, that we just have to have it."[54] The mayor of Elizabeth City noted that he had heard "nothing but universal praise for the manner in which these camps were conducted and all the farmers with whom I have talked were most gratefully pleased in that they eliminated the necessity of frequent trips into Elizabeth City in an endeavor to recruit labor as was the custom in prior years." He added his own commendation to the camp program "for going a long way in solving a heretofore vexatious problem." Migrating labor movements in previous years had brought disease, fire and sanitation hazards, disorderly conduct, drunkenness, "affrays and even murder." "These faults have been alleviated," he noted, "by the establishment of the camps. The laborers are now well-housed; their health conditions are periodically checked and the camps' authorities exercise a good control over their conduct." "It is with pleasure," he concluded, "that I heartily endorse the Migratory Labor Camps as a most worthwhile project."[55]

Growers were willing to back the program when it supplied them with labor, but in areas where FSA officials arrived to remove farmworkers, growers' reactions ranged from outrage to armed resistance. Most of the domestic workers relocated by the transportation program came from the boot heel region of Missouri and from around Memphis, areas that the USES had designated "good places of recruitment because of the large number of underemployed farmers and share croppers who might be interested in aiding the war effort and obtaining much needed supplements to their meagre annual incomes." Elsewhere the program encountered only isolated acts of resistance. The governor of South Carolina threatened to arrest any USES agent recruiting labor in his state, and the Spartanburg police arrested two Florida farm labor agents for soliciting labor without a state license. Moreover, when the USES recruited several hundred farmworkers in South Florida for work at Campbell Soup in New Jersey, the Florida growers were outraged, calling it the "most high-handed act of labor piracy ever perpetrated in this state."[56]

Some protested these alleged acts of labor piracy; others cooperated grudgingly with the Labor Transportation Program. Still, over the course of 1942, farmers grew more frustrated with farm labor policy. They directed most of their ire not at the transportation program but at the camps themselves or, to be more precise, at the increasingly militant farmworkers who resided in them.

The object of their frustration was obvious. Like farmworkers during Reconstruction and the First World War, farmworkers were using their improved position to drive up their wages. The supply of labor did not have to be substantially diminished for farmworkers to take advantage of farmers' fears of labor scarcity. And those who lived in the camps were particularly well placed to bargain with employers. They could not be evicted from a grower's property or denied relief. The camps gave them security, and growers' fears of labor scarcity gave them leverage.

Farmworkers did not have to picket, protest, or even organize to any great extent to win higher wages. They only had to tell growers the rate for which they would work and then wait while the highly perishable truck crops ripened in the fields. The Vienna, Maryland, camp manager reported that they "had a few incidents where farmers promised to pay them one rate and paid another—always lower. These farmers were never able to get any of the campers to work for them again."[57] The manager of the Everglades Farm Labor Supply Center noted that, due to the drop in the piece work rate for beans, the bulk of their 872 campers refused to go to work.[58] The chairman of the Florida Farm Bureau's Vegetable Committee complained to Secretary Wickard that "50% of the crops are wasting in the fields on approximately 30,000 acres of winter vegetables and 25,000 acres of sugar cane with 1,000 farm laborers idle in the communities and a majority of those working effectively employing delaying tactics."[59]

In their complaints to federal officials, most growers described these actions as their predecessors had during Reconstruction and the First World War. Black farmworkers who held out for higher wages were not ambitious but lazy, willing to work only until their pockets were full. "There is not a shortage of farm labor," one Homestead, Florida, farmer insisted, "They just wont stay on the job long enough to do any work." Another complained in a telegram: "My tomato crop is wasting in field today because insufficient labor available. Such labor available will not work regularly is principally illiterate irresponsible American Negro." Another telegram stated, "I have not struck nor sat down[.] My labor ha[s] several times. . . . Such domestic labor as I have been able [to] procure only works part time[.] Remainder they loaf gamble drink chase women, that is our American negro citizens illiterate no patriotism whatsoever."[60]

Growers were quick to blame the camps for the rising tide of militancy among farmworkers. As long as camp managers refused to evict workers who rejected offers of work at what they considered to be depression wages, the camps posed an enormous threat to growers producing highly perishable crops. James Beardsley of Clewiston, Florida, was troubled by rumors that farmworkers could stay in the camps and pay their rent by "pushing a lawnmower along on the grass" if they had to. While he failed to find an adequate number of men to cut sugarcane, farmworkers idled in the camps: "There is no compulsion on them to go out and make a living. They pick beans for 1 day and make $2.50, and that's all they need."[61] A Dade County farmer, "in the business for 30 years," complained that "such help as we have left to do farm work cannot be depended upon." He lost a good portion of his crop the previous season, he complained, "and now it looks as if I will have to lose one half or more this season. At this rate I cannot think of planting another crop as I borrow money to do this farming. 10 years ago I paid .25/hamper for bean picking and my pickers would very often make as high as $6.00/day. Now we are offering and paying as high as .70 per hamper. There is not a shortage of farm labor. They just wont stay on the job long enough to do any work." The problem, he concluded, was that "this same help that is making this trouble has been fed by the government or through relief channels for the last six or eight years and they still think they can get a living without working for it. I am anxious and able to do my part in an all out war effort as a food producer only with your help."[62] After workers in the Back Bay, Virginia, camp struck for higher wages, Northampton County growers rejected the idea of a mobile camp for their own community. Fearing "organized labor trouble," they blocked the camp's construction, though they admitted that without one they would be hard pressed to get workers at all.[63]

One "outstanding source of complaint" in Florida was the U.S. Sugar Company, which was having difficulty attracting workers despite wages it claimed were up to $4 a day. Workers brought in by U.S. Sugar and housed at the FSA camps would quit within a few days to work as bean pickers. Cane cutters worked at least ten hours a day, while bean pickers could earn as much working fewer hours, with far less effort and little risk of injury. U.S. Sugar complained to camp managers that their employees had "stopped all work and were loafing while housed in our camps." FSA officials investigated but determined that the men U.S. Sugar had recruited had simply gone to work for other farmers. The camp managers concluded that "it is not within [their] power to require individuals to work at any specified point."[64]

Although there are many examples of farmers who forced laborers to work against their will during the war, few growers had the means or perhaps the will to compel farmworkers to work by threat of violence.[65] Likewise there is little evidence of a widespread movement to reenact or enforce work-or-fight measures, as there was during the First World War, and little discussion of stopping black migration to the North, though the scale of out-migration was far greater than it had been during the First World War.

Growers had little call to use force during the Second World War because the FSA had shown them another path, a more effective route to the same end. If local workers would not work at wages farmers deemed acceptable, East Coast farmers would get an alternative source of labor from abroad. One woman wrote to the secretary of agriculture, saying, "I want 6 Bahama Laborers and need them now. Bahamians are far better help than riffraff now walking our roads and shooting craps in our fields." Another wrote, "Floridas Farm War effort has been sabotaged by McNutts [*sic*] continued refusal to allow us to import Bahaman labor [McNutt was the head of the War Manpower Commission (WMC)].... A part of present crops will be lost and next years crops greatly reduced unless you take immediate action.... Your action will show whether you are working for the allies or the axis." Another added, "To Hell with your increase in production[;] let McNutt and his advisors produce it. I am through."[66]

They had good reason to believe that their demands could be met, since the FSA was already supplying West Coast growers with Mexican nationals. The existing system could be expanded to serve the East Coast. But preserving and expanding the FSA system was one thing; keeping it under FSA management was another. As long as the Labor Transportation Program fell within the jurisdiction of the FSA, farmers could not be sure that they would secure foreign workers at favorable terms. Their desire, therefore, was to keep the migrant labor program, but under different leadership.

This was, in essence, the goal of House Resolution 96, which was written by the American Farm Bureau Federation with the added support of the Associated Farmers, the National Council of Farmer Cooperatives, and the National Grange of the Patrons of Husbandry. In a joint statement in support of the bill, they recommended that "the administration of this program be decentralized as far as possible so as to enable each State and each county to develop programs best adapted to the needs of their area." The bill was thus a restatement of the Farm Bureau's two-year-old demand that the Migratory Camp Program be turned over to the locally controlled Extension Service. "With respect to workers imported from Mexico and other foreign nations," the statement recommended that immediate agreements be modified "to remove existing impractical and unnecessary restrictions and requirements." Finally, the joint statement insisted "that all workable, hampering restrictions and controls, including the fixing of minimum wages, restrictions of hours, housing standards, unionization of workers be immediately discontinued," and it asked Congress to prohibit the use of farm labor recruitment funds for those purposes.[67] In other words, these growers' associations were demanding that the farm labor recruitment program be retained so long as it could *not* be used to improve farmworkers' conditions. House Resolution 96 passed with only minimal opposition in April 1943.[68]

The new law, called Public Law 45, turned the FSA's remaining programs over lock, stock, and barrel to the newly created War Food Administration (WFA), which was responsible for all aspects of agricultural production for the duration of the war. The WFA's Office of Labor would take over the migratory camps, which were renamed farm labor supply centers. The name change was apt, for under the new Emergency Farm Labor Supply Program the camps would serve the needs of growers, not the welfare of migrant farmworkers. Moreover, where necessary, the camps would be reserved for foreign workers.

More importantly, perhaps, under the new law transportation program funds could not be used to fix minimum wages, set maximum work hours, regulate housing standards, or enforce collective bargaining agreements, except where required to meet the demands of contracts with foreign governments. Domestic workers would not enjoy the same protections as the importees. Public Law 45 also prohibited the transportation of farmworkers from their home counties without the prior consent in writing of the county agricultural extension agents. Because these officials were interested in protecting their local labor supply and would rarely sign such releases, the law had the intended effect of gutting the domestic labor transportation program.[69]

A few months later, in July 1943, the president signed the "death appropriation bill," which finally defunded and dissolved the FSA.[70] But the FSA brigantine had been commandeered, not sunk. It was defunded and dissolved only in the sense that it lost its leaders and its authority to make decisions; otherwise the agency remained intact. The WFA simply took over the FSA's existing operation, assuming authority for both its facilities and personnel.[71]

With WFA officers safely aboard, the FSA crew set the ship on a new course. It expanded the existing program dramatically to provide the nation's farm employers with both foreign workers and prisoners of war. By the end of 1943 the transportation program was importing 7,000 Mexican nationals a month as well as placing West Indians and POWS on American farms. Puerto Ricans were included in the program the following year. The domestic transportation program was insignificant in comparison. In 1945 the WFA transported fewer than 11,000 domestic farmworkers, while it moved and employed 122,000 POWS and 56,000 foreign workers (not counting the Puerto Rican migrants, who were of course citizens).

The expansion of the Labor Importation Program and the construction of legal barriers to domestic migration did not eliminate the American-born migrant worker. On the East Coast, African American migrants continued to move about on their own, although they encountered gas and tire shortages at every turn. Wherever they went, moreover, they found themselves in competition with foreign workers, both for work and for spaces in the farm labor supply centers. Bahamians arrived at the Okeechobee Camp in 1943, although the camp's staff thought that the domestic labor supply had been adequate the previous year. "The farmer had more than necessary labor" in 1942, one staff member noted. With the addition of the Bahamians "many farm laborers were without day work," she added. In 1944 the camp was "filled to capacity" by the time the bean harvest got under way. The camp manager noted in his monthly report for October that "daily we turn down hundreds of applicants who are so anxious to call this their home."[72]

Having made promises to foreign governments that their citizens would be properly housed, the WFA reserved a number of camps for importees only. An official of the Division of Farm Population and Rural Welfare reported, after a visit to the Swedesboro, New Jersey, camp, that of the 300 or so people in the camp, all but 25 were Jamaicans. The African American migrants who had come to the camp in family groups early in the year "were permitted to stay," but no new native families were accepted. He noted, however, that "the Jamaicans and the Negro migrants" were housed separately.[73]

Even some growers were outraged by "regulations which prevented American citizens being housed in Federal farm labor supply centers." However, to the administrators of the labor supply program the exclusion of domestic migrants meant more efficient use of federal facilities. In recommending that the Pahokee camp be used for Bahamians rather than for domestic white migrants, Paul Vander Schouw, noted that domestic workers' children simply took up space. During the previous year's peak season, he pointed out, the camp had housed only 213 workers old enough to work, although it was filled to capacity. If the camp was used for Bahamians only, he argued, it could house at least 800 "easily."[74]

Barred from many farm labor supply centers, African Americans also found that they were hired only as a last resort on many farms. Growers in the Fort Pierce area preferred Bahamians, whom they found "*very satisfactory.*" They based this assessment on attendance, tractability, adaptability, production, and conduct. The Fort Pierce camp manager noted that most employers "considered Bahamians, all things considered, as superior to native American workers," adding that "in some instances, the Bahamians have out cut the domestics who have been cutting fruit all their lives." He observed that "most of the Bahamians were quite contented and happy. It is said that they are that way by nature anyway."[75]

Competition for housing and work led, not surprisingly, to resentment toward imported workers. At Azucar, the camp built especially to house cane cutters recruited for U.S. Sugar, hostility between Jamaicans and African Americans occasionally flared into violent confrontations. Such a conflict occurred in March 1945 after a movie shown in the camp to an audience of domestic and imported workers. According to a Jamaican worker's account, after the film one of the American workers backed his car into a crowd of Jamaicans, saying, "Kill these damn Jamaicans." That set off a brawl during which one Jamaican was shot. He added that on another occasion, "They line up the streets with guns decided to shoot any body who pass. They say they must kill some Jamaican before they leave here."[76]

Whether this particular conflict stemmed from the displacement of domestic workers by the importees is unclear. What is clear is that hostility between importees and African Americans ultimately benefited the growers who hired them. The Reverend David Burgess, sent by the STFU to minister to the migrant population, noted that West Indians and African Americans were housed in two separate camps in Belle Glade. Because the camps were no more than a mile apart, growers could drive from one to the other, forcing wages down by telling each group that the other had underbid it. There was no shortage of labor, Burgess insisted. The importation program was simply a means to break strikes and depress wages.[77]

If this was indeed its purpose, the program seems to have worked. Competition led to a marked decline in the militancy of domestic workers by the end of the war. One Farm Labor Supply official noted in 1945 that he "could have had 450 to 500 Domestic colored in the Homestead Camp by the 20th of January. . . . The Domestic colored did a swell job in harvesting the vegetable crop. They never once asked for higher prices than prevailed in that area."[78]

The decline in strikes among African Americans did not bring peace on the farm labor front in the latter years of the war because foreign workers could also strike, and they did so quite frequently. However, growers had less reason to fear their collective actions because the importees could be promptly and unceremoniously deported and replaced. Moreover, although strikes remained a constant problem under the Emergency Labor Supply Program, growers did not have to contend with them personally. Like turn-of-the-century berry growers in New Jersey, truck farmers during the Second World War had absolved themselves of responsibility for recruiting, housing, and disciplining their workforce. But while the berry growers relied on Italian padroni, World War II truck farmers had Uncle Sam.

The manager of the Pahokee labor camp reported, for example, that "approximately 75 workers held a strike against the 50 cents an hour paid them which was the prevailing wage at that time. This strike was caused by three workers only and a hearing was held for the three workers involved and they were turned over to the Border Patrol for deportation." He noted that "no other trouble has occurred since."[79] In Hebron, Maryland, in 1944 workers protested wages that were lower than wages in other areas they had worked. "Many of the Bahamians have refused to work at these rates," the camp manager reported. He noted that they had had "quite a number" of workers repatriated due to complaints about living conditions, wage rates, food debts, and other matters. "In many cases the workers wanted to pick their own jobs and dictate to the farmer the wage rate they wanted to get." Another camp manager reported that the 681 importees working in the vicinity of the Burlington, New Jersey, camp were "forever dickering for higher wages," and "in some cases," he added, they "have left the fields and refused to work for the prevailing rate of pay." In Palmetto, Florida, too, workers "refused to accept employment" at the proffered wages. As a result, it had been "necessary to make some repatriations."[80]

The WFA interpreted these actions in a variety of ways. The Redland, Florida, camp manager thought that the Bahamians were simply picking up bad habits from African Americans. "Bahaman workers are becoming Americanized to the extent that they are choosing the days they work." "On fields when they can make $35.00 to $60.00 per week they work every day but in fields when they can only earn $25.00 they refuse to work," he explained. Other officials simply counted the number of "refusals to work" while admitting that they did not understand what was causing them.[81]

Federal officials discovered, at the very least, that the padrone's job was not an enviable one, and being padrone to a whole nation involved a host of difficult and often unforeseeable problems. From the very beginning, for example, there were conflicts over where workers should be placed. For the first year of the program, the government of the British West Indies refused to allow Jamaican citizens to be placed "south of the Mason-Dixon line" for fear that they would be treated as poorly as African Americans. Consular officials eventually relented, but only after extended negotiations. Even then they insisted that before the first shipment of 800 Jamaicans arrived in Clewiston, Florida, the WFA would have to provide funds for a Jamaican camp manager and an assistant manager for each camp, an assistant liaison officer from Jamaica to be stationed in Florida, and an American area supervisor to work in conjunction with the Jamaican liaison.[82]

The importation of Puerto Ricans involved additional difficulties. The WFA had been reluctant to include Puerto Ricans in the program because, as U.S. citizens, they could not be "repatriated" at the end of a contracted period. The solution, settled on in 1944, was to withhold a portion of each worker's pay and deposit it in a Puerto Rican bank. The workers' contracts stipulated that they could not withdraw these funds until they returned home, an interesting twist on the long-standing practice of withholding pay to guarantee that workers stayed until the end of the season.

While some of these problems could be resolved by careful planning, others persisted throughout the war. Prisoners of war were particularly troublesome. The use of POWS in agriculture was first planned in April 1943, and the first prisoners arrived in the United States just a month later. Because most of the prison camps were located in the southern part of the United States for reasons of security, almost 200,000 were available to southern employers, including growers. Moreover, POWS had to be kept under heavy guard, so they were only made available to large growers or to groups of growers. This led to charges that some of the largest growers in the South were using POWS to depress already low harvest wages. As one critic put it rather emphatically, "FIRE THOSE NAZIS — and see to it the jobless Americans are offered a decent price for picking cotton. That'll get the crop in in time!"[83]

The WMC issued new rules in August 1943 that stipulated that POWS could only be used when no other labor was available, and they were not to be used to lower wage rates. The WFA insisted publicly that growers assigned POWS were required to pay prevailing wages; however, privately they admitted that few states actually held hearings to determine what "prevailing rates" were. County agents would sometimes just poll local growers and settle on a figure, and these same officials determined whether a labor shortage actually existed.[84] Necessary or not, POWS were employed in agriculture in large numbers: 41,000 in 1943, 102,000 in 1944, and 122,000 in 1945.[85]

If critics of the program were unhappy about the wages paid to POWS, the POWS were even less enamored with the system, for they only received 80 cents of their earnings a day. The rest went to the WFA and the War Department to defray the cost of the program.[86] In Fitzgerald, Georgia, POWS held at a temporary camp struck for two weeks, forcing the WFA to intervene to save the region's peanut crop.[87] In Arizona 200 members of the German Submarine Service refused to pick cotton at 80 cents a day. The WFA resolved such conflicts by feeding the prisoners nothing but bread and water until they agreed to go back to work. However, even when POWS did agree to work, their output was poor. One official estimated that Italian POWS used in ditch clearing "never averaged an output better than seventy-two percent of free labor and then only for a short time."[88]

POWS represented a particular challenge to federal authorities, because although the enlisted men could be forced to work under the Geneva Convention, they could hardly be fired or deported. They were in some ways in a position analogous to that of slaves, but unlike slaves, they could be neither whipped nor sold.

Although the WFA found itself in the uncomfortable position of having to break strikes by threat of deportation and even starvation, most of its tasks as federal padrone were far more mundane. Among forty-nine workers returned to the Bahamas in September 1943, nine were repatriated for "refusing to work," but five were considered "disorderly," twenty-four were sick or injured, one was pregnant, and seven were needed at home.[89] The WFA had assumed responsibility not simply for a program but for several hundred thousand individuals, all with their own needs, problems, and personalities.

The business of disciplining a workforce spread over an entire nation was daunting to say the least. It put an enormous burden on the camp managers, who found themselves responsible for both the care and the behavior of their charges. When importees left their assigned camp in search of higher farm wages or industrial work, the camp managers would have to find them and convince them to stick to the terms of their contracts or else face repatriation hearings. The Gould, Florida, camp manager reported, for example, that "we have had quite a few workers go A.W.O.L., leaving one camp and going to another," although he noted that in South Florida, "we happen to be fortunate in having immigration officers to help us out on this problem."[90] When women became pregnant, the camp managers had to arrange for their deportation "because of their inability to perform heavy agricultural work, the hazardous conditions under which the infant would be reared and the question of citizenship of the infant." This action resulted in "a considerable number of induced abortions," according to the East Coast field medical officer.[91]

Besides putting female importees in the position of having to choose between deportation and abortion, the camp managers also found themselves having to guide people of color who were not Americans through the minefield of American racial "customs." For example, the Hebron, Maryland, camp manager took it upon himself to explain the rules of the Jim Crow South to a Jamaican worker who insisted on attending a white church. "It is hard for these workers to realize that they can have only the privileges of the local colored people," he noted.[92]

Even the process of transporting workers could be complicated. In November 1943 a mutiny aboard a naval transport vessel carrying 4,000 workers back to Jamaica resulted in the death of one worker who fell overboard during the fracas. "From the beginning of the voyage, the workers seemed restless and anxious to return home as quickly as possible." These feelings of frustration were aggravated by the fact that the overcrowded vessel was traveling at only six knots. When the workers were asked to clean their quarters, they told the WFA officials to "go to hell," pointing out that they were paying passengers (as their fare had been deducted from their pay) and that they "were not supposed to perform such degrading tasks." Twelve days into the voyage, while the ship was anchored in Guantanamo Bay, the Jamaicans stormed the galley during mealtime, overwhelmed the crew, and took possession of the ship. A detachment of marines had to be sent from the base to recapture the ship.[93]

Even while WFA officials struggled to control the imported population, they also had to fill growers' labor needs. This was, after all, their purpose. It was also, perhaps, the most difficult task of all. The monthly report submitted in June 1944 by George Winston, the Pahokee camp manager, reveals the extent and complexity of the labor supply effort. Winston noted that the population of the camp at the beginning of the month was 592, 500 of whom were working ten hours a day in U.S. Sugar's cane fields at 40 cents an hour for men and 30 cents for women. On June 13 all workers were called in from the cane fields because Winston had been advised to have them ready to leave the camp on June 16, "which was later cancelled until June 18." On June 18 the camp shipped 778 Bahamians by special train to Cheriton, Nassawadox, Melfa, and Mapesville, Virginia. One hundred fifty-four of the 778 had been brought in only that morning from the Okeechobee camp. This shipment left about 52 workers in Camp Pahokee, but on June 19, workers began arriving "from all parts of Florida, and from Nassau." In four days the camp's population had increased to about 672 workers. On June 23, 617 of these workers were shipped to Bloxton and Melfa, Virginia, and to Hendersonville, North Carolina. On June 25, 80 workers were sent by bus to Pungo, Virginia, "this shipment taking our COUNCIL who had helped very much in the camp's operation," Winston noted. On June 30, workers were sent to Salisbury, Maryland, via West Palm Beach, and 30 women, just in from Nassau, were sent to various places in Florida to join their husbands. At the time of his report the camp population was 325. This was just one camp's activities for one month.

Clearly, the vast labor exchange system, conceived during Reconstruction, schemed about during the Progressive Era, and attempted during the First World War, had finally been put into action.[94] The federal government had taken command of the nation's farm labor supply and was moving farmworkers from harvest to harvest, but by the end of the war the "soldiers on the food production front" were imported workers and prisoners of war. Yet the same agencies that imported foreign workers freely admitted that the nation's problem was not a labor shortage but a maldistribution of labor. If domestic workers had been carefully directed to labor-scarce regions, their numbers would have been adequate to meet the demands of agricultural war production. Why, then, such a vast expenditure of effort to generate new sources of labor if domestic workers were available?

The answer is that domestic workers were not inanimate farm commodities to be shipped here or there at some official's whim. Nor were they overwhelmed by the prospect of steady work at slightly increased wages. Rather, they had used the security and independence afforded by the FSA camps to strike for higher wages. Within a year of the U.S. declaration of war, farmworkers had transformed the migrant camps from places of shelter and relief into a staging ground for an odd sort of labor movement. It was a movement without union elections, sit-down strikes, or flying pickets. It required little in the way of organization or leadership. It was in a sense a sedentary variant on the age-old practice of voting with one's feet. Based in the camps, farmworkers could simply wait while frightened growers panicked themselves into a bidding war.

This was a struggle that growers could not have won alone without either an open display of force, in the manner of C. F. Seabrook, or access to an alternative source of labor. With the help of the state, growers pursued the latter alternative. Thus the state entered the affairs of farm labor relations in order to compensate for growers' Achilles' heel — their vulnerability to farm labor strikes — and native-born farmworkers lost their opportunity to transform the conditions of East Coast agriculture by organizational resolve and collective will.

The Union as Padrone

The "Underground Railroad"
during the Second World War

THE EASE WITH WHICH the War Food Administration (WFA) commandeered the welfare apparatus set up for migrant farmworkers suggests the danger of dependence on the state. It also suggests an alternative course of action. If workers cannot depend on the state for aid and
assistance, then by implication they must look to each other for strength.
Yet nothing we have seen so far testifies to the power of farm labor
unionism. For their efforts among farmworkers in 1913 Wheatland, California, Industrial Workers of the World organizers found themselves in
prison on trumped-up murder charges. In 1934 the fledgling Agricultural and Cannery Workers' Industrial Union at Seabrook Farms had
victory within its grasp one moment and found itself removed from the
bargaining table the next. Farmworkers living in Farm Security Administration (FSA) migratory labor camps in 1942 used the security the
camps afforded to bargain up their wages and, for their efforts, found
themselves locked out of the camps and thrown into competition with
workers imported from abroad. These struggles may have given the
workers who participated in them pride in their own courage, but beyond that there is little to recommend them.

Each of these efforts shared a common strategy, which was to push for
concessions just prior to the harvest, when growers were most vulnerable. The problem with this strategy was that without collective bargaining rights (and perhaps even with them), it led only one of two ways:
growers either capitulated or struck back with all the force at their dis-

posal. In 1913 and 1934 they fought back with guns, tear gas, and fire-hoses. In 1942 they were aided by the WFA, which wielded the Labor Importation Program as its weapon.

In 1943, however, two unions — the Southern Tenant Farmers' Union and the Amalgamated Meat Cutters and Butcher Workmen — collaborated on a different strategy. Instead of organizing strikes, they offered to organize growers' labor supply, assuming for themselves the dual role of padrone and protector. Compared with the federal government's Emergency Labor Supply Program, the unions' labor supply campaign was tiny; it provided only a fraction of the labor needed in New Jersey's fields and canneries. Yet it was significant not for what it achieved but for what it suggested might have been achieved by legally sanctioned agricultural unions.

THE ORIGINAL IDEA for this joint union venture came from the Camden, New Jersey, local of the Amalgamated Meat Cutters and Butcher Workmen of North America, an American Federation of Labor affiliate. Chartered in February 1941, Local 56, known as the Meat and Cannery Workers' Union, got from the International the right to organize cannery workers in New Jersey (cannery workers had the right of collective bargaining, according to the National Labor Relations Board's reading of the Wagner Act). Local 56 was remarkably successful in this effort, winning eight closed-shop agreements — the first in agriculture — in the first two years of its charter.[1]

Still, in the course of its campaigns the local encountered unforeseen problems, most notably the difficulty of organizing a workforce that doubled in size for a few months of every year. At one South Jersey cannery, for example, 500 workers labored year-round, but during the harvest rush their numbers were dwarfed by 4,000 migrant workers. As Leon Schachter, the local's business agent and later secretary, explained, year-round workers were hostile to the seasonal employees "because the migrant worker has been used in the past as a cushion for the employer to offset any protest that the regular worker might want to make." This enmity was an obstacle to organization in the rush season, when both groups of employees worked side by side in the canneries. Organizing was even more difficult during the off-season because local workers competed for a limited number of positions and were reluctant to do anything that might jeopardize their jobs.[2]

Eventually the union succeeded in courting year-round workers, but only by acquiescing to their prejudices against migrants. Under the terms of the Meat and Cannery Workers' closed-shop agreements, seasonal workers were required to pay union dues but were excluded from union membership. They received few of the benefits that year-round workers won for themselves, and they labored at wage rates below the union scale.[3]

The first of these agreements was with none other than Seabrook Farms.[4] Signed in March 1941, the contract gave Seabrook's permanent workers a guarantee of year-round employment, a wage increase of 10 to 20 percent, seniority rights, preference for promotions, and (completely unheard-of in agriculture) a week's vacation with pay. That C. F. Seabrook agreed to this deal is nothing short of remarkable; he was pushed into it, however, by a combination of idealism and avarice.

According to the leaders of Local 56, the impulse to negotiate came from C. F. Seabrook's three sons, who returned from college to manage the company with engineering degrees and "new ideas about labor relations." "Theirs is a new light," noted the Amalgamated's newspaper, adding that "throughout the Seabrook system lies a deep vein of human kindness." Had anyone said this in 1934, Seabrook's employees would have laughed themselves silly. Yet twenty-six-year-old Jack, by then labor manager at the farm, admitted to having been "bitten by the desire to do something for the Negro." He instituted a nondiscriminatory hiring policy and moved African Americans into management positions.[5]

The Seabrook boys were clearly taking the corporation in a new ideological direction, but there were also economic motives behind their willingness to bargain. Seabrook Farms was the world's leading producer of frozen foods, and it continued to expand its productive capacity. Vegetables still grew according to the seasons, of course, but once harvested, they would be frozen and stored in the farm's four-story cold storage facility, allowing the farm to sign contracts to supply vegetables a year in advance. Jack, who became general manager during the war, could estimate costs and know precisely what the crops would earn before the seeds ever touched the ground. In other words, C. F. Seabrook and sons were out of the fresh vegetable market; they produced vegetables like Henry Ford produced cars.

Unlike other farm employers, who felt pressured to squeeze down on farm wages when produce prices were low at harvest, the Seabrooks knew exactly what they could afford to pay their workers. They were better placed than any other agricultural employer in the country to offer their 500 year-round employees security, relatively high wages, and skilled work. All they needed in return was the ability to plan ahead, and this was what Local 56 offered. While other farms and canners faced

Japanese American and African American women hand-weighing
packages of green beans on the Seabrook Farms packing line
(Seabrook Educational and Cultural Center Museum)

spiraling wages, Seabrook enjoyed a no-strike guarantee and a contract
that capped wages for at least a year.[6]

With $1 million in sales in 1940 alone, Seabrook was by far the leading
vegetable processor in the Northeast, if not in the world. Once the Meat
and Cannery Workers settled with Seabrook, the farm's major competi-
tors fell into line. By the time Local 56 concluded its organizing drives in
1943, it had closed-shop agreements with eight canneries, including
Venice Maid, Stokely Foods, and H. J. Heinz.[7]

These were unprecedented victories for a union of farmworkers, but
the local's failure to organize seasonal workers still galled. Leon Schachter was particularly committed to improving the lives of migrant farmworkers and to extending the existing contracts to include migrant workers. He also feared, however, that as long as seasonal workers were not
union members, they could be used against the union the day Seabrook's vein of human kindness ran dry.[8]

By the time the local signed its eighth contract with a New Jersey
cannery in 1943, the union was already beginning to feel a bit parched.
Growers' and canners' complaints of harvest labor shortages were ring-
ing loudly in the halls of Congress. Their appeals were particularly compelling because half of the canning industry's output went directly to the

armed forces. Once the WFA took over the FSA's programs in the spring of 1943, the federal response was rapid: the army provided agricultural employers in New Jersey — including Seabrook — with soldiers, then prisoners of war. The WFA flew in farmworkers from Puerto Rico and the West Indies, and Jack Seabrook recruited Japanese Americans released from western internment camps.

Since Local 56 had a closed-shop contract with Seabrook Farms, all of these new workers were required to pay dues to the union (the company paid the dues for the POWS), but the idea of a closed shop in agriculture was not widely accepted.[9] Union leaders found themselves in the uncomfortable position of having to demand dues checkoff from soldiers who had "volunteered" to help pick and process essential war crops (they were, in fact, paid for the work, and their wages supplemented their regular army pay). During the 1944 harvest season the union's effort to collect dues from "Nazis" made national news. In each instance, Schachter noted, the union had to maintain "a forceful attitude toward the employer" to uphold its contract and the security of its members. By the summer of 1943 Local 56 was in an open fight to enforce the contracts it had so recently won. There was, after all, little to prevent Seabrook Farms from reneging on the union contract if labor became more plentiful.[10]

The union's future was looking dim when Leon Schachter had a revelation. The union itself would supply New Jersey's canner/growers with however many seasonal workers they needed, providing that the workers arrived as union members under improved conditions. They would find available workers where everyone knew they were: way down south in Dixie.

Schachter contacted H. L. Mitchell of the Southern Tenant Farmers' Union (STFU) to explain his plan. The STFU would round up its members: migrant workers, displaced sharecroppers, tenant farmers, even some who still farmed but were available between the planting of the cotton in spring and the harvest in fall. Under the federal "job freeze" order, such people could not be removed from their home counties without the permission of the local agricultural agent. To get around this the STFU would transfer its members temporarily to the membership rolls of the Meat and Cannery Workers. In that instant the workers would be transformed from surplus labor stuck in the South to unemployed members of Local 56, eligible to be moved to jobs wherever the New Jersey union could find them.[11]

That this sleight of hand worked is even more remarkable than a closed-shop contract with Seabrook Farms, but as Schachter explained, "When they became our *own* unemployed members, we were able to

Seabrook Farms employees Jim Mitsui and a German prisoner of war
(Seabrook Educational and Cultural Center Museum)

demand from the War Manpower Commission the right to make them
available for employment under our Union hiring hall status, which
[was] recognized by the WMC." The WMC, having already announced
that its policy was to provide POWS only when domestic workers were un-
available, could hardly refuse a union's offer to locate and transport un-

employed Americans to an essential defense industry. It also did not hurt that the STFU was willing to displace members of the United Cannery, Agricultural, Packing, and Allied Workers of America, or UCAPAWA, the CIO-affiliated, communist cannery union that already had members at Campbell Soup. The WMC agreed that it would override the authority of local agricultural agents who might prevent unemployed southern workers from leaving their home counties.[12]

The STFU had compelling reasons for jumping at Schachter's scheme. When growers' complaints of labor scarcity reached Congress in 1942, H. L. Mitchell had done his best to call "attention to the fact that there were thousands of farm people in the southern states who normally were employed only four to six months each year." These were the STFU's constituents: the cotton tenants and sharecroppers of Arkansas, Missouri, and Oklahoma, who were among the poorest people in the nation. But Mitchell's efforts paid off only briefly. In the summer of 1942, when the FSA was just getting into the labor transportation business, the STFU was able to get 2,000 of its members moved to California, where they picked long-staple cotton for parachutes before returning home. The following winter 500 members went to Florida to work in the fruit and vegetable harvest. The wages STFU members received on these voyages were often more than three times higher than the wages they could earn in their home states, but in 1942 the FSA was not long for this world. As Mitchell put it, "The big cotton planters of the south got frightened. . . . They feared that once men and women were paid $5.00 a day they would never again work for $1.00 per day." "The Farm Bureau," he argued, "cooked up a scheme to bring in foreign workers, Mexicans, Bahamians, Jamaicans to work on the farms in the north, the east and west and to let the poor white and Negro workers of the south stay down there, work for whatever they could get and at such times as they were needed." Indeed, it was the Farm Bureau's bill that prevented the transportation of domestic workers without the written permission of county agricultural agents. From April 1943, when Public Law 45 went into effect, until November 1944, Mitchell reported, "not a single farm worker" was provided transportation from the states where most STFU members lived, although the union gave the WFA a list of 2,200 workers who were ready to participate in the Labor Transportation Program.[13]

In late November the WFA finally secured the release of a few hundred farmworkers in southeastern Missouri for two months' work picking cotton in the West. Few of these people were STFU members, however, and Mitchell felt certain that if the local county agents knew there were union members among the group, "not a single one would have secured transportation."[14] When Mitchell sent out a survey asking members if they were having difficulty getting releases from their county agents, the results were clear. Willie Reeves wrote from Forrest City, Arkansas, that the St. Frances County agent would not send any workers out of the county. The county agent serving Lexington, Tennessee, told J. R. Hatchett that he would not sign the release but would get him a job on a local farm at $1.50 for a twelve-hour day. Over 150 surveys came back within two weeks from workers who had been denied permission to leave their counties. Only one had been granted a release.[15]

Without the "underground railway," as Mitchell called the interunion clearance scheme worked out by Local 56, the STFU's members would, in his view, be frozen on cotton plantations "under a new form of peonage." Local 56's plan was advantageous to the STFU in another way as well. Since every farmworker who wanted to participate in the plan would have to join the STFU first, the union could expect a much needed boost in membership.[16]

Thus together the STFU and the Meat and Cannery Workers initiated a venture that merged the functions of padrone and protector. The unions would both supply workers and see to their welfare with the cooperation of the WMC. Federal involvement "prevented any *state* regulations from interfering with our activities," Schachter noted, "although such attempts were made."[17]

The STFU began sending workers north in November 1943. Since there was little need for farmworkers in New Jersey at that time of the year, the program started off slowly; by December the STFU had sent 73 tenants and sharecroppers and 42 unemployed day laborers to the Edgar F. Hurff Company in Swedesboro, New Jersey. By the end of the following summer, however, the STFU had sent 1,047 men and women to New Jersey, as well as a few to Delaware. There they were made temporary members of Local 56 for periods ranging from six weeks to four months.[18]

Union-supervised migration seemed the solution to everyone's problem: the unions, the employers, the workers, and the government's labor supply agencies. That it benefited the workers is clear. As Schachter remarked after the close of the 1944 harvest season, "We were able to discover a solution to the general problem of migration." The "organized migration" helped the Amalgamated Meat Cutters to organize the unorganized. It established "better feeling between the organized and the seasonal worker," and that cooperation resulted in better Union

Raw recruits from the South in front of the Seabrook Farms employment office
(Seabrook Educational and Cultural Center Museum)

security for its members, in the off-season as well as in the peak season.
"We have achieved the *respect* of the Employer," he concluded, "the
cooperation of the government agencies, and the *loyalty* of the Workers."[19]

Indeed, the unions' efforts to ensure decent living conditions and
steady wages were effective. As the STFU required employers to send rail
or bus fare for each worker recruited, even the workers' trips north were
quicker and safer than the traditional journey in the back of a crew
leader's truck. On August, 1, 1944, such a group made its way to Camden with the help of the Reverend David Burgess, the union's "minister
to the migrants." Destined for Campbell Soup, the eighty-six black workers, wearing war worker pins so that Burgess could identify them, met as
instructed at the Memphis train station. Burgess later reported that they
arrived in Camden "without much trouble despite a rapid change in
Washington, [and] some Jim Crow restrictions." One man got his finger
jammed in a door; but otherwise all went well, and "the men were very
cooperative."[20]

Arriving in Camden, they joined 239 STFU members already at
Campbell, plus 200 Barbadians, 200 Floridians who were members of
UCAPAWA, and 400 to 500 Puerto Ricans. Burgess's group found the
company slow to feed them, their accommodations crowded, and no safe

THE UNION AS PADRONE

place to store their belongings. This was not unusual for migrants. What was unusual was that they had a union representative with them who expressed their concerns to the company.

power of the union

Burgess presented a "memorandum" to Mr. Heap, the company's employment manager, in which he objected to these conditions, but his dealings with Heap were "rather unfortunate." "At first I delt [*sic*] with him verbally," Burgess reported, "but his attitude toward me and slowness and frequent refusals to do anything forced me to put my requests in writing." Eventually these memorandums reached Mr. Worden, Heap's immediate superior. "[Then] I got a little action," Burgess noted, but Worden turned out to be "a very dictatorial boss" and poorly acquainted with the migrants' problems. "Like the other Campbell officials," Burgess wrote, "he has a *very* low opinion of the Negro." This was made plain by Worden's remarks, upon visiting the overcrowded barracks, that "he attributed the lack of ventilation to the 'natural stench' of the Negro."[21] The company was slow to deal with the ventilation and storage problems, but in the following days Burgess was able to handle difficulties with foremen, get the company to cover a can line that ran noisily through the barracks, and reinstate a worker who was fired after being injured on the job.[22]

Every Sunday afternoon, after church services, the union would hold its meetings. The first of such gatherings took place on the Sunday after the STFU group arrived in Camden. A workers' quartet sang. Burgess preached. Schachter talked. Then Burgess explained the contract, the grievance procedure, "and the like." The workers' shop stewards, Anderson Johnson and Sam James, also addressed the group. "Grievances were then considered — and they were many."

By the end of the month three workers' committees were functioning at Campbell Soup. The Grievance Committee, led by Johnson and James, met frequently. "Mr. Johnson and Mr. James are constantly in the office," Burgess noted, "and I find them very effective and most respected by the men." The Barracks Council also brought frequent complaints, and the Church Committee helped to plan the Sunday services and acted as ushers. "Fortunately or unfortunately," Burgess quipped, "we have a considerable number of Reverends in our midst."

Burgess worked out of the Local 56 office in Camden, from where he dealt with a steady stream of problems: injured workers, illnesses, men who wanted to return home, even a special trip to pick up a trunk for a union member. He also notified the STFU when workers received word that their families were being intimidated at home in their absence. One man reported that the sheriff had visited his wife a few days after he left home, and another "had his field plowed over by the bosses' hands — an act showing that the boss is threatening to remove him."[23]

The success of the organized migration required constant attention to the workers' grievances. The 150 STFU members sent to the Hurff Company in Swedesboro, New Jersey, encountered the most problems. The Meat and Cannery Workers had not been able to organize Hurff's, and as a result, placing union members there was risky. Arriving in Swedesboro in June 1944, the STFU group joined 350 African Americans, white West Virginians, and Puerto Ricans who were not union members. Together they got in two weeks' work before the crop failed as a result of bad weather. Although he had no work for them, Hurff still expected the group to reimburse him for the expense of advancing their fares. Instead of taking $3.00 from each week's check over the course of the summer, he deducted $18.80 from a single $21.54 pay check. One worker wrote Mitchell that after taxes, rent, and 25 cents in union dues, she was left with 25 cents for a week's work. Combining this with the $2.64 that remained from her previous week's pay, she had "$2.89, no job, and no protection." W. C. Banks, the leader of the union members at the Hurff camp, reported that "more than half of our members" had left the camp, "some wint back home others went to other jobs where they can get more money." Again, this was not an unusual experience for migrant workers. What was different was that the union sent David Burgess to settle workers' claims and move them to other farms where there was enough work to make the journey worthwhile.[24]

All told, the unions' leaders found the workers well pleased with their efforts. "Despite their bad living quarters," the Campbell shop steward Sam James estimated "that 80% of the men are perfectly satisfied."[25] Sent by the STFU to check on its members, F. R. Betton reported from Camden that there were many complaints by the members, but that most of them were due to misunderstandings of the terms of the union's contract with the company. With Burgess's help, he reported, he had "just about got them all adjusted here at Cambell's [sic]." He added that he wished he could have arrived earlier to thoroughly organize the group, but, he concluded, "they all are highly pleased with the STFU and are promising to help secure more members when they return home."[26]

The STFU and Local 56 did more than just intercede on the workers' behalf to satisfy their needs; they tried to school new members in the culture and workings of a trade union, to empower them to address grievances themselves. This educational process had a negative aspect, moreover, in that the unions had to discipline their members to resist the impulse to bolt when they were dissatisfied with a position. Burgess

because they were empowered

noted, for example, that he refused to back a worker who insulted a foreman and walked off the job.

Such discipline problems were particularly difficult at the beginning and the very end of the seasons. "Though they signed contracts and agreed to stay at least six weeks," Burgess explained, "many of [the] men, homesick and a little lost in the industrial set-up, wanted to go home at the first opportunity. I attempted to show the men the necessity of living up to their contract if they and the Unions were to have good reputations with the Company." As the end of the summer approached, moreover, it was harder to keep the workers on the job, as many were anxious to return home in time for the cotton harvest. Burgess reported in August 1944 that "there has been a great number of men in this office requesting to go home, and in only three cases have I given official sanction to their departure." "The requests for going home are increasing daily," he added, "mostly because the men fear that land owners will persecute them when they return. In a few cases, the opening of the cotton has made several men greatly concerned." It was up to Burgess and the Meat and Cannery Workers' business agent to decide which workers could go and which had to stay.[27]

There was a positive side to this disciplinary action, however, as the two unions were trying to get the workers to hold their ground and demand improved conditions instead of voting with their feet. Burgess and Schachter were particularly instrumental in this educational process. When Burgess arrived in Swedesboro, for example, he "got acquainted with the people slowly, was elected to their Council, and labored in the cannery alongside of them."[28] He met with the council frequently, took up grievances with them rather than for them, and in his words, "attempted in a rather feeble way to educate the membership in Parliamentary law." He quickly determined that the council members were ineffective in stating their grievances to the manager of the plant: "They didn't know how to argue, being Southern Negroes," he reported. Upon his recommendation the council removed the obsequious Reverend W. C. Banks from his position as spokesperson and replaced him with another council member chosen from among the younger and more militant leaders. Burgess also helped the council to simplify its grievance procedure so that the chain of authority would be clear and the head steward "would be less inclined to be servile before the white 'bossman.'"[29]

The unions' leaders taught other lessons at Seabrook Farms. When the first 400 Japanese Americans arrived at Seabrook Farms from internment camps, white and black employees alike reacted with hostility, convinced "that the presence of these Japanese-Americans threatened their job security, and constituted a device of the employer to split the workers and eventually to break the union itself." With the help of the Reverend Mineo Katagiri, a Hawaiian Japanese graduate of Union Seminary, the leaders of Local 56 attempted "to educate the white and Negro workers" so that they would "realize that economic strength lies only in racial unity."[30]

The difference between the advice that Burgess and Schachter offered and the experience that the FSA officials had provided in the migratory labor camps was significant. The FSA helped camp residents form councils with which they governed themselves. These camp councils prohibited drinking and unruly behavior, arranged "wholesome" recreational activities, and even raised money to send children to college, but they had nothing to do with workers' negotiations with employers. When workers left the camps to board the back of a grower's truck, they were on their own. The union grievance committees also advocated moral discipline and organized social activities to enliven the work season, but their primary aim was to empower workers to negotiate with their employers.

One group of workers sent to New Jersey became particularly involved in the unions' educational mission. These were women from black colleges throughout the South recruited to work at Seabrook Farms. Students at Morehouse, Bennett, Hampton, Virginia Union, Shaw University, and other black colleges across the South journeyed to Seabrook and to its subsidiary, the Deerfield Packing Company, in order to support the war effort and earn tuition money.

The STFU did not really intend for the "negro college girls" to interact with its regular members. Indeed, H. L. Mitchell promised "the college officials that these girls would not be too closely associated with the low type of transient workers, especially in their living and recreation activities."[31] However, by the end of their stay in New Jersey, most of the students had been changed by their experience.

When the first group arrived at the Deerfield Packing House (also owned by C. F. Seabrook), they complained of "unhealthful living conditions," long work hours at night, "obscenity" visible from the young men's rooms, and "undesirable social contacts" with the other workers at the company. Thirty-five students left because of these problems, but the ninety-one who remained threw themselves into their work and into the union's activities. Although they had been promised special housing, they decided as a group not to press for it, fearing that the other workers would resent their being treated differently. Instead they stayed, without "any inter-racial conflicts," in the Seabrook dormitories with 700 other

College students from Tennessee and Mississippi in a DC-3 en route to
Seabrook Farms. H. L. Mitchell is standing to the left of the door. (Southern
Historical Collection, Library of the University of North Carolina, Chapel Hill)

workers, including black and white migrant workers from the South and
Americans of Japanese descent. Local 56 had arranged for a College
Girls Committee to meet apart from the Tenants Council, which spoke
for all the workers in the Seabrook dormitory. However, the students
voted against a separate grievance procedure, deciding instead to use
the College Girls Committee to organize open discussions on the labor
movement.[32]

The students' efforts to foster a system of self-government that united
all the various groups represented at Seabrook seems to have worked. "It
was quite apparent," Mitchell noted, "that the student group had already become an influence for good in the project. . . . The Japanese and
the Negro college girls set an example for others in their behavior." Even
the dean of women at Hampton University, who arrived in response to
the students' early complaints, found the conditions inadequate but "no
tension whatsoever." "The inter-racial relations were fine" and a "credit
to the project," she concluded.[33] With the help of their student members, union leaders were so successful at easing hostility among the vari-

ous groups of workers at Seabrook Farms and other unionized canneries and farms that even the workers brought to South Jersey by the federal government on contracts from Puerto Rico and Barbados sought to join the union.[34]

The participation of the college women was perhaps the most interesting aspect of the union-organized migration, but, ironically, it is also a sign of the movement's weakness. Leon Schachter had wanted to improve the lives of migrant farmworkers by supplanting the soldiers, foreign workers, and POWS supplied by the federal government. H. L. Mitchell had sought a way to break the hold of the job freeze order that prevented poor southerners from reaping the benefits of the war economy. But it is difficult to see how placing college women in summer jobs fulfilled either mission. Mitchell noted that the students might go on to become advocates for civil rights and trade unionism in the South, but this was as much rationalization as design.[35] Mitchell was recruiting college students because he was having trouble supplying anyone else.

The task of providing labor was apparently no less difficult when unionists tried their hands at it than when philanthropists, progressive reformers, and Terence V. Powderly were behind it. The STFU and Local 56 had to recruit workers, hire supervisors, arrange transportation, and negotiate with employers. They had to move workers from one contract to another when work slowed in one location and picked up elsewhere, and they had to inform the workers of when and where they were going, of the terms of their contracts, and of the penalties for breaking them.[36] The padrone's role was constant and complex.

In the end, it appears the STFU could not live up to its end of the bargain. H. L. Mitchell was able to send about 1,200 active STFU members and a couple of hundred college students to New Jersey, but the task of recruiting and relocating thousands of unemployed or underemployed tenant farmers who were spread across the South proved to be too difficult for his limited staff, which consisted of a vice-president and an office manager.[37] Mitchell could recruit students with the help of college administrators because they were easily accessible during summer holidays. Unorganized individuals with families and sharecrop contracts were not so easily rounded up and transported to jobs hundreds of miles away, however much they needed the work.

The union-organized migration lasted for two years after the war ended. Indeed, due to a rail strike, college women were flown to New Jersey in the summer of 1946, most of them boarding airplanes for the first time in their lives.[38] Although the program reached its peak by transporting 3,000 workers that year, it never matched the number of

importees and war prisoners employed in New Jersey's food processing plants alone. And there were many more West Indians, Puerto Ricans, and POWS at work in the fields. Union-sponsored migration never
added more than a drop to the sea of workers delivered to farm employers by the U.S. government.

The summer after Japan's surrender, 250 STFU members struck at
Starkey Farms in Morrisville, Pennsylvania, where farmworkers had demanded a new deal in 1934. Little had changed in twelve years. This
time the workers demanded a raise from 45 cents to 65 cents an hour,
better living conditions, clean drinking water, and the elimination of
child labor. More than any other event since the start of the union-
organized migration, the Starkey strike demonstrated what a union had
to offer migrant farmworkers. Citing "primitive and unsanitary conditions," Local 56 backed its migrant members, bringing 1,000 sympathiz-
ers to join their picket line. Carrying signs that stated, "We are backin
you—Keep up the fight" and "Don't Give into Starkey's Thugs," members of seven locals of the Meat and Cannery Workers' Union arrived at
the protest with clothing, canned foods, and a side of beef, turning an
initially tense strike into a jubilant celebration of a new era of labor
unionism in agriculture.[39] At the time the Starkey strike seemed to welcome migrant farmworkers into an already buoyant labor movement. In
retrospect it seems more like a wake than a coming-out party, for the
fledgling farm labor movement was about to be dealt a death blow.[40]

Five months after the war ended in the summer of 1945, Congress
extended the life of the Labor Importation Program.[41] In 1946 the use
of war prisoners ended, but the importation of foreign workers did not.
In 1947, a year after the Starkey strike, Congress enacted Public Law 76,
which did much more than just extend the importation program. It
renewed the provisions of Public Law 45, the 1943 law that had banned
the use of federal funds to improve wage rates, hours, or conditions for
American farmworkers and ended the administrative life of the FSA.
Public Law 76 also removed any vestiges of the FSA's earlier welfare
efforts from the government's labor supply programs. While it institu-
tionalized the Farm Labor Importation Program, it gave the U.S. Department of Agriculture (USDA) the authority to dispose of the migrant
labor camps "for such prices and under such terms as the Secretary
determined to be reasonable." The camps were to be sold "to any public
or semi-public agency or nonprofit association *of farmers* . . . who would
agree to operate and maintain the facilities for housing farm laborers
and to relieve the Government of all responsibility in connection with
the facilities." The secretary apparently thought $1.00 a reasonable

price, and for that amount the camps were sold to growers' associations around the country.[42]

The 1947 law also put an end to the state-supported migration organized by Local 56 and the STFU. Besides reaffirming Congress's prohibition against collective bargaining in agriculture, it banned collective bargaining agreements between farmworkers placed by a government agency and their employers, thus outlawing even voluntary agreements between employers and farmworkers. Even the Taft-Hartley bill, "denounced as slavery for the industrial worker," did not go as far as this legislation, noted the *Union Reporter*.[43] Farmworkers would get no new deal in the postwar era.

As the war was drawing to a close, H. L. Mitchell had expressed the hope that the STFU's arrangement with Local 56 would be just the beginning of a much larger supply effort. He envisioned union hiring halls around the country channeling farmworkers to the "best paying jobs" and the best living facilities. He had come to believe that only by stepping into the shoes of the padrone could a union hope to organize migratory farmworkers. He would not realize his dream.[44]

Together the STFU and Local 56 of the Amalgamated Meat Cutters and Butcher Workmen's Union brought thousands of black and white southerners to South Jersey to work in the fields and canneries under wartime union contracts. They succeeded in defying southern planters' efforts to keep low-wage workers frozen in the South. They vastly improved the conditions under which migrants worked in the North. They struggled to make undisciplined migrants into disciplined trade unionists. And they demonstrated to other New Jersey union members the necessity of bringing migrants into the union fold.

The union-organized underground railroad, however, came nowhere near meeting the labor needs of New Jersey's corporate farmers. Two unions acting alone lacked the means to act as padrone to canneries in a single state, let alone to a nation. The scale and complexity of labor distribution demanded the power of the state. The FSA's labor transportation program had been successful (and therefore worth taking over in the eyes of farm employers) because it pulled together an enormous bureaucracy made up of U.S. Employment Service officials, USDA county agents, FSA doctors, social workers, writers, and even photographers. It took this sort of administrative muscle to physically relocate farmworkers from state to state and farm to farm. Dependence on state power may have been dangerous, but the efforts of two unions alone inspired little hope for long-term gains.

If farmworker unions could not succeed as padroni without the added muscle of the welfare state, the union-organized migration of farmworkers during the Second World War did reveal the importance, even the necessity, of a militant labor movement. Without such a movement, farmworkers had no say in the making and implementation of state policy. Even the most autonomous, well-intended state agencies failed in their best efforts to act as neutral employment services. The Freedmen's Bureau, T. V. Powderly's Division of Information, and the FSA all demonstrated that neutrality was an administrative impossibility. Once federal officials delivered farmworkers into the hands of farm employers, they could not see to their welfare. They could not guarantee that the workers' pay would be as promised, that their shelters would have roofs, that their injuries would be attended to, or that their children would be well cared for. Only workers—organized and vigilant—could enforce their own bargains.

Epilogue

THE DECISION to import workers during the Second World War shaped the course of farm labor history over the next fifty years. In the aftermath of the war, Puerto Rican farmworkers replaced Italians in New Jersey and New York. In Florida, Bahamians and Jamaicans monopolized all but a few hundred of the 8,000 to 10,000 cane cutting jobs. In the 1970s Haitians began arriving, making Belle Glade, for a time, the second largest Haitian community in the United States. But in the 1980s the Haitians found themselves passed over in favor of Mexicans and Central Americans, who remain the farmworkers of choice in the East. Thus a story that began with the transformation of East Coast agriculture by western grain ends with an influx of western labor.[1]

The Atlantic Coast farm labor market has been westernized in another crucial way as well. Before the Second World War, growers on the East and West Coasts manipulated their labor supply in very different ways. Only California growers were able to defeat farmworkers' organizational efforts with ethnic reserve armies. When Chinese contract laborers organized in the mid-nineteenth century, the Japanese arrived in California to replace them. When the Japanese organized and demanded higher wages, growers turned to Filipinos. White and African American workers flooded the labor pool in the 1930s, and Mexicans and Mexican Americans were available all along.[2]

In contrast, East Coast farmworkers were mostly African Americans (although Italians in New Jersey got more press), and eastern growers employed traditionally southern solutions to their labor supply problems. They chased labor recruiters out of their communities, used vagrancy laws to keep workers in the fields, invented a wartime work-or-fight campaign reminiscent of Confederate Army labor drafts, used tar and feathers on occasion, and even sponsored a cross burning in New Jersey. None of these methods had to be used very often, however, because debt, boll weevils, and federal crop reduction programs kept the fields well stocked with labor for much of the twentieth century.

Yet when the federal Labor Importation Program and its recent manifestation, the H2 program, gave the nation's growers the power to seek labor from abroad at taxpayers' expense, Atlantic Coast growers began to employ western methods of labor control. The result was a strategically diversified labor force in the East, in which one group of migrants could be pitted against another. In Belle Glade after the Second World War, African Americans were last hired in almost every instance.

This diversity has persisted. Haitians now do the cane planting, Jamaicans the cane cutting, and Mexicans most of the corn harvesting and all of the highly paid lettuce cutting. Florida growers have so successfully played one group against the others that in 1977 and 1978 strikes by Latino farmworkers in South Florida were broken by African American strikebreakers, and Rural Legal Services sued two growers for laying off Haitians and African Americans in favor of Latinos. The westernization of the East Coast was almost complete. The final step was the institutionalization of illegal workers. There are now so many *sindocumentos* among the Latin Americans that growers have all but stopped pressing for the extension of the H2 or temporary labor importation program. Illegal workers are cheaper, more vulnerable, less likely to complain, and well worth the risk, as long as the Immigration and Naturalization Service continues to punish workers, not employers, for violating immigration law.[3]

For workers there remains much to complain about. Conditions and wages are generally considered worse in the East than on the West Coast. Housing is not only as poor as it was in the 1940s, it sometimes *is* what it was in the 1940s. In Belle Glade the Osceola and Okeechobee migrant labor camps, built by the FSA and sold to growers for a dollar each at the end of the war, are still in use. They remain outside the city limits, which means that black workers, despite their numbers, do not control city politics. Within the city, housing for farmworkers is as overpriced and undermaintained as it ever was. Only a handful of growers now provide housing; most farmworkers have to shift for themselves.[4]

East Coast field workers are also distinguished by their ill health. A 1991 study of migrant workers laboring in five North Carolina counties found a 3.6 percent rate of active tuberculosis among African American migrants, more than 300 times the national average. Sixty-two percent of those tested had been exposed to TB. The researchers were quick to point out that this was not an imported problem brought by farmworkers from countries where medical care is a luxury of the very rich; the Latin

American migrants had only a .47 percent active TB rate. The causes of the problem, they concluded, were all homegrown: poverty, poor nutrition, and living conditions as unsanitary and crowded as the sheds and barns that housed Italians on turn-of-the-century cranberry bogs.[5]

Social reformers did not give up their efforts to improve such conditions, despite the demise of the FSA. Advocates for farmworkers, especially church groups, succeeded in winning the Crew Leader Regulation Act in 1963, the Migrant Health Act in 1965, the inclusion of farmworkers in the Fair Labor Standards Act in 1966, and an amendment making them eligible for unemployment insurance in 1977. But all these efforts have been undermined by minimal funding, lax enforcement, and, increasingly, a hostile federal judiciary.

Too much of reformers' attention has been focused, perhaps, on the workings of the crew leader system. Journalistic exposés have highlighted cases of outright enslavement, physical abuse, or crew members kept in debt by supplies of wine or crack. But most growers do not want addicts in their fields any more than turn-of-the-century bog owners wanted small children tearing up their vines. And most farmworkers are not members of "wino crews."[6]

The majority of migrants today, like the Italian families and African American migrants of the Progressive Era, are strivers, self-exploiters, sojourners. They take stereos and televisions back to Jamaica, send remittance checks back to Mexico, and if they stay in the United States, get out of field work as soon as possible. Most migrant farmworkers are too ambitious or too needy to stay long with a crew leader who is physically abusive or who would enslave them in what the *Raleigh News and Observer* called "almost medieval shackles of dependency." These are the sensational stories, the stories meant to shock, to make us pause before we buy a head of lettuce or cut into a tempting tomato. They reveal little about the causes of migrant poverty.[7]

Crew leaders do sometimes pocket workers' unemployment insurance deductions, skim off so much of their pay that they rarely receive the minimum wage, charge farmworkers exorbitant fees for trips to migrant health clinics, and cause deadly accidents by failing to maintain their vehicles. Yet crew leaders are a symptom, not the cause, of farmworkers' troubles. Though they are more destructive than they were when they ruled the berry rows in turn-of-the-century New Jersey, they are only as strong as farmworkers are weak. They become dangerously exploitive when fields are oversupplied with labor and when farmworkers can choose among neither labor contractors nor employers.

It is the supply of labor, not the grip of the padrone, that dictates whether farmworkers will have the power to demand higher pay or improved conditions. Even if crew leader, housing, and health laws were enthusiastically enforced, they would still be undercut by federal immigration policy. And there will never be enough federal and local officials to investigate housing conditions on every farm or check every worker's pay stub to see if the proper piece rate has been paid. Only farmworkers themselves can enforce their own bargains. As long as farmworkers have to compete among themselves for a finite number of poorly paid jobs, however, they will be in a poor position to do so.

Conditions remain dismal, therefore, not because poverty is an inevitable feature of modern agriculture or because crew leaders trap migrants into a new sort of debt peonage. They are dismal because the federal government intervened on behalf of growers, undermining farmworkers' bargaining power and relieving growers of the need to recruit labor by improving wages and conditions.

Not all federal labor supply efforts were intended to be so partisan; the turn-of-the-century Division of Information tried to match labor-hungry growers with unemployed workers but found neutrality an impossibility in a world where workers and employers were not equals. Officials of the Department of Labor's USES tried to supply farmworkers to growers during the First World War on the condition that employers met some minimal standards of pay and housing. They were stymied by southern planters' cries of carpetbaggery and trade unionism.

None of these labor supply efforts were particularly successful both because growers were reluctant to accept the dictates of state managers and because the federal bureaucracy was too skeletal in the early twentieth century to assume control of the nation's farm labor supply and actually meet growers' labor demands. It was easier just to open the border to Mexico in the West and to recommend that planters resort to tried and true methods of labor control in the South.

Federal labor supply efforts only became effective when New Dealers built a vast administrative structure capable of counting, moving, and housing large numbers of workers. Acting on a policy of welfare reform designed to uplift and rehabilitate farmworkers so that they would abandon the migratory life, New Dealers created a reform apparatus on an unprecedented scale. But it was that apparatus, that combination of staff, buildings, media contacts, and operational procedures, that became the foundation for the vast and transformed labor supply efforts of the Second World War. When African American farmworkers tried to turn uplift into empowerment, using labor camps as strike headquarters and federally supplied food and shelter as strike funds, growers' allies in

Congress commandeered the ship of reform. While the wartime U.S. Department of Agriculture filled federal labor camps with foreign workers supplied to growers under fixed-wage, no-strike contracts, Congress made it illegal for any federal funds to be used for the improvement of farmworkers' wages or working conditions. By the end of the war, African Americans, who were still the majority population in the East Coast migrant stream, were returned to obscurity, rendered invisible once again by the more remarkable presence of foreign workers.

The only exception to this story of defeat and displacement was the "underground railroad" that supplied New Jersey growers and canners with labor, with the STFU and the Amalgamated Meat Cutters acting the part of padrone. However trivial this experience was in comparison with the federal labor supply program, it demonstrated that in a tight labor market, with the ability to bargain collectively, farmworkers were able to win higher wages, improved housing, better food, and greater respect—all without striking.

What might have happened if this experience had become the model for postwar farm labor policy, we can scarcely imagine. No great leaders emerged from the ranks of East Coast farm labor in the postwar period, perhaps because those ranks changed so dramatically. Would there have been a farmworker movement in the East if the federal government had not assumed the role of padrone? We will never know. Will there be a farmworker movement so long as the federal government shapes U.S. immigration policy to growers' needs? Probably not. We have seen what farmworkers got for fighting without the right of collective bargaining and without the ability to control the supply of labor: a volley of tear gas, a no-vacancy sign on the door of federal labor camps, a free ticket back to Jamaica. The state that walked unscathed out of the Second World War was a giant among dwarves. Farmworkers can only hope to transform it from a formidable enemy to an unreliable ally. To achieve this would require a revitalized labor movement—organized, vigilant, and sanctioned by law. Without such a movement, farmworkers will never reap the fruits of their labor.

Notes

Abbreviations and Acronyms

In addition to the abbreviations and acronyms found in the text, the following are used in the notes:

Beecher Testimony	John Beecher, Testimony before the Civil Liberties Committee, May 15, 16, 1940. Box 9, file AD-124, region 5, migratory labor, 1940, Record Group 96, National Archives and Records Administration, Washington, D.C.
Dillingham Commission, *Recent Immigrants in Agriculture*	U.S. Senate, Immigration Commission. *Report of the Immigration Commission*. Pt. 24, vols. 21 and 22, *Recent Immigrants in Agriculture*. 61st Cong., 2d and 3d sess. S. Doc. 633. Washington, D.C.: Government Printing Office, 1911.
FLSC	Farm Labor Supply Center
Local 56 Papers	Local 56 of the Amalgamated Meat Cutters and Butcher Workmen Papers
NARA	National Archives and Records Administration, Washington, D.C.
NDMH	U.S. House of Representatives. Select Committee Investigating National Defense Migration. *Hearings*. 77th Cong., 2d sess. Washington, D.C.: Government Printing Office, 1943.
NYT	*New York Times*
RG	Record Group
Robinson and Horne, "Florida Migratory Workers"	Robinson, Aubrey Clyde, and Glenore Fisk Horne. "Florida Migratory Workers." Confidential report to the resettlement administrator, June 1937. Box 9, file AD-124, region 5, migratory labor, 1940, Record Group 96, National Archives and Records Administration, Washington, D.C.

Schachter, "Report"   Schachter, Leon B. "Report on the First Organized Migration of Union Labor through the
Cooperation of Local 56 and the Southern
Tenant Farmers' Union during the Summer of
1944, as a Possible Solution to the Problem of
Migratory Seasonal Labor in the Canning Industry, and as a Means of Organization." Nov.
19, 1944, #3472, box 52, folder 963, Southern
Tenant Farmers' Union Papers, Southern Historical Collection, University of North Carolina, Chapel Hill, N.C.

Tolan Hearings   U.S. House of Representatives. Select Commit-
tee to Investigate the Interstate Migration of
Destitute Citizens (Tolan Committee). *Hear-
ings before the Select Committee to Investigate the
Interstate Migration of Destitute Citizens.* 76th
Cong., 3d sess., 1940–41. Washington, D.C.:
Government Printing Office, 1941.

Introduction

1. This description is taken almost verbatim from Lawrence E. Will, self-proclaimed "cracker historian," but with references to "jigaboos" and "young
bucks" excised from the account. See Will, *Swamp to Sugar Bowl*, pp. 189–93. See
also Robinson and Horne, "Florida Migratory Workers."

2. Will, *Swamp to Sugar Bowl*; Beecher Testimony, pp. 23–24.

3. Will, *Swamp to Sugar Bowl*.

4. The best known of these authors are the economist Paul Taylor and his
student Carey McWilliams. In *On the Ground in the Thirties*, Taylor wrote up the
research he did as an expert witness for the 1939 LaFollette hearings, which
documented the exploitation of farmworkers on the West Coast. McWilliams,
who assisted in that inquiry, probably reached a wider audience with his *Factories
in the Field* and *Ill Fares the Land*. Author of several books, including the brilliantly
titled *Spiders in the House and Workers in the Field*, Ernesto Galarza was a farm labor
unionist in California. See also Moore, *Slaves We Rent*; Dale Wright, *They Harvest
Despair*; and, more recently, Jones, *The Dispossessed*, pp. 167–204.

5. See, for example, Radosh and Rothbard, *New History of Leviathan*.

6. Polantzas, *Political Power and Social Classes*; Skocpol, *States and Social Revolutions*.

7. Tomlins, *The State and the Unions*, pp. xiii–xiv.

8. Skocpol, "Political Responses to Capitalist Crisis" and *Protecting Soldiers and
Mothers*; Finegold, "From Agrarianism to Adjustment"; Hooks, "From an Autonomous to a Captured State Agency."

9. Linda Gordon, *Pitied but Not Entitled*; Gilbert and Howe, "Beyond 'State vs.
Society.' "

10. On the relationship between the state and white supremacy, see, for example, Quadagno, *Transformation of Old Age Social Security* and *Color of Welfare*. On the gendered nature of the Social Security Act, see the extended Internet debate on H-State between April 19 and April 24, 1995.

11. Calavita makes this point clearly in *Inside the State*.

12. The symbiotic relationship between the USDA and the American Farm Bureau Federation has been well documented by Gladys L. Baker, *County Agent*; Campbell, *Farm Bureau and the New Deal*; and McConnell, *Decline of Agrarian Democracy*.

13. Other historians have already demonstrated the problems caused by a federal department of agriculture so intimately tied to growers' lobbies. See, for example, McConnell, *Decline of Agrarian Democracy*, and Campbell, *Farm Bureau and the New Deal*.

14. Miriam Cohen, e-mail communication, Aug. 5, 1994, H-State list.

15. See, for example, Edward Berkowitz's critique of those who focus exclusively on race and gender when discussing the state, Apr. 19, 1995, H-State list, Internet.

Chapter One

1. Wolf, *Europe and the People without History*, pp. 354–84; Hobsbawm, *Age of Empire*, pp. 112–41.

2. Coulter, *Industrial History of the Valley*.

3. Shannon, *Farmer's Last Frontier*, p. 158; Coulter, *Industrial History of the Valley*, p. 48.

4. Shannon, *Farmer's Last Frontier*, p. 246.

5. Danhof, "Agricultural Technology," pp. 140–41.

6. Ibid., pp. 141–45.

7. Ibid., p. 145.

8. Ibid., p. 146.

9. Shannon, *Farmer's Last Frontier*, p. 159.

10. Coulter, *Industrial History of the Valley*, p. 62; *World To-Day* 8 (1905): 162; *Harper's New Monthly Magazine* 60, no. 358 (1869): 530.

11. *Harper's New Monthly Magazine* 60, no. 358 (1869): 532, 535.

12. Ross, "Expansion of Agriculture," p. 388; U.S. Bureau of the Census, *11th Census, Agriculture*, p. 6; U.S. Bureau of the Census, *12th Census*, vol. 6, *Agriculture*, pt. 2, plate no. 3; Morison et al., *Concise History of the American Republic*, pp. 424, 426; Shannon, *Farmer's Last Frontier*, p. 154.

13. Shannon, *Farmer's Last Frontier*, p. 154.

14. Coulter, *Industrial History of the Valley*, p. 64.

15. Shannon, *Farmer's Last Frontier*, p. 245.

16. U.S. Bureau of the Census, *11th Census*, pp. 1–2; Shannon, *Farmer's Last Frontier*, p. 246.

17. Connecticut Board of Agriculture, "Past and Future of Connecticut Agriculture," p. 165; "The Labor Question in Massachusetts," *Nation*, June 8, 1871,

p. 398; *Century Magazine* 48 (1894): 30, 792; New Jersey State Board of Agriculture, *Annual Report*, 1890–91, p. 395.

18. *Century Magazine* 48 (1894): 30, 792.

19. *Cosmopolitan Magazine* 15 (1883): 220.

20. Agriculturalists usually distinguish between "market gardeners," who produce a variety of crops, and "truck farmers," who concentrate on a single product adapted to local conditions. However, contemporaries rarely drew this distinction, so I have not. See Shannon, *Farmer's Last Frontier*, p. 260.

21. New Jersey State Board of Agriculture, *Annual Report*, 1874, p. 341; ibid., 1904, p. 108.

22. Ibid., 1874.

23. Ibid.

24. Ibid., 1882, p. 32; Massey, "Development of Marketing Gardening."

25. In the 1850s steamers ran from Savannah, Charleston, and Norfolk to northern ports, but the vegetables and fruits they carried amounted to only a few hundred packages a year. The sluggish pace of ocean transport inhibited further expansion of the industry because the longer it took to make a journey along the coast, the more bruised and decayed the produce would be when it finally arrived at its destination. Shipments to the North resumed in 1866, but not until the consolidation of the South's fragmentary railroads into great systems in the 1880s were northern markets made truly accessible to southern growers of perishable crops. See Earle, "Development of Trucking Interests," pp. 439–40.

26. On the rule rather than the exception, see C. Van Woodward, *Origins of the New South*, pp. 179–80.

27. Massey, "Development of Marketing Gardening," pp. 144–45.

28. Bruce, *Rise of the New South*, p. 64; Andrew M. Soule, "Vegetable, Fruit, and Nursery Products," p. 127.

29. Andrew M. Soule, "Vegetable, Fruit, and Nursery Products," pp. 146–48.

30. Although vegetables were extremely valuable to individual southern farmers, in the South as a whole they were worth only 8 percent of the total crop value. See Andrew M. Soule, "Vegetable, Fruit, and Nursery Products," pp. 130, 155, and Shannon, *Farmer's Last Frontier*, pp. 123–24.

31. Hourwich, *Immigration and Labor*, pp. 104–8, and Wallace, *Rockdale*.

32. New Jersey State Board of Agriculture, *Annual Report*, 1891, p. 28; USIC, *Reports*, 10:82–99, 124.

33. Cox, "American Agricultural Wage Earner," pp. 97–99.

34. U.S. Department of Labor, "Hand and Machine Labor," pp. 25, 91, 93.

35. Ibid.

36. Testimony of Franklin Dye, secretary of the New Jersey State Board of Agriculture, USIC, *Reports*, 10:82–83.

37. Cox, "Agricultural Labor in the United States," p. 11.

38. Ibid., pp. 29–35.

39. Between 1876 and 1914 7.5 million Italians emigrated to the United States, more than from any other country during this period of peak immigration. See Starr, *Italians of New Jersey*, pp. 3–5.

40. Iorizzo and Mondello, *Italian Americans*, pp. 19, 58; Starr, *Italians of New Jersey*, p. 3.

41. On their arrival in the United States, Italians were set, quite literally, to deepening the foundations of American industry. They were so often hired to lay track, dig ditches, and excavate tunnels that the *sciabola*, the shovel, became the symbol of Italian immigrant workers. See Vecoli, "Italian American Workers," p. 26; Cinel, "Seasonal Emigrations of Italians," pp. 48–50; Bodnar, *Transplanted*, p. 45.

42. Starr, *Italians of New Jersey*, pp. 11–12; New Jersey, *Report of the New Jersey Commission of Immigration*, p. 33; Schuyler, "Italian Immigration in the United States," p. 481, cited in Cinel, "Seasonal Emigrations of Italians," p. 43.

43. Cinel, "Seasonal Emigrations of Italians," pp. 52–60.

44. John Bodnar shows, for example, that between 1890 and 1916 a family of five living in Buffalo, New York, needed an income of $650 to $752 a year simply to subsist, but the average Italian laborer earned only $364 to $624. See Bodnar, *Transplanted*, pp. 75–6; see also Caroline Manning, *Immigrant Woman and Her Job*, pp. 46–49.

45. U.S. Commissioner Carroll D. Wright's 1893 study of immigrant communities in Philadelphia found that the earnings of women and children nearly doubled their families' incomes. The average male wage in "the slums" of Philadelphia was $9.54 a week, or under $500 a year; however, the average family wage was $19.01, or $988 a year. See Carroll D. Wright, *Slums of Baltimore, Chicago, New York, and Philadelphia*, pp. 59–64; Caroline Manning, *Immigrant Woman and Her Job*, pp. 12, 22, 39; Van Kleeck, *Artificial Flower-Makers*, pp. 94–95; Bodnar, *Transplanted*, p. 79.

46. Italians represented 75 percent of the women working in the men's and boy's clothing industry and 93 percent of the women doing hand embroidery in New York City. Seasonality in the garment- and hat-making industries remained a problem well into the 1940s. See Bodnar, *Transplanted*, p. 64; Van Kleeck, *Artificial Flower-Makers*, pp. 40–51; Greig, *Seasonal Fluctuations in Employment*; Caroline Manning, *Immigrant Woman and Her Job*, pp. 3–4, 100–102.

47. There is no way to estimate the numbers of Italian immigrants who worked in South Jersey's fields. Because the census was taken in spring, census takers would find berry pickers in the tenements of Philadelphia and New York, not in New Jersey's berry fields and bogs. The timing of the census has long been an obstacle to those who have sought to estimate numbers of migrant workers. Year-round farmworkers appear in the census, but migrant workers are statistically invisible. This leaves us, unfortunately, with contemporaries' estimates of the number of berry pickers.

48. Keyssar, *Out of Work*, p. 157; Dillingham Commission, *Recent Immigrants in Agriculture*, 21:71, 22:522–23.

49. Dillingham Commission, *Recent Immigrants in Agriculture*, 22:523.

50. Ibid.

51. Carroll D. Wright, *Slums of Baltimore, Chicago, New York, and Philadelphia*, p. 66. See also Caroline Manning, *Immigrant Woman and Her Job*, p. 46, and Keyssar, *Out of Work*, p. 112.

52. Dillingham Commission, *Recent Immigrants in Agriculture*, 21:70, 101.

53. Gavin Wright, *Old South, New South*, p. 65.

54. USIC, *Reports*, 10:19. See also Cox, "American Agricultural Wage Earner," p. 109.

55. Mandle, *Not Slave, Not Free*, p. 26.

56. Giles R. Wright, *Afro-Americans in New Jersey*, pp. 13–15; Price, *Freedom Not Far Distant*, p. 131; New Jersey Conference of Social Work, *Negro in New Jersey*, p. 17.

57. Mandle, *Not Slave, Not Free*, pp. 21–32, contains a useful discussion of why more African Americans did not venture north prior to the First World War. Gavin Wright argues that the U.S. labor force was divided along sectional lines but does not explain why southerners did not cross that invisible line and seek higher wages in the North prior to the First World War. See Gavin Wright, *Old South, New South*.

58. U.S. Bureau of the Census, *12th Census*, vol. 47, *New Jersey*, Middlesex County.

59. New Jersey State Board of Agriculture, *Annual Report*, 1904, p. 315; USIC, *Reports*, 10:124, 132–34, and 11:90–91.

60. Giles R. Wright, *Afro-Americans in New Jersey*, p. 46; Foster, "Institutional Development in the Black Community," pp. 34–35; New Jersey Conference of Social Work, *Negro in New Jersey*, p. 25.

61. More women than men settled permanently. As a result, in 1910 there were 1,000 black women to every 945 men, and most came from Virginia and the Carolinas. See New Jersey Conference of Social Work, *Negro in New Jersey*, pp. 19–20.

62. Giles R. Wright, *Afro-Americans in New Jersey*, p. 45, and New Jersey Conference of Social Work, "Survey of Negro Life in New Jersey," Community Report no. 13.

63. U.S. Bureau of the Census, *12th Census*, vol. 47, *New Jersey*, Middlesex County; New Jersey Conference of Social Work, "Survey of Negro Life in New Jersey," Community Report no. 23.

64. The African American death rate from tuberculosis was four times higher than the white rate. See New Jersey Conference of Social Work, *Negro in New Jersey*, 43.

65. By 1932 the illiteracy rate for the state as a whole was only 3.8 percent and for its black population 5.1 percent. In Bloomfield, just above Newark, where most black residents worked as domestic servants, the illiteracy rate among African Americans was actually 2.1 percent lower than the rate of the town as a whole. When, in 1932, the Interracial Committee of the New Jersey Conference of Social Work surveyed 81 black residents of Monmouth County who had graduated from high school over the previous five years, they found that 13 of the 27 men were attending normal school or college. Of the 14 who were working, 1 worked as a postal clerk, 1 was employed in a New York bank, 1 was an undertaker, and another was trying to get money to go back to college. Of the 54 women surveyed, 11 were attending college, 12 were housewives, 6 were teach-

ing, 11 were nursing, and 11 were "working." See New Jersey Conference of Social Work, "Survey of Negro Life in New Jersey," Community Reports nos. 8 and 13.

66. Price, *Freedom Not Far Distant*, p. 191.

67. New Jersey State Board of Agriculture, *Annual Report*, 1904, p. 99.

68. Maine Board of Agriculture, *Report*, 1881, p. 39, quoted in Cox, "Agricultural Labor in the U.S.," p. 15.

69. Cox, "Agricultural Labor in the United States," p. 16.

70. New Jersey State Board of Agriculture, *Annual Report*, 1904, p. 108.

Chapter Two

1. The reformers who chose New Jersey berry pickers as their cause were members of what Mary Furner calls the "democratic collectivist" school of progressive reform. Unlike "voluntarists," who promoted collective bargaining and opposed government intervention because they thought that industrial order would best be achieved through voluntary cooperation between capital and labor, democratic collectivists advocated a positive state role in the regulation of corporations and in efforts to protect the rights of labor. See Furner, *Knowing Capitalism*; see also Wunderlin, *Visions of a New Industrial Order*.

2. In 1905 the Philadelphia and New Jersey consumers' leagues published the results of their investigation of working and living conditions on the bogs, and five years later the National Child Labor Committee reinvestigated the industry. The National Consumers' League was founded in 1882 by reformers who sought to use consumer boycotts to bring about broad social reforms. Unlike other groups that sought to improve the healthfulness and safety of products for consumers' sake, the National Consumers' League promoted boycotts of products whose manufacturers failed to safeguard the health and safety of the workers they hired. In 1911 the Child Labor Committee undertook a more thorough investigation in light of growers' charges of libel and exaggeration, only to uncover the same conditions reported the year before. In response to their complaints, the State of New Jersey created a commission of its own (the Commission of Immigration), which investigated sixteen bogs and held hearings at which both growers and representatives of the Child Labor Committee testified. In the same year a federal commission on immigration, the United States Immigration Commission, chaired by Republican Senator William P. Dillingham of Vermont, published the results of its massive study of recent immigrants in the United States, including in its forty-one-volume report extensive information on the conditions of work in New Jersey's berry fields and bogs. Together these commissions and inquiries provide the main sources of information on migrant farmworkers in turn-of-the-century New Jersey. See New Jersey, *Report of the New Jersey Commission of Immigration*; Dillingham Commission, *Recent Immigrants in Agriculture*; Markham et al., *Children in Bondage*, pp. 188, 190, 199–202; Ginger, "In Berry Field and Bog," p. 166.

3. Richard P. McCormick, "Historical Overview," p. 10.

4. Dillingham Commission, *Recent Immigrants in Agriculture*, 22:493; Chute, "Cost of the Cranberry Sauce."

5. Lipari, " 'Padrone System' "; Koren, "Padrone System and Padrone Banks."

6. Ginger, "In Berry Field and Bog," pp. 163–64; Dillingham Commission, *Recent Immigrants in Agriculture*, 22:493–520.

7. Dillingham Commission, *Recent Immigrants in Agriculture*, 22:493; New Jersey, *Report of the New Jersey Commission of Immigration*, pp. 36–37; Ginger, "In Berry Field and Bog"; New Jersey State Board of Agriculture, *Annual Report*, 1904, p. 112.

8. Dillingham Commission, *Recent Immigrants in Agriculture*, 21:70, 100; Ginger, "In Berry Field and Bog."

9. Dillingham Commission, *Recent Immigrants in Agriculture*, 22:528; Ginger, "In Berry Field and Bog," pp. 166–67; New Jersey, *Report of the New Jersey Commission of Immigration*, pp. 36–37.

10. Ginger, "In Berry Field and Bog," pp. 166–67.

11. On the seventeen bogs visited by the National Child Labor Committee, 32 percent of the pickers were under age fourteen and 18 percent were under age ten, and on twelve bogs a number of children under five worked as well. See Chute, "Cost of the Cranberry Sauce," p. 1283; Ginger, "In Berry Field and Bog," p. 166; New Jersey, *Report of the New Jersey Commission of Immigration*, p. 38; Dillingham Commission, *Recent Immigrants in Agriculture*, 22:528.

12. Markham et al., *Children in Bondage.* pp. 190, 199–202; Ginger, "In Berry Field and Bog," p. 166.

13. Ginger, "In Berry Field and Bog," p. 164.

14. Chute, "Cost of the Cranberry Sauce," p. 1283.

15. Ginger, "In Berry Field and Bog," p. 166.

16. Ginger tracked fifty children aged six to fourteen who worked in the strawberry section. She discovered that by October 5 only twenty-four had returned to their classrooms. See ibid., pp. 166, 188.

17. Ibid., p. 166. See also Chute, "Cost of the Cranberry Sauce," pp. 1281–82, and Markham et al., *Children in Bondage*, pp. 185–204.

18. With the exception of Dino Cinel, historians have also treated the padrone system as a peculiarity of Italian immigration. See Cinel, "Seasonal Emigrations of Italians," pp. 48–50.

19. Vecoli, "Italian American Workers"; Lipari, " 'Padrone System' "; Juliani, "Italian Community in Philadelphia"; Koren, "Padrone System and Padrone Banks."

20. The Italian berry growers of Vineland and Hammonton tended to keep their farms small (their average acreage was fifteen) in order to avoid the need for outside labor. The Dillingham Commission estimated that berry farms under twenty-five acres could be managed without hired help. See Dillingham Commission, *Recent Immigrants in Agriculture*, 21:95–98.

21. For their services most bosses were paid wages, and some received a commission on each bushel picked. See Dillingham Commission, *Recent Immigrants*

in Agriculture, 22:524; Chute, "Cost of the Cranberry Sauce"; New Jersey State Board of Agriculture, *Annual Report*, 1904, p. 112.

22. Dillingham Commission, *Recent Immigrants in Agriculture*, 22:524–30.

23. New Jersey State Board of Agriculture, *Annual Report*, 1904, pp. 112–13.

24. Dillingham Commission, *Recent Immigrants in Agriculture*, 22:524.

25. European emigration to the United States was virtually cut off during the First World War, and it was limited by law after 1924. But when New Jersey's Department of Labor surveyed the berry-picking population in 1930, it found 567 Italian families on 214 farms. These berry pickers were not the children of Italians who had entered the country in the late nineteenth century; all but two of the men and one of the women were born in southern Italy. They too worked with their children alongside them, but ultimately they and their children would move on to other work. See New Jersey Department of Labor, *Why New Jersey Farmers Employ Italian Family Labor.*

26. New Jersey, *Report of the New Jersey Commission of Immigration.*

27. Hall et al., *Like a Family*, pp. 96–97.

28. Dillingham Commission, *Recent Immigrants in Agriculture*, 22:525.

29. Ginger, "In Berry Field and Bog," pp. 167–69.

30. Chute, "Cost of the Cranberry Sauce," p. 1283.

31. *Survey*, Jan. 11, 1913, p. 485.

32. Long after the decline of the progressive movement, self-appointed advocates for migrant children continued to press for prohibitions against child labor in agriculture. In 1927 they finally succeeded in bringing a bill to the New Jersey state assembly designed to prohibit the employment of out-of-state children in agriculture during the school year. When the bill was defeated, the Pennsylvania Bureau of Women and Children made an investigation of Philadelphia children working on New Jersey farms, which resulted in a new bill. This one was also defeated. New Jersey finally passed a law at the height of the depression in 1937 restricting children from working in the fields during school hours, only to repeal it when growers complained of labor scarcity during the Second World War. See New Jersey Assembly no. 182, Feb. 7, 1927, and Assembly no. 32, Jan. 16, 1928, in New Jersey, *Report of the Commission to Investigate the Employment of Migratory Children*, p. 3; "Employment of Philadelphia Children at Farm Labor."

33. USIC, *Reports*, 10:82–99; New Jersey State Board of Agriculture, *Annual Report*, 1904, p. 112.

34. New Jersey State Board of Agriculture, *Annual Report*, 1904, pp. 98–99.

35. "In the Berry Fields of New Jersey," *Charities and the Commons*, Sept. 1, 1906, p. 531.

36. Growers were still defending their use of child labor in 1930. In that year the American Cranberry Growers' Association asked New Jersey's Department of Labor to undertake a new study, which resulted in the report *Why New Jersey Farmers Employ Italian Family Labor.* The report, submitted to the governor in 1931, did no more than reveal that in fifty years little had changed in New Jersey agriculture. The perishability of vegetable and fruit crops required "steady,

reliable and experienced forces" to pick the crops the day they were ready, the report concluded, and according to the 101 farmers interviewed, local help was insufficient. Alongside the hundreds of Italian men and women at work in the fields, the Department of Labor found 1,342 children between the ages of six and fifteen. See New Jersey Department of Labor, *Why New Jersey Farmers Employ Italian Farm Labor*; New Jersey, *Report of the New Jersey Commission of Immigration*, p. 36.

Chapter Three

1. Bowers, *Country-Life Movement.*

2. *Survey*, Oct. 7, 1911, p. 927.

3. Tosti, "Agricultural Possibilities of Italian Immigration," p. 472; *Survey*, Apr. 17, 1909, p. 112; Carey, "Progressives and the Immigrants," p. 28.

4. Furner, *Knowing Capitalism*, chap. 8; USIC, *Reports*, vol. 10.

5. USIC, *Reports*, 10:xviii and 11:79–80 (emphasis mine). At the same time, the report conceded that, at $215 a year, agricultural workers were "the lowest paid of all the great groups of occupations."

6. Ibid., 10:viii.

7. Though a decade later the Dillingham Commission interviewed hundreds of farmworkers, the USIC's members made no visits to farms or labor camps and did not attempt to bring farmworkers to testify.

8. USIC, *Reports*, 11:79.

9. Ibid., 11:73.

10. Ibid., 11:87 and 10:62, 66.

11. To strengthen his argument, Brown noted that "no man in the State . . . lives under pleasanter relations with the negro than I do, and I work a good many of them" (ibid., 10:xiv, xiii, cxxxii–cxxxiii, and 62).

12. Ibid., 11:73.

13. Carey counts among supporters of labor distribution Mary McDowell, Florence Kelly, Jane Addams, Lillian Wald, and other notables in the reform world. See Carey, "Progressives and the Immigrants," pp. 108–10.

14. Tosti, "Agricultural Possibilities of Italian Immigration."

15. *Survey* 25 (1911): 587.

16. Ibid., p. 589.

17. Emily Fogg Meade, "The Italian Immigrant on the Land," *Charities and the Commons* 13 (1905) 544, 595.

18. *NYT*, July 23, 1905.

19. *Survey* 25 (1911): 594.

20. Tosti, "Agricultural Possibilities of Italian Immigration," p. 474 (emphasis his).

21. *Survey* 25 (1911): 594.

22. Alice Bennett, "Italian-American Farmers," *Survey* 22 (1909): 173. See also Claghorn, "Protection and Distribution of Immigrants"; Weyl, "Immigration and Industrial Saturation"; Senner, "Immigration from Italy."

23. Claghorn, "Protection and Distribution of Immigrants."

24. Charles B. Phipard, "The Philanthropist-Padrone," *Charities and the Commons* 12 (1904): 470–72.

25. *NYT*, Feb. 11, 13, 1909.

26. Carey, "Progressives and the Immigrants," pp. 674–77.

27. Ibid., p. 111.

28. On November 26 of that same year, President Roosevelt, evidently in reaction to reformers' lobbying, suggested to Secretary of Agriculture James Wilson that he inquire into the practicability of organizing the distribution of immigrants among farmers. See Letters Sent by the Secretary's Office, 1893–1941, RG 16, NARA. On the relationship between the panic of 1907 and the renewed concern for labor distribution, see "A Great Emergency," New York City Charity Organization Society *Bulletin*, Mar. 4, 1914, p. 1, cited in Carey, "Progressives and the Immigrants," p. 111.

29. Report of the Commission-General of Immigration, 1908, p. 173, quoted in Lombardi, *Labor's Voice in the Cabinet*, p. 144. See also Babson, *W. B. Wilson and the Department of Labor*, and Jonathan P. Grossman, *Department of Labor*. On the first labor exchanges, see Terrell, *United States Department of Labor*; Sautter, *Three Cheers for the Unemployed*; Shelby M. Harrison, *Public Employment Offices*.

30. For an extended discussion of state and federal efforts to alleviate unemployment before the New Deal, see Sautter, *Three Cheers for the Unemployed*. Sautter argues that the creation of the Division of Information was motivated by antinativist sentiment, not by concern for the unemployed.

31. Agitation for a department of labor with executive status began immediately after the Civil War. In 1868 the National Labor Union Congress passed the first recorded resolution calling for a labor department and cabinet post in New York City. A bureau of labor statistics was established within the Department of the Interior in 1884, and in 1888 an independent Department of Labor was created, though without Cabinet rank. See Lombardi, *Labor's Voice in the Cabinet*, pp. 15–74.

32. Straus, *Under Four Administrations*, quoted in Lombardi, *Labor's Voice in the Cabinet*, p. 60. On Terence V. Powderly and the Knights of Labor, see Fink, *Workingmen's Democracy*; Powderly, *Path I Trod*; Falzone, *Terence V. Powderly*.

33. Martin and Gelber, *Dictionary of American History*, p. 466.

34. *NYT*, Sept. 16, 1907.

35. *NYT*, Sept. 29, 1907.

36. Lombardi, *Labor's Voice in the Cabinet*, p. 146.

37. Ibid., pp. 147–48.

38. Ibid., pp. 148–49, 151.

39. Powderly felt so constrained by his opponents that when, in December 1909, he was invited by members of the American Civic Alliance to address them on the question of labor distribution, he declined "because I might be accused of undue activity in opposing the wishes of someone" (Green to Powderly, Dec. 11, 1909, reel 80, Powderly Papers). Unfortunately most of the papers from Powderly's Division of Information years are letters congratulating him on his appointment or letters from men seeking similar federal positions. The papers

reveal little of Powderly's activities and views during his tenure as chief of the Information Division.

40. Lombardi, *Labor's Voice in the Cabinet*, p. 145.

41. Secretary James Wilson's private secretary to Mr. C. A. Schweizer, Okawville, Ill., Letters Sent by the Secretary's Office, 1893–1941, 132:73, and to William Morgan, July 1, 1909, 131:429, both in RG 16, NARA. See also letters dated July 3, 1909, 131:466; July 2, 14, 1909, 132:73; July 3, 1910, 136:459; July 8, 1910, 137:39; Aug. 25, 1910, 142:91.

42. Dillingham Commission, *Recent Immigrants in Agriculture*, 21:13–14, 40.

43. *NYT*, Aug. 14, 1913.

44. Parker, *Casual Laborer*, p. 65.

45. No one was indicted for the murder of the two hops pickers. For accounts of these events, see Parker, *Casual Laborer*; Cletus Daniel, *Bitter Harvest*, pp. 88–90.

46. From the preamble to the 1905 IWW convention, reproduced in Kornbluh, *Rebel Voices*, p. 12.

47. CIR, "Land Question and the Condition of Agricultural Labor," in *Final Report* (known as the Manly Report after Basil M. Manly, director of research and investigation), pp. 86–89.

48. For more on the ideology and intent of the USIC and the CIR, see Furner, *Knowing Capitalism*; Wunderlin, *Visions of a New Industrial Order*; Adams, *Age of Industrial Violence*.

49. CIR, *Final Report*, p. 101.

50. Ibid., pp. 114–15.

51. Adams, *Age of Industrial Violence*.

52. *Southern Cultivator*, May 1, 1917. Advertised as "A Real Farm Paper" and "The Representative of Southern Agriculture," the *Southern Cultivator* was a bimonthly paper published in Atlanta, Georgia.

Chapter Four

1. Walter White's Report on Florida, reel 23, Papers of the NAACP.

2. For a similar account of white southern reaction to the Great Migration, see James R. Grossman, "Black Labor Is the Best Labor." Grossman and I differ on the timing of the various reactions to black migration and on the federal role in southern farm labor relations during the war.

3. Genung, "Agriculture in the World War Period," p. 276.

4. Litwack, *Been in the Storm So Long*; Cohen, *At Freedom's Edge*; C. Mildred Thompson, *Reconstruction in Georgia*; Eric Foner, *Reconstruction*; Jaynes, *Branches without Roots*.

5. Lombardi, *Labor's Voice in the Cabinet*.

6. The May 1914 law was the Smith-Lever Act. See Gladys L. Baker, *County Agent*; McCune, *Farm Bloc*; Gaus and Wolcott, *Public Administration and the U.S.D.A.*

7. Mandel introduction, pp. 66–67; Marx, *Capital*, pp. 274–75.

8. Thanks to Alex Lichtenstein for suggesting this term.

9. Coleman, *History of Georgia*, p. 261.

10. Dittmer, *Black Georgia*, pp. 23–24.

11. Woofter, "Migration of Negroes from Georgia," p. 28.

12. Ibid., p. 18.

13. Woofter's 1920 study of African American population movements in Georgia shows that, before 1910, changes in black population at the county level correspond to opportunities for land ownership. See ibid., pp. 106–17.

14. Both cited in Gaston, "Negro Wage Earner in Georgia," pp. 133, 177.

15. Ibid., pp. 170–72; Berthoff, "Southern Attitudes toward Immigration."

16. *Georgia Laws, 1903*, no. 394, pp. 46–47, and no. 307, pp. 91–92; *Southern Cultivator*, Dec. 1, 1912, quoted in Gaston, "Negro Wage Earner in Georgia," p. 130. On the widespread movement to reenact labor control measures, see Cohen, *At Freedom's Edge*, p. 239.

17. Besides nullifying the principle that a defendant is innocent until proven guilty, this law violated the most basic tenet of contract law: the notion that contracts are made to be broken and that those who break them are liable only for the damage caused to the other party. In 1911 the U.S. Supreme Court struck down as unconstitutional a virtually identical law in Alabama, but Georgia's courts refused to consider the law nullified and continued to enforce it until the 1940s. See Gaston, "Negro Wage Earner in Georgia," pp. 142–43.

18. Lynching peaked in most other states between 1880 and 1900 and declined thereafter, but white Georgians lynched more African Americans after 1900 than before. See Dittmer, *Black Georgia*, p. 131, and Brundage, *Lynching in the New South*.

19. Gavin Wright, *Old South, New South*; Cohen, *At Freedom's Edge*.

20. Southern farm wages peaked in 1860 and 1880, but generally over the course of the nineteenth century they fell in relation to northern farm wages. In 1899 farm wages in Georgia and South Carolina were just over 50 percent of northern farm wages. See Lebergott, *Manpower in Economic Growth*, p. 539, and Gavin Wright, *Old South, New South*, pp. 75–78.

21. In 1914 over a million immigrants entered the country, but the next year they were followed by just 300,000 new arrivals. Almost half a million immigrants returned home between 1915 and 1918. See U.S. Bureau of Immigration, *Annual Reports of the Commissioner-General of Immigration*.

22. On early twentieth-century black migration, see James R. Grossman, *Land of Hope*; Fligstein, *Going North*; Gottlieb, *Making Their Own Way*; Florette, *Black Migration*; Johnson and Campbell, *Black Migration in America*; Jones, *Labor of Love, Labor of Sorrow*, p. 156; Kirby, "Southern Exodus"; Meier and Rudwick, *From Plantation to Ghetto*; and, more recently, Trotter, *Great Migration in Historical Perspective*, and Alferdteen Harrison, *Black Exodus*. See also U.S. Bureau of the Census, *Negroes in the United States*, p. 25.

23. The outbreak of the war was devastating for cotton producers. Indeed, cotton commodity exchanges shut down to prevent a market crash in the fall of 1914. As a result, labor demand was low, and the effects of this out-migration were not immediately felt. The temporary closing of cotton markets left Georgia

planters sitting on the biggest cotton crop in the state's history, and the price of cotton plummeted from 14 cents to just 6 cents a pound. The international market for cotton was soon reorganized, and prices began to rise. See Hibbard, *Effects of the Great War on Agriculture*, p. 44.

24. Finney, "Study of Negro Labor."

25. Ibid., pp. 73–77; U.S. Department of Labor, *Negro Migration*, p. 121.

26. U.S. Department of Labor, *Negro Migration*, p. 108.

27. Finney, "Study of Negro Labor," p. 78.

28. Ibid., pp. 84–94.

29. U.S. Department of Labor, *Negro Migration*, p. 80.

30. *Congressional Record*, vol. 56, pt. 2, 65th Cong., 2d sess., Jan. 25, 1918, p. 1256.

31. The *Florida Times-Union* reported that potato growers in St. Johns County, Florida, made so much money in 1917 that "they are fitting their farms up with city conveniences." Seventy farmers had abandoned lamps for electric lights in their homes, a display of "the right spirit," according to the *Times-Union*, and evidence that St. Johns County would have "no trouble keeping the boys and girls on the farm" (*Manufacturers Record*, Aug. 2, 1917).

32. *Southern Cultivator*, July 1, 1917.

33. U.S. Department of Labor, *Negro Migration*, p. 99.

34. The one advantage to this situation, according to the *Record*, was that income from the peanut crop would belong to the grower instead of "so much of it going to the colored hands" (*Manufacturers Record*, Nov. 8, 1917).

35. *Southern Cultivator*, Jan. 1, Feb. 15, 1918, Nov. 15, 1917, and July 15, 1918.

36. Williams, "Negro Exodus from the South"; Woofter, "Migration of Negroes from Georgia," pp. 78–98.

37. Woofter, "Migration of Negroes from Georgia."

38. Wertenbaker, *Norfolk*, p. 286.

39. Ibid., pp. 306–8. See also Earl Lewis, *In Their Own Interest*.

40. The Eastern Shore region shipped approximately 3 million barrels of early potatoes to northeastern markets in 1916. See *Manufacturers Record*, July 19, 1917.

41. *Virginian-Pilot*, Jan. 29, Feb. 2, 3, 5, 1918; Wertenbaker, *Norfolk*, p. 307.

42. Wertenbaker, *Norfolk*, pp. 306–8; Earl Lewis, *In Their Own Interest*.

43. In 1917 Georgia, USES field workers found adequate numbers of workers in both rural and urban districts, although they reported that they could "find many instances of individual employers who need more Negro labor." T. J. Woofter Jr., an investigator for the Department of Labor's Bureau of Negro Economics, found farm labor "disturbed only in spots" in Georgia. See U.S. Department of Labor, *Negro Migration*, pp. 12–13, 77; Ready, "Georgia's Entry into World War I"; Dittmer, *Black Georgia*, pp. 23–24.

44. W. J. Spillman identifies the postwar course of the East Coast migrant stream in *Farm Management*, p. 381.

45. *Manufacturers Record*, Nov. 8, 1917.

46. Charles Lewis, "Thirty Cent Cotton and the Negro." This particular ac-

count has been cited by other historians as proof of black prosperity during the war. It is rarely substantiated or corroborated with other observations. Robert Higgs uses this anecdote uncritically, though he criticizes other historians for making broad assertions without factual evidence. See Higgs, "Boll Weevil," and Tindall, *Emergence of the New South*.

47. *Manufacturers Record*, Jan. 10, 1918.

48. Ibid., June 15, 1917.

49. Ibid., July 1, 1917.

50. Ibid., Aug. 30, 1917.

51. Cited in *Savannah Tribune*, May 26, 1917.

52. Ibid., Jan. 13, 1917.

53. *Manufacturers Record*, Sept. 13, 1917.

54. Ibid. Sept. 13, 15, 1917. In nearby Jacksonville, Florida, the city council passed an ordinance requiring agents to pay a $1,000 license fee. Soliciting labor without such a license could be punished by a $600 fine and sixty days in a workhouse. See Finney, "Study of Negro Labor," p. 80.

55. Memorandum of Understanding Concerning Cooperation Between the U.S.D.L and the U.S.D.A. in Securing Labor for Farm Work During the Crisis Arising from the Entrance of the United States in the European War, Apr. 24, 1917, general correspondence, box 402, file Labor-laborers (1917), RG 16, NARA.

56. Acting secretary to Mr. Charles McCarthy, May 23, 1917, Letters Sent by the Secretary's Office, RG 16, NARA, 1:207.

57. Box 3, file 54200/2 (New York Zone), RG 85, NARA.

58. Director of employment to the commissioner-general, May 1, 1917, box 3, file 54200/4 (Baltimore), RG 85, NARA.

59. Lewis Bryant, commissioner, to A. Caminetti, commissioner-general, May 24, 1917, box 3, file 54200/21 (New Jersey), RG 85, NARA.

60. Ibid., file 54200/3 (Philadelphia).

61. Mr. Harrison to R. A. Pearson, assistant to the secretary of agriculture, June 18, 1917, general correspondence, box 402, file Labor-laborers (1917), RG 16, NARA.

62. *Manufacturers Record*, Mar. 28, 1918; *World's Work*, quoted in *Southern Cultivator*, July 1, 1917; memo of Louis F. Post to E. Goyle, Apr. 4, 1919, quoted in Finney, "Study of Negro Labor," pp. 102–3. See also "End Labor Competition: Concerns Warned to Stop Large Advertising for Workers," *NYT*, Jan. 23, 1918.

63. Louis Post was assistant secretary of labor and responsible for the department's labor supply effort. A single-taxer and close friend of Henry George, Post was cofounder of the Progressive weekly *The Public*. Finney calls him "one of the few men of genuine liberal sentiment that held a responsible position in the Wilson administration" ("Study of Negro Labor," p. 148). Impeachment proceedings were brought against him in 1920 because he opposed blanket deportations of radical aliens. He finished his term in office but died in 1928. See "End Labor Competition: Concerns Warned to Stop Large Advertising for Workers," *NYT*, Jan. 23, 1918.

64. Mr. Harrison to R. A. Pearson, assistant to the secretary of agriculture, June 18, 1917, general correspondence, box 402, file Labor-laborers (1917), RG 16, NARA.

65. R. A. Pearson, assistant to the secretary of agriculture, to Mr. Harrison, June 21, 1917, RG 16, NARA.

66. G. I. Christie, assistant to the secretary, and Clarence DuBose, special assistant, "Supplying the Farm Labor Need: Organization, Cooperation and the Government's Interest," July 1918, box 565, file Labor (Aug.) 1918, RG 16, NARA.

67. It is even more remarkable that the wartime regulations not only waived the restrictions against contract labor, but they *required* that aliens entering for temporary farmwork have contracts for the duration of their stay. Box 242, file 54261/202, RG 85, NARA, documents changes made in immigration regulations to admit temporary agricultural workers from Mexico and Canada. On the abrogation of departmental orders authorizing the admission of Mexican, Bahamian, and other laborers for war emergency reasons, see Bureau of Immigration to commissioners of immigration and inspectors in charge of district, Dec. 18, 1918, ibid.; Department of Labor Bureau circular no. 54261/202, Apr. 21, 1918, ibid.; "Aid for Canadian Farmers/Our Army of Wheat Harvesters Will Help Them Gather in Crop," *NYT*, July 27, 1918; and Guerin-Gonzales, *Mexican Workers and American Dreams*, pp. 44, 61–63.

68. Guerin-Gonzales, *Mexican Workers and American Dreams*, p. 44.

69. Close to 260,000 women were employed on the land in Great Britain in 1917. See press release, office of the assistant secretary of agriculture, Feb. 11, 1918, general correspondence of the office of the secretary, box 564, file Labor (Feb.), RG 16, NARA. See also *NYT*, Feb. 3, 1918.

70. Secretary James Wilson to John S. Bryan, June 18, 1979, Letters Sent by the Secretary's Office, 1893–1941, RG 16, NARA, 1:261; *Manufacturers Record*, July 19, 1917.

71. Organizations involved in mobilizing women for farmwork included the Women's Land Army of America, the National League of Women's Service, the Bureau of Registration and Information in Washington, D.C., the Women's War Service Branch of the National Council of Defense, and the Women's Division of the Department of Labor's Employment Service. See Secretary James Wilson to Mrs. Howard W. Beal, Feb. 20, 1918, Letters Sent by the Secretary's Office, 1893–1941, RG 16, NARA, 1:425.

72. *NYT*, Feb. 24, Oct. 27, 1918.

73. *NYT*, July 29, 1918.

74. *NYT*, Mar. 31, 1918.

75. *NYT*, Jan. 30, 1918.

76. *NYT*, Feb. 25, 1918.

77. *Manufacturers Record*, Apr. 4, 1918.

78. Ibid. Both Hunnicutt and Ousley agreed that food conservation and preparation were appropriate tasks for women. "I can think of no finer thing for a city woman to do in this war emergency," Ousley noted, "than to go to the farm to help her country sister to bear these burdens of kitchen and farm." Hun-

nicutt added that officers' wives, in particular, "should be drafted and put to some hard work which would be good for their nerves and digestions." "These women are as a rule foot-loose," he asserted. "Why should they not, in our present need of labor, hire out to the farm women and do their share to help win the war?" (*Southern Cultivator*, Aug. 1, 1918).

79. In the spring of 1917, for example, the Philadelphia Bourse and the Commercial Exchange established a volunteer farm labor exchange on the "floor" of the Bourse. Within two weeks, according to the Department of Labor, it proved so successful that it was made a branch of the Philadelphia office of the USES, with the assistant secretary of the Bourse in charge. The exchange sent out several thousand farmworkers to farms in Pennsylvania, Delaware, and New Jersey that summer and was, according to the Employment Service, "responsible for saving many a crop" (*U.S. Employment Service Bulletin* 1, no. 11 [Apr. 9, 1918], general correspondence, box 565, file Labor [Apr.] 1918, RG 16, NARA).

80. *Memphis Commercial Appeal*, Oct. 31, 1918, cited in reel 23, subject Compulsory work laws, Papers of the NAACP.

81. W. J. Spillman to the secretary of agriculture, general correspondence, box 563, file Labor (Jan.) 1918, RG 16, NARA.

82. Ousley to Spillman, ibid.

83. Statement by Secretary Houston, Mar. 6, 1918, reproduced in *Monthly Labor Review* 6 (1918): 835. Houston became secretary of agriculture when Woodrow Wilson assumed office on March 4, 1913. He was a graduate of the University of South Carolina and had done graduate work in government and economics at Harvard. President of Texas A&M College in 1902 and of the University of Texas in 1905, he had been appointed chancellor of Washington University in St. Louis in 1908.

84. "Farm Workers from City/Volunteers Relied upon to Help Make Bumper Crops This Year," *NYT*, Mar. 31, 1918.

85. Press release, Feb. 11, 1918, general correspondence, box 564, file Labor (Feb.), RG 16, NARA.

86. Ibid.

87. W. J. Spillman, "The Farmer's Part in Securing Labor," Jan. 26, 1918, general correspondence, box 563, file Labor (Jan.) 1918, RG 16, NARA.

88. "The Farm Labor Problem," office of the assistant secretary, Feb. 11, 1918, box 564, file Labor (Feb.), RG 16, NARA.

89. Mandel Sener, secretary-manager, New Bern, N.C., Chamber of Commerce, to Clarence Ousley, assistant secretary of agriculture, Feb. 25, 1918, general correspondence, box 564, file Labor (Mar.), RG 16, NARA.

90. *Manufacturers Record*, Mar. 6, 1918.

91. Ibid., Apr. 18, 1918.

92. Ousley to the secretary, Apr. 24, 1918, and Mayor Pierpont to Ousley, Apr. 22, 1918, general correspondence, box 565, file Labor (Apr.), RG 16, NARA.

93. Philip B. Perlman, "Maryland Law Which Makes Everybody Work/Conscription of the Unemployed Rich and Poor Has Begun in One State, and Congress Has Before It a Similar Plan for the Nation," *NYT*, Jan. 13, 1918.

94. Ibid.

95. *NYT*, Mar. 23, 1918; Chapter 55, *Laws of 1918*, issued by proclamation of Walter E. Edge, governor of New Jersey, cited in *NYT*, Mar. 10, 15, 19, 1918.

96. Clarence Ousley to Dr. True, Mar. 27, 1918, general correspondence, box 564, file Labor, RG 16, NARA.

97. Director to Bradford Knapp, chief, office of extension work, Apr. 5, 1918, general correspondence, box 565, file Labor (Apr.) 1918, and J. F. Duggor, director, Alabama extension service to Clarence J. Ousley, May 25, 1918, box 565, file Labor (May) 1918, both in RG 16, NARA.

98. Leslie Gilbert to Ousley, June 3, 1918, and "Six Days of Work Would Help Win War," May 14, 1918, unidentified clipping, box 565, file Labor (June) 1918, both in RG 16, NARA.

99. *Manufacturers Record*, Apr. 18, 25, 1918.

100. *NYT*, Mar. 3, 1918.

101. Not all congressmen jumped on the work-or-fight bandwagon. One questioned the constitutionality of such a measure, and another asked if the Civil War had not been fought over the question of "denying to a man the profits of his own labor." But these arguments were minority opinions in both houses. See *Congressional Record*, vol. 56, pt. 1, 65th Cong., 2d sess., Jan. 27, 1918, pp. 991–92, and *Appendix*, pt. 12, pp. 170. The bill was H.R. 8001. See also pt. 2, Jan. 25, 1918, p. 1219; Feb. 1, 1918, pp. 1582–85; Mar. 1, 1918, pp. 2886–92. On opposition to labor draft, see pt. 3, Mar. 2, 1918, pp. 2905–9.

102. *Manufacturers Record*, Apr. 18, 1918.

103. According to the *NYT*, the new order was aimed at idle men of draft age who were hanging around poolrooms and racetracks; men of draft age affiliated with the IWW movement; men serving food or drink in hotels, public places, and social clubs; elevator operators; doormen; footmen; ushers; and persons connected with games, sports, and amusements. Asked what effect the new regulation would have on strikers, Secretary of War Baker replied that "the regulation is silent upon that subject, but it is not the intention of the department to permit the draft regulations to be used to affect any such labor controversy" (*NYT*, May 26, 24, 1918).

104. Crowder's order caused considerable panic over whether professional baseball players would be classified as ineffective. Crowder ruled that the game was a sport, not an occupation, and that all players between the ages of twenty-one and thirty-one would fall within the scope of the regulations. See *NYT*, May 25, June 4, 22, 1918, and July 2, 1917.

105. *NYT*, July 2, 1917, and July 2, 1918.

106. *NYT*, July 7, 12, 11, 1918.

107. *NYT*, July 13, Aug. 14, 1918.

108. *Monthly Labor Review* 7 (1918): 1810.

109. L. F. Post to W. B. Wilson, Oct. 5, 1918, cited in Phillip S. Foner, *History of the Labor Movement*, pp. 194–95.

110. Walter White's report on Alabama and *Montgomery Journal*, Oct. 18, 1918, reel 23, Papers of the NAACP.

111. J. H. McConico to John R. Shillady, Oct. 9, 1918; Walter White to John R. Shillady, Nov. 14, 1918; Walter White's Reports on Mississippi and Alabama;

Walter White to F. R. Belcher, Aug. 22, 1918; James Jordan to NAACP, Aug. 14, 1918; G. R. Hutto to Walter White, Oct. 21, 1918; secretary of Edward Waters College to John R. Shillady, Oct. 26, 1918; *Little Rock Gazette*, Sept. 22, 1918, all in reel 23, Papers of the NAACP.

112. Louis F. Post, "The Farm Labor Problem," *U.S. Employment Service Bulletin* 1, no. 11 (Apr. 9, 1918), general correspondence, box 565, file Labor (Apr.) 1918, RG 16, NARA. The AFL also asserted throughout the war that claims of labor scarcity were exaggerated. At its Buffalo, New York, convention in 1918 the AFL drew up a pamphlet for public distribution that made that argument precisely: "The general situation relative to farm labor is not of sufficient departure from the normal to cause any loud complaint. . . . The farmers must be prepared to pay for transportation, for adequate housing and the wages which the men are demanding. . . . What has occurred in this country relative to labor supply has been the development of a slight opportunity for a laborer to choose the conditions in which he will take employment and the shifting of the common labor supply from economic slaves to relative free men." See American Federation of Labor, "The Alleged Shortage of Labor," *Report of Committee Appointed by the AFL to Investigate This Question — Report Indorsed by the Buffalo Convention*, general correspondence, box 564, file Labor (Mar.) 1918, RG 16, NARA.

113. *Manufacturers Record*, May 2, 1918.

114. Ibid.

115. We should not conclude that Labor Department officials were above racism. Particular individuals certainly expressed opinions about black workers that had more in common with Clarence Ousley's views than with Louis Post's. See, for example, the statements of John B. Densmore, the director-general of the USES, and M. A. Coykendall, the head of the Employment Service's Farm Service Division, *NYT*, Aug. 1, 1918, and *Manufacturers Record*, May 23, 1918. The difference between the two agencies is that, although a Labor Department official such as Coykendall might show sympathy for compulsory work laws due to his own racist views, he violated departmental policy by advocating such measures. The Department of Agriculture based its policy on the kind of views that Coykendall expressed.

116. *Memphis News Scimitar*, Dec. 27, 1918, in reel 13, subject Migration 1917–1919 Clippings, Papers of the NAACP.

117. The Bureau of Negro Economics was defunded in 1919. See Perlman, "Stirring the White Conscience"; reel 9, subject Labor, general, Jan.–Apr. 1919, Papers of the NAACP; "South Aroused over Wilson's Labor Policies," *New York Tribune*, Apr. 21, 1919; Finney, "Study of Negro Labor," pp. 242–45, 251–55.

118. "Open Letter to the Chamber of Commerce of Pine Bluff, Ark. and to the Public" and J. H. McConico to John R. Shillady, Oct. 9, 1918, reel 23, Papers of the NAACP.

119. Oct. 26, 1918, ibid.

120. G. R. Hutto to Walter F. White, Oct. 21, 1918, ibid.

121. Walter White to John Shillady, Oct. 26, 1918, ibid.; L F. Post to W. B. Wilson, Oct. 5, 1918, cited in Phillip Foner, *History of the Labor Movement*, p. 194.

122. Walter White's Report on Georgia, reel 23, Papers of the NAACP.

123. Walter White's Report on Florida, ibid.; *Savannah Tribune*, Aug. 24, 1918.

Chapter Five

1. In 1911 there were just 4,000 gasoline-powered tractors in use in the United States. By the end of the war there were 242,000 more. Likewise, farmers' use of trucks increased from 15,000 in 1914 to 111,000 at the war's end, and farmers bought automobiles at an amazing rate: 343,000 in 1914 and 1.76 million in 1919. In their effort to grow the most on every acre, farmers doubled their use of nitrogen fertilizer and tripled their use of lime. See Faulkner, *Decline of Laissez-Faire*, p. 337.

2. Willard W. Cochrane notes that exports stayed roughly at this level until 1932, when they plunged to $662 million. See Cochrane, *Development of American Agriculture*, pp. 100–111; Stine, "World's Agriculture Much Changed."

3. Cochrane, *Development of American Agriculture*, pp. 100–101.

4. William F. Holmes, "Economic Developments," p. 263.

5. Ham, *Seasonal Farm Labor in the Southeast*, pp. 3–4.

6. In the early 1930s migrants picked and packed most of the state's citrus crop, but the citrus industry lengthened the production period, allowing the pickers, who were usually white, to settle in the citrus regions. As a result citrus pickers were less likely to be migrants than were vegetable harvesters. See Testimony of A. Frederick Smith (Florida Industrial Commission), Tolan Hearings, pt. 2, pp. 483–88, 563.

7. Dovell, "The Everglades," p. 187; Douglas, *The Everglades*, pp. 5–23; Fritzie P. Manuel, "Land Development in the Everglades," NDMH, pt. 33, p. 12863.

8. Rail service extended into the Everglades in 1915 when the Florida East Coast Railway reached Okeechobee City from New Smyrna. The Atlantic Coast Line Railroad reached Moore Haven in 1918 and Clewiston in 1922. See Dovell, "The Everglades," p. 191.

9. Those who responded to the "ten acres and independence" slogan did not receive title to any particular parcel of land. The location of each plot was determined by lottery. When the buyers discovered that "their land" had been neither surveyed nor flooded, many tried to sue the sellers. They were unsuccessful. See Fritzie P. Manuel, "Land Development in the Everglades," NDMH, pt. 33, p. 12884; Douglas, *The Everglades*, p. 323.

10. Dovell, "The Everglades," pp. 190–91.

11. In 1935 only one-quarter of the white residents in Florida's three southeastern counties were natives of the state. Twelve percent hailed from Georgia. See Douglas, *The Everglades*, p. 356; *Miami Herald*, Feb. 9, 1930; Joan Pascal and Harold G. Tipton, "Vegetable Production in South Florida," NDMH, pt. 33, p. 12907.

12. Individual attempts to drain the land were fruitless. For example, George E. Sebring (after whom Sebring, Florida, is named) bought steam-operated pumps to drain his several hundred acres in the 1920s. During one heavy rain-

fall the boiler exploded, and his avocado seedlings were lost because of flooding. He replaced this equipment with a stationary engine and replanted his avocados; but two years later the engine broke, and he lost all his trees again. The settlers might not have anticipated these problems, but the men who sold them the land knew its limitations. In 1910 the Office of Experiment Stations prepared to publish a report which concluded that "the drainage of the Everglades is entirely feasible from an engineering standpoint" but "the value of the lands when drained is still largely problematical. Some small drained tracts on the edge of the glades have produced very satisfactory crops of vegetables; usually, but not always, large quantities of fertilizers have been used." Agents of the Florida Everglades Land Company demanded that the circular be suppressed, and it was never published. See Testimony of James E. Beardsley and Fritzie P. Manuel, NDMH, pt. 33, pp. 12560–61, 12873; Douglas, *The Everglades*, pp. 327–29, and Tebeau, *History of Florida*, p. 373.

13. Douglas, *The Everglades*, p. 337. See also Tindall, "Bubble in the Sun," pp. 76–83, 109–11, and Tebeau, *History of Florida*.

14. Douglas, *The Everglades*, has the number of dead at 18,000, but I gather this is a typographical error. The Department of Justice received a number of letters complaining about the conscription of black labor under armed guard to assist in the cleanup. See Telegram to Calvin Coolidge from the Associated Negro Press, Sept. 25, 1926; NAACP to the U.S. Attorney General, Sept. 27, 1926; clippings from *Chicago Tribune*, *Chicago Herald*, and the *Examiner*, all in correspondence, box 10789, file 50-18-7, classified subject files 50 (peonage), RG 60, NARA. For another description, see Dovell, "The Everglades," pp. 192–93.

15. According to Douglas, it shrank a foot a year in the first five years and is still shrinking. The erosion is controlled by rotating crops with cattle grazing but continues albeit at a slower pace. See Douglas, *The Everglades*, pp. 348–49, 361–62.

16. Fritzie P. Manuel, "Land Development in the Everglades," NDMH, pt. 33, pp. 12864–65.

17. Howard Haney, one of the most successful truck farmers in Belle Glade, estimated that to start a profitable farm in 1942, a Glades grower would need at least 640 acres and $35,000 worth of equipment. A used precooler alone cost between $12,000 and $18,000. See Haney Testimony, pp. 12576, 12597–98, 12600, and Joan Pascal and Harold G. Tipton, "Vegetable Production in South Florida," p. 12917, both in NDMH, pt. 33.

18. Haney testimony, NDMH, pt. 33, pp. 12576, 12597–98, 12600.

19. South Florida tenancy rates fell during the 1930s but were still extremely high. In Broward County the tenancy rate was 70.9 percent in 1930, 68.9 percent in 1935, and 59.5 percent in 1940. In Palm Beach County the tenancy rate was 54.6 percent in 1930, 50.3 percent in 1935, and 34.9 percent in 1940. See U.S. Bureau of the Census, *16th Census*, County Table 2, Farm Tenure.

20. The pressure on growers to plant beans brought remarkable results. In 1919 farmworkers harvested 8,522 acres of beans worth almost half a million dollars. In 1939 they brought in almost 64,000 acres valued at $5.5 million. See ibid., p. 682. The quote is from Robinson and Horne, "Florida Migratory Workers," pp. 36, 43–44. See also Terrell Cline, social worker in charge of research at

Belle Glade, to John Beecher, research supervisor, FSA, May 14, 1939, box 20, file RP-M-85-183-01, monthly reports, RG 96, NARA.

21. Federal researchers Pascal and Tipton noted that supply dealers who extended credit sometimes required borrowers to plant beans because the growers could plant several crops in succession and increase the volume of the dealer's trade: "Growers in these areas able to do so, however, curtailed their bean acreages and expanded their plantings of more cold-resistant crops." Quoted in "Vegetable Production in South Florida," NDMH, pt. 33, p. 12896. See also testimony of Joseph G. Cassellius, Pahokee, Apr. 26, 1942, and M. M. Carter, Belle Glade, Apr. 25, 1942, ibid., pp. 12767–70, 12775–76.

22. Testimony of Joseph G. Cassellius, Pahokee, Apr. 26, 1942, ibid., p. 12772.

23. Testimony of Luther Jones, Belle Glade, Apr. 24, 1942, ibid., pp. 12659–60.

24. Even in 1919, vegetables were the largest part of South Florida agriculture. In Broward County, vegetables brought $730,686, while fruits and nuts only earned farmers $68,341 and cereals only $15,075. In Palm Beach County, vegetables brought $755,308 in 1919, compared with only $275,308 for fruits and nuts and $33,359 for cereals. In Dade County, vegetables sold for over $2 million, compared with $1 million for fruits and nuts and $10,798 for cereals. See U.S. Bureau of the Census, *14th Census*, p. 375. By 1939 there were over 30,000 acres in sugarcane in Florida but over 185,000 in vegetables. See U.S. Bureau of the Census, *16th Census*, p. 682. See also Pascal and Tipton, "Vegetable Production in South Florida," NDMH, pt. 33, p. 12893.

25. U.S. Bureau of the Census, *16th Census*, p. 682.

26. Beecher Testimony, p. 28.

27. Ibid. See also testimony of C. M. Swindle, Belle Glade, Apr. 25, 1942, NDMH, pt. 33, pp. 12706–10.

28. Harvests on farms of over 500 acres increased in Broward County from 15.7 to 41.1 percent and in Dade County from 18.9 to 38.3 percent between 1929 and 1939. See Pascal and Tipton, "Vegetable Production in South Florida," NDMH, pt. 33, p. 12911.

29. U.S. Bureau of the Census, *14th Census* and *16th Census*.

30. Another corporation had 70,000 acres in a single block, with less than 2,000 acres in cultivation. Adjoining the growing celery district were twelve square sections, which reputedly belonged to a northern land company. Cuban interests also acquired large holdings. The largest farms by far were the ones in Okeechobee County. In 1920 the average acreage of farms in Broward County was 72.9; Dade, 155.2; Palm Beach, 60.1; Lee, 76.8; and Monroe, 68.1. The average acreage of farms in Okeechobee County was 3,183.4! See Beecher Testimony, p. 29; U.S Bureau of the Census, *14th Census*, pp. 364–69; testimony of B. E. Lawton, Broward County agricultural agent, Apr. 28, 1942, NDMH, pt. 33, pp. 12779–80.

31. Pascal and Tipton, "Vegetable Production in South Florida," NDMH, pt. 33, p. 12911.

32. Ibid., p. 12924.

33. Florida farms spent almost $21 million on wages in 1939. The next largest expense was $13 million for fertilizer. See U.S. Bureau of the Census, *16th Census*, p. 749.

34. Terrell Cline to John Beecher, May 14, 1939, box 20, file RP-M-85-183-01, monthly reports, RG 96, NARA.

35. According to several sources, bean pickers' earnings fell from 40 cents an hour in the 1920s to 25 cents an hour in the 1930s. The basis for this statistic is a mystery since bean pickers were paid by the hamper, not the hour. See Pascal and Tipton, "Vegetable Production in South Florida," NDMH, pt. 33, p. 12924; Tolan Hearings, pt. 1, p. 77, and pt. 2, pp. 327, 487, 536, 598; Douglas, *The Everglades*, pp. 356–57; Donald E. Grubbs, "Story of Florida's Migrant Farm Workers," pp. 106–7.

36. NDMH, pt. 33, pp. 12739–42.

37. James Beardsley of Clewiston, Florida, recalls that truck farmers near Lake Okeechobee hired their first "Sau Niggers" (i.e., residents of Nassau) in 1920. See NDMH, pt. 33, p. 12565. The two best sources on Bahamian laborers in early twentieth-century Florida are Raymond A. Mohl, "Black Immigrants," and Howard Johnson, "Bahamian Labor Migration to Florida." Johnson argues that the passage of the Johnson-Reed Act in 1924, which limited all immigration to the United States according to a quota system, resulted in the virtual exclusion of Bahamians from the United States and thus from Florida's labor market. As we well know, immigration restrictions often go unenforced. Indeed, Mohl's findings confirm the presence of Bahamian laborers in Florida after 1924.

38. Testimony of Jacob McMillan, Belle Glade, Apr. 25, 1942, NDMH, pt. 33, pp. 12651–53.

39. As a rule, black workers kept to the fields and white workers to the packing sheds. As the depression wore on into the 1930s, however, and more and more white people joined the ranks of the mobile poor, whites began to compete with black workers for field work. However, when blacks and whites did the same work, the piece rate for blacks would invariably be half to two-thirds of the rate for whites. In Belle Glade, where white women packed beans, tomatoes, and other vegetables, packing paid 25 cents an hour. In Sanford, north of Orlando, where celery washhouses hired only black workers, packing paid 12½ to 17 cents an hour. In 1937 black workers in Belle Glade reported to federal investigators that white workers were coming into the fields and working side by side with them in increasing numbers. Observers counted 7,000 to 8,000 black migrants and 2,000 white migrants in Belle Glade in 1937, reputedly an increase of 1,000 white workers over the previous year. See Max Egloff to John Beecher, May 15, 1939, box 20, file RP-M-85-183-01, monthly reports, RG 96, NARA; Robinson and Horne, "Florida Migratory Workers," p. 24.

40. Testimony of A. Frederick Smith (Florida Industrial Commission), Tolan Hearings, pt. 2, pp. 483, 583; John Beecher, research supervisor, Resettlement Division, Region 5, to Max A. Egloff, chief of research and investigations, Labor Relations Division, May 15, 1939, box 20, file RP-M-85-183-01, monthly reports, RG 96, NARA.

41. Eatonville—better known because it was the birthplace of Zora Neale Hurston—is farther north in central Florida.

42. Arthur S. Evans Jr. and David Lee conducted twenty-seven oral interviews with Pearl City residents in 1984 and 1985. The result of their project was *Pearl City, Florida: A Black Community Remembers*. The book, while interesting, is problematic because the authors took the liberty of consolidating all twenty-seven interviews into one composite story, without attention to the age, sex, or experience of their informants. However, thanks to the generosity of the Boca Raton Historical Society Library, which funded the oral history project, I was given access to transcripts of the original interviews. Interviews are cited hereafter as Pearl City Oral History Project.

43. Of the 690 workers interviewed in the winter of 1936–37 by Aubrey Clyde Robinson and Glenore Fisk Horne for their 1937 report, titled "Florida Migratory Workers," 79.3 percent were from southern states, 39.7 percent were from Georgia, and 10.4 percent were from Alabama.

44. Pearl City Oral History Project.

45. See also the testimony of William Yearby, Belle Glade, Apr. 26, 1942, NDMH, pt. 33, pp. 12653–56.

46. Testimony of A. Frederick Smith of the Florida Industrial Commission, Tolan Hearings, pt. 2, pp. 483, 583; John Beecher to Max A. Egloff, May 15, 1939, box 20, file RP-M-85-183-01, monthly reports, RG 96, NARA.

47. The quote is from Douglas, *The Everglades*, pp. 356–57. See also Donald E. Grubbs, "Story of Florida's Migrant Farm Workers," pp. 106–7. One Belle Glade truck farmer noted that when he arrived in 1936, "colored people were paying 25 cents a night to sleep on a truck body, just an ordinary stake truck with bean bags on the platform and a tarpaulin over it, simply because there was no place for them to live." The reason for these conditions, he explained, was that the development of the truck farming industry in the area simply outstripped the pace of housing construction. However, he added an additional justification: "There is no particular profit in maintaining quarters, unless you do charge more than seems reasonable, because this type of colored help have no respect for property and those quarters, as poor as they were, virtually need rebuilding each year" (testimony of Howard Haney, NDMH, pt. 33, p. 12604).

48. The truck driver is quoted in Robinson and Horne, "Florida Migratory Workers," p. 39.

49. To the dismay of federal investigators, the state of Florida turned a blind eye to migrant health and housing conditions. Local boards of health had the "authority to proceed" against the most flagrant abusers of housing regulations, but there is no evidence that they ever invoked this authority. Likewise health officials provided little in the way of health services to migrants. Although most of the state's migrant population worked in Palm Beach County, and 42 percent of the county's black population tested positive for syphilis, the county employed only one health officer, who served a population of perhaps 60,000. See Tolan Hearings, pt. 2, pp. 541, 591; Beecher Testimony; Donald E. Grubbs, "Story of Florida's Migrant Farm Workers," pp. 107–8.

50. Robinson and Horne, "Florida Migratory Workers," p. 36.

51. Hurston, *Their Eyes Were Watching God*, pp. 192–93.

52. Ibid., p. 197.

53. Beecher Testimony, pp. 23–24.

54. Robinson and Horne, "Florida Migratory Workers," p. 42.

55. Ibid., pp. 45–46.

56. When, in 1940, a severe freeze ruined the vegetable harvest, "thousands of migrants were stranded and faced virtual starvation." See Tolan Hearings, pt. 2, pp. 483–88; testimony of Dorothea Brower, district welfare supervisor, West Palm Beach, Apr. 29, 1942, NDMH, pt. 33, pp. 12792–95.

57. Maryland State Employment Service, *Proceedings of Interstate Conference on Migratory Labor*, Feb. 12–13, 1940, office of the secretary, general subject file, 1940–45, box 151, file Migrant labor, RG 174, NARA; Robinson and Horne, "Florida Migratory Workers."

58. A labor contractor noted to federal investigators that ten to sixty trucks would line up at a particular corner in Belle Glade every morning during the season. At 7 o'clock the police would blow a whistle, and the workers would board the truck of their choice. See testimony of Norman Hall, Belle Glade, Apr. 26, 1942, NDMH, pt. 33, p. 12640; Beecher Testimony, pp. 24–25.

59. Pearl City Oral History Project.

60. Elnore Jackson managed to remain year-round in Belle Glade with her husband and four children by doing washing and ironing while her husband picked up what farmwork he could find. Still, the six of them had to live in a 10-x-12-foot room in a Belle Glade boardinghouse without running water or a toilet. They could have returned to their home in Cordele, Georgia, where they had more room, but they made more money in Belle Glade. See NDMH, pt. 33, pp. 12630–31.

61. Pearl City Oral History Project; Robinson and Horne, "Florida Migratory Workers," p. 48; John Beecher to Max A. Egloff, May 15, 1939, box 20, file RP-M-85-183-01, monthly reports, RG 96, NARA.

62. Free-lancers were more common on the East Coast than the West Coast because of the predominance of young and single people among the Atlantic migrant population. Of the 4,119 black migrants enumerated in New Jersey in 1939 by the State Employment Service, 3,356 were men, 677 were women, and only 86 were children. The New Jersey State Employment Service counted a total of 474 families. See Liss, "Farm Migrants in New Jersey."

63. Testimony of Mr. Engler, Maryland State Employment Service, *Proceedings of Interstate Conference on Migratory Labor*, Feb. 12–13, 1940, office of the secretary, general subject file, 1940–45, box 151, file Migrant labor, RG 174, NARA. C. W. E. Pittman of North Carolina's Farm Placement Service described the three-year migration pattern of one particularly large group of 200 farmworkers. They started in Okeechobee, Florida, in November, and after three and a half months they went south to Dade County, where they spent a month. From there they went north to Hastings, Florida, where they spent almost two months. After that they spent two-thirds of a month in South Carolina; the same amount of time in North Carolina; about a month in Exmore, Virginia; a couple of weeks in Pocomoke City, Maryland; a month in Freehold, New Jersey; and a half-

month in Long Island City. They then returned home. In all, they traveled 1,660 miles. See Pittman, "Migratory Agricultural Workers on the Atlantic Seaboard," quoted in testimony of Arthus J. Edwards, Tolan Hearings, pt. 1, p. 380.

64. Robinson and Horne, "Florida Migratory Workers," pp. 19, 26–27.

65. Tolan Hearings, pt. 1, p. 235.

66. A Belle Glade grower's description of the crew leader system might just as well explain the Italian padrone system in 1890:

These Negroes arrive in the "muck" broke and hungry. The leader [contractor] puts them up and feeds them, arranges jobs for them, and takes his advances out of their pay later. The employer pays them in the field, but the labor leader has got them in debt to him, and he gets it back from them. The leader owns all the concessions, the barbecue, and fish-fry stands, the barber shops, stores, funeral parlors. He supplies housing, several hundred in one place. Usually this is just a big barracks-like building; sometimes small packing houses are taken over for living quarters. . . . The Negro leader makes a profit coming and going, both from the workers and the employers. (Robinson and Horne, "Florida Migratory Workers," p. 37)

67. NDMH, pt. 33, p. 12642.

68. A 1930 survey counted 580 Italian families doing seasonal farmwork in New Jersey. According to the report of the Committee to Investigate the Employment of Migratory Children in the State of New Jersey, more than half of the 3,719 Italian migrant workers were children between the ages of six and fifteen. Ten years later the New Jersey Department of Agriculture and the State Employment Service estimated that New Jersey growers continued to employ approximately 5,000 Italian migrants. See Liss, "Farm Migrants in New Jersey."

69. Ibid., p. 2.

70. Ibid., p. 3.

71. Ibid.

72. Thirty-seven of the growers relied on the same "gang" of workers to return each year. Twenty-five went south for labor themselves, and the remaining ninety-eight contracted with crew leaders. The 320 growers surveyed as to why they hired black migrants responded as follows: 101 said that black migrants were good workers, willing to help at all hours; 86, that they hired black migrants because local help was not available; 27, that migrants were the only labor available to do the type of work required; 28, that the migrants "were always available and dependable"; 19, that local help was not satisfactory; 18, that local labor on WPA would not or could not do the work; 26, that black migrants were the most satisfactory labor for potato digging; 16, that they used the same labor year after year; 6, that the WPA had spoiled local labor; and 5, that the temporary nature of the work made it hard for WPA workers to accept without losing their access to relief. See ibid.; Maryland State Employment Service, *Proceedings of Interstate Conference on Migratory Labor*, office of the secretary, general subject file, 1940–45, box 151, file Migrant labor, RG 174, NARA, pp. 24–25; Tolan Hearings, pt. 1, pp. 70–78.

73. Letter of W. R. Valentine, principal, Manual Training School, Borden-

town, New Jersey, to Lieut. Lawrence A. Oxley, chief, Division of Negro Labor, Aug. 10, 1934, RG 174, NARA.

74. *Cranbury Press*, Aug. 3, 1934; Tolan Hearings, pt. 1, p. 239.

75. Tolan Hearings, pt. 1, pp. 70–78, 102–3.

76. Testimony of Edith E. Lowry, executive secretary, Council of Women for Home Missions, ibid., pp. 313–14.

77. Testimony of James C. Ewart, ibid., pp. 46, and Lowry testimony, ibid., p. 315.

78. Tolan Hearings, pt. 1, p. 86.

79. Ibid., p. 314.

80. With the help of the Workers Defense League, the seven victims filed a civil suit in federal court for damages totaling $250,000. They won $14,000, none of which they ever received as far as I can tell. See Jean Yatrofsky, "Jersey Joads: The Story of the Cranbury Case," May 15, 1940, folder 24, and press release, May 10, 1940, folder 23, both in box 154, Workers Defense League Papers, Archives of Labor History and Urban Affairs.

Chapter Six

1. Congress enacted the Emergency Relief and Construction Act in July 1932. It was succeeded by the Federal Emergency Relief Act in May 1933, which provided $500 million for poor people who could not meet state residency requirements for local relief. By the end of February 1934, 85 transient bureau camps in 44 states and the District of Columbia were providing assistance to over 100,000 people a day. Two months later there were 190 camps providing jobs as well as food, clothing, shelter, and medical care. FERA would provide aid to unemployed farm laborers; in fact, nearly half of FERA's relief recipients had been farm laborers. However, working migrant farmworkers were ineligible, even if they could not subsist on their wages. Under FERA rules the term "transient" did not "apply to people who do not secure sufficient wages from their labor to meet living requirements. Responsibility for their care rests upon the States in which, and the employers for whom, they work." See Webb, *Migratory and Casual Worker*, pp. ix–x; Webb, *Transient Unemployed*, p. 48; Ryan, *Migration and Social Welfare*, pp. 8–10; Ellen C. Potter, "After Five Years: The Unsolved Problem of the Transient Unemployed, 1932–37," included in the testimony of Bertha McCall, general director, National Travelers Aid Association, Tolan Hearings, pt. 1, New York City Hearings, p. 54; Carothers, *Chronology of the Federal Emergency Relief Administration*, pp. 25, 81.

2. According to Sidney C. Sufrin's study, which is based on Bureau of Agricultural Economics statistics, by April 1933 farmers were offering only three jobs where they would normally have offered five. At the same time the farm labor supply had increased. By January 1933 there were five workers available for every two jobs. In 1934 labor demand increased, and by summer there were only three workers for every two jobs. See Sufrin, "Labor Organization in Agricultural America," p. 350.

3. The period from 1930 to 1933 saw a decline in militancy and membership in both rural and urban unions. Stuart Jamieson recorded only eight farm strikes involving 8,600 workers in 1930, just five strikes involving 3,000 workers in 1931, and ten much smaller strikes involving fewer than 3,200 workers in 1932. Moreover, most of these strikes were about access to and the adequacy of relief, rather than about wages and working conditions. Sufrin recorded far fewer strikes (two in 1931, one in 1932, nine in 1933, fifteen in 1934, and ten in 1935), but he appears to be counting only strikes organized by trade unions. See Jamieson, *Labor Unionism in American Agriculture*, p. 16; Sufrin, "Labor Organization in Agricultural America," pp. 546, 555. See also Cletus Daniel, *Bitter Harvest*, p. 220, and Taylor and Kerr, "Uprisings on the Farm," p. 19.

4. *Philadelphia Record*, Sept. 1, 1933.

5. Jamieson, *Labor Unionism in American Agriculture*, p. 16.

6. In 1914 state militia fired on the tents of striking miners' families, killing eleven people.

7. For a fascinating account of the 1933 cotton strike in California, see Cletus Daniel, *Bitter Harvest*.

8. Folsom, "Farm Laborers in the United States."

9. For a chronology of the strike, see Dusinberre, "Strikes in 1934."

10. According to C. F.'s grandson John, in 1911 C. F. met with some financiers about borrowing money to expand the farm. The financiers then bought out his father's share for less than half of its estimated value. See John Seabrook, "Spinach King"; John M. "Jack" Seabrook, *Henry Ford of Agriculture*, p. 2; Jack Seabrook to the author, June 1, 1995, p. 2.

11. Jack Seabrook to the author, June 1, 1995, p. 2.

12. Dusinberre, "Strikes in 1934," p. 37. As Jack Seabrook points out, the varieties of vegetables suitable for canning or the fresh market were not necessarily appropriate for freezing. Seabrook Farms brought to the partnership the know-how to develop new varieties in large quantities quickly. See John M. Seabrook, *Henry Ford of Agriculture*, for the corporate history of Seabrook Farms and the history of Seabrook's role in the development of the frozen food industry.

13. *New York Sun*, July 10, 1934.

14. "Canner Strike Is Settled as U.S. Mediates," *New York Post*, July 10, 1934.

15. "Peace Agreed on in Farm Walkout but Jersey Strikers Must Ratify Conference Terms," *New York Sun*, July 10, 1934.

16. For coverage of the Campbell Soup strike, see *Camden Post*, Apr. 5, 1934; *Daily Worker*, Apr. 23, 1934; *Camden Argus*, May 4, 1934; *NYT*, Apr. 5, 1934; *Camden Post*, Apr. 6, 1934; and *Philadelphia Labor Record*, Apr. 6, 1934. Clippings on the Campbell Soup strike and the Seabrook Farms strike can be found in the American Civil Liberties Union Papers.

17. Granger, "Negro Joins the Picket Line."

18. Busnardo and Broadwell were interviewed in 1968 by Lloyd S. Kelling. See Kelling, "Historical Study of a Strike."

19. Ibid., p. 28, and *NYT*, July 7, 1934. A copy of the contract, dated Apr. 10, 1934, is in case file 270/9817, Seabrook Farms, RG 280, NARA.

20. In 1928 Donald Henderson and Rexford Tugwell coauthored a book of

study questions designed for college economics courses. Eleanor joined the Communist Party in 1931 and ran for Congress as a party member in 1934. Donald joined in 1932 and went on to serve as an officer in various party organizations. The Agricultural and Cannery Workers' Industrial Union was part of the Communist Party's Trade Union Unity League. The Hendersons would go on to found UCAPAWA in 1937. The quote is from Granger, "Negro Joins the Picket Line." See also Kelling, "Historical Study of a Strike," pp. 31–34.

21. The American Civil Liberties Union investigators agreed that the federal government was partly to blame for the strike. The Farm Credit Administration, which had taken over the responsibilities of Hoover's Reconstruction Finance Corporation, had targeted the Seabrook loan for liquidation, believing that it was unsound. However, the ACLU also noted that the credit administration had extended the Seabrook loan in an effort to "carry the enterprise along." The latest extension had been negotiated four months prior to the strike, so it is quite possible that federal pressure to repay the loan had diminished and that Seabrook was using the loan as an excuse to slash wages. See *New York Post*, July 10, 11, 1934.

22. It is not clear who these people were. Some were obviously the farm's foremen; others, the owners and operators of large farms in the vicinity.

23. Sufrin, "Labor Organization in Agricultural America." Kelling interviewed Saunders in 1968 for Kelling, "Historical Study of a Strike," pp. 19–20, 35–36.

24. Kelling, "Historical Study of a Strike," p. 36; *NYT*, July 7, 1934; *New York Herald Tribune*, June 27, 1934; *Daily Worker*, June 27, 1934; *Philadelphia Record*, Aug. 13, 1934.

25. Henderson and Dahl's hearing was scheduled to take place the next day, but the justice of the peace deferred it for a week when more than 100 strikers blocked traffic in front of his office. See *Daily Worker*, July 5, 1934; *New York Post*, July 6, 1934; and *Camden Post*, Mar. 3, 1934.

26. *Bridgeton Evening News*, July 10, 1934.

27. The account of Busnardo's rescue is from Kelling, "Historical Study of a Strike," p. 45. See also *New York Post*, July 9, 1934; *Daily Worker*, July 7, 1934; and *Camden Post*, July 7, 1934.

28. *New York Post*, July 9, 1934.

29. Schwarzkopf is the father of Col. Norman Schwarzkopf of Gulf War fame. See *New York Post*, July 9, 1934; *Millville Republican*, July 20, 1934; *New York Sun*, July 10, 1934.

30. *Millville Republican*, July 10, 1934; *Bridgeton News*, July 10, 1934; *Daily Worker*, July 7, 1934.

31. *New York Herald Tribune*, July 10, 1934. This article refers to workers blocking the gates to the fields, but as C.F.'s son Jack pointed out, there were no gates or fences. Apparently C.F. had a phobia about farm fences and had them pulled down whenever he bought new property. This supports Jack Seabrook's contention that many journalists reported on the strike from afar. See John M. Seabrook to the author, May 22, 1995; *New York Herald Tribune*, July 10, 1934.

32. *Camden Post*, July 19, 1934.

33. Ibid.; *Millville Republican*, July 10, 1934.

34. *Camden Post*, July 19, 1934; *New York Herald Tribune*, July 10, 1934.

35. *New York Sun*, July 10, 1934; *Camden Post*, July 19, 1934.

36. Legal scholar Austin Morris notes that the wording of the NIRA did not exclude farmworkers, and it is not entirely clear that Congress intended to exclude them. If groups of farm employers had submitted codes of fair conduct, their employees would have been covered by the act. However, none did. The government could have imposed codes, but it did not. Morris continues, "The incentive spurring industry to formulate codes — freedom from the restrictions of antitrust law — did not operate with any force on agriculture. The latter industry obtained the same essential benefits without submitting codes by entering the marketing agreements and crop support programs of the AAA" (Morris, "Agricultural Labor and National Labor Legislation," p. 1948).

37. An interdepartmental report on labor in the Florida citrus industry noted, for example, that "the legislative history of that Act contains some indication that farm labor was not intended to be brought within its labor provisions, though it is not conclusive on the point and a strong argument to the contrary may be made from the terms of the Act itself" (ibid.).

38. The administrative decree was the President's Re-employment Agreement. See Cletus Daniel, *Bitter Harvest*, pp. 167–221.

39. This particular wording is attributed to Dr. Leo Wolman, chairman of the Labor Advisory Board, according to Morris, "Agricultural Labor and National Labor Legislation," p. 1949.

40. Ibid., p. 1950.

41. Petition addressed to Frances Perkins from the Farmers and Workers Union of America, Apr. 9, 1934, and H. L. Kerwin, director of conciliation, to Ernest J. Johnson, Apr. 24, 1934, case file 170/9817, Seabrook Farms, RG 280, NARA.

42. George Creel had earlier assumed what Cletus Daniel calls the "role of patron-savior" in the 1933 cotton pickers' strike in California's San Joaquin Valley. Creel had been appointed head of the Western District of the NRA. "Though the federal government, having excluded agricultural workers from the application of the NIRA, lacked any statutory authority to intervene in the cotton strike, Creel had no intention of letting technicalities stand in the way of a progressive reformation." He also had no intention of recognizing the workers' radical union, which, he believed, "would disappear along with the 'handful of tramp agitators'" once a fair settlement was imposed. When the union rejected Creel's negotiated settlement, he launched a "back-to-work" campaign, which denied relief supplies to strikers who refused to return to the fields. The strikers refused to be intimidated, returning to work only at the union's urging. See Cletus Daniel, *Bitter Harvest*, pp. 174–217.

43. Telegram from John A. Moffett to H. L. Kerwin, Department of Labor, July 7, 1934, case file 270/9817, Seabrook Farms, RG 280, NARA; *Camden Post*, July 10, 1934; *Millville Republican*, July 10, 1934; *New York Sun*, July 10, 1934.

44. *New York Post*, July 10, 1934; *New York Sun*, July 10, 1934.

45. *NYT*, July 11, 12, 1934.

46. Tuso was, interestingly enough, the prosecutor at O'Donnell's trial. O'Donnell began a hunger strike that succeeded in bringing national attention to his cause. After only twenty-three days prosecutor Tuso apparently decided that keeping O'Donnell in prison was more trouble than letting him go free, so he vacated the charges against him. See Vineland, New Jersey, *Evening-Journal*, July 31, 1934; *Camden Post*, Aug. 2, 1934; *Philadelphia Record*, Aug. 13, 1934; *New York Post*, Nov. 20, 1934; *NYT*, Nov. 25, 26, Dec. 8, 1934; *New York Telegram*, Nov. 26, 1934; *Camden Post*, Nov. 29, 1934.

47. The towns were Bridgeton, Millville, Vineland, and Salem. See *NYT*, July 20, 1934.

48. Granger, "Negro Joins the Picket Line."

49. John M. Seabrook, *Henry Ford of Agriculture*, pp. 39–42.

Chapter Seven

1. Linder, "Farm Workers and the Fair Labor Standards Act."

2. Baldwin, *Poverty and Politics*, pp. 326–27, 348, 361–62.

3. The Senate report on hearings on the Wagner bill cites only "administrative reasons" for the agricultural exclusion. There was only one brief mention of the bill's applicability to agriculture in these 1934 hearings, according to Austin Morris. It came during a discussion of the difficulties of imposing the measure on small employers. Dr. William Leiserson noted, "You might want to except a small farmer with a few employees, *but you certainly would not want to except him in a situation like the one you have out in the Imperial Valley now, with a great number of people working in agricultural employment.*" Senator Walsh, the committee chairman, replied, "As the bill is drafted, *there is no limitation at all.*" What happened between this exchange and the redrafting of the bill to exclude farmworkers, Morris cannot say with certainty. He concludes that political pressures were more important than any administrative reasons. "Senator Wagner wrote to Norman Thomas that the opposition of the farm bloc made coverage of agricultural labor under his bill out of the question." See Morris, "Agricultural Labor and National Labor Legislation," pp. 1951–55.

4. Ibid., pp. 1962–63.

5. The NLRB's logic was affirmed by Judge Stephens in *North Whittier Heights Citrus Association v. NLRB*, 109 F2d 76, 80 (9th Cir.), *cert. denied*, 310 U.S. 632 (1940). According to the judge's opinion, farmworkers were like the other groups excluded from the Wagner Act—children employed by their parents and domestic servants:

There never would be a great number [of agricultural workers] suffering under the difficulty of negotiating with the actual employer and there would be no need for collective bargaining [providing that the term was] not enlarged beyond the usual idea the term suggests.... When every detail of farming from plowing to delivering the produce to the consumer was done by the farmer and his "hired man", this common denominator was present. But when in the transition . . . to the great industry of the present in which the fruit is passed . . . to a corporation for treatment in a packing house owned and run by such corporation . . . we think the common denominator has ceased to exist. (Morris, "Agricultural Labor and National Labor Legislation," p. 1963)

6. Robinson and Horne, "Florida Migratory Workers," pp. 45–46; Tebeau, *History of Florida*, p. 403.

7. Robinson and Horne, "Florida Migratory Workers," p. 40.

8. Baldwin, *Poverty and Politics*, p. 54.

9. Ibid., chap. 3.

10. "Parity" referred to parity between agricultural and industrial products. The goal was to raise agricultural produce prices so that farmers would have the buying power they enjoyed in the period before the First World War known as the "Golden Age of Agriculture." See ibid., p. 54.

11. Mary Hines, interview by Annie L. Bowman, reel 1, #2, Federal Writers' Project Life Histories.

12. Baldwin, *Poverty and Politics*, pp. 76–87.

13. "History of Farm Labor Activities of the Farm Security Administration," FSA Pub. 132, RG 287, NARA; John Fischer, director of information, FSA, USDA, to Paul H. Appleby, asst. to the secretary, Dec. 9, 1939, general correspondence, camps, migratory labor, 1939, RG 16, NARA.

14. Statement by Paul Vander Schouw, supervisor, Florida Migratory Labor Camps, West Palm Beach, Florida, NDMH, pt. 33, pp. 12745–47; "History of Farm Labor Activities of the Farm Security Administration," FSA Pub. 132, RG 287, NARA, pp. 5–6; John Fischer to Paul H. Appleby, Dec. 9, 1939, general correspondence, camps, migratory labor, 1939, RG 16, NARA, pp. 5–8; FSA, "Memorandum of Interstate Farm Family Migrations," Mar. 17, 1939, correspondence concerning migratory labor camps, 1935–1943, box 8, file AD-124, migratory labor, general, all regions, 1939, RG 96, NARA.

15. John Fischer to Paul H. Appleby, Dec. 9, 1939, general correspondence, camps, migratory labor, 1939, and testimony by Dr. W. W. Alexander, FSA, Senate Civil Liberties Commission, May 23, 1940, Office of Agricultural Defense Relations, general correspondence, 1939–1941, box 40, file Labor-migratory, both in RG 16, NARA.

16. Mobile camps did not go into operation until the 1942–43 season. See Statement by Paul Vander Schouw, NDMH, pt. 33, pp. 12745–47; John Beecher to Dr. W. W. Alexander, June 17, 1940, correspondence concerning migratory labor camps, 1935–1943, box 9, file AD-124, region 5, migratory labor, 1940, RG 96, NARA.

17. Testimony of Edith Lowry, Tolan Hearings, pt. 1, p. 307.

18. Ibid.

19. Statement by Paul Vander Schouw, NDMH, pt. 33, pp. 12745–47; "History of Farm Labor Activities of the Farm Security Administration," FSA Pub. 132, RG 287, NARA.

20. C. B. Baldwin to Senator Claude Pepper, July 29, 1941, box 9, file AD-124,

region 5; FSA, "Community and Family Services Bulletin," Feb. 28, 1941, migrant labor camps correspondence, 1935–1943, box 16, file RP-M-169-publications; John F. O'Malley, Elba, New York, narrative report for period ending Oct. 4, 1942, box 19, file RP-M-183, migratory region 1, reports, all in RG 96, NARA.

21. Statement by Paul Vander Schouw, NDMH, pt. 33, pp. 12745–47; migrant labor camp correspondence, box 17, file RP-M-163, region 1, 1941, RG 96, NARA.

22. Monthly narrative report for Florida migrant labor camps, Apr. 1942, migrant labor camps correspondence, 1935–1943, box 20, file RP-M-85-183-Reports, RG 96, NARA.

23. NDMH, pt. 33, pp. 12655–56.

24. Ibid., p. 12603.

25. Ibid., p. 12761.

26. Tolan Hearings, pt. 2, pp. 497–502.

27. Ibid., pp. 574–83.

28. NDMH, pt. 33, p. 12742.

29. Ibid., pp. 12570–74.

30. Ibid., pp. 12625–28.

31. Ibid., pp. 12574–77.

32. Ibid., p. 12603.

33. Baldwin, *Poverty and Politics*, p. 54.

34. *Yearbook of Agriculture*, 1940, p. 908; John R. Fleming to administrative officers of department, "Labor that Might be Transferred out of Agriculture into other channels in a War Emergency," Oct. 12, 1939, cited in Rasmussen, *Emergency Farm Labor Supply Program*, p. 13. On farm wages, see N. Gregory Silvermaster, director, Labor Division, FSA, to Wayne N. Darrow, director, Agricultural Labor Administration, Mar. 20, 1943, Office of Labor, FSA correspondence, box 75, file 4-FLT-R36, labor estimates, RG 224, NARA. On the persistent problems of farm labor surplus, see also Office of Agricultural War Relations, general correspondence, 1939–1941, report no. 4, Aug. 14, 1940, and report no. 9, Sept. 18, 1940, box 6, file Admin.-progress reports (advisory committee) 1–4, RG 16, NARA.

35. Testimony of Howard Haney, NDMH, pt. 33, Apr. 23, 26, 1942, p. 12603.

36. James Cheseburough to Franklin Delano Roosevelt, Jan. 20, 1942. This letter and others like it are in Office for Agricultural War Relations, general correspondence, 1942, box 145, file Employment 3 wages (Jan. 1–July 31), RG 16, NARA.

37. *Farm Labor Notes*, June 20, 1942, marked "Confidential, USDA, Bureau of Agricultural Economics," secretary of agriculture, general correspondence, employment, 1-4 Farm, May 14–July 15, 1942, RG 16, NARA.

38. Office for Agricultural War Relations, general correspondence, 1942, box 138-144, file Employment 1-1 labor, and box 189, RG 16, NARA; resolution from Charlotte City, Virginia War Board, June 30, 1943, general correspondence, 1943, box 26, file Resolutions-petitions, RG 224, NARA.

39. Clipping in correspondence concerning migratory labor camps, 1935–1943, box 9, file RP-M-127, employment, RG 96, NARA.

40. Wages climbed slightly between October 1, 1942, and January 1, 1943, but farmworkers made 39 percent of what unskilled factory workers earned in both years. The Bureau of Agricultural Economics's breakdown of wages by state is a bit misleading because it suggests that farmworkers were making substantially more in the Northeast than they were in the South. The bureau's numbers only reveal what growers had to pay, however, not what workers were actually earning. Harvest workers in the North were much more likely to be working for labor contractors who would have been taking a large bite out of their earnings, so their actual earnings would be far less that what the Bureau of Agricultural Economics reported. These figures are included in N. Gregory Silvermaster's report to Wayne H. Darrow, director, Agricultural Labor Administration, Mar. 20, 1943, FSA correspondence, box 75, file 4-FLT-R36, labor estimates, RG 224, NARA; "Farm Labor Notes," June 20, 1942, general correspondence, employment, 1-4 Farm, May 14–July 15, 1942, RG 16, NARA, p. 5.

41. The Agricultural Marketing Service concurred with the Interbureau Coordinating Committee's conclusion that the farm labor supply was not seriously reduced. The committee's studies showed an increase in wages between 1940 and 1941, but no drop in the number of hired laborers in agriculture. According to the Marketing Service, average monthly wages with board were $37 in July 1940 and $45 in 1941. See Report of the Interbureau Planning Committee on Farm Labor, "Review of the Farm Labor Situation in 1941," Dec. 31, 1941, general correspondence, subject employment, file Labor Oct. 4 to — [1941?], RG 16, NARA.

42. For a more detailed discussion of the FSA's changed priorities, see Baldwin, *Poverty and Politics*, pp. 326–35.

43. Harold Ballou, regional information adviser, to John Fischer, chief of the Information Division, May 5, 1941, correspondence concerning migratory labor camps, 1935–1943, box 9, RG 96, NARA.

44. Baldwin, *Poverty and Politics*, pp. 329–31; N. Gregory Silvermaster, director, Labor Division, FSA, to Mr. C. B. Baldwin, re: proposed expansion of FSA Camp Program to meet agricultural defense production needs, undated, correspondence concerning migratory labor camps, 1935–1943, box 2, file RP-85 M-060, projects, 1941, RG 96, NARA.

45. Grover Hill, asst. secretary of agriculture, to Paul V. McNutt, chair, WMC, July 14, 1942, general correspondence, employment 1 labor, Feb. 4–Feb. 21, 1942, RG 16, NARA.

46. Rasmussen, *Emergency Farm Labor Supply Program*, p. 25.

47. General correspondence, employment, 1-4 farm, and Office of Information press release, May 22, 1942, box 188, RG 16, NARA.

48. Baldwin, *Poverty and Politics*, p. 346.

49. This was the Byrd Committee, so called after its chair, Senator Harry F. Byrd. All but one member were avid FSA critics, and the committee predictably concluded that the FSA should be abolished and its war-related agencies "transferred to some more suitable agency" (ibid., pp. 347–48).

50. Ibid., pp. 353–54, 356–61.

51. Ibid., pp. 360–61.

52. Calavita, *Inside the State*, 18–22; Rasmussen, *Emergency Farm Labor Supply Program*, pp. 27–29; Thomas J. Flavin, asst. to the secretary, to H. G. Winsor, director, WMC, Northwest District, Seattle, Oct. 10, 1942, correspondence concerning migratory labor camps, 1935–1943, box 7, file Migratory-120-A thru G, RG 96, NARA.

53. Of the domestic workers transported, there were 114 from Virginia, 46 from Ohio, 287 from West Virginia, 531 from Texas, 1,508 from Missouri, 58 from New Jersey, 1,508 from Kentucky, 85 from North Carolina, 1,517 from Tennessee, 318 from Mississippi, 22 from Georgia, 96 from Louisiana, 656 from Illinois, and 62 from Alabama. Workers were moved to harvests in New York, New Jersey, Connecticut, Michigan, Florida, California, Arizona, New Mexico, and Washington. See Rasmussen, *Emergency Farm Labor Supply Program*, pp. 27–28; Laurence I. Hewes Jr., FSA regional director in charge, Mexican Labor Transportation Program, to Howard Norton, *Baltimore Sun*, Dec. 4, 1942, correspondence concerning migratory labor camps, 1935–1943, box 7, file Migratory-120-A thru G, RG 96, NARA.

54. Herman G. Agle, chairman, Erie County Farm Bureau, to James M. Mead, U.S. Senate, Apr. 8, 1942, correspondence concerning migratory labor camps, 1935–1943, box 1, RG 96, NARA. The remaining letters of support are in box 16, file Migratory-84-160 and file Migratory 160-01-general.

55. Jerome B. Flora, mayor, Elizabeth City, to Howard H. Gordon, regional director, FSA, Aug. 31, 1942, migratory labor camps correspondence 1935–1943, box 16, file Migratory-84-160 and file Migratory 160-01-general, RG 96, NARA.

56. Memorandum, Oct. 29, 1942, general correspondence, employment-1-labor, file 4/23–12/31/42, RG 16, NARA; Mason Barr, director, Management Division, FSA, to Watson B. Miller, asst. administrator, Federal Security Agency, Jan. 16, 1943, correspondence concerning migratory labor camps, 1935–1943, box 7, file Migratory-120-A thru G, RG 96, NARA; Harry L. Askew, chairman, Joint Industry Committee, to Marvin Jones, WFA, Aug. 9, 1943, general correspondence, 1943–44, box 61, file 6-R15-Florida, July–Dec. 1943, RG 224, NARA.

57. James W. Vann, Aug. 1942, general correspondence, box 16, file RP-M-85-183, monthly reports, RG 96, NARA.

58. General correspondence, box 51, file C2-R36, narrative reports FLSC, Florida, 1944, May–Dec., RG 224, NARA; Irwin R. Holmes, Monthly Narrative Report, Aug. [1942?], correspondence concerning migratory labor camps, 1935–1943, box 16, file RP-M-81-183, RG 96, NARA.

59. L. L. Stuckey, chairman, Vegetable Committee, Florida Farm Bureau Federation, Pahokee, Florida, to Claude R. Wickard, Feb. 10, 1942, correspondence concerning migratory labor camps, 1935–1943, box 7, file Migratory-120-A thru G, RG 96, NARA.

60. Correspondence, 1943–1944, box 75, file 4-FLT-R57, RG 224, NARA.

61. Testimony of James E. Beardsley, Clewiston, Apr. 26, 1942, NDMH, pt. 33, pp. 12565–66.

62. Telegram from J. L. Murray, Homestead, Florida, to Secretary Wickard, Feb. 4, 1943, correspondence, 1943–44, box 75, file 4-FLT-R57, RG 224, NARA.

63. Fred Wallace to H. W. Parisius, July 9, 1942, no. 208, box 160, file Meetings 8, State War Board Meetings 8 (Virginia), RG 16, NARA.

64. Paul Vander Schouw, supervisor, Florida Migratory Labor Camps, January 1942, FSA, correspondence concerning migratory labor camps, 1935–1943, box 20, file RP-M-85-183, monthly reports, RG 96, NARA.

65. The most notable is the case of U.S. Sugar, whose managers were charged with kidnapping, imprisoning, and shooting at workers in 1942. On U.S. Sugar, see the *Tampa Tribune*, Nov. 5, 1942. The sheriffs of Lake County and Broward County, Florida, used their official powers and their guns to generate labor for themselves and their neighbors' farms. Sheriff Willis McCall of Lake County (near Orlando) would have his officers sweep through black neighborhoods, arresting whomever they found out and about. Convicted of vagrancy within a matter of hours, his victims would then be "allowed" to work off their fines on his farm. In 1944 the Workers Defense League secured more than sixty affidavits from African Americans, mostly longshoremen, who had been charged with vagrancy and forced to work off the fines and court costs in the bean fields. The FBI investigated and ultimately brought the case before the federal grand jury. No indictment was rendered. The Workers Defense League filed civil suits on behalf of twelve of the plaintiffs and collected damages in 1948. On Broward and Lake County cases, see "Peonage and Other Forms of Forced Labor in the United States," Apr. 1949, box 171, folder 2; "Preliminary Memorandum on Lake County, Florida, and Sheriff Willis V. McCall," box 171, folder 14; depositions of plaintiffs, box 128, folders 33, 11; Aron S. Gilmartin, Workers Defense League, to Senator Claude A. Pepper, Aug. 15, 1944, box 170, folder 16; and numerous letters in box 170, folder 18, all in Workers Defense League Papers, Archives of Labor History and Urban Affairs.

66. Office of Labor, FSA correspondence, 1943–44, box 75, file 4-FLT-R57, RG 224, NARA, contains over fifty telegrams to Secretary Wickard from South Florida potato, bean, and tomato growers demanding imported farm labor, particularly Bahamian labor. They are all dated Jan. 29, 1943, because growers sent them after a meeting in Homestead to discuss ways to stabilize wages. I have quoted from telegrams from C. K. Gossman, Mrs. William J. Krome, W. H. Owens, L. L. Chandler Wickard, and E. A. Ames.

67. U.S. Congress, House Committee on Appropriations, 1943–44, *Hearings . . . Farm Labor Program . . . 1943–1944*, cited in Rasmussen, *Emergency Farm Labor Supply Program*, p. 42.

68. Both the NAACP and the STFU opposed the bill, but neither organization was in a particularly good position to influence Congress. On NAACP opposition, see *Atlanta Daily World*, May 4, 1943, clipping in general correspondence, 1943, box 25, file Publications 1-1, Negro Press, RG 224, NARA. On the opposition of the STFU, by then renamed the National Agricultural Workers Union, see the STFU Papers.

69. Baldwin, *Poverty and Politics*, p. 394.

70. Ibid.

71. Rasmussen, *Emergency Farm Labor Supply Program*, pp. 58, 62–63.

72. Reports by Sadye E. Pryor, home management supervisor, Okeechobee Cen-

ter, Sept. 1943, and Henry O. Earwood, Okeechobee Camp manager, Oct. 1944, general correspondence, 1943–44, box 51, file C2-R36-Florida, RG 224, NARA.

73. Walter C. McKain Jr. to Dr. Carl C. Taylor, director, Division of Farm Population and Rural Welfare, June 4, 1943, box 11, file Camps, June 1943, and Albert A. Richards, agricultural labor specialist, region 1, to Colonel Philip G. Bruton, Office of Labor, WFA, Aug. 24, 1943, box 61, file 6-R15, Jamaicans, RG 224, NARA.

74. Monthly Narrative Report, Aug. 1943, box 51, file C2-R36, Florida, RG 224, NARA.

75. S. C. Merritt, manager, Fort Pierce, FLSC Report for Oct., Nov. 5, 1945, general correspondence, 1945, box 78, file Camps 11-1, and John V. Wright, manager, Fort Pierce Labor Supply Center, Jan. [1944?], box 51, file C2-R36, Florida, RG 224, NARA.

76. W. W. Francis (Jamaican worker) to WFA, Mar. 20, 1945, box 86, file Laborers 3, claims-complaints, RG 224, NARA.

77. Oral interview by the author, May 1990.

78. Sherwood Brantley, Fort Pierce, FLSC manager, Jan. 31, 1945, general correspondence, 1945, box 78, file Camps 11-1, RG 224, NARA.

79. George E. Winston, Pahokee Farm Labor Center, Apr. 1944 Report, general correspondence, 1943–44, box 51, file C2-R36, Florida, RG 224, NARA.

80. Hebron FLSC monthly report, Oct. 2, 1944, general correspondence, 1943–44, box 52, file C2-R36 MD; D. W. Green, Burlington, New Jersey, FLSC monthly report, Aug. 31, 1945; Palmetto, Florida, FLSC monthly report, Apr. 30, 1945; and Erwin C. Thompson, Black Horse, Maryland, FLSC monthly report, Aug. 1, 1945, box 78, in files marked Camps 11-1, RG 224, NARA.

81. Reports for the week ending June 10, 1944, reveal that, of the 152 Bahamian workers housed at the Okeechobee Mobile Center, 18.8 percent refused to work. The following week, 36.6 percent of the 13 Bahamians and 106 domestic nontransported workers housed at Canal Point refused to work. At Morehead City 21.3 percent of 105 Bahamians and 133 domestic nontransported workers refused to work, and as did 14 percent of the 127 Bahamians and 13 domestic nontransported workers in Castle Hayne, North Carolina. See Hudson Wren, chief of operations, WFA, to Philip Bruton, June 27, 1944, general correspondence, 1943–44, box 59, file 6-A19, agreements, Jan. 1944; Redland, Florida, FLSC Monthly Report, Feb. 1945, box 78, file Camps 11-1, Florida; George E. Winston, manager, Pahokee Camp, narrative report, Nov. 30, 1945, file Camps 11-1, United States Sugar Corporation, Florida, 1945, all in RG 224, NARA.

82. Philip G. Bruton to Sidney de la Rue, special asst., Anglo-American Caribbean Commission, Washington, D.C., June 14, 1944, and Labour Adviser, Labour Dept., Jamaica, B.W.I., to Colonel Bruton, May 1, 1944, general correspondence, 1943–44, box 61, file 6-R15, Jamaicans, 1944, RG 224, NARA.

83. John B. Wentworth, Tenants Harbor, Maine, to Clinton Anderson, no date, general correspondence, 1945, box 94, file Wage stabilization 2, wage ceilings-orders-regulations, RG 224, NARA.

84. Milton Rossoff, Office of Labor, to George W. Hill, chief, Program Branch, Dec. 9, 1943, box 53, file C2-R36, inspection reports, 1943, RG 224, NARA.

85. Rasmussen, *Emergency Farm Labor Supply Program*, pp. 97–99.

86. Ibid., pp. 66–97.

87. Stephen Pace to Lieut. Col. Wilson Buie, Sept. 2, 1943, and telegram from Willard A. Munson to Buie, Sept. 19, 1944, general correspondence, 1943–44, box 59, file Recruitment and request for assistance W-WP-R15, RG 224, NARA.

88. Thomas W. Skuce, wage rate analyst, to W. C. Holly, Office of Labor, Sept. 23, 1944, general correspondence, 1943–44, box 59, file 4-WP-W2 (wages), RG 224, NARA.

89. Marvin O. Dickerson and Verdie A. Kile, farm labor supply assistants, to Mason Barr, chief, Office of Labor, WFA, Nov. 22, 1943, box 62, file 6-R59, repatriation, Jan. 1944, RG 224, NARA.

90. K. A. Butler, regional director, Indiana, to Mason Barr, Jan. 27, 1944, box 62, file 6-R59, repatriation, Jan. 1944, and Roy Litchfield, Gould, Florida, FLSC manager, Jan. 1944, box 51, file C2-R36, Florida, RG 224, NARA.

91. John Newdorp to Philip G. Bruton, July 1, 1944, box 62, file 6-R59, repatriation, Jan. 1944, RG 224, NARA.

92. Hebron, Maryland, FLSC Report, May 4, 1945, box 78, file Camps 11-1, RG 224, NARA.

93. Marvin O. Dickerson and Verdie A. Kile, farm labor supply assistants, to Mason Barr, chief, Office of Labor, WFA, Nov. 22, 1943, box 62, file 6-R59, repatriation, Jan. 1944, RG 224, NARA; *Journal and Guide* (Norfolk, Va.), June 5, 1943; *Pittsburgh Courier*, May 22, 1943.

94. George E. Winston, monthly narrative, June 1944, box 51, C2-R36, Florida, RG 224, NARA.

Chapter Eight

1. Schachter, "Report."

2. Ibid.

3. Ibid.

4. Jack Seabrook claims that he and his brother Belford "selected" Schachter and Local 56 when they realized that an industrial union would target their canneries. See personal correspondence with the author, June 1, 1995.

5. C. F. was increasingly at odds with his sons. When Belford announced that he was joining the military after Pearl Harbor, C. F. effectively disowned him, and Jack stepped into his shoes. But Jack and C. F. waged a bitter war in the 1950s that resulted in C. F. selling the company to keep it from his sons. See John Seabrook's painful account of his family's history in "Spinach King." See also *Butcher Workman*, 27, no. 8 (Aug. 1941), and "Racial Discrimination Forbidden at Giant Seabrook," *Philadelphia Record*, no date, clipping in box 103, Local 56 Papers.

6. Jack Seabrook confirmed in a recent letter that "it was well worth the extra cost of a Union to have workers we could really count on before the season started" (Jack Seabrook to the author, June 1, 1995).

7. *Philadelphia Daily News*, Mar. 14, 1941; *Butcher Workman*, 27, no. 8 (Aug.

1941); unidentified clipping, "Seabrook Farms Signs Contract with A.F.L. Union," all in box 103, Local 56 Papers; Schachter, "Report."

8. Schachter, "Report."

9. John M. Seabrook notes that the owners of Campbell Soup Company were "more hostile to unionization than old Henry Ford, if that's possible" and they "regarded the union contract at Seabrook as heresy" (personal correspondence to the author, June 1, 1995).

10. Jack Seabrook agrees that Local 56 took "a beating in the press" over the issue of collecting dues from the POWs and U.S. soldiers but denies any part in undermining the union's control over the seasonal workforce. See personal correspondence, June 1, 1995, and Schachter, "Report." For news coverage on the dues collection issue, see *Philadelphia Inquirer*, Sept. 17, 1943, Feb. 10, 1944; *Courier-Post* (Camden), *New York Herald*, and *Birmingham Post*, Feb. 11, 1944; *Wichita Beacon*, *Savannah Morning News*, and *Florida Times-Union*, Feb. 12, 1944, clippings in Local 56 Papers.

11. Schachter, "Report."

12. The union already at Campbell Soup was the UCAPAWA, founded by Eleanor and Donald Henderson of Seabrook Farms fame. Having concentrated most of its organizing efforts on the West Coast, the CIO affiliate had a small presence in New Jersey, including Campbell. UCAPAWA and the STFU were already bitter rivals due to an attempted merger, or takeover (depending on whose account you read), of the STFU. When Campbell contracted with the STFU for workers, UCAPAWA threatened a walkout of its members but eventually backed down. Each accused the other of racism, raiding each other's members, and selling out to companies. H. L. Mitchell's account of this controversy is well documented in the STFU Papers; however, UCAPAWA's position is less clear. Some of its newsletters survive, but they are not particularly useful. As a result, at present I am not able to delve more deeply into the history of this interunion conflict. UCAPAWA was renamed the Food, Tobacco and Agricultural Workers Union in 1944. See the *FTA News* during the war years for UCAPAWA's side. On the agreement between Schachter, the STFU, and the WMC, see Schachter, "Report," and "Report of the Executive Council," pt. 2, 11th Annual STFU Convention, box 52, file 959, STFU Papers.

13. "Special to Newspaper Meat and Cannery Local 56," by H. L. Mitchell, [1944], box 52, file 976, STFU Papers.

14. H. L. Mitchell, "The 1944 Farm Labor Supply Bill," box 52, folder 975, STFU Papers.

15. Memorandum from H. L. Mitchell, [1943?], box 52, folder 975, STFU Papers.

16. H. L. Mitchell to Dan Bell, June 15, 1944; H. L. Mitchell, "The March of the Machines on the Land," report of the Executive Council, 11th Annual STFU Convention, box 52, file 959, STFU Papers, p. 4.

17. The most notable of these attempts occurred in Forrest City, Arkansas, on July 31, 1944. STFU organizers Sam James and Anderson Johnson were about to drive eighty men to Memphis, where they were scheduled to board a train for Campbell Soup in Camden, New Jersey. Although James and Johnson had a letter

from the WMC giving them the authority to move the group, they were arrested, along with four truck drivers, by the local manager of the USES and charged with enticing labor and transporting workers out of the state. STFU lawyers got all six out of jail and back on the road, and the USES manager was later reprimanded by the WMC. See various letters dated August 1944 in box 51, STFU Papers.

18. Schachter, "Report," pp. 9, 13; "Chart of Members transferred by August 1944," STFU Papers.

19. Schachter, "Report," pp. 9, 13 (emphasis is his).

20. David Burgess, "Progress Report," Aug. 22, 1944, STFU Papers.

21. David Burgess, "Labor and the Church Cooperate," Final Report, Oct. 1, 1944, box 51, folder 950, STFU Papers, pp. 19–20.

22. David Burgess, "Progress Report," Aug. 22, 1944, and "Labor and the Church Cooperate," Final Report, Oct. 1, 1944, box 51, folder 950, STFU Papers.

23. David Burgess, "Progress Report," Aug. 22, 1944, and "Labor and the Church Cooperate," Final Report, Oct. 1, 1944, box 51, folder 950, STFU Papers.

24. Mrs. Violet Leola Walker to H. L. Mitchell, June 9, 1944, and W. C. Banks to H. L. Mitchell, June 5, 1944, STFU Papers.

25. David Burgess, "Progress Report," Aug. 22, 1944, STFU Papers.

26. F. R. Betton to H. L. Mitchell, Sept. 6, 1944, box 51, folder 944, STFU Papers.

27. David Burgess to H. L. Mitchell, Aug. 30, 1944, folder 942, and Burgess, "Labor and the Church Cooperate," Final Report, Oct. 1, 1944, box 51, folder 950, STFU Papers, p. 16.

28. David Burgess, "Labor and the Church Cooperate," Final Report, Oct. 1, 1944, box 51, folder 950, STFU Papers.

29. Ibid.

30. Ibid., p. 10.

31. June 8, 1944, STFU Papers.

32. Minutes of Meeting with College Girls Committee at Seabrook Housing Project, July 18, 1944, STFU Papers.

33. E. Marie Miles, asst. to the dean, Hampton Institute, to H. L. Mitchell, June 26, 1944, folder 932; H. L. Mitchell to John Egar, project management director, National Housing Authority, July 17, 1944, folder 934; Dean of Women to H. L. Mitchell, July 26, 1944, folder 937, all in box 50, STFU Papers.

34. H. L. Mitchell to Oswalt Escrique, leader of Barbadians at Campbell Soup, Sept. 19, 1944, box 51, folder 947, STFU Papers.

35. June 3, 1944, and H. L. Mitchell to Student Members, Sept. 1, 1944, STFU Papers.

36. See, for example, various letters in box 50, folder 932, STFU Papers.

37. The STFU survived on charitable contributions and dues of just $1.00 a month. Its papers are filled with requests for funding.

38. *Labor Vanguard,* June 1946; *Brewery Worker,* June 19, 1946; *Progressive News,* June 8, 1946; *Memphis Press-Scimitar,* June 1946, all clippings in box 106, STFU Papers.

39. *Philadelphia Record,* July 15, 1946, in box 106, STFU Papers.

40. "Canneries Urged to Oust POW's, Hire Americans," *Philadelphia Record,* Aug. 22, 1945, in box 103, Local 56 Papers.

41. Passed on December 28, 1945, Public Law 269 extended the life of the Farm Labor Supply Appropriation Act through December 31, 1946. Foreign workers were to be permitted to enter the United States within the provisions of the act of 1944, despite the cessation of hostilities. Growers' organizations testified in support of the bill, complaining only that the appropriation was too small. Public Law 521, passed July 23, 1946, extended the program through June 30, 1947. See Rasmussen, *Emergency Farm Labor Supply Program,* pp. 50–52.

42. Public Law 76 was passed on May 26, 1947. See ibid., p. 56.

43. The *Union Reporter* was a publication of the National Farm Labor Union, which was the STFU's postwar incarnation. See the issue for July 1947 in the STFU Papers.

44. "Farm Organization in the South," Sept. 6, 1944, box 51, folder 944, STFU Papers.

Epilogue

1. On the postwar period, see William H. Metzler, *Migratory Farm Workers in the Atlantic Coast Stream: A Study in the Belle Glade Area of Florida,* circular no. 966 (Washington, D.C.: U.S. Department of Agriculture, 1955); *Puerto Rican Farm Workers in the Middle Atlantic States: Highlights of a Study* (Washington, D.C.: U.S. Department of Labor, Bureau of Employment Security, 1954); McCoy and Wood, "Caribbean Workers in the Florida Sugar Cane Industry"; Weintraub and Ross, *"Temporary" Alien Workers in the United States.* Also see Schell interview.

2. *NYT,* Apr. 20, 1978; Schell interview; Cletus Daniel, *Bitter Harvest.*

3. Schell interview. For the fullest discussion of imported and illegal workers in agriculture since the Second World War, see Calavita, *Inside the State.*

4. Schell interview.

5. On farmworkers and tuberculosis, see *NYT,* Apr. 3, 1991; on AIDS in Belle Glade, see *Los Angeles Times,* Jan. 28, 1993; and on exposure to pesticides, see *NYT,* Aug. 19, 1990. See also "Migrant Workers Straining the South's Health Safety Net," *Raleigh News and Observer,* Oct. 29, 1989.

6. " 'Wine Book' Tells of N.C. Migrant Workers' Debt, Servitude," *Raleigh News and Observer,* Oct. 31, 1989, and "Crop Failure: Homeless Are Drawn into a Miserable Life on Farm 'Wino Crews,' " *Wall Street Journal,* Oct. 19, 1992.

7. *Raleigh News and Observer,* Oct. 31, 1989.

Bibliography

Primary Sources

Manuscript Collections

Chapel Hill, North Carolina
    Southern Historical Collection, University of North Carolina
        Penn School Papers
        Southern Tenant Farmers' Union Papers
Detroit, Michigan
    Archives of Labor History and Urban Affairs, Walter Reuther Library, Wayne
    State University
        Workers Defense League Papers
Durham, North Carolina
    Perkins Library, Duke University
        Radical Farm Organizations (microfilm)
New Brunswick, New Jersey
    Rutgers University Libraries, Special Collections
        Local 56 of the Amalgamated Meat Cutters and Butcher Workmen Papers
Philadelphia, Pennsylvania
    National Archives and Records Administration, Philadelphia Branch
        RG 224, Records of the Office of Labor (War Food Administration) relat-
        ing to New Jersey
Princeton, New Jersey
    Princeton University Library
        American Civil Liberties Union Papers (microfilm reel 110)
Trenton, New Jersey
    New Jersey Department of State, Division of Archives and Records Manage-
    ment
        New Jersey Ethnic Survey
    New Jersey Historical Commission
        New Jersey Ethnic Life Series

Washington, D.C.
  Catholic University of America
    Terence V. Powderly Papers, series B, Immigration, part 2, Correspondence of Chief, Information Division, Bureau of Immigration, 1906–22 (microform)
  Library of Congress, Manuscript Division
    Carter G. Woodson Collection of Negro Papers and Related Documents (microfilm)
    National Consumers League Records (microfilm)
    National Urban League Papers (microfilm)
    Papers of the National Association for the Advancement of Colored People (NAACP), part 10, Peonage, Labor, and the New Deal, 1913–1939 (microfilm)
  National Archives and Records Administration
    RG 16, Records of the Office of the Secretary of Agriculture, including the records of the Office for Agricultural War Relations
    RG 60, General Records of the Department of Justice
    RG 85, Records of the Immigration and Naturalization Service, including the records of the Bureau of Immigration of the Department of Commerce and Labor
    RG 86, Records of the Women's Bureau
    RG 96, Records of the Farmers Home Administration, including the Records of the Farm Security Administration and the Resettlement Administration
    RG 174, General Records of the Department of Labor
    RG 183, Records of the U.S. Employment Service
    RG 211, Records of the War Manpower Commission
    RG 224, Records of the Office of Labor (War Food Administration)
    RG 280, Records of the Federal Mediation and Conciliation Service

Newspapers and Contemporary Magazines

Agricultural Worker, continued as *The Rural Worker* (1935–37), *The CIO News: UCAPAWA Edition*, and *FTA News*
Belle Glade Record
Bridgeton Evening News
Camden Post
Canal Point News
Century Magazine
Charities and the Commons, continued as *The Survey* and as *Survey Graphic*
Clewiston News
The Cosmopolitan
Cranbury Press
The Crisis
Daily Worker
Florida Agricultural Interests

Florida Agriculturalist
Florida Dispatch
Florida Times-Union
Harper's New Monthly Magazine
Illustrated World
Journal and Guide (Norfolk, Virginia)
Manufacturers Record
Miami Herald
Millville Republican
Monthly Labor Review
Nation
New Jersey Afro-American
New Jersey Labor Herald
New Republic
New York Herald Tribune
New York Post
New York Sun
New York Times
Opportunity
Palm Beach Post
Philadelphia Inquirer
Philadelphia Record
Pittsburgh Courier
Savannah Tribune
Sharecroppers Voice
Southern Cultivator
STFU News, continued as *The Tenant Farmer, The Farm Worker* (1943–44), *Farm Labor News* (1945), and *Union Reporter* (1946) (Perkins Library, Duke University [microfilm])
The Survey
Tampa Tribune
Vineland Evening-Journal
World To-Day
Yearbook of Agriculture

Oral Histories

Burgess, David. Interview by the author. Newark, New Jersey. May 29, 1990.
Federal Writers' Project Life Histories. Southern Historical Collection. Library of the University of North Carolina, Chapel Hill.
Pearl City Oral History Project. Boca Raton Historical Society Library.
Schell, Greg. Florida Rural Legal Services. Interview by the author. Belle Glade, Florida. July 16, 1994.
Sorn, George F. Interview by the author. Orlando, Florida. July 17, 1994.
Wright, Giles R., comp. *Looking Back: Eleven Life Histories*. New Jersey Ethnic Life Series (10). New Jersey Historical Commission, Department of State, 1986.

Government Publications

FEDERAL

Beck, Philip G., and M. C. Foster. *Six Rural Problem Areas: Relief—Resources—Rehabilitation: An Analysis of the Human and Material Resources in Six Rural Areas with High Relief Rates*. Research Monograph 1. Washington, D.C.: Federal Relief Administration, 1935. Reprint. New York: Da Capo, 1971.

Belle Glade Area of Florida. Circular no. 966. Washington, D.C.: U.S. Department of Agriculture, 1955.

Bernert, E. H., and G. K. Bowles. *Farm Migration, 1940–45*. Washington, D.C.: U.S. Bureau of Agricultural Economics, 1947.

Carothers, Doris. *Chronology of the Federal Emergency Relief Administration, May 12, 1933, to December 31, 1935*. WPA Research Monograph 6. Washington, D.C.: GPO, 1937.

Carpenter, Niles. *Immigrants and Their Children*. U.S. Bureau of the Census. Census Monograph no. 7. Washington, D.C.: GPO, 1927.

Congressional Record. Washington, D.C.: GPO.

Ducoff, L. J., and M. J. Hagood. *Wages and Wage Rates of Seasonal Farm Workers in Special Crop Areas of Florida, Feb.–March 1945*. Report 1. Washington, D.C.: U.S. Bureau of Agricultural Economics, 1945.

Earle, F. S. "Development of Trucking Interests." In *Yearbook of Agriculture 1900*, pp. 437–52. Washington, D.C.: GPO, 1901.

Farm Security Administration. *Annual Reports of the Administrator*. Washington, D.C.: GPO, 1938–43.

Folsom, Josiah C. "Farm Laborers in the United States Turn to Collective Action." In *Yearbook of Agriculture 1935*, pp. 188–91. Washington, D.C.: GPO, 1935.

———. "Farm Labor in Massachusetts, 1921." *USDA Department Bulletin no. 1220* (Apr. 1924): 1–25.

———. *Wage Ceilings in Florida Citrus Groves, Season of 1943–44*. Washington, D.C.: U.S. Bureau of Agricultural Economics, 1950.

———, comp. *Migratory Agricultural Labor in the United States: Annotated Bibliography of Selected References*. Washington, D.C.: GPO, 1953.

Folsom, Josiah C., and O. E. Baker. *A Graphic Summary of Farm Labor and Population*. Miscellaneous Publication 265. Washington, D.C.: U.S. Department of Agriculture, 1937.

Genung, A. B. "Agriculture in the World War Period." In *Yearbook of Agriculture 1940: Farmers in a Changing World*, pp. 277–96. Washington, D.C.: GPO, 1940.

Ham, William J. "Farm Labor in an Era of Change." In *Yearbook of Agriculture 1940: Farmers in a Changing World*, pp. 911–12. Washington, D.C.: GPO, 1940.

Ham, William T. *Seasonal Farm Labor in the Southeast*. Statement made at the Interstate Conference on Migratory Labor, Atlanta, Ga., Dec. 17 and 18, 1940. Washington, D.C.: U.S. Bureau of Agricultural Economics, 1940.

Holley, William C., Ellen Winston, and T. J. Woofter Jr. *The Plantation South, 1934–1937*. WPA Research Monograph 22. Washington, D.C.: GPO, 1940.

Jamieson, Stuart. *Labor Unionism in American Agriculture*. U.S. Department of Labor. Bureau of Labor Statistics. Bulletin no. 836. Washington, D.C.: GPO, 1945. Reprint. New York: Arno, 1976.

Koren, John. "The Padrone System and Padrone Banks." *Bulletin of the Department of Labor*, no. 9 (Mar. 1897): 113–29.

Manning, Caroline. *The Immigrant Woman and Her Job*. New York: Arno, 1970. Reprint of U.S. Department of Labor. *Bulletin of the Women's Bureau*, no. 74. Washington, D.C.: GPO, 1930.

Meade, Emily. "The Italians on the Land: A Study in Immigration." *Bulletin of the U.S. Bureau of Labor* 14 (May 1907): 473–533.

Oemler, A. "Truck Farming." In *Report of the Commissioner of Agriculture*, pp. 583–627. Washington, D.C.: GPO, 1885.

Rasmussen, Wayne D. *A History of the Emergency Farm Labor Supply Program, 1943–1947*. Bureau of Agricultural Economics Monograph 13. Washington, D.C.: U.S. Bureau of Agricultural Economics, 1951.

Resettlement Administration. *Annual Report*. Washington, D.C.: GPO, 1936.

Strikes and Lockouts in 1944. U.S. Bureau of Labor Statistics Bulletin 833. Washington, D.C.: GPO, 1945.

Taylor, William H. "The Influence of Refrigeration on the Fruit Industry." In *Yearbook of Agriculture 1900*, pp. 561–80. Washington, D.C.: GPO, 1901.

True, Alfred Charles. *A History of Agricultural Extension Work in the United States, 1785–1923*. Washington, D.C.: GPO, 1928.

U.S. Bureau of Immigration. *Annual Reports of the Commissioner-General of Immigration*. Washington, D.C.: GPO, 1913–19.

U.S. Bureau of the Census. *11th Census of the United States, Agriculture, 1890*. Washington, D.C.: GPO, 1895.

———. *12th Census of the United States, 1900*. Washington, D.C.: GPO, 1902.

———. *14th Census of the United States, Agriculture, 1920*. Vol. 6, pt. 2, *The Southern States*. Washington, D.C.: GPO, 1922.

———. *16th Census of the United States, Agriculture, 1940*. Vol. 1, pt. 3, *The South Atlantic States*. Washington, D.C.: GPO, 1942.

———. *Negroes in the United States, 1920–1932*. Washington, D.C.: GPO, 1935.

U.S. Commission on Civil Rights. North Carolina Advisory Commission. *When Miles Outrate Men: Migrant and Seasonal Farmworkers in North Carolina: A Report*. Washington, D.C.: GPO, 1979.

U.S. Department of Agriculture. *Yearbooks of Agriculture*. Washington, D.C.: GPO, 1894–1955.

U.S. Department of Labor. *Annual Reports of the Secretary*.

———. *The Anvil and the Plow: A History of the U.S. Department of Labor*. Washington, D.C.: GPO, 1963.

———. *Hand and Machine Labor: Introduction and Analysis*. Vol. 1 of *13th Annual Report, 1898*. Washington, D.C.: GPO, 1899.

———. *Negro Migration in 1916–1917*. Washington, D.C.: Division of Negro Economics, U.S. Department of Labor, 1919.

———. Children's Bureau. *Work of Children on Truck and Small-Fruit Farms in South New Jersey*. Bureau Pub. no. 132. Washington, D.C.: GPO, 1924.

U.S. House of Representatives. *Hearings on Appropriation for the Farm Labor Program, 1943*. 78th Cong., 1st sess. Washington, D.C.: GPO, 1943.

———. Select Committee Investigating National Defense Migration. *Hearings*. 77th Cong., 1st and 2d sess., 1941–43. Washington, D.C.: GPO, 1943.

———. Select Committee of the House Committee on Agriculture to Investigate the Activities of the Farm Security Administration. *Hearings*. 78th Cong., 1st sess. Washington, D.C.: GPO, 1944.

———. Select Committee to Investigate the Interstate Migration of Destitute Citizens (Tolan Committee). *Hearings before the Select Committee to Investigate the Interstate Migration of Destitute Citizens*. 76th Cong., 3d sess., 1940–41. Washington, D.C.: GPO, 1941.

U.S. Industrial Commission. *Reports*. Vol. 10, *Report of the Industrial Commission on Agriculture and Agricultural Labor*, and vol. 11, *Report of the Industrial Commission on Agriculture and on Taxation in Various States*. House of Representatives, 57th Cong., 1st sess., H. Doc. no. 179. Washington, D.C.: GPO, 1901.

U.S. President's Commission on Migratory Labor. *Migratory Labor in American Agriculture: Report of the President's Commission on Migratory Labor*. Washington, D.C.: GPO, 1951.

U.S. Senate. *Hearings of the Senate Sub-Committee on Agricultural Appropriation*. 77th Cong., 2d sess. Washington, D.C.: GPO, 1943.

———. Commission on Industrial Relations. *Final Report and Testimony Submitted to Congress by the Commission on Industrial Relations*. Vol. 1. 64th Cong., 1st sess., S. Doc. 415. Washington, D.C.: GPO, 1916.

———. Immigration Commission (Dillingham Commission). *Reports of the Immigration Commission*. Pt. 24, vols. 21 and 22, *Recent Immigrants in Agriculture*. 61st Cong., 2d and 3d sess. S. Doc. 633. Washington, D.C.: GPO, 1911.

Webb, John N. *The Migratory and Casual Worker*. WPA Research Monograph 7. Washington, D.C.: GPO, 1937.

———. *The Transient Unemployed*. WPA Research Monograph 3. Washington, D.C.: GPO, 1935.

Williams, W. T. B. "The Negro Exodus from the South." In *Negro Migration in 1916–1917*, edited by U.S. Department of Labor, Division of Negro Economics. Washington, D.C.: GPO, 1919.

Woofter, T. J. "Migration of Negroes from Georgia, 1916–1917." In *Negro Migration in 1916–1917*, by U.S. Department of Labor, pp. 75–91. Washington, D.C.: Division of Negro Economics, U.S. Department of Labor, 1919.

Wright, Carroll D. *The Slums of Baltimore, Chicago, New York, and Philadelphia*. 7th Special Report of the Committee of Labor. Washington, D.C.: GPO, 1894.

STATE

Connecticut Board of Agriculture. "The Past and Future of Connecticut Agriculture." *24th Annual Report*, 1890.

Florida Legislative Council and Legislative Reference Bureau. *Migrant Farm Labor in Florida*. Tallahassee, Fla., 1963.

Hendrickson, Clarence Irving. *An Economic Study of the Agriculture of the Connecti-*

cut Valley. Connecticut Agricultural Experiment Station Bulletin 174. Storrs, Conn., 1931.

Jackson, Nelson C. *Negroes on the Road: A Survey of the Negro Transient in New Jersey*. Trenton, N.J.: State Employment Relief Administration, 1935.

Koos, Earl Loman. *They Follow the Sun*. Jacksonville, Fla.: Bureau of Maternal and Child Health, Florida State Board of Health, 1957.

Lunberg, Emma O. *Social Welfare in Florida*. Publication no. 4. Tallahassee, Fla.: State Board of Public Welfare, 1934.

Massey, W. F. "The Development of Marketing Gardening Southward and Its Lesson to the Northern Trucker." In *Annual Report* of New Jersey State Board of Agriculture, pp. 149–59. Trenton, N.J.: New Jersey State Printers, 1905.

New Jersey. *Report of the Commission to Investigate the Employment of Migratory Children in the State of New Jersey*. Trenton, N.J.: New Jersey State Printers, 1931.

———. *Report of the New Jersey Commission of Immigration*. Trenton, N.J.: New Jersey State Printers, 1914.

New Jersey Department of Labor. *Why New Jersey Farmers Employ Italian Family Labor*. Trenton, N.J.: New Jersey State Printers, 1931.

New Jersey State Board of Agriculture. *Annual Reports*. Trenton, N.J.: New Jersey State Printers, various years.

Woodward, Carl R. *The Development of Agriculture in New Jersey, 1640–1880*. New Brunswick, N.J.: New Jersey Agricultural Experiment Station, 1927.

Woodward, Carl R., and Ingrid N. Waller. *New Jersey's Agricultural Experiment Station, 1880–1930*. New Brunswick, N.J.: New Jersey Agricultural Experiment Station, 1932.

Wright, Giles R. *Afro-Americans in New Jersey: A Short History*. Trenton, N.J.: New Jersey Historical Commission, Department of State, 1988.

Secondary Sources

Adams, Graham. *Age of Industrial Violence, 1910–1915: The Activities and Findings of the U.S. Commission on Industrial Relations*. New York: Columbia University Press, 1966.

Ahearn, Daniel J., Jr. *The Wage of Farm and Factory Laborers, 1914–1944*. New York: Columbia University Press, 1945.

Anderson, Henry P. *The Bracero Program in California*. Chicano Heritage Series. New York: Arno, 1976.

Anderson, Nels. *Men on the Move*. Chicago: University of Chicago Press, 1940.

Anthony, David W. "The Cranbury Terror Case." *The Crisis* 46 (Oct. 1939): 295–96, 314.

Argersinger, Peter H., and Jo Ann E. Argersinger. "The Machine Breakers: Farmworkers and Social Change in the Rural Midwest of the 1870s." *Agricultural History* 58 (1984): 393–410.

Ashby, Richard. "Florida, 1920–1935: A Case of Inter-State Migration." Ph.D. dissertation, University of North Carolina, 1938.

Atkinson, Raymond C., Louise C. Odencrantz, and Ben Deming. *Public Employment Service in the United States*. Chicago: Public Administration Service, 1938.

Ayers, Edward L. *The Promise of the New South: Life after Reconstruction*. New York: Oxford University Press, 1992.

——. *Vengeance and Justice: Crime and Punishment in the Nineteenth-Century American South*. New York: Oxford University Press, 1984.

Babson, Roger W. *W. B. Wilson and the Department of Labor*. New York: Brentano's, 1919.

Bach, Robert L. "Mexican Immigration and the American State." *International Migration Review* 12 (1978): 536–58.

Badger, Anthony J. *Prosperity Road: The New Deal, Tobacco, and North Carolina*. Chapel Hill: University of North Carolina Press, 1980.

Bailey, Joseph Cannon. *Seaman A. Knapp: Schoolmaster of American Agriculture*. New York: Columbia University Press, 1945.

Baily, Samuel L. "The Italians and Organized Labor in the U.S. and Argentina, 1880–1910." *International Migration Review* 1 (1967): 55–66.

Baker, Gladys L. *The County Agent*. Chicago: University of Chicago Press, 1939.

Baker, Ray Stannard. "The Negro Goes North." *World's Work* 34 (July 1917): 314–19.

Baldwin, Sidney. *Poverty and Politics: The Rise and Decline of the Farm Security Administration*. Chapel Hill: University of North Carolina Press, 1968.

Barger, Harold, and Hans H. Landsberg. *American Agriculture, 1899–1939: A Study of Output, Employment, and Productivity*. New York: National Bureau of Economic Research, 1942.

Bartley, Numan V. *The Creation of Modern Georgia*. Athens: University of Georgia Press, 1983.

Barton, Amy E. *Campesinas: Women Farm Workers in the California Agricultural Labor Force*. Sacramento, Calif.: Committee on the Status of Women, 1978.

Beck, Henry C. *Forgotten Towns of Southern New Jersey*. New Brunswick, N.J.: Rutgers University Press, 1961.

Becket, James W. "Agricultural Labor Skills — Past, Present, Future." In *Fruit and Vegetable Harvest Mechanization: Manpower Implications*, edited by B. C. Cargill and G. E. Rossmiller, pp. 257–66. East Lansing: Rural Manpower Center, Michigan State University, 1969.

Beecroft, Eric, and Seymour Janow. "Toward a National Policy for Migration." *Social Forces* 16 (May 1938): 475–92.

Benedict, Murray. *Farm Policies of the United States, 1790–1950*. New York: Octagon, 1966.

Berger, Samuel R. *Dollar Harvest: The Story of the Farm Bureau*. Lexington, Mass.: Heath Lexington, 1971.

Bernstein, Irving. *A History of the American Worker, 1920–1933: The Lean Years*. Baltimore: Penguin, 1960.

Berthoff, Rowland. "Southern Attitudes toward Immigration, 1865–1914." *Journal of Southern History* 17 (1951): 328–60.

Billinger, Robert D., Jr. "With the Wehrmacht in Florida: The German POW Facility at Camp Blanding, 1942–1946." *Florida Historical Quarterly* 58, no. 2 (Oct. 1979): 160–73.

Bishop, C. E., ed. *Farm Labor in the United States*. New York: Columbia University Press, 1967.

Block, Fred. "The Ruling Class Does Not Rule: Notes on the Marxist Theory of the State." *Socialist Revolution* 33 (May–June 1977): 6–28.

Block, William Joseph. *The Separation of the Farm Bureau and the Extension Service*. Urbana: University of Illinois Press, 1960.

Blum, A. A. "The Farmer, the Army, and the Draft." *Agricultural History* 38 (1964): 34.

Bodnar, John. *The Transplanted: A History of Immigrants in Urban America*. Bloomington: Indiana University Press, 1987.

Bowers, William L. *The Country-Life Movement in America, 1900–1920*. Port Washington, N.Y.: Kennikat Press, 1974.

Brandfon, Robert L. "The End of Immigration to the Cotton Fields." *Mississippi Valley Historical Review* 50 (1964): 591–611.

Breen, William. "The Mobilization of Skilled Labor in World War I: 'Voluntarism,' the U.S. Public Service Reserve, and the Department of Labor, 1917–1918." *Labor History* 32, no. 2 (1991): 253–72.

"Bringing the Italians to Vineland." *Vineland Historical Magazine* 53 (1977): 28–29.

Brooks, Robert Preston. *Georgia Studies: Selected Writings of Robert Preston Brooks*. Athens: University of Georgia Press, 1952.

Bruce, Philip Alexander. *The Rise of the New South*. Vol. 17 of *The History of North America*. Edited by Guy Carleton Lee. Philadelphia: George Barrie & Sons, ca. 1905.

Brundage, W. Fitzhugh. *Lynching in the New South: Georgia and Virginia, 1880–1930*. Urbana: University of Illinois Press, 1993.

Brunner, Edmund S., and E. Hsin Pao Yang. *Rural America and the Extension Service*. New York: Bureau of Publications, Teachers College, Columbia University, 1949.

Calavita, Kitty. *Inside the State: The Bracero Program, Immigration, and the INS*. New York: Routledge, 1992.

Campbell, Christiana McFadyen. *The Farm Bureau and the New Deal: A Study of the Making of National Farm Policy, 1933–1940*. Urbana: University of Illinois Press, 1962.

Carey, John J. "Progressives and the Immigrants, 1885–1915." Ph.D. dissertation, University of Connecticut, 1968.

Churchill, Charles W. *The Italians of Newark: A Community Study*. Reprint. New York: Arno, 1975.

Chute, Charles. "Cost of the Cranberry Sauce." *Survey*, Dec. 2, 1911, pp. 1281–84.

Ciccolella, Erasmo S. *Vibrant Life, 1886–1942: Trenton's Italian Americans*. New York: Center for Migration Studies of New York, 1986.

Cinel, Dino. "The Seasonal Emigrations of Italians in the Nineteenth Century:

From Internal to International Destinations." *Journal of Ethnic Studies* 10 (Spring 1982): 43–68.

Claghorn, Kate. "The Protection and Distribution of Immigrants." *Proceedings of the Academy of Political Science in the City of New York* 2 (July 1912): 199–206.

Clarke-Hazlett, Christopher. "The Road to Dependency: Policy, Planning, and the Rationalization of American Agriculture, 1920–1945." Ph.D. dissertation, University of Rochester, 1986.

Cobb, James C., and Michael V. Namorato, eds. *The New Deal and the South.* Jackson: University Press of Mississippi, 1984.

Cochrane, Willard W. *The Development of American Agriculture: A Historical Analysis.* Minneapolis: University of Minnesota Press, 1979.

Cohen, William. *At Freedom's Edge: Black Mobility and the Southern White Quest for Racial Control.* Baton Rouge: Louisiana State University Press, 1991.

———. "Negro Involuntary Servitude in the South, 1865–1940: A Preliminary Analysis." *Journal of Southern History* 42 (1976): 31–60.

Colburn, David R. *Racial Change and Community Crisis: St. Augustine, Florida, 1877–1980.* New York: Columbia University Press, 1985.

Coleman, Kenneth, ed. *History of Georgia.* Athens: University of Georgia Press, 1977.

Coles, Robert. *Migrants, Sharecroppers, Mountaineers.* Boston: Little, Brown, 1971.

Collins, Henry Hill. *America's Own Refugees: Our 4,000,000 Homeless Migrants.* Princeton, N.J.: Princeton University Press, 1941.

Conner, Valerie. *The National War Labor Board: Stability, Social Justice, and the Voluntary State in World War I.* Chapel Hill: University of North Carolina Press, 1983.

Conrad, David E. *The Forgotten Farmers: The Story of the Sharecroppers in the New Deal.* Urbana: University of Illinois Press, 1965.

Conway, Alan. *The Reconstruction of Georgia.* Minneapolis: University of Minnesota Press, 1966.

Coulter, John Lee. *Industrial History of the Valley of the Red River of the North.* Vol. 3. Bismarck: North Dakota State Historical Society, 1910.

Cox, LaWanda Fenlason. "Agricultural Labor in the United States, 1865–1900, with Special Reference to the South." Ph.D. dissertation, University of California, Berkeley, 1942.

———. "The American Agricultural Wage Earner, 1865–1900: The Emergence of a Modern Labor Problem." *Agricultural History* 22 (1948): 95–114.

Craig, Richard B. *The Bracero Program: Interest Groups and Foreign Policy.* Austin: University of Texas Press, 1971.

Cunningham, Barbara, ed. *The New Jersey Ethnic Experience.* Union City, N.J.: Wise, 1977.

Danbon, David B. *The Resisted Revolution: Urban America and the Industrialization of Agriculture, 1900–1930.* Ames: Iowa State University Press, 1979.

Danhof, Clarence H. "Agricultural Technology to 1880." In *The Growth of the American Economy,* 2d ed., edited by Harold F. Williamson, pp. 113–40. New York: Prentice-Hall, 1951.

Daniel, Cletus. "Agricultural Unionism and the Early New Deal: The California Experience." *South California Quarterly* 59, no. 2 (1977): 185–215.

———. *Bitter Harvest: A History of California Farmworkers, 1870–1941*. Ithaca, N.Y.: Cornell University Press, 1981.

Daniel, Pete. *Breaking the Land: The Transformation of Cotton, Tobacco, and Rice Cultures since 1880*. Chicago: University of Illinois Press, 1985.

———. *The Shadow of Slavery: Peonage in the South, 1901–1969*. Chicago: University of Illinois Press, 1972.

Davis, Edward D. *A Half-Century of Struggle for Freedom in Florida*. Orlando, Fla.: Drakes, 1981.

Davis, Lance E., Richard A. Easterlin, William N. Parker, Dorothy S. Brady, Albert Fishow, et al., eds. *American Economic Growth*. New York: Harper and Row, 1972.

Decker, Phil. "Cleselia." *Migration Today* 13, no. 2 (1985): 18–29.

DeWitt, Howard. *Violence in the Fields: California Filipino Farm Labor Unionization during the Great Depression*. Saratoga, Calif.: CZI, 1980.

Dickinson, Joan Younger. *The Role of Immigrant Women in the United States Labor Force, 1890–1910*. New York: Arno, 1980.

Dittmer, John. *Black Georgia in the Progressive Era, 1900–1920*. Urbana: University of Illinois Press, 1977.

Douglas, Marjory Stoneman. *The Everglades: River of Grass*. New York: Rinehart, 1947.

Dovell, Junius E. "The Everglades, a Florida Frontier." *Agricultural History* 22 (1948): 187–97.

Dovring, F. "Review Article: Bondage, Tenure, and Progress: Reflections on the Economics of Forced Labour." *Comparative Studies in Society and History* 2 (1964): 309–23.

Dunn, James William. "The New Deal and Florida Politics." Ph.D. dissertation, Florida State University, 1971.

DuPont, Patricia, Carl H. Feuer, and Jean Kost. "Black Migrant Farmworkers in New York State." *Afro-Americans in New York Life and History* 12, no. 1 (Jan. 1988): 7–26.

Durland, Kellog. "Immigrants on the Land: Italian Colonists." *Chautauquan* 5 (1908): 89–90.

Dusinberre, William W. "Strikes in 1934, with a Case Study of a Strike of New Jersey Farm Workers." Master's thesis, Columbia University, 1953.

Dyson, Lowell K. "The Southern Tenant Farmers' Union and Depression Politics." *Political Science Quarterly* 88 (1973): 230–52.

Ebeling, Walter. *The Fruited Plain: The Story of American Agriculture*. Berkeley: University of California Press, 1977.

Emerson, Robert D. *Seasonal Agricultural Labor Markets in the United States*. Ames: Iowa State University Press, 1984.

"Employment of Philadelphia Children at Farm Labor." *Monthly Labor Review* 28 (1928): 82–83.

Engerrand, Steven W. " 'Now Scratch or Die': The Genesis of Capitalist Agricultural Labor in Georgia, 1865–1880." Ph.D. dissertation, University of Georgia, 1981.

Evans, Arthur S., Jr., and David Lee. *Pearl City, Florida: A Black Community Remembers*. Boca Raton: Florida Atlantic University Press, 1990.

Fair, Laura. "Migrants as a Social and Educational Problem in New Jersey." Master's thesis, Rutgers University, 1931.

Falzone, Vincent J. *Terence V. Powderly, Middle-Class Reformer*. Washington, D.C.: University Press of America, 1978.

Fanning, John William. "Negro Migration: A Study of the Exodus of the Negroes between 1920 and 1925 from Middle Georgia Counties as That Exodus Was Influenced or Determined by Existing Economic Conditions." *Bulletin of the University of Georgia* 30 (June 1930): 34–35.

Farm Management. New York: Orange Judd, 1923.

Faulkner, Audrey Olsen, Marsel A. Heisel, Wendell Holbrook, and Shirley Geismar, eds. *When I Was Comin' Up: An Oral History of Aged Blacks*. Hamden, Conn.: Archon, 1982.

Faulkner, Harold U. *The Decline of Laissez-Faire, 1897–1917*. Vol. 7 of *Economic History of the United States*. Edited by Henry David, Harold U. Faulkner, Louis M. Hacker, Curtis P. Nettels, and Fred A. Shannon. New York: Rinehart, 1951.

Federal Writers' Project. *Stories of New Jersey: Its Significant Places, People, and Activities*. New York: Barrows, 1938.

Fickle, James E. "Management Looks at the Labor Problem: The Southern Pine Industry during World War I and the Post War Era." *Journal of Southern History* 40 (1974): 61–76.

Fields, Barbara J. "Ideology and Race in American History." In *Region, Race, and Reconstruction: Essays in Honor of C. Van Woodward*, edited by J. Morgan Kousser and James M. McPherson. New York: Oxford University Press, 1982.

Finegold, Kenneth. "From Agrarianism to Adjustment: The Political Origins of New Deal Agricultural Policy." *Politics and Society* 11 (1981): 1–27.

Fink, Leon. *Workingmen's Democracy: The Knights of Labor and American Politics*. Urbana: University of Illinois Press, 1983.

Finney, John Dustin, Jr. "A Study of Negro Labor during and after World War I." Ph.D. dissertation, University of Georgia, 1967.

Fite, Gilbert C. *Cotton Fields No More: Southern Agriculture, 1865–1980*. Lexington: University Press of Kentucky, 1984.

Fitzpatrick, Joseph P. *Puerto Rican Americans: The Meaning of Migration to the Mainland*. 2d ed. Ethnic Groups in American Life Series. Englewood Cliffs, N.J.: Prentice-Hall, 1987.

Fligstein, Neil. *Going North: Migration of Blacks from the South, 1900–1950*. London: Academic, 1982.

Florette, Henri. *Black Migration: Movement North, 1900–1920*. Garden City, N.Y.: Anchor, 1975.

Florida Farm Bureau Yearbook. Vol. 1. Winter Park, Fla.: Rollins, 1945.

Flynn, Charles L., Jr. *White Land, Black Labor: Caste and Class in Late Nineteenth Century Georgia*. Baton Rouge: Louisiana State University Press, 1983.

Foerster, Robert F. *The Italian Emigration of Our Times*. Cambridge, Mass.: Harvard University Press, 1924.

Foner, Eric. *Nothing but Freedom: Emancipation and Its Legacy*. Baton Rouge: Louisiana State University Press, 1983.

———. *Reconstruction: America's Unfinished Revolution, 1863–1877*. New York: Harper and Row, 1988.

Foner, Nancy, and R. Napoli. "Jamaican and Black Migrant Farm Workers: A Comparative Analysis." *Social Problems* 25, no. 4 (Apr. 1978): 491–503.

Foner, Phillip S. *History of the Labor Movement in the United States*. Vol. 7, *Labor and World War I, 1914–1918*. New York: International Publishers, 1987.

Foster, Herbert J. "Institutional Development in the Black Community of Atlantic City, New Jersey: 1850–1930." In *The Black Experience in Southern New Jersey*, edited by David C. Munn, pp. 32–48. Papers presented at a symposium, Feb. 11 and 12, 1984, Camden County Historical Society. Camden, N.J.: Camden County Historical Society, 1985.

Friedland, William H., and Dorothy Nelkin. *Migrant: Agricultural Workers in America's Northeast*. New York: Holt, Rinehart and Winston, 1971.

Friedland, William H., Amy E. Barton, and Robert J. Thomas. *Manufacturing Green Gold: Capital, Labor, and Technology in the Lettuce Industry*. Cambridge: Cambridge University Press, 1981.

Fuchs, Lawrence H. "Immigration Reform in 1911 and 1981: The Role of Select Commissions." *Journal of American Ethnic History* 3, no. 1 (1983): 58–89.

Furner, Mary O. "Knowing Capitalism: Public Investigation and the Labor Question in the Long Progressive Era." In *The State and Economic Knowledge: The American and British Experiences*, edited by Mary O. Furner and Barry Supple, pp. 241–86. Cambridge: Cambridge University Press, 1990.

———. *Knowing Capitalism: Public Investigation and the Labor Question in the Long Progressive Era*. Forthcoming.

Gabaccia, Donna R. *From the Other Side: Women, Gender, and Immigrant Life in the United States, 1820–1990*. Bloomington: Indiana University Press, 1994.

Galarza, Ernesto. *Farm Workers and Agribusiness in California, 1947–1960*. Notre Dame, Ind.: University of Notre Dame Press, 1977.

———. *Spiders in the House and Workers in the Field*. Notre Dame, Ind.: University of Notre Dame Press, 1976.

Galloway, Beverly Thomas. "Intensive Farming." In *The Making of America*, edited by R. M. LaFollette, 5:322–42. Philadelphia: John D. Morris, 1905.

Garcia y Griego, Larry Manuel. "The Bracero Policy Experiment: U.S.–Mexican Responses to Mexican Labor Migration, 1942–1955." Ph.D. dissertation, University of California, Los Angeles, 1988.

Gaston, Edward Aaron. "A History of the Negro Wage Earner in Georgia, 1890–1940." Ph.D. dissertation, Emory University, 1957.

Gaus, John M., and Leon O. Wolcott. *Public Administration and the U.S.D.A.* Chicago: Public Administration Service, 1940.

George, Paul. "Colored Town: Miami's Black Community, 1896–1930." *Florida Historical Quarterly* 56, no. 4 (Apr. 1978): 432–47.

Gilbert, Jess, and Carolyn Howe. "Beyond 'State vs. Society': Theories of the

State and New Deal Agricultural Policies." *American Sociological Review* 56 (Apr. 1991): 204–20.

Ginger, Mina. "In Berry Field and Bog." *Charities and the Commons*, Nov. 4, 1905, pp. 162–69.

Gold, Bela. *Wartime Economic Planning in Agriculture*. New York: Columbia University Press, 1949.

Goldfarb, Ronald L. *Migrant Farm Workers: A Caste of Despair*. Ames: Iowa State University Press, 1981.

Gompers, Samuel. *American Labor and the War*. Englewood, N.J.: J. S. Ozer, 1974.

Goodrich, Carter, Bushrod W. Allin, C. Warren Thornthwaite, et al. *Migration and Economic Opportunity*. Philadelphia: University of Pennsylvania Press, 1936.

Goodwyn, Lawrence. *Democratic Promise: The Populist Moment in America*. New York: Oxford University Press, 1976.

Gordon, Asa H. *The Georgia Negro: A History*. Ann Arbor, Mich.: Edwards Brothers, 1937.

Gordon, Linda. *Pitied but Not Entitled: Single Mothers and the History of Welfare*. New York: Free Press, 1994.

Gottleib, Peter. *Making Their Own Way: Southern Blacks' Migration to Pittsburgh, 1916–1930*. Urbana: University of Illinois Press, 1987.

Granger, Lester B. "The Negro Joins the Picket Line." *Opportunity*, Aug. 1934, pp. 248–49.

Gregory, Clifford V. "The American Farm Bureau Federation and the AAA." *Annals of the American Academy of Political and Social Science* 179 (May 1935): 152–57.

Greig, Gertrud Berta. *Seasonal Fluctuations in Employment in the Women's Clothing Industry in New York*. Studies in History, Economics, and Public Law, no. 554. New York: Columbia University Press, 1949.

Griffith, David Craig. "The Promise of a Country: The Impact of Seasonal U.S. Migration on the Jamaican Peasantry." Ph.D. dissertation, University of Florida, 1983.

Griffith, David Craig, and Ed Kissan. *Working Poor: Farmworkers in the United States*. Philadelphia: Temple University Press, 1995.

Grossman, James R. "Black Labor Is the Best Labor: Southern White Reactions to the Great Migration." In *Black Exodus: The Great Migration from the American South*, edited by Alferdteen Harrison, pp. 51–71. Jackson: University Press of Mississippi, 1991.

——. *Land of Hope: Chicago, Black Southerners, and the Great Migration*. Chicago: University of Chicago Press, 1989.

Grossman, Jonathan P. *The Department of Labor*. New York: Praeger, 1973.

Grubbs, Donald E. "A History of the Atlantic Coast Stream of Agricultural Migrants." Master's thesis, University of Florida, 1959.

——. "The Story of Florida's Migrant Farm Workers." *Florida Historical Quarterly* 40, no. 2 (Oct. 1961): 103–22.

Grubbs, Frank L. *Samuel Gompers on the Great War: Protecting Labor's Standards*. Wake Forest, N.C.: Meridional Publications, 1982.

Guerin-Gonzales, Camille. *Mexican Workers and American Dreams: Immigration, Repatriation, and California Farm Labor, 1900–1939*. New Brunswick, N.J.: Rutgers University Press, 1994.

Hall, Jacquelyn Dowd, James Leloudis, Robert Korstad, Mary Murphy, LuAnn Jones, and Christopher B. Daly. *Like a Family: The Making of a Southern Cotton Mill World*. Chapel Hill: University of North Carolina, 1987.

Halter, Marilyn. "Working the Cranberry Bogs: Cape Verdeans in Southeastern Massachusetts." *Spinner: People and Culture in Southeastern Massachusetts* 3 (1984): 70–83.

Harrison, Alferdteen, ed. *Black Exodus: The Great Migration from the American South*. Jackson: University Press of Mississippi, 1991.

Harrison, Shelby M. *Public Employment Offices: Their Purpose, Structure, and Methods*. New York: Russell Sage Foundation, 1924.

Haun, Steven. *The Roots of Southern Populism: Yeomen Farmers and the Transformation of the Georgia Upcountry, 1850–1890*. New York: Oxford University Press, 1985.

Hellwig, David J. "Black Leaders and U.S. Immigration Policy, 1917–1929." *Journal of Negro History* 66, no. 2 (1981): 110–27.

Henderson, Donald H. "The Negro Migration of 1916–1918." *Journal of Negro History* 6, no. 4 (1921): 383–498.

Hibbard, Benjamin Horace. *Effects of the Great War on Agriculture in the United States and Great Britain*. New York: Oxford University Press, 1919.

Higgs, Robert. "The Boll Weevil, the Cotton Economy, and Black Migration, 1910–1930." *Agricultural History* 50 (1976): 335–50.

———. *Cooperation and Coercion: Blacks in the American Economy, 1865–1914*. New York: Cambridge University Press, 1977.

———. *The Transformation of the American Economy, 1865–1914*. New York: Wiley and Sons, 1971.

Hill, Mozell Clarence. *Rural Survey of Clarke County, Georgia, with Special Reference to the Negroes*. Bulletin of the University of Georgia 15, no. 3 (Mar. 1925).

History Task Force, Centro de Estudios Puertorriqenos. *Labor Migration under Capitalism: The Puerto Rican Experience*. New York: Monthly Review Press, 1979.

Hobsbawm, Eric. *The Age of Empire, 1875–1914*. New York: Pantheon, 1987.

Hoffman, P. *Ministry of the Dispossessed: Learning from the Farmworker*. Los Angeles: Wallace, 1987.

Holmes, Michael S. "From Euphoria to Cataclysm: Georgia Confronts the Great Depression." *Georgia Historical Quarterly* 58 (1974): 313–30.

Holmes, William F. "Economic Developments, 1890–1940." In *A History of Georgia*, edited by Kenneth Coleman, pp. 257–338. Athens: University of Georgia Press, 1977.

———. "Labor Agents and the Georgia Exodus, 1899–1900." *South Atlantic Quarterly* 79 (1980): 436–48.

Hooks, Gregory. "From an Autonomous to a Captured State Agency: The Decline of the New Deal in Agriculture." *American Sociological Review* 55 (Feb. 1990): 29–43.

Horgan, James J. "The Union Makes a Difference: The UFW Organizes in Florida." *Southern Exposure* 11, no. 6 (1983): 62–65.

Hourwich, Isaac A. *Immigration and Labor: The Economic Aspects of European Immigration to the United States.* New York: Putnam, 1912.

Howard, Louise E. *Labor in Agriculture.* London: Oxford University Press, 1935.

Howard, Robert P. *James R. Howard and the Farm Bureau.* Ames: Iowa State University Press, 1982.

Hunter, Tera W. "Household Workers in the Making: Afro-American Women in Atlanta and the New South, 1861 to 1920." Ph.D. dissertation, Yale University, 1990.

Hurston, Zora Neale. *Their Eyes Were Watching God.* Chicago: University of Illinois Press, 1978.

Iorizzo, Luciano J. "Italian Immigration and the Impact of the Padrone System." Ph.D. dissertation, University of Syracuse, 1966.

———. *Italian Immigration and the Impact of the Padrone System.* New York: Arno, 1980.

———. "The Padrone and Immigrant Distribution." In *The Italian Experience in the U.S.,* edited by Silvano M. Tomasi and Madeline H. Engel, pp. 43–76. New York: Center for Migration Studies, 1970.

Iorizzo, Luciano J., and Salvatore Mondello. *The Italian Americans.* Boston: Twayne, 1980.

Jacob, Samuel. "Immigrant Farm Colonies in Southern New Jersey." *Monthly Labor Review* 12 (1921): 1–22.

Jaynes, Gerald D. *Branches without Roots: Genesis of the Black Working Class in the American South, 1862–1882.* New York: Oxford University Press, 1986.

Jenkins, J. Craig. *The Politics of Insurgency: The Farm Worker Movement in the 1960s.* New York: Columbia University Press, 1985.

Jenks, Jeremiah W., and W. Jett Lauck. *The Immigration Problem: A Study of Immigrant Conditions and Needs.* New York: Funk and Wagnalls, 1913.

Johnson, Charles S., Edwin R. Embree, and W. W. Alexander. *The Collapse of Cotton Tenancy.* Chapel Hill: University of North Carolina Press, 1935.

Johnson, Daniel M., and Rex R. Campbell. *Black Migration in America: A Social Demographic History.* Durham, N.C.: Duke University Press, 1981.

Johnson, Howard. "Bahamian Labor Migration to Florida in the Late 19th and Early 20th Centuries." *International Migration Review* 22 (1988): 84–103.

Johnston, Helen J. "An Overview of the Growth and Development of the United States Migrant Health Program." *Migration Today* 12, no. 4–5 (1984): 8–14.

Jones, Jacqueline. *The Dispossessed.* New York: Basic Books, 1992.

———. *Labor of Love, Labor of Sorrow: Black Women, Work, and the Family, from Slavery to the Present.* New York: Vintage, 1985.

Juliani, Richard N. "The Italian Community in Philadelphia." In *Little Italies in North America,* edited by Robert F. Harney and J. Vincenza Scarpaci, pp. 85–104. Toronto: Multicultural History Society of Ontario, 1981.

———. *The Social Organization of Immigration: The Italians in Philadelphia.* New York: Arno, 1980.

Kelling, Lloyd S. "Historical Study of a Strike at Seabrook Farms, Inc., 1934." Unpublished seminar paper, Glassboro State College, 1969.

Kester, Howard. *Revolt among the Sharecroppers*. New York: Covici, Friede, 1936. Reprint. New York: Arno, 1969.

Key, V. O. *Southern Politics in State and Nation*. New York: Knopf, 1945.

Keyssar, Alexander. *Out of Work: The First Century of Unemployment in Massachusetts*. Cambridge: Cambridge University Press, 1986.

Kharif, Wali Rashash. "The Refinement of Racial Segregation in Florida after the Civil War." Ph.D. dissertation, Florida State University, Tallahassee, 1983.

Kirby, Jack Temple. *Darkness at the Dawning: Race and Reform in the Progressive South*. Philadelphia: Lippincott, 1972.

———. *Rural Worlds Lost: The American South, 1920–1960*. Baton Rouge: Louisiana State University Press, 1987.

———. "The Southern Exodus, 1910–1960: A Primer for Historians." *Journal of Southern History* 49 (1983): 585–600.

———. "The Transformation of Southern Plantations, 1920–1960." *Agricultural History* 57 (1983): 257–76.

Koedel, Craig. *South Jersey Heritage: A Social, Economic, and Cultural History*. Washington, D.C.: University Press of America, 1979.

Kornbluh, Joyce L., ed. *Rebel Voices: An I.W.W. Anthology*. Ann Arbor: University of Michigan Press, 1968. Reprint, 1972.

Korstad, Robert Rogers. "Daybreak of Freedom: Tobacco Workers and the CIO, Winston-Salem, North Carolina, 1943–1950." Ph.D. dissertation, University of North Carolina, 1987.

Kramer, Peter. *The Offshores: A Study of Foreign Farm Labor in Florida*. St. Petersburg, Fla: Community Action Fund, 1966.

Kritz, Mary, Charles B. Keely, and Silvano M. Tomasi, eds. *Global Trends in Migration: Theory and Research on International Population Movements*. New York: Center for Migration Studies, 1981.

Kusmer, Kenneth Leslie. "The Underclass: Tramps and Vagrants in American Society, 1865–1930." Ph.D. dissertation, University of Chicago, 1980.

LaGodna, Martin Michael. "The Florida State Department of Agriculture during the Administration of Nathan Mayo, 1923–1960." Master's thesis, University of Florida, 1970.

La Gumina, Salvatore J. "Reflections of an Italian American Worker." *Journal of Ethnic Studies* 3 (Summer 1975): 65–77.

LaMar, Howard. "From Bondage to Contract: Ethnic Labor in the American West, 1600–1890." In *The Countryside in the Age of Capitalist Transformation*, edited by Steven Haun and Jonathan Prude, pp. 293–324. Chapel Hill: University of North Carolina Press, 1985.

Lebergott, Stanley. *Manpower in Economic Growth*. New York: McGraw-Hill, 1964.

Lee, Guy. "The General Records of the U.S. Department of Agriculture in the National Archives." *Agricultural History* 19 (1945): 242.

Lewis, Charles. "Thirty Cent Cotton and the Negro." *Illustrated World*, May 1918, p. 470.

Lewis, Earl. *In Their Own Interest: Race, Class, and Power in Twentieth-Century Norfolk, Virginia*. Berkeley: University of California Press, 1991.

Lewis, Edward E. "The Southern Negro and the American Labor Supply." *Political Science Quarterly* 48 (1933): 172–83.

Lichtenstein, Nelson. *Labor's War at Home: The CIO in World War II*. New York: Cambridge University Press, 1983.

Linder, Marc. "Farm Workers and the Fair Labor Standards Act: Racial Discrimination in the New Deal." *Texas Law Review* 65 (1987): 1335–93.

Lipari, Marie. " 'The Padrone System': An Aspect of American Economic History." In *The Italians: Social Background of an American Group*, edited by Francesco Cordasco and Eugene Bucchioni, pp. 377–79. Clifton, N.J.: Augustus M. Kelley, 1974.

Liss, Samuel. "Farm Migrants in New Jersey." *Land Policy Review* 4, no. 6 (1941): 29–37.

Litwack, Leon F. *Been in the Storm So Long: The Aftermath of Slavery*. New York: Knopf, 1981.

Lombardi, John. *Labor's Voice in the Cabinet: A History of the Department of Labor from Its Origin to 1921*. New York: Columbia University Press, 1942.

Long, Francis Taylor. "The Negroes of Clarke County, Georgia, during the Great War." *Bulletin of the University of Georgia* 19 (Sept. 1919): 49–55.

Lowery, Edith E. *They Starve That We May Eat: Migrants of the Crops*. New York: Council of Women for Home Missions, 1938.

Lowi, Theodore. *The End of Liberalism: Ideology, Policy, and the Crisis of Public Authority*. New York: Norton, 1969.

Luke, George W. "New Jersey Agriculture from 1850–1950: An Economic Analysis." Ph.D. dissertation, New York University, 1956.

McConnell, Grant. *The Decline of Agrarian Democracy*. Berkeley: University of California Press, 1953.

McCorkle, James L., Jr. "Moving Perishables to Market: Southern Railroads and the 19th century origins of Southern Truck Farming." *Agricultural History* 66 (1992): 42–67.

McCormick, Fowler. *The Development of Farm Machines*. Princeton, N.J.: Newcomer Society, 1941.

McCormick, Richard P. "An Historical Overview." In *Politics in New Jersey*, edited by Alan Rosenthal and John Blyndenburgh, pp. 1–28. New Brunswick, N.J.: Rutgers University, 1979.

McCoy, Terry L., and Charles H. Wood. "Caribbean Workers in the Florida Sugar Cane Industry." Paper no. 2, Center for Latin American Studies, University of Florida, Dec. 1982.

MacCulloch, Campbell. "Who Picked Your Cranberries?" *Good Housekeeping*, Nov. 1913, pp. 669–77.

McCune, Wesley. *The Farm Bloc*. Garden City, N.Y.: Doubleday, 1943.

McKay, Janet S. *Pennsylvania Children on New Jersey Cranberry Farms*. Philadelphia: Public Education and Child Labor Association of Pennsylvania, 1923.

MacNeil, Douglas Harrison. *Seven Years of Unemployment Relief in New Jersey, 1930–1936*. Washington, D.C.: Committee on Social Security, Social Science Research Council, 1938.

McWilliams, Carey. *Factories in the Field: The Story of Migratory Farm Labor in California.* Boston: Little, Brown, 1940.

——. *Ill Fares the Land: Migrants and Migratory Labor in the United States.* New York: Barnes and Noble, 1941. Reprint, 1967.

Maddox, James G. "The Farm Security Administration." Ph.D. dissertation, Harvard University, 1950.

Majka, Linda C., and Theo J. Majka. *Farm Workers, Agribusiness, and the State.* Philadelphia: Temple University Press, 1982.

Maldonado, Edwin. "Contract Labor and the Origins of the Puerto Rican Community in the United States." *International Migration Review* 13 (1979): 103–21.

Mandel, Ernest. Introduction to *Capital*, by Karl Marx, 1: 11–86. New York: Vintage, 1977.

Mandle, Jay R. *Not Slave, Not Free: The African-American Economic Experience since the Civil War.* Durham, N.C.: Duke University Press, 1992.

——. *The Roots of Black Poverty: The Southern Plantation Economy after the Civil War.* Durham, N.C.: Duke University Press, 1978.

Manning, Robert D. "From Orange to Green 'Gold': The Roots of the Asparagus Fern Industry in Florida." *Florida Historical Quarterly* 62, no. 4 (Apr. 1984): 464–84.

Markham, Edwin, Benjamin B. Lindsey, and George Creel. *Children in Bondage: A Complete and Careful Presentation of the Anxious Problem of Child Labor. . . .* New York: Hearst International Library, 1914. Reprint. New York: Arno Press and the *New York Times*, 1969.

Marks, Carole. "Black Workers and the Great Migration North." *Phylon* 46, no. 2 (1985): 148–61.

——. *Farewell — We're Good and Gone: The Great Black Migration.* Bloomington: Indiana University Press, 1989.

Martin, Michael, and Leonard Gelber. *Dictionary of American History.* Totowa, N.J.: Littlefield, Adams, 1972.

Martin, Philip. *Seasonal Workers in American Agriculture: Background and Issues.* Washington, D.C.: National Commission for Employment Policy, 1985.

Martlett, Penny. "The Woman's Land Army, World War I." In *Clio Was a Woman: Studies in the History of American Women*, edited by Mabel E. Deutrick and Virginia C. Purdy, pp. 136–46. Washington, D.C.: Howard University Press, 1980.

Marx, Karl. *Capital.* Vol. 1. New York: Vintage, 1977.

Meade, Emily. "Italian Immigration into the South." *South Atlantic Quarterly* 4 (1905): 217–23.

Mehra, Rekha. "International Labor Migration and Florida Sugarcane Production: A Political and Economic Analysis." Ph.D. dissertation, University of Florida, 1984.

Meier, August, and Elliott M. Rudwick. *From Plantation to Ghetto.* New York: Hill and Wang, 1966.

Meister, Dick, and Anne Loftis. *A Long Time Coming: The Struggle to Unionize America's Farm Workers.* New York: Macmillan, 1977.

Merlino, S. "Italian Immigrants and Their Enslavement." *Forum* 15 (1893): 183–90.

Mertz, Paul E. *New Deal Policy and Southern Rural Poverty*. Baton Rouge: Louisiana State University Press, 1978.

Mills, C. Wright, Clarence Senior, and Rose Goldsen. *Puerto Rican Journey*. New York: Harper and Row, 1950.

Mitchell, Stuart. *Farmwork and Farmworkers in New York State*. Albany, N.Y.: New York State Impact, 1981.

Mohl, Raymond A. "Black Immigrants: Bahamians in Early Twentieth-Century Miami." *Florida Historical Quarterly* 65, no. 3 (Jan. 1987): 271–97.

Mohl, Sandra M. "Migrant Farmworkers in America: A Florida Case Study." Master's thesis, Florida Atlantic University, 1981.

Money, Edgar Lowell, Jr. "An Analysis of Civilian Public Service Camp Twenty-Seven F, Orlando, Florida." Master's thesis, Florida Atlantic University, 1975.

Montgomery, David. *Workers' Control in America: Studies in the History of Work, Technology, and Labor Struggles*. New York: Cambridge University Press, 1979.

Moore, Truman. *The Slaves We Rent*. New York: Random House, 1965.

Morales, Rebecca. "Unions and Undocumented Workers." *Southwest Economy and Society* 6, no. 1 (1982): 3–11.

Morison, Samuel Eliot, Henry Steele Commager, and William E. Leuchtenburg. *A Concise History of the American Republic*. New York: Oxford University Press, 1983.

Morris, Austin P. "Agricultural Labor and National Labor Legislation." *California Law Review* 54 (1966): 1939–89.

Motolinsky, Melvyn. "Migrant Farm Labor in New Jersey." B.A. thesis, Rutgers University, 1964.

Murray, Stanley N. "Railroads and the Agricultural Development of the Red River Valley of the North, 1870–1890." *Agricultural History* 31 (1957): 57–66.

The Negro in New Jersey: Report of a Survey by the Interracial Committee of the New Jersey Conference of Social Work. New York: Negro Universities Press, 1932.

Nelkin, Dorothy. *On the Season: Aspects of the Migrant Labor System*. Ithaca, N.Y.: Cornell University Press, 1970.

Nelli, Humbert S. "The Italian Padrone System in the United States." *Labor History* 5, no. 2 (1964): 153–64, and 17, no. 3 (1976): 406–12.

New Jersey Conference of Social Work, Interracial Committee. *The Negro in New Jersey: Report of a Survey by the Interracial Committee of the New Jersey Conference of Social Work*. New York: Negro Universities Press, 1932.

————. "Survey of Negro Life in New Jersey." Community Reports nos. 8, 13, and 23, 1932.

Nijeholt, G. Thomas-Lycklama A. *On the Road for Work: Migratory Workers on the East Coast of the United States*. Boston: Martinus Nijhoff, 1980.

Nobles, Gregory. "Capitalism in the Countryside: The Transformation of Rural Society in the United States." *Radical History Review* 41 (Spring 1988): 163–76.

Novak, Daniel A. *The Wheel of Servitude: Black Forced Labor after Slavery*. Lexington: University Press of Kentucky, 1978.

Padfield, Harland, and William E. Martin. *Farmers, Workers, and Machines: Technological and Social Change in Farm Industries of Arizona*. Tucson: University of Arizona Press, 1965.

Painter, Nell Irwin. *Exodusters: Black Migration to Kansas after Reconstruction*. New York: Knopf, 1977.

Parker, Carleton. *The Casual Laborer and Other Essays*. New York: Harcourt, Brace and Howe, 1920.

Pecarini, Alberto. "The Italian as an Agricultural Laborer." *Annals of the American Academy of Political and Social Science* 3 (1909): 380–99.

Peck, Samuel H. "How New Jersey Tamed Their Wild Blueberry." *New Jersey Compass* 1 (Aug. 1947): 25–27.

Perkins, Van L. *Crisis in Agriculture: The AAA and the New Deal, 1933*. Berkeley: University of California Press, 1969.

Perlman, Daniel. "Stirring the White Conscience: The Life of George Edmund Haynes." Ph.D. dissertation, New York University, 1972.

Perlo, Victor. *The Negro in Southern Agriculture*. New York: International Publishers, 1953.

Persch, Louis. "An Analysis of the Agricultural Migratory Movements on the Atlantic Seaboard and the Socio-Economic Implications for the Community and the Migrants, 1930–1950." Ph.D. dissertation, American University, 1953.

Petras, Elizabeth McLean. *Jamaican Labor Migration: White Capital and Black Labor, 1850–1930*. Boulder, Colo.: Westview Press, 1988.

Piore, Michael J. *Birds of Passage: Migrant Labor and Industrial Societies*. New York: Cambridge University Press, 1979.

Pitt, Dimitry T. "Migratory Child Labor on New Jersey Farms." Master's thesis, Columbia University, 1933.

Polantzas, Nicos. *Political Power and Social Classes*. Translated by Timothy O'Hagen. London: New Left Books, 1973.

Polenberg, Richard. *War and Society: The United States, 1941–1945*. Philadelphia: Lippincott, 1972.

Powderly, Terence V. *The Path I Trod: The Autobiography of Terence V. Powderly*. New York: AMS Press, 1968.

Price, Clement Alexander. *Freedom Not Far Distant: A Documentary History of Afro-Americans in New Jersey*. Newark, N.J.: New Jersey Historical Society.

Quadagno, Jill. *The Color of Welfare: How Racism Undermined the War on Poverty*. New York: Oxford University Press, 1994.

———. *The Transformation of Old Age Social Security: Class and Politics in the American Welfare State*. Chicago: University of Chicago Press, 1988.

Radosh, Ronald, and N. Rothbard, eds. *A New History of Leviathan: Essays on the Rise of the Corporate State*. New York: Dutton, 1972.

Ramsey, Elizabeth. *The History of Tobacco Production in the Connecticut Valley*. Northampton, Mass.: Smith College Studies in History, 1930.

Ransom, Roger L., and Richard Sutch. *One Kind of Freedom: The Economic Consequences of Emancipation*. New York: Cambridge University Press, 1977.

Raper, Arthur Franklin. *Tenants of the Almighty*, 1943.

Ready, Milton L. "Georgia's Entry into World War I." *Georgia Historical Quarterly* 52 (1968): 262.

Reed, Ellery F. *Federal Transient Program: An Evaluative Survey.* New York: Committee on Care of Transient and Homeless, 1934.

Reisler, Mark. *By the Sweat of Their Brow: Mexican Immigrant Labor in the United States, 1900–1940.* Westport, Conn.: Greenwood, 1976.

Rosengarten, Theodore. *All God's Dangers: The Life of Nate Shaw.* New York: Knopf, 1974.

Ross, Earle R. "The Expansion of Agriculture." In *The Growth of the American Economy,* 2d ed., edited by Harold F. Williamson, pp. 388–417. New York: Prentice-Hall, 1951.

Rouson-Gosset, Vivian Reissland, ed. *Like a Mighty Banyan: Contributions of Black People to the History of Palm Beach County.* Palm Beach, Fla.: Palm Beach Junior College Press, 1982.

Ryan, Philip Elwood. *Migration and Social Welfare.* New York: Russell Sage Foundation, 1940.

Saloutos, Theodore. *The American Farmer and the New Deal.* Ames: Iowa State University Press, 1982.

——. "Edward O'Neal: The Farm Bureau and the New Deal." *Current History* 28 (June 1955): 356–61.

Sautter, Udo. *Three Cheers for the Unemployed: Government and Unemployment before the New Deal.* New York: Cambridge University Press, 1991.

Sawada, Mitziko. "After the Camps: Seabrook Farms, New Jersey, and the Resettlement of Japanese Americans, 1944–47." *Amerasia* 13, no. 2 (1986–87): 117–36.

Schmidt, Benno C., Jr. "Principle and Prejudice: The Supreme Court and Race in the Progressive Era." Part 2, "The Peonage Cases." *Columbia Law Review* 82, no. 4 (May 1982): 646–718.

Schmidt, Hubert G. *Agriculture in New Jersey: A 300-Year History.* New Brunswick, N.J.: Rutgers University Press, 1973.

——. *Rural Hunterdon.* New Brunswick, N.J.: Rutgers University Press, 1947.

Schultz, Theodore W. *The Economic Organization of Agriculture.* New York: McGraw-Hill, 1953.

Schuyler, Eugene. "Italian Immigration in the United States." *Political Science Quarterly* 4 (1899): 480–95.

Scott, Emett J. *The American Negro in the World War.* Washington, D.C.: Negro Historical Publishing, 1919.

——. *Negro Migration during the War.* New York, Oxford University Press, 1920. Reprint. New York: Arno, 1969.

——, comp. "Additional Letters of Negro Migrants of 1916–1918." *Journal of Negro History* 4, no. 4 (1919): 412–65.

——. "Letters of Negro Migrants of 1916–1918." *Journal of Negro History* 4, no. 3 (1919): 290–340.

Scroggs, W. C. "Inter-State Migration of Negro Population." *Journal of Political Economy* 25 (Dec. 1917): 1034–43.

Seabrook, John (Jr.). "The Spinach King," *New Yorker*, Feb. 20–27, 1995, pp. 222–35.

Seabrook, John M. *The Henry Ford of Agriculture: Seabrook Farms, 1893–1959, and Charles F. Seabrook, 1881–1964*. Seabrook, N.J.: Seabrook Educational and Cultural Center, 1995.

Senner, Joseph H. "Immigration from Italy." *North American Review* 162 (1896): 649–57.

Shannon, Fred A. *The Farmer's Last Frontier: Agriculture, 1860–1897*. Vol. 5 of *Economic History of the United States*. Edited by Henry David, Harold U. Faulkner, Louis M. Hacker, Curtis P. Nettels, and Fred A. Shannon. New York: Farrar & Rinehart, 1959.

Shofner, Jerrell H. "Custom, Law, and History: The Enduring Influence of Florida's Black Code." *Florida Historical Quarterly* 55, no. 3 (Jan. 1977): 277–98.

———. "Florida and the Black Migration." *Florida Historical Quarterly* 57, no. 3 (Jan. 1979): 267–89.

———. "Forced Labor in the Florida Forests, 1880–1950." *Journal of Forest History* 25, no. 1 (1981): 14–25.

———. "The Legacy of Racial Slavery: Free Enterprise and Forced Labor in Florida in the 1940s." *Journal of Southern History* 47 (1981): 411–26.

———. "Militant Negro Laborers in Reconstruction Florida." *Journal of Southern History* 39 (1973): 397–408.

———. "Postscript to the Martin Tabert Case: Peonage as Usual in the Florida Turpentine Camps." *Florida Historical Quarterly* 60, no. 2 (1981): 161–73.

Skocpol, Theda. "Political Responses to Capitalist Crisis: Neo-Marxist Theories of the State and the Case of the New Deal." *Politics and Society* 10 (1980): 155–201.

———. *Protecting Soldiers and Mothers: The Political Origins of Social Policy in the United States*. Cambridge, Mass.: Belknap Press of Harvard University Press, 1992.

———. *States and Social Revolutions: A Comparative Analysis of France, Russia, and China*. Cambridge: Cambridge University Press, 1979.

Skowronek, Stephan. *Building a New American State: The Expansion of National Administrative Capacities, 1877–1920*. Cambridge: Cambridge University Press, 1982.

Smith, Darrell H. *The Bureau of Immigration: Its History, Activities, and Organization*. Baltimore: Johns Hopkins University Press, 1924.

———. *The U.S. Employment Service: Its History, Activities, and Organization*. Baltimore: Johns Hopkins University Press, 1923.

Sosnick, Stephen H. *Hired Hands: Seasonal Farm Workers in the United States*. Santa Barbara, Calif.: McNally and Loftin, West, 1978.

Soule, Andrew M. "Vegetable, Fruit, and Nursery Products and Truck Farming in the South." In *South in the Building of the Nation*, 6:127–35. Richmond: Southern Publication Society, 1909.

Soule, Henry George. *Prosperity Decade: From War to Depression*. Vol. 8 of *Economic History of the United States*. Edited by Henry David, Harold U. Faulkner,

Louis M. Hacker, Curtis P. Nettels, and Fred A. Shannon. New York: Rinehart, 1947. Reprint. New York: Harper and Row, 1968.

Spargo, John. *The Bitter Cry of the Children*. New York: Macmillan, 1906.

Spillman, William J. *Farm Management*. New York: Orange Judd, 1923.

Starr, Dennis J. *The Italians of New Jersey: A Historical Introduction and Bibliography*. Collections of the New Jersey Historical Society, vol. 20. Newark, N.J.: New Jersey Historical Society, 1985.

Stein, Walter J. *California and the Dust Bowl Migration*. Westport, Conn.: Greenwood, 1973.

———. "The 'Okie' as Farm Laborer." *Agricultural History* 49 (1975): 202–15.

Stellhorn, Paul A., ed. *New Jersey's Ethnic Heritage*. Papers presented at the 8th Annual New Jersey History Symposium, Dec. 4, 1976. Trenton, N.J.: New Jersey Historical Commission, 1978.

Stine, O. C. "World's Agriculture Much Changed by the War and the Results." In *Agriculture in the United States: A Documentary History*, edited by Wayne D. Rasmussen, 3:2604–7. New York: Random House, 1975.

Stockbridge, Frank Parker, and John Holliday Perry. *Florida in the Making*. New York: de Bower, 1926.

Straus, Oscar S. *Under Four Administrations: From Cleveland to Taft*. New York: Hougton Mifflin, 1922.

Street, James H. *The Revolution in the Cotton Economy*. Chapel Hill: University of North Carolina Press, 1957.

Sufrin, Sidney C. "Labor Organization in Agricultural America, 1930–1935." *American Journal of Sociology* 43 (1938): 544–59.

Taylor, Paul. "The American Hired Man: His Rise and Decline." *Land Policy Review* 6, no. 1 (1943): 3–16.

———. *On the Ground in the Thirties*. Salt Lake City: Gibbs M. Smith, 1983.

Taylor, Paul S., and Clark Kerr. "Uprisings on the Farm." *Survey Graphic* 24 (Jan. 1935): 19–22, 44.

Tebeau, Charlton W. *A History of Florida*. Coral Gables, Fla.: University of Miami Press, 1971.

Terrell, John Upton. *The United States Department of Labor: A Story of Workers, Unions, and the Economy*. New York: Meredith, 1968.

Thernstrom, Stephan. "Urbanization, Migration, and Social Mobility in Late Nineteenth-Century America." In *Towards a New Past: Dissenting Essays in American History*, edited by Barton J. Bernstein, pp. 158–75. New York: Pantheon, 1968.

Thistlethwaite, Frank. "Migration from Europe Overseas in the Nineteenth and Twentieth Centuries." In *Population Movements in Modern European History*, edited by Herbert Moller, pp. 73–91. New York: Macmillan, 1964.

Thomas, Brinley. *Migration and Economic Growth: A Study of Great Britain and the Atlantic Economy*. 2d ed. Cambridge: Cambridge University Press, 1973.

Thompson, C. Mildred. *Reconstruction in Georgia: Economic, Social, Political, 1865–1872*. Savannah, Ga.: Beehive Press, 1972.

Thompson, J. A. *Reformers and War: American Progressive Publicists and the First World War*. Cambridge: Cambridge University Press, 1987.

Thornthwaite, C. Warren. *Internal Migration in the United States*. Philadelphia: University of Pennsylvania Press, 1934.

Tindall, George B. "The Bubble in the Sun." *American Heritage* 16 (Aug. 1965): 76–83.

———. *The Emergence of the New South, 1913–1945*. Baton Rouge: Louisiana State University Press, 1967.

Tomlins, Christopher L. *The State and the Unions: Labor Relations, Law, and the Organized Labor Movement in America, 1880–1960*. New York: Cambridge University Press, 1985.

Tosti, Gustavo. "Agricultural Possibilities of Italian Immigration." *Charities and the Commons* 12 (1904): 472–76.

Trattner, Walter I. *Crusade for the Children: A History of the National Child Labor Committee and Child Labor Reform in America*. Chicago: Quadrangle Books, 1970.

Trotter, Joe William, Jr., ed. *The Great Migration in Historical Perspective*. Bloomington: Indiana University Press, 1991.

Tucker, Barbara M. "Agricultural Workers in World War II: The Reserve Army of Children, Black Americans, and Jamaicans." *Agricultural History* 68 (1994): 54–73.

Vance, Rupert B. *Human Factors in Cotton Culture: A Study in the Social Geography of the American South*. Chapel Hill: University of North Carolina Press, 1929.

Van Kleeck, Mary. *Artificial Flower-Makers*. New York: Survey Associates, 1913.

Vecoli, Rudolph J. "Italian American Workers, 1880–1920: Padrone Slaves or Primitive Rebels?," In *Perspectives in Italian Immigration and Ethnicity*, edited by S. M. Tomasi, pp. 25–50. New York: Center for Migration Studies, 1977.

Vittoz, S. *New Deal Labor Policy and the American Industrial Economy*. Chapel Hill: University of North Carolina Press, 1987.

Wallace, Anthony. *Rockdale: The Growth of an American Village in the Early Industrial Revolution*. New York: Knopf, 1978.

Wanger, Peter H. "Farmers and the Immigration Act of 1924." *Agricultural History* 49 (1975): 647–52.

Washington, Ray, ed. *A Voice for Agriculture: The First 40 Years of the Farm Bureau in Florida*. Gainesville, Fla.: Florida Farm Bureau Federation, 1983.

Weeks, Jerry Woods. "Florida Gold: The Emergence of the Florida Citrus Industry, 1865–1895." Ph.D. dissertation, University of North Carolina, 1977.

"We Go Cranberry Harvesting." *South Jersey Magazine* 1 (Winter 1972): 2–5.

Weintraub, Sidney, and Stanley R. Ross. *"Temporary" Alien Workers in the United States: Designing Policy from Fact and Opinion*. Boulder, Colo.: Westview Press, 1982.

Weisberger, Bernard A. "Here Comes the Wobblies!" In *American Vistas: 1877 to the Present*, 6th ed., edited by Leonard Dinnerstein and Kenneth T. Jackson, pp. 104–23. New York: Oxford University Press, 1987.

Wertenbaker, Thomas J. *Norfolk: Historic Southern Port*. Durham, N.C.: Duke University Press, 1931. Reprint, 1962.

Wesley, Charles H. *Negro Labor in the United States*. New York: Vanguard, 1927.

Weyl, Walter. "Immigration and Industrial Saturation." *Proceedings of the National Conference of Charities and Corrections* 32 (1905): 365–75.

Whatley, Warren C. "A History of Mechanization in the Cotton South: The Institutional Hypothesis." *Quarterly Journal of Economics* 100, no. 4 (1985): 1191–1215.

———. "Labor for the Picking: The New Deal in the South." *Journal of Economic History* 43, no. 4 (1983): 905–29.

Wiener, Jonathan M. *Social Origins of the New South: Alabama, 1860–1885*. Baton Rouge: Louisiana State University Press, 1978.

Wilcox, Walter W. *The Farmer in the Second World War*. Ames: Iowa State College Press, 1947.

Wilkinson, Alec. *Big Sugar: Seasons in the Cane Fields of Florida*. New York: Knopf, 1989.

Will, Lawrence E. *Swamp to Sugar Bowl: Pioneer Days in Belle Glade*. St. Petersburg, Fla.: Great Outdoors, 1968.

Wilson, Margaret Gibbons. *Floridians at Work Yesterday and Today*. Gainesville: University of Florida Press, 1989.

Wilson, Walter. *Forced Labor in the United States*. New York: International Publishers, 1933.

Winokur, L. A., and Chip Hughes. "Workers of the Harvest." *Southern Exposure* 11, no. 6 (1983): 55–61.

Wiser, Vivian. *Two Centuries of American Agriculture, 1775–1975*. Washington, D.C.: Agricultural History Society, 1976.

Wolf, Eric. *Europe and the People without History*. Berkeley: University of California Press, 1982.

Wood, Charles H., and Terry L. McCoy. "Migration, Remittances, and Development: A Study of Caribbean Cane Cutters in Florida." *International Migration Review* 19 (1985): 251–77.

Woodman, Harold D. "Sequel to Slavery: The New History Views the Postbellum South." *Journal of Southern History* 43 (1977): 523–54.

Woodruff, Nan Elizabeth. "Pick or Fight: The Emergency Farm Labor Program in the Arkansas and Mississippi Deltas during World War II." *Agricultural History* 64 (1990): 74–85.

Woodson, Carter Goodwin. *A Century of Negro Migration*. New York: Russell and Russell, 1969.

———. *The Rural Negro*. New York: Russell and Russell, 1930.

Woodward, C. Van. *Origins of the New South, 1877–1913*. Baton Rouge: Louisiana State University Press, 1951.

Woody, Robert H. "The Labor and Immigration Problem of South Carolina during Reconstruction." *Mississippi Valley Historical Review* 18 (1931): 196–202.

"Work of Children on New Jersey Truck Farms." *Monthly Labor Review* 18 (1924): 1047–48.

Wright, Dale. *They Harvest Despair: The Migrant Farm Worker*. Boston: Beacon, 1965.

Wright, Gavin. "American Agriculture and the Labor Market: What Happened to Proletarianization?" *Agricultural History* 62 (1988): 182–209.

———. *Old South, New South: Revolutions in the Southern Economy since the Civil War*. New York: Basic Books, 1986.

Wunderlin, Clarence E., Jr. *Visions of a New Industrial Order: American Social Science and Labor Theory in the Progressive Era.* New York: Columbia University Press, 1992.

Yans-McLaughlin, Virginia. *Family and Community: Italian Immigrants in Buffalo, 1880–1930.* Ithaca, N.Y.: Cornell University Press, 1977.

Young, Ruth C., Bruce M. John, Christopher Hermann, and Delos R. Whitman. *Migrant Farmworkers in Western New York.* Ithaca, N.Y.: Department of Rural Sociology, Cornell University, 1979.

Zeichner, Oscar. "The Legal Status of the Agricultural Laborer in the South." *Political Science Quarterly* 55 (1940): 412–28.

Zepp, Glenn A. *Effects of Harvest Mechanization on the Demand for Labor in the Florida Sugarcane Industry.* Gainesville: University of Florida Press, 1975.

Zieger, Robert H. *The CIO, 1935–1955.* Chapel Hill: University of North Carolina Press, 1995.

———. "Toward the History of the CIO: A Bibliographic Report." *Labor History* 26, no. 4 (1985): 485–516.

Zimmerman, Diana. "America's Nomads." *Migration Today* 9, no. 3 (1981): 24–32, and no. 4–5 (1981): 34–38.

Index

Addams, Jane, 61
AFL. *See* American Federation of Labor
African Americans, 6, 12, 28, 217 (n. 18)
—during Progressive Era: compared to Italians, 32; migration within the South, 33; migration north before World War I, 33–37, 39, 210 (nn. 57, 61); reformers' attitudes toward, 59–60, 76–77; gains of, 83–84, 217 (n. 13); and growers' reactions to, 84–85, 217 (n. 17); and illiteracy rate of, 210 (n. 65)
—during World War I: effects of outbreak on, 85; migration to Connecticut, 85–86; Great Migration of, 86–88; migration from Georgia, 88; opportunities for in South, 88–90; and white media's reaction to, 90–91; African American press's reaction to, 91–92; blamed for labor scarcity in South, 99–103; as objects of work-or-fight campaigns, 104–8; defended by U.S. Department of Labor, 108–9; and Bureau of Negro Economics, 109–11; resistance to forced labor campaigns, 111–12
—during Great Depression, 114–16; as victims of hurricane, 118; migration from Georgia to Florida, 124–30; migration up coast, 130–31; and crew leader system, 131–32; as harvest workers in New Jersey, 132–37; at Campbell Soup, 141; at Seabrook Farms, 141–50; and collective bargaining law, 151; as strikers in depression era Florida, 154
—during World War II: as objects of forced labor campaigns, 9, 164–65; as residents of FSA migrant labor camps, 156–62; militance of, 171–72; displaced by Caribbean importees, 175–77; at Seabrook Farms, 184; at Campbell Soup, 191; as part of union-organized migration, 192–96
—since World War II: supplanted by immigrant labor, 200–201, 203–4; as strikebreakers, 201; tuberculosis rate among, 201–2
Agricultural Adjustment Administration, 8–9, 146–47, 155. *See also* New Deal; U.S. Department of Agriculture
Agricultural and Cannery Workers' Industrial Union, 142–46, 148–50, 182, 232 (n. 20)
Agricultural Extension Service, 167, 173
Agricultural labor. *See* Labor/Laborers, agricultural

275

to redistribute, 56–78; World War I efforts to redistribute, 79–112; in Florida during Great Depression, 114–16, 122–28; in New Jersey during Great Depression, 132–37, 231 (n. 2); during World War II, 150–53, 162–66, 185–89, 238 (n. 41); manipulated by Florida State Police during bean pickers' strike, 154; as key to farmworkers' poverty, 202–4
Labor, industrial, 2, 4, 6, 29–32, 36, 197
Labor exchanges. *See* U.S. Department of Labor
Labor Importation Program. *See* Farm Security Administration—Labor Importation Program
Local 56. *See* Amalgamated Meat Cutters and Butcher Workmen of North America
Louisiana, 62, 107, 109
Lowry, Edith, 134–35
Lynching, 32–33, 35, 217 (n. 18). *See also* Violence

McNutt, Paul V., 173
Maine, 28, 36, 96, 163–64
Maryland, 23, 94, 103, 106–7, 163–65, 171, 177, 179
Massachusetts, 19–20, 89, 107, 139, 163
Meat and Cannery Workers' Union. *See* Amalgamated Meat Cutters and Butcher Workmen of North America
Mechanization. *See* Farming—mechanization of
Men, 3, 6, 29–37, 48
Mexican Americans, 6, 12
Mexicans, 6, 12, 77, 96, 152, 167–69, 173–74, 188, 200–201
Michigan, 160
Migrant. *See* Labor/Laborers, agricultural—migratory
Migrant Health Act of 1965, 202

Migratory Camp Program. *See* Farm Security Administration—Migratory Camp Program
Minnesota, 17
Mississippi, 107, 109
Missouri, 109, 170, 188
Mitchell, H. L., 186, 188–89, 194–96, 198, 243 (n. 12). *See also* Southern Tenant Farmers Union
Moffett, John A., 146, 148–50
Montana, 107
Moore, Harry, 144
Murrow, Edward R., 7

National Association for the Advancement of Colored People, 79, 108, 136, 240 (n. 68)
National Child Labor Committee, 41, 45, 51–54, 211 (n. 2)
National Consumers' League, 41, 45–46, 51–53, 211 (n. 2)
National Council of Farmer Cooperatives, 173
National Grange of the Patrons of Husbandry, 173
National Industrial Recovery Act. *See* Collective bargaining
National Labor Relations Act. *See* Collective bargaining
National Recovery Administration. *See* Collective bargaining: under National Industrial Recovery Act
National Urban League, 85, 110, 211 (n. 2)
Nebraska, 109
New Deal, 8–13, 138–40, 146–81, 203–4. *See also* Collective bargaining; Farm Security Administration; Race; Relief; Unions
New England, 18–20
New Jersey, 5–7; African American and Italian migrants move to, 15, 28, 32–37; rise of truck farming in, 20–23, 132; decline of rural industry in, 24; depopulation of countryside, 25; demand for migrant

farmworkers in, 25–29; mechanization of farming in, 26–28; farm labor in, 29–37, 38–54; farm labor wages in, 164; farmworkers recruited for, 170, 175, 183; Caribbean importees on strike in, 177; union-organized migration to, 183–98, 243 (n. 17); use of Japanese American internees in, 186, 193–95; use of prisoners of war in, 186–87, 196–97; Puerto Ricans replace Italians in, 200. *See also* Campbell Soup; Seabrook Farms

New Jersey Board of Agriculture, 21–22, 25, 28, 34, 36, 48, 54

New Jersey Commission of Immigration, 29, 52, 211 (n. 2)

New Jersey Employment Service, 132–35

New Jersey State Potato Growers Association, 133–34

New York, 5, 20–21, 28, 36, 57, 66; Italian agricultural colonies in, 62–63; Division of Information branch in, 71; World War I farm labor migration to, 89; impact of federal work-or-fight order on, 106–7; FSA migratory labor camp in, 169; Puerto Ricans replace Italians in, 200

New York Association for Improving the Condition of the Poor, 66

New York Bowery Mission, 66

New York Tenements Department, 67

North Carolina, 23–24, 27–28, 34, 87, 101–3, 164, 169, 201

North Dakota, 109

Northern Pacific Railroad, 15–18

Ohio, 71

Oklahoma, 188

Ousley, Clarence, 98, 100–102, 104

Packinghouses: rise of in Florida, 119–22; white workers employed by, 124; and National Industrial Recovery Act, 138, 147; at Seabrook Farms, 141; and National Labor Relations Act, 153–54; and FSA housing, 161. *See also* Collective bargaining; Seabrook Farms; Unions

Padroni: as recruiters of immigrants from Italy, 29; defined, 39; as organizers of New Jersey's farm labor supply, 40–41, 212 (n. 21); proliferation of, 42; and child labor, 43–47; growers' dependence on, 47–50, 212 (n. 18), 213 (n. 25); farmworkers able to choose, 49–51; reformers' efforts to supplant, 65–67; Division of Information as, 70–72; Farm Security Administration as, 166–81; union as, 182–83, 186–99; compared to crew leaders in the 1990s, 202–3. *See also* Crew leaders: system

Panic of 1907, 68–69

Pearl City, Fl., 124–25, 228 (n. 42)

Pennsylvania, 20–21, 76, 139. *See also* Philadelphia, Pa.

Perkins, Frances, 146–47, 149. *See also* U.S. Department of Labor

Philadelphia, Pa., 5, 26, 30–32, 35, 51, 61

Planters. *See* Growers

Police, 140, 142–46, 149, 154, 229 (n. 58)

Populism, 58–59

Post, Louis, 95–96, 108–10, 219 (n. 63)

Poverty: in historiography, 7; progressive reformers' views of, 57–58; during Great Depression, 113–16, 122–29, 132–34; exacerbated by Agricultural Adjustment Administration, 155; Farm Security Administration's efforts to eradicate, 155–56; labor supply key to, 202–4. *See also* Crew leaders; Farm Security Administration; Housing; Padroni; Relief

Powderly, Terence V., 68, 70–72, 75–76, 196, 199, 215 (n. 39)

Preston, Frances, 135–37

Preston, Jake, 135–37

Prices, crop, 35

—in late nineteenth century: wheat, 18; grain compared to truck, 23; and timing of African American and Italian migration, 32

—during Progressive Era: berry, 42; wheat, 58, cotton, 83

—during World War I: cotton, 90; increase in compared to wages, 109; effect of outbreak on, 217 (n. 23)

—during Great Depression: collapse after World War I, 113–14; in Florida, 118–22; cotton, 137; C. F. Seabrook's ability to control, 141

—during World War II, 184

Prisoners of war (POWs), 6, 152, 174, 178–79, 186

Progressive farming. See Farming

Progressive reformers, 10, 211 (nn. 1, 2); background, 38–39; lack of interest in African American farmworkers, 39; opposition to padrone system, 39–47, 212 (nn. 11, 16), 213 (n. 32); views on poverty, 57–58; and immigration restriction, 61–78. See also Commission on Industrial Relations; National Child Labor Committee; National Consumers' League; U.S. Industrial Commission

Public Law 45. See House Resolution 96

Puerto Rico, 152, 174, 178, 186, 196, 200

Race: and federal policy, 11–13, 207 (n. 10); progressive reformers' views of, 57, 59–60, 76–77; and World War I labor supply, 79–83, 109, 223 (n. 115); and Seabrook strike, 141, 144, 148, 150; and divi-

sion of labor in Florida agriculture, 155; and segregation of migratory labor camps, 156–57; and World War II forced labor campaigns, 164–65; and complaints of labor scarcity, 171–72; and Labor Importation Program, 174–77, 179–80; and interracial union in New Jersey, 192–96

Red River Valley, 15–18

Reform: paradox of, 9–12; movement in Progressive Era, 38–54; labor distribution as, 55–77; decline of, during World War I, 77–78; necessity of, in view of U.S. Department of Labor, 81; lack of, during early New Deal, 138–40; and Farm Security Administration migratory labor camps, 151–53, 155–63; efforts and World War II, 166; prohibited by wartime Congress, 173–74; and union-organized migration to New Jersey, 185–99; legislation, inadequacy of, 202–4

Relative state autonomy. See State

Relief: use of to hold labor, 128; claims that workers were spoiled by, 132; exclusion of farmworkers from, 138–39, 231 (n. 1); lack of for striking bean pickers, 154

Resettlement Administration. See Farm Security Administration

Rhode Island, 60, 107

Roosevelt, Eleanor, 156

Roosevelt, Franklin Delano, 138, 146, 154

Roosevelt, Theodore, 55, 68, 107, 215 (n. 28)

Row bosses, 42, 50. See also Padroni

Rural Legal Services, 201

Saunders, Jack, 142–43

Schachter, Leon, 183, 185–91, 193–94, 196, 242 (n. 4)

Schwarzkopf, H. Norman, 144, 149, 233 (n. 29)

United Cannery, Agricultural, Packing, and Allied Workers of America, 188, 232 (n. 20), 243 (n. 12)

United Citrus Workers, 139

U.S. Boys' Working Reserve, 97

U.S. Conciliation Service, 146, 148–50

U.S. Congress, 41–42, 58, 68; and World War I debate over drafting labor, 105–6, 222 (n. 101); and investigation into interstate migration of destitute citizens, 133–35; attack on Farm Security Administration, 151–52, 165, 167–68, 173; H. L. Mitchell's testimony before, 188

U.S. Department of Agriculture, 9–11, 71, 80, 81
—during World War I: plans for national labor exchange, 92–93; as critic of U.S. Department of Labor's efforts, 96; as opponent of using women as farm laborers, 98; and work-or-fight campaign, 99–112
—during Great Depression: and collective bargaining law, 146–47; and Resettlement Administration, 154–56
—during World War II: commandeering of Migratory Camp Program, 152; analysis of labor supply, 163, 165; reconstituted as War Food Administration, 173–81

U.S. Department of Labor, 9–10, 26, 77, 81, 215 (n. 31)
—during Progressive Era: Division of Information's efforts to redistribute labor, 56, 67–72, 75–76, 81, 215 (n. 39)
—during World War I: labor distribution efforts of, 80–96; Bureau of Negro Economics's analysis of southern labor supply, 88, 218 (n. 43); U.S. Employment Service and labor exchange program,

93–95, 98–99, 109; Bureau of Immigration's wartime migration policy of, 96, 220 (n. 67); efforts to recruit volunteers, 97; and Women's Land Army, 97–99; opposition to forced labor schemes, 108–10; George Haynes sent south to improve race relations, 109–11
—during Great Depression: U.S. Conciliation Service and Seabrook Farm strike, 146, 148–50; and debate over extension of collective bargaining rights to agriculture, 147
—during World War II: U.S. Employment Service and labor distribution campaign, 166–70; War Manpower Commission and immigrants, 173; and prisoners of war, 178–79; and union-organized migration to New Jersey, 186–89, 243–44 (n. 17)

U.S. Employment Service. See U.S. Department of Labor

U.S. Industrial Commission, 25–26, 28, 33–34, 56–61, 74–75, 135, 215 (n. 7), 216 (n. 48)

U.S. Sugar Corporation, 121–22, 153, 161, 172, 176, 180, 240 (n. 65). See also Sugar cane production

Urban League. See National Urban League

USDA. See U.S. Department of Agriculture

USES. See U.S. Department of Labor—during World War I

USIC. See U.S. Industrial Commission

Vagrancy laws, 6, 84, 101–2, 240 (n. 65). See also Work-or-fight campaigns

Vander Schouw, Paul, 159–60, 175

Vermont, 28, 163

Violence: against African American farmworkers, 4, 35, 135–37; in the South during World War I, 107,

112; and farm labor strikes, 140,
142–46, 149–50; between African
Americans and Jamaicans, 176;
during World War II, 240 (n. 65)

Virginia, 23, 28

—as source of migrant labor, 28, 34,
60, 135

—during World War I: complaints of
labor scarcity in, 87–89, 95, 100;
difficulty of mobilizing farm labor
volunteers in, 101; U.S. Department of Labor finds labor supply
adequate in, 109

—during World War II: farm wages
in, 164; labor demand in, 167;
farm labor strikes in, 172

Wages, agricultural, 3–6, 25–28, 33,
58, 73, 217 (n. 20)

—during World War I: and labor
supply, 81–82, 109; rising, 88–89;
and resistance to white supremacy,
89–92; and foreign workers, 96;
and African American women, 107

—during Great Depression: in
Florida, 122–23, 127–28, 130, 227
(nn. 35, 39); in New Jersey, 131,
133–35; in North and South, 137;
farmworkers' efforts to raise,
139–50

—during World War II: fall of, at
start of war, 163; lowest where
growers complain loudest, 164–65;
and backlash against FSA, 165–66;
and Mexican importees, 168; farmworkers' efforts to raise, 170–72;
prohibition against minimum,
173–74; at Seabrook Farms, 184–
86; earned by STFU members in
California and Florida, 188; slight
climb of, in 1942, 238 (n. 40)

—since World War II: extension of
ban on minimum wage in agriculture, 197; minimum wage law
extended to, 202

Wages, industrial, 25–26, 29–32

Wagner Act. *See* Collective bargaining: under National Labor Relations Act

Wallace, Henry A., 155

Walsh, Frank, 74

War Food Administration, 89, 92,
173–81, 182–83, 186, 188

War Manpower Commission, 173,
178–79, 187–89, 243–44 (n. 17).
See also U.S. Department of
Labor—during World War II

West Coast, 5–6, 12, 15–21, 167–69,
186, 201, 203, 229 (n. 62), 234
(n. 42). *See also* California; Wheatland Riot

West Indians, 118, 123–24, 128,
172, 175–77, 188, 190, 196, 200–
202, 227 (nn. 17, 37). *See also*
Immigrants

West Virginia, 107

Wheat. *See* Farming—wheat

Wheatland Riot, 72–78, 182

White, Walter, 79, 112

Whites: Italians as, 59; as migrant
workers, progressive reformers'
views of, 76–77; in the South,
opposed to use of white women as
farm labor volunteers, 98; in the
South, and manual labor, 98–99;
as laborers in Florida agriculture,
124, 224 (nn. 6, 11), 227 (n. 39);
hostile to African American
migrants in New Jersey, 134–37;
in interracial agricultural unions,
141–45, 147–50; as residents of
segregated migratory labor camps,
160–61; from South as part of
union-organized migration,
186–96

Wickard, Claude, 167–68, 171

Wilson, William B., 80–81, 96

Wilson, Woodrow, 77, 80

Wisconsin, 109

Wobblies. *See* Industrial Workers of
the World

Woerner, W. T., 21–22

Women: and maternalist reforms, 8–9; farmworkers as sign of declining civilization, 19–20; Italian, as farmworkers in New Jersey, 30–32, 35–37; African American, as migrants on Jersey shore, 34; as settlers on New Jersey farms, 34–35; relation to padroni, 49; Women's Land Army as farm labor volunteers during World War I, 97–99, 220 (nn. 69, 71, 78); as strikers, 141–46, 149; importees deported if pregnant, 179; college students at Seabrook, 194–96

Women's Land Army, 97–99, 220 (nn. 69, 71). *See also* Women

Workers Defense League, 136, 231 (n. 80), 240 (n. 65)

Work-or-fight campaigns, 9, 103–12, 172, 222 (nn. 103, 104)

World War I, 9–10, 12–13; and decline of agrarian ideal, 57; and Commission on Industrial Relation, 77–78; effect of on supply of labor, 79–80, 81–83, 85, 217 (n. 21); and African-American migration, 85–89; and expansion of truck farming along East Coast, 89–90; opportunities for African American southerners during, 89–92; federal labor supply efforts, 93–96, 221 (n. 79); immigration policy during, 96, 220 (n. 67); and U.S. Boys' Working Reserve, 97; and Women's Land Army, 97–99, 220 (nn. 69, 71); and U.S. Department of Agriculture's work-or-fight campaign, 99–107; and southern forced labor campaigns, 107–8; and African American resistance, 110–12, 152, 172

World War II, 3–4, 10–13; and farm labor supply, 162–65; and roll back of New Deal programs, 165–66; and transformation of Farm Security Adminstration, 166–67; and importation of Mexican labor, 167–69; and Labor Transportation Program, 169–70; and growers' complaints of labor scarcity, 170–73; labor freeze, 173–74; Emergency Farm Labor Supply Program, 174–80; union-organized migration during, 183–99